THE UNITED NATIONS AT THE MILLENNIUM

The Principal Organs

Edited by

PAUL TAYLOR

and

A. J. R. GROOM

CONTINUUM

London and New York

Continuum

The Tower Building, 11 York Road, London SE1 7NX
370 Lexington Avenue, New York, NY 10017-6503

First published 2000

British Library Cataloguing-in-Publication Data
A catalogue record for this book is available from the British Library.

ISBN 0-8264-4777-5 (hardback)
      0-8264-4778-3 (paperback)

Library of Congress Cataloging-in-Publication Data
The United Nations at the millennium: the principal organs/edited by Paul Taylor and A. J. R. Groom.
        p. cm.
    Includes bibliographical references and index.
      ISBN 0-8264-4777-5 — ISBN 0-8264-4778-3 (pbk.)
    1. United Nations 2. International agencies I. Taylor, Paul Graham II. Groom, A. J. R.
    JZ5005 .U527 2000
    341.23—dc21   00-059037

Typeset by Centraserve, Saffron Walden, Essex
Printed and bound in Great Britain by Creative Print and Design Wales, Ebbw Vale

CONTENTS

Abbreviations   vii

Contributors   xi

Preface   xvii

1   Getting to 'Go': The Birth of the United Nations System   1
    A. J. R. Groom

2   The General Assembly: Grandeur and Decadence   21
    Marie-Claude Smouts

3   The Security Council   61
    Juergen Dedring

4   Managing the Economic and Social Activities of the United
    Nations System: Developing the Role of ECOSOC   100
    Paul Taylor

5   The Trusteeship Council: A Successful Demise   142
    A. J. R. Groom

6   The International Court of Justice   177
    B. G. Ramcharan

7   The United Nations Secretariat: Reform in Progress   196
    Yves Beigbeder

8   States Groups at the United Nations and Growth of Member
    States at the United Nations   224
    Sally Morphet

9   NGOs and the Principal Organs of the United Nations   271
    Carolyn M. Stephenson

10   The Institutions of the United Nations and the Principle of
    Consonance: An Overview   295
    Paul Taylor

Select Bibliography
(prepared by *Yuji Uesugi*) 327

Index 351

ABBREVIATIONS

ACABQ	The Advisory Committee for the Administrative and Budgetary Questions
ACC	Administrative Committee on Co-ordination
AFL	American Federation of Labor
ASEAN	Association of South East Asian Nations
BINGO	Business International Non-governmental Organization
CAMDUN	Campaign for a More Democratic UN
CCAQ	Consultative Committee on Administrative Questions
CGIAR	Consultative Group on International Agricultural Research
CIO	Congress of Industrial Organizations
CONGO	Conference of Non-governmental Organizations
COPA	Cross Organizational Programme Analysis
COW	Committee of the Whole
CPC	Committee for Program and Co-ordination
CSD	Commission on Sustainable Development
CSW	Commission on the Status of Women
DAC	Development Assistance Committee
DAF	Development Assistance Frameworks
DGDIEC	Director General for Development and International Economic Cooperation
DPI	Department of Economic and Social Affairs
DSG	Deputy Secretary-General
ECAFE	Economic Commission for Asia and the Far East
ECE	Economic Commission for Europe
ECOSOC	Economic and Social Council
ENGO	Environmental Non-governmental Organization
EPTA	Expanded Programme of Technical Assistance
FAO	Food and Agriculture Organization
FCO	Foreign and Commonwealth Office
FICSA	Federation of International Civil Servants' Associations
GA	General Assembly
IACB	Inter-Agency Consultative Board
IAEA	International Atomic Energy Agency
IALANA	International Association of Lawyers Against Nuclear Arms

IBRD	International Bank of Reconstruction and Development
ICAO	International Civil Aviation Organization
ICCPR	International Covenant on Civil and Political Rights
ICESCR	International Covenant on Economic and Social Rights
ICSC	International Civil Service Commission
IDA	International Development Association
IFC	International Finance Corporation
IFAD	International Fund for Agricultural Development
IGO	Intergovenmental Organization
ILC	International Law Commission
ILO	International Labour Organization
IMCO	International Governmental Maritime Consultative Organization
IMF	International Monetary Fund
IMO	International Maritime Organization
INSTRAW	International Training and Research Institute for the Advancement of Women
IPPNW	International Physicians for the Prevention of Nuclear War
IRO	International Relief Organization
ITC	International Trade Centre
ITO	International Trade Organization
ITU	International Telecommunication Union
IUOTO	International Union of Official Travel Organizations
JIU	Joint Inspection Unit
MIGA	Multilaterial Investment Guarantee Agency
NATO	North Atlantic Treaty Organization
NGLS	Non-governmental Liaison Services
NGO	Non-governmental Organization
NIEO	New International Economic Order
OHRM	Office of Human Resources Management
OIC	Organization of the Islamic Conference
OIOS	Office of Internal Oversight Services
ONUC	Opérations des Nations Unies pour le Congo
OPEC	Organization of Petroleum Exporting Countries
POC	Peace Observation Commission
QUANGO	Quasi-non-governmental Organization
RINGO	Religious International Non-government Organization
SUNFED	Special UN Fund for Economic Development
UNCED	UN Conference on Environment and Development
UNCHS	UN Centre on Human Settlement
UNCTAD	UN Conference on Trade and Development
UND	UN Department
UNDAF	UN Development Assistance Framework

UNDCP	UN International Drug Control Programme
UNDG	UN Development Group
UNDP	UN Development Programme
UNEF	UN Emergency Force
UNEP	UN Environment Programme
UNESCO	UN Educational, Scientific and Cultural Organization
UNFPA	UN Fund for Population Activities
UNHCR	UN High Commission for Human Rights
UNICEF	UN Children's Fund
UNIDO	UN Industrial Development Organization
UNIFEM	UN Development Fund for Women
UNITAR	UN Institute for Training and Research
UNRRA	UN Refugee and Rehabilitation Administration
UNRWA	UN Relief and Work Administration
UNSCOB	UN Special Conference on Broadcasting
UNSCOP	UN Special Conference on Population
UNTEA	UN Temporary Executive Authority
UNU	UN University
UPU	Universal Postal Union
WEOG	Western European and Other States group
WFP	World Food Programme
WHO	World Health Organization
WIPO	World Intellectual Property Organization
WMO	World Meteorological Organization
WTO	World Trade Organization
WTUC	World Trade Union Congress

CONTRIBUTORS

Yves Beigbeder worked as a personnel officer for the Food and Agriculture Organization of the UN from 1951 to 1955 and for the World Health Organization from 1955 to 1984. He has lectured on international organizations and administrations for UNITAR as a Senior Fellow, and for various universities in France, Switzerland and North America. He teaches at Webster University in Geneva as Adjunct Professor. He has written books and articles on the internal management of UN organizations, on WHO, UNHCR, non-governmental organizations and international criminal Tribunals.

Juergen Dedring was born and raised in (West) Germany. He holds degrees from the Free University Berlin, and Harvard University. He has taught at the Free University Berlin, Harvard University, Dartmouth College, Long Island University and, since 1996, at SUNY and New York University. Following two years (1972–74) as Research Associate dealing with peace and conflict research at UNITAR, New York, he served from 1975 until August 1996 as Political Officer in the UN Secretariat, the first 13 years in the Political and Security Council Affairs department. Since leaving UN service in 1996, he has undertaken academic teaching and research on international relations, especially international organizations, in conflict resolution and peace-making, and in comparative politics, with a focus on Europe. He is currently involved in a book-length study of the UN Security Council in the post-Cold War era.

A. J. R. Groom is Professor and Head of the Department of Politics and International Relations at the University of Kent at Canterbury. He studied at University College London and in the United States and Switzerland. His Dr.ès.scipol. is from Geneva and he was recently awarded a doctorate *honoris causa* from the University of Tampere. A former chairman of the British International Studies Association and vice-president of the International Studies Association and board member of ACUNS (Academic Council on the UN System), he founded the European International Relations Standing Group. He is currently on the Executive Committee of the European Consortium for Political Research, Director for the Centre for Conflict Analysis and Chairman of the International Studies Co-ordinating Committee of world international studies associations. He has written, edited and co-edited 17 books and monographs, several with Paul Taylor, and well over 100 articles and chapters. His academic interests lie in international relations theory, international organization, conflict studies and European international relations. He has British and Swiss nationality. He is a faithful supporter of his home town football club, Lincoln City.

Sally Morphet was educated in the Middle East, the United States and the United Kingdom. She has worked as a research analyst in the United Kingdom Foreign and Commonwealth Office since the mid-1960s. She specialized first on South and South-East Asia, and from 1974 on general international and UN questions. She has published articles and chapters in books on human rights, the environment and NGOs, the non-aligned, peacekeeping and the Security Council. She is currently on the Board of Directors of ACUNS (Academic Council on the UN System).

Bertie Ramcharan is Deputy United Nations High Commissioner for Human Rights, at the Assistant Secretary-General level. Previously he was Director of the Africa I Division in the Department of Political Affairs. He has been with the United Nations for the past 25 years. He is Adjunct Professor of International Human Rights Law at Columbia University and has taught at several other universities, including the Geneva Graduate Institute of International Studies. He is the author of several books on international law of human rights, the International Law Commission, the United Nations, early warning and preventive diplomacy, the good offices of the Secretary-General, and fact-finding. He has extensive field experience in diplomacy and has been on a number of fact-finding missions for the United Nations. He has a doctorate in International Law from the LSE and is also a barrister-at-law of Lincoln's Inn.

Marie-Claude Smouts is Director of Research at the French National Centre for Scientific Research (Centre d'études et de recherches internationales) and Professor at the Institut d'études politiques de Paris. She has written many books and articles on multilateral diplomacy and sociology of international relations. Her most recent publications are *Les organisations internationales* (1995) and *Les nouvelles relations internationales* (ed.), (1998). Her book with Bertrand Badie, *Le retournement du monde*, is now in its third edition. Her current research concerns international protection of the environment, especially tropical forests. She is Vice-President of l'Association française de science politique, a board member of ACUNS and a member of the Steering Committee of the European Standing Group for International Relations.

Carolyn M. Stephenson is Associate Professor of Political Science at the University of Hawaii at Manoa. She teaches international relations, especially international organization, and also conflict resolution. Educated at Mount Holyoke College, and with a PhD (1980) from Ohio State University, she is editor of the book *Alternative Methods for International Security* (1982). She is also the author of *Common Sense and the Common Defense* (to be published by Syracuse University Press), which examines the conditions under which conflict resolution, non-violent action and sanctions, and peacekeeping are effective at the international level. She was Director of Peace Studies at Colgate, and Co-Editor of *Peace and Change: A Journal of Peace Research*, for a number of years. She served as a member of the governing board of the International Studies Association and as Chair of its Peace Studies Section and currently serves as Chair of the Peace Movements Commission of the International Peace Research Association. Her current research is in the areas of UN peacekeeping and mediation as well as non-governmental organizations and UN conference diplomacy in the areas of environment, women and disarmament. She attended the UN's 'Earth Summit' in Rio in 1992 and has been doing participant observation of the UN Commission on Sustainable Development. She attended all four of the UN conferences on women, in Mexico City in 1975, Copenhagen in 1980, Nairobi in 1985, and Beijing in 1995, attending both the official UN conference and the Non-governmental Organization (NGO) Forum, as well as the three Special Sessions on disarmament.

Paul Taylor is Professor of International Relations and Chair of the Department at the London School of Economics, where he specializes in international organization within the European Union and the United Nations system. He has published on the history and theory of international organization, on the economic and social arrangements of the United Nations and on the politics of the institutions of the European Union. Most recently he has published *International Organization in the Modern World* (London: Pinter, 1993), and *The European Union in the 1990s* (Oxford: Oxford University Press, 1996). He has edited and contributed to a number of books on international organization, with A. J. R. Groom, and most recently with Sam Daws and Ure Adamczick-Gerteis (*Documents on the Reform of the United Nations*, London: Ashgate, 1997), and was editor of the *Review of International Studies*. He is a graduate of the University College of Wales, Aberystwyth, and of the LSE.

For
Bronwen and Elizabeth

PREFACE

The year 1995 saw an impressive number of seminars, workshops and conferences on the subject of the United Nations in acknowledgement, not just of its fiftieth anniversary, but also in the context of a growing interest in the question of global governance. However, not all aspects of the UN system have been reviewed in a comprehensive and thorough manner. This is particularly the case with some of the principal organs of the United Nations.

The United Nations Charter indicates that there are six principal organs, namely the General Assembly, the Security Council, the Economic and Social Council, the Trusteeship Council, the Secretariat, and the International Court of Justice. In the recent spate of UN seminars, a great deal of discussion has been concentrated on the role and function of the Security Council and to a lesser extent that of the Secretariat and General Assembly. The Economic and Social Council, the Trusteeship Council and the International Court of Justice have been largely ignored. Yet, if the United Nation system is to work effectively, it must fire on all cylinders and if some of the principal organs are no longer adequate or appropriate, then they must be reformed or dispensed with and new organs fashioned to take their place to reflect the world of the second half-century of the UN rather than its past.

The Trusteeship Council is a case in point. There are now no UN Trust Territories, yet it is still open for members of the United Nations to put their dependent territories under the control of the Trusteeship Council. Moreover, as the UN faces up to the awesome prospect of collapsed or failing states and what to do about them, it may be possible to find a functional equivalent as an important element in global governance. This may not involve an amendment of the Charter, if the analogy of peace-keeping is to be followed, since that activity has no mention in the Charter whatsoever.

Much has been written about the role of the Security Council in such questions as the Kuwait affair, humanitarian intervention and the Secretary-General's proposals for *An Agenda for Peace*. There have been many arguments for a change of membership of the Security Council, yet little progress has been made. It is not hard to think of reasons why this is so, but what effect will that fact have on the continued efficacy of the Security Council in the context of global governance overall? Is the Security Council likely to become a minor principal organ, as it was in the 1950s, or is it likely to continue its recent enhanced status? In this context, what pointers does the Kosovo conflict give?

As the Security Council has waxed and waned in its influence, so have the General Assembly, the Secretary-General and the Secretariat. At the present time the General Assembly is not the force that it once was, but as there is a reaction to the leadership of the permanent members of the Security Council and to the failure to change the Security Council, will the General Assembly reassert its role? Moreover, there are many suggestions for the reform of the Secretariat and some changes have been made. There can be little doubt that the UN system requires an effective Secretariat, but how effective a Secretariat and Secretary-General do the member states wish the United Nations to have?

The Economic and Social Council has never really found a role in the UN system. It has failed to act as a central co-ordinating instrument of the specialized agencies and other programmes of the UN system. On the other hand, the need for an Economic Security Council has been mooted by many and this is a role to which ECOSOC might aspire. Could it be amalgamated with G7 and the governing bodies of the World Bank, the World Trade Organization and the IMF? Will it merely stumble on as in the past, more dead than alive? Or is it finally getting to grips with the notion of a UN system including not just the principal organs and their programmes but also the specialized agencies and global conferences? Is there now a political will to think systemically and at different levels – global, regional and national – with integrated trans-sectional programmes?

And what of the International Court of Justice? It is the object of much pious support, yet states are not flocking to take cases to the Court. Is this because the other methods of dealing with disputes in the UN Charter have proved to be far more effective than judicial processes, and, if so, would it be possible to envisage new roles for the ICJ? Or is the ICJ quietly forging the legal norms, rules and practices of a global civil society?

Our starting point has been the principal organs of the UN. We have set out the historical background and traced the evolution of each of the organs and assessed likely future developments. We have tried to see how the organs might constitute an integrated system. We have also seen how caucuses have formed as a means of working the system and making the system work. We have chronicled the tentative steps to reach out to civil society. The UN system is a political organization that has its own needs and which adapts – sometimes well and sometimes badly – to both its internal and external environments. It has enormous potential, some real accomplishments and many inadequacies. It is what we make it, but one thing is sure: if it did not exist we would have to invent it. And without some such system we would be even more prey to the blind and unthinking processes of globalization.

Any enterprise of this nature requires the goodwill and intellectual contribution of a team of scholars. Our team is international, hailing from Britain, France, Germany, Guyana and the United States, but our concerns and interests are shared. We are a mixture of academics and practitioners as well as, for once, men and women. As editors we have enjoyed the stimulation that our team has provided and we can only thank them not only for what they have done but also for the manner in which they have done it – their co-operation has been exemplary. Two other words of thanks are in order: the first is to those who have commented on drafts. Secondly, even in the electronic age high quality support skills are at a premium. For these services our warmest thanks go to Nicola Cooper, Ann Hadaway and, as always, Marilyn Spice.

AJRG
PGT
January 2000

CHAPTER 1

GETTING TO 'GO': THE BIRTH OF THE UNITED NATIONS SYSTEM

A. J. R. Groom

On 10 January 1946, the United Nations General Assembly began its first session in London. The debate about the nature of a future general international organization, which had begun in the early days of the Second World War, had come to fruition in the negotiation of the UN Charter at San Francisco in 1945. The first session of the General Assembly marked the practical beginning and was a dramatic recognition of a pressing need for a general and universal international organization associated with a number of specialized agencies and open to an increasing range of non-governmental organizations. That this was taken for granted by all but a few was in itself an implicit tribute to the League of Nations, the first such organization, which had been established barely a quarter of a century previously. The League had laid down roots to the extent that it was unthinkable to governments of states large and small, as they lifted their eyes from war to the post-war world emerging on the horizon, that a similar organization should not be created, drawing on the lessons, both salutary and otherwise, of the League's experience.

From the perspective of the new millennium, there seems to be nothing extraordinary in this since the notion of a general, universal world organization is now so much a part of the political, economic, social and cultural landscape. However, international organization in the sense that we know it is of recent provenance. At the end of the Napoleonic Wars there existed hardly any international organizations in modern form. Now there are literally thousands, be they intergovernmental, non-governmental, profit-making or hybrid. They may be universal, regional or transregional in their membership and activities, as well as their financing. They cover virtually all aspects of human endeavour. Some are highly formal with constitutions, secretariats, budgets and formal membership. Others are no more than networks and can indeed be criminal as well as legal. Why, then, has this great growth of organization and institution-building occurred in the last two centuries of our millennium?

THE ROOTS OF THE UNITED NATIONS SYSTEM

International organization is one response to the growing tension in world society between the process of integration and the desire for separation. Greatly strengthened by the Industrial Revolution, capitalism spread to virtually all corners of the globe, created an integrated world economy and at the same time promoted the movement of ideas and people, as well as that of goods and services. This was the key step towards what has become a commonplace: the idea of globalization. At the same time, the growth of nationalism, particularly strong in eighteenth- and nineteenth-century Europe and more widely in the twentieth century, signified a demand for separation. State boundaries were first demarcated and then became increasingly an impediment to the free flow of people, ideas, goods and services. Moreover, loyalties escaped from the personal bonds of feudalism and became focused on the territorial state. Subjects became citizens and there was a tendency to a sharper demarcation of identities based on language, religion, ethnicity and the like. How, then, could the aspiration of the state to police its boundaries and organize life within those boundaries, in security and political terms, as well as economic, social and cultural terms, be reconciled with the growth of global markets, which tended not only to redefine the territorial base of economies but also of societies and even cultures? The tension between global integration and state separation was tempered by the growth of international organization. The growth of international organization enables the state to play a gate-keeping role by means of an international institution, the function of which is to promote and regulate transactions, to deal with problems within and between states, and to take advantage of opportunities and necessities in particular areas of human intercourse. The need to recognize and work with forces for integration as well as separation had to be acknowledged by the founders of the United Nations. The system reflects what has gone before, but also a dialectic that is inherent in modern international society.

The growth of international organization, like most experiments in governance, is a massive attempt at social and political engineering and reflects the spirit of the times, particularly of the nineteenth century and early twentieth century. It is a product of the Enlightenment project. As two of the traditional curses of humankind – famine and plague – were for the most part being eradicated in Western Europe and the North American Atlantic seaboard, war assumed a greater absolute and relative importance as the last great curse of the 'developed' world. In particular, the application of the Industrial Revolution to organized warfare, first made abundantly evident in the American Civil War, together with the motivation of citizens to defend *'la patrie'*, which the French Revolution had promoted, presented a challenge that was not refused. The dominant ideas of Western Europeans and North Americans were that progress was possible and that rational and reasonable men could co-operate for the common advantage, whether it be through the hidden hand of Adam Smith in his challenge against mercantilism or the cosmopolitan law of Kant arguing the case for perpetual peace. Thus the ideas of democracy, nationalism, integration, the rights and duties of citizens and states, and the universality of human needs and values took root and were reflected in the growth of international organization.

This was in the mood of the eighteenth and nineteenth centuries, a *Zeitgeist* that underpinned a quest for progress and suggested that what existed could be improved if reason and scientific method were properly applied. There was no magic wand that could produce a new world order in the biblical twinkling of an eye simply because of a functional need. Rather, there was an evolutionary process, which gradually led to the metamorphosis of older institutional frameworks. For example, the Concert system, particularly as it emerged after the independence of Belgium in 1830, was a system of great power governance to deal with questions likely to endanger international peace and security through a challenge to the interests of the great powers of the day. In this it worked well, insofar as the interests of the great powers collectively were concerned, but this was often at the expense of others. The informal institutionalization of the conferences of ambassadors and ministers was formalized in the Council of the League of Nations and even more dramatically in the establishment of the Security Council of the United Nations, with its permanent members holding a veto. But, at the same time as the institutionalization of the management of the balance of power, there was a growth of institutional frameworks for the management of disputes, often in the form of arbitration. For example, Britain and the United States settled their very real differences in the Alabama case in the aftermath of the American Civil War, not by going to war, which was certainly a real possibility given the tension between the United States and British North America throughout much of the nineteenth century, but by going to arbitration. In the Americas, the newly independent republics began to create a network of arbitration agreements, as did powers in other parts of the world, and this gave rise, at the beginning of the twentieth century, to the Permanent Court of Arbitration, decided upon at the First Hague Peace Conference in 1899, from which the Permanent Court of International Justice (PCIJ) of the League of Nations and the International Court of Justice (ICJ) of the UN are descended.

The Hague became the international law capital of the world as the PCIJ and ICJ were and are located there, as is the current War Crimes

Tribunal concerned with the former Yugoslavia. But that town is also associated with another important trend in international organization, which affected both the Covenant of the League and the Charter of the UN, namely the Hague Peace Conferences. Held in 1899 and 1907, these conferences were a major step forward in arms control and, to a lesser degree, disarmament. Both arms control and disarmament are integral elements of the Covenant and the Charter, although the process as a whole is much wider than the UN system.

The nineteenth century saw the growth of international public unions that were often concerned with setting standards and facilitating the growing integration of the world economy and political, social and economic systems. Post and telecommunications were clearly in need of international organization and this happened at an early date.[1] So too did the protection of intellectual property. There was also a need to establish standards of weights, measures, distance and the like, and to begin the evolution of a standard of rights and duties in social areas. In response to this a plethora of governmental and especially non-governmental organizations was set up. Moreover, a wide range of what we would now call epistemic communities, especially in the area of science, were founded and flourished. With the establishment of a general international organization in 1920 with a permanent secretariat and a mandate to be universal, this tendency was further stimulated: as the Bruce Committee reported in 1939, the development of functional co-operation was one of the great successes of the League. This was recognized in the UN system by the establishment of specialized agencies as separate bodies, each with their own constitution, membership, budget and secretariat, several of which grew out of sections of the League Secretariat or associated bodies. In short, the United Nations is not only an organization made up of its six principal organs and their subsidiary bodies, but is also a system with a wide network of agencies and programmes (see figure 1.1).

The development of international organization, including its intergovernmental aspects, owes a great deal to the growth of national, transnational and international non-governmental organizations. Indeed, the proposals and lobbying of such bodies were of direct benefit to the League of Nations in that they provided a powerful stimulus in the late nineteenth century and early twentieth century to the setting up of the organization. It can be said that the League was a beneficiary of the development of civil society. Without the pressures from this source, governments might have been tempted to water down even more than they did the proposal for some form of general international organization. The nineteenth century saw the birth of a wide range of influential non-governmental bodies such as the International Committee of the Red Cross in 1864 and the Anti-Slavery League, which fought first against the slave trade, and then

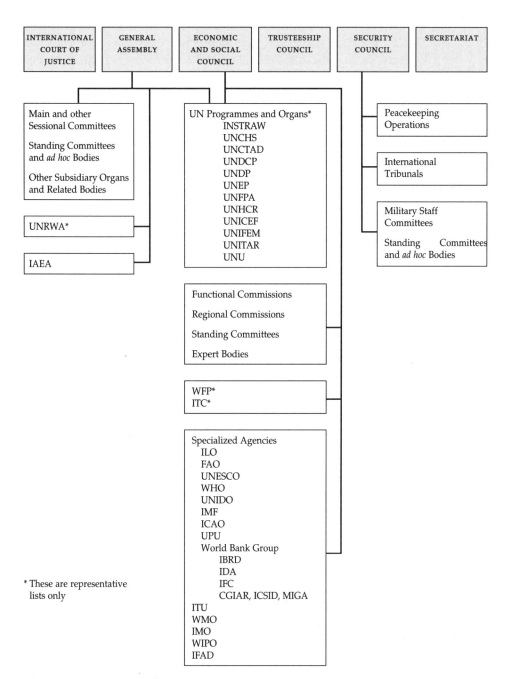

Figure 1.1 The United Nations system

Source: The UN Handbook 1999 (Wellington: Ministry of Foreign Affairs and Trade, 1999), p. 8.

for the abolition of the institution of slavery. The UN Charter begins with the words 'We the Peoples . . .', but in practice there was little place for NGOs until the growth of the global special conferences, which developed agendas in a wide range of specific areas of activity. These brought together parts of the UN system with the representatives of governments as well as non-governmental actors, whether within the spheres of the environment, women's interests and rights, habitat, disarmament and the like. Non-state actors cannot be ignored since they command loyalties, resources and affect outcomes in virtually every dimension of human life. While NGOs were important in the procuring of support for a general universal international organization, slowly the system is learning not to keep them at arm's length because, willy-nilly, the system cannot function effectively without them.

Thus the United Nations system reflected an evolutionary development of international governance, although, to be sure, it had some innovative aspects, particularly in the provisions for enforcement action in Chapter VII and in human rights. Its immediate predecessor was the League of Nations, but the antecedents of the system that was entering into operation in 1946 can be clearly seen in the nineteenth-century history, principally of Europe and the Americas. More generally, the notion of global social and political engineering to which it aspires finds its roots in the Enlightenment project and reflects a view of humankind that acknowledges that if we are in a mess it is at least in part our own fault and therefore it is up to us to set matters right. This was very much the spirit behind the League of Nations and later the UN, which was also influenced by the ideas behind the New Deal in the United States and Keynesian projects in the UK. However, at the time the system reflected a highly truncated vision of humankind, since very few of the 51 signatories of the UN Charter in San Francisco came from Africa or Asia.

THE LEAGUE OF NATIONS

One of the central ideas behind the League of Nations was the notion of collective security, and this also became, with some modifications, the central principle of the UN. Put at its simplest, the theory is that a group of states will meet together to decide upon what henceforth shall be the principles that will govern their mutual relations and the manner in which those principles may be changed. Once having agreed upon the basis for the relationship and the method for peaceful change, the actors in the system of collective security also pledge that they will do what is appropriate to ensure, if necessary by coercive action, that all members of the system will abide by the agreed principles and the methods of changing them. In the practice of the League of Nations, it was certainly viewed by the liberal internationalists that a system of collective security would work best if the states were democratic in their internal form of government, and if they were made up of peoples who had implicitly or explicitly exercised the principle of self-determination. This arrangement also applies to the UN, with the major difference that in this organization primary responsibility for action to protect international security is given to the Security Council, and is not attached equally to all states.

The League of Nations reflected a purer form of collective security: a general and unavoidable obligation to act for all states. It was not intended to be a world government, nor to be some form of international federation; it was intended to enhance the degree of international community and to ameliorate and facilitate relationships. It was to be the framework within which the harmony of interests could flourish, bringing the enhanced benefits of co-operation. The organization certainly fulfilled a key heuristic purpose in that it demonstrated that a general, universal, international organization was necessary for the maintenance of a lasting peace and the protection of international security. It involved the notion of a collective international responsibility, not just of the great powers, as through the Concert system, but through the notion of a collective security. The League's Covenant set out elaborate procedures through which major disputes might be broached and indeed it had a certain degree of success, a classic case being the settlement of the Aland Islands dispute. A potentially highly dangerous dispute in the Baltic region was resolved and the solution found has survived to the present day. But the League, as we have already intimated, also sought to enhance functional co-operation and in this it was highly successful. It began to traverse the difficult way towards decolonization, which became a major feature of world politics in the third quarter of the twentieth century. In short, through the establishment of the Secretariat and its principal organs, the League altered world politics. Whatever its failings, it was an innovation that became a harbinger for the future.

The failings of the League are of course well known. Collective security, in the stricter sense of all for all, did not so much fail as was never tried. This was due to flaws in the conception of system, but also because of the initial absence of the major revisionist powers, Germany and the Soviet Union, and the self-exclusion of a major potential pillar of the system, the United States. This meant that League action was constantly at risk of being perceived as the work of the remaining members, constituted as an alliance rather than an international organization embodying collective security. The lesson was obvious: if an international organization with universal pretensions seeks to establish a system of collective security, it must include all major global actors – a mistake that the United Nations was not to make, except for the period following the Communist Revolution in China until the Peking regime occupied China's place in the organization.

Thus the League was quietly buried after the Second World War. Its failures were obvious, but it had its successes, such as the resolution of the Aland Islands dispute and in functional co-operation, which were largely unsung. The overall decision of the great powers during the Second World War was that on balance it was better not to resurrect the League, particularly as the United States had never been a member, and given the unhappy experience of the Soviet Union with it. It seemed prudent to start again, and in taking the enterprise forward the lead was given by Britain, the United States and the Soviet Union.

THE COVENANT AND LESSONS FOR THE CHARTER

The Covenant of the League is a brief document of 26 Articles. It sets out an institutional structure of an Assembly, a Council, and a permanent Secretariat, all of which are specified in Article 2. Article 14 presages a Permanent Court of International Justice, the proposal for which was to be formulated by the Council, while Article 22 on the mandates system refers to a permanent commission subsidiary to the Council 'on all matters relating to the observance of the mandate'. Article 23 lists six economic and social areas in which the League promises to be active, most of which gave rise to specialized agencies in the United Nations system. The remit of the Assembly is wide (Article 3), since it 'may deal . . . with any matter within the sphere of action of the League or affecting the peace of the world' and in the meetings of which each member shall have one vote. The Council (Article 4) had a restricted membership consisting of 'Representatives of the Principal, Allied and Associated Powers, together with Representatives of four other Members of the League', who will be '. . . selected by the Assembly from time to time in its discretion'.[2] The Council could, with the approval of the majority of the Assembly, add additional permanent members to the Council. The Council's area of competence was the same as that of the Assembly and each member of the Council had one vote. Article 5 stated that, unless otherwise expressly provided for, '. . . decisions at any meeting of the Assembly or of the Council shall require agreement of all the Members of the League represented at the meeting'. This is a framework that would not have been alien to a Metternich, a Tallyrand or a Castlereagh. But Article 6 contains an innovation, since a 'permanent Secretariat shall be established . . . [and] shall comprise a Secretary-General and secretaries and staff as may be required . . . [who] shall be appointed by the Council with the approval of the majority of the Assembly'.

The Permanent Court of International Justice referred to in Article 14 was proposed in the Covenant but had yet to be established. It would 'be competent to hear and determine any dispute of an international character which parties thereto submit to it. A Court may also give an advisory opinion upon any dispute or question referred to it by the Council or by the Assembly.' Article 22 deals with the question of mandates and the constitution of a permanent commission 'to advise the Council on all matters relating to the observance of the Mandates', while Article 23 deals, as we have seen, with a range of economic and social activities.

In its two decades of active life, the Covenant was interpreted, developed, ignored and stretched as the new organization and its principal institutional instruments came to broach the real world. In so doing, practices emerged of which due account was taken when the time came to draft the Charter of the United Nations. Thus, notwithstanding the fact that the League was treated by those charged with negotiating the Charter of the United Nations as an elderly relative whom one would rather like to ignore, they nevertheless drew liberally on the practice and experience of the League and the working of its organs. The United Nations Charter revealed an evolutionary practice rather than a sharp break with the past. This was hardly surprising given that the men and women who were concerned with negotiating the new organization had themselves often participated in the work of its predecessor. How, then, did this evolution take shape?

The League of Nations was tarred with the brush of the Treaty of Versailles, of which it formed part. Criticisms against the Treaty therefore frequently also brushed off upon the League, and such criticisms of the Treaty were many and varied from all quarters. This meant that the United States in particular was careful to ensure that the process of negotiating the Charter would be kept separate from the question of peace treaties, in order that the new organization might start with a *tabula rasa*. Indeed, the notion that there was a need for a new start, building on and developing the experience of the League of Nations, was one that was widely shared.[3]

As we have seen, the League Assembly operated on the unanimity principle, whereas the UN General Assembly can make recommendations on the basis of a two-thirds majority. Nevertheless, in practice, the League Assembly could adopt a *vœu* on a majority basis which had a standing and influence not dissimilar from a General Assembly recommendation. The differences, however, are greater when a comparison is made between the League Council and the Security Council.

The League Council, like the Assembly, operated on the basis of unanimity. What is more, both organs could deal with 'any matter within the sphere of action of the League or affecting the peace of the world'. The remit of the General Assembly stated in Article 10 of the Charter is that it 'may discuss any questions or any matters within the scope of the present Charter or related to the powers and functions of any organs provided for in the present Charter, and . . . may make recommendations . . .' except when the Security Council is 'exercising . . . the functions assigned to it . . .' (Article 12). The Security Council, which is the nearest equivalent to the League Council, operates on the basis of a qualified majority, with each of the five permanent members able to exercise a veto and non-permanent members or a group thereof able to exercise a collective veto.[4] Moreover, while the League Council included only the major powers, the Security Council includes representatives from each of the major regions of the world, chosen informally by the caucuses from those regions. It is therefore much more democratic and representative than the League Council. Indeed, Brazil, which aspired to great power status, left the League because it was not included in the Council. Moreover, the Security Council can take binding decisions under Chapter VII, including the obligation to apply military sanctions. Indeed, under Article 12 of the Charter, when it 'is exercising in respect of any dispute or situation the functions assigned to it in the present Charter, the General Assembly shall not make any recommendation with regard to that dispute or situation unless the Security Council so requests'. Thus in certain matters the Security Council is supreme and this is reinforced by the existence of the Military Staff Committee and the obligation of states to provide military forces on the basis of agreements negotiated with it. Even such innovations as the Uniting for Peace Resolution of 1950, which allowed the General Assembly to take over responsibility for security if the Security Council was unable to act, reflected this principle. It only applied if a permanent member vetoed action and needed a majority vote of Council members to which the veto did not apply.

The other two organs newly created in the UN system, namely the Economic and Social Council (ECOSOC) and the Trusteeship Council, are both subordinate to the General Assembly, even though they have the same status as principal organs. Nevertheless, while the League had two bodies with a general competence, the UN has only one. As we shall see below, the status of principal organ for both the ECOSOC and the Trusteeship Council was a late addition to the framework of the UN Charter but it was admirably presaged by the League experience. The Bruce Committee of the League recommended the establishment of a Central Committee for economic and social questions and the Mandates Commission, in its practice, developed a role not far below that assigned to the Trusteeship Council in the Charter.

Many aspects of the role of the Secretariat were taken over by the United Nations and incorporated, following upon the League's experience. However, there is one important development in Article 99, which states: 'The Secretary-General may bring to the attention of the Security Council any matter which in his opinion may threaten the maintenance of international peace and security.' This gives a political role to the Secretary-General that was absent from the practice and behaviour of Sir Eric Drummond (UK), Joseph Avenol (France) and Sean Lester (Ireland). The political development of the role of the Secretary-General in the UN has far exceeded that of the League's Secretaries-General. Nevertheless, Drummond gave the League a flexible administrative structure – a useful 'fairy godmother's' gift which passed on to the UN.

Just as in the League experience in which the Permanent Court of International Justice was initially a promise, so the International Court of Justice in the UN system only came on the scene late in the day during the negotiations at San Francisco. Both legal bodies have their own statutes and neither of them played the role within the system that some had hoped for and others might have feared. Both institutions were, from the point of view of the principal organs, the Cinderella of their respective systems.

We can see, therefore, the learning process in devising the principal organs of the UN Charter derived from the Covenant of the League of Nations and its experience in practice. The process was essentially evolutionary, derived from that practice and from the logical development of new ideas based on past experience. Thus ECOSOC and the specialized agencies were added. But the whole did not spring into being at San Francisco. It evolved primarily through the diplomacy of Britain, and the United States in the early years of the war, and later involved the Soviet Union, with a quickening pace from 1943 onwards. It is to this evolution that we now turn.

THE PATH TO SAN FRANCISCO

Reflecting that 'the forces of totalitarianism, international disorganization and national irresponsibility produced the greatest and most disastrous of conflicts – World War Two', Inis Claude noted that

> this total collapse of world order produced not so much a sense of the futility and hopelessness of international organization as a vivid awareness of the need for and a resolute determination to achieve an improved system of international organization. It became clear that the modern

world had developed the habit of responding to catastrophe by intensifying its quest for effective organization.[5]

This process was, of necessity, mainly a governmental one. There could
be no effective discussion in Nazi-occupied Europe. The Soviet Union was
not a pluralistic political entity and in Britain much of the intellectual
capacity to reflect on questions of organization was already incorporated
into governmental or quasi-governmental structures. However, the
League of Nations Union, under the leadership of Cecil, did make an
independent contribution. On the other hand, figures like David Mitrany,
whose ideas about a working peace system were influential in leading to
a functionalist strategy for the emerging UN system, were playing their
role in a quasi-governmental framework. In the United States, it was
rather more difficult for government to be involved ostentatiously in the
early days, since the United States had yet to enter the war. It had not
joined the League of Nations, and the spirit of isolation was still abroad.
This left the field open to private organizations, such as the Commission
to Study the Organization of Peace led by James Shotwell, which was
founded in 1939 and contributed a number of reports that were influential
in the following years. John Foster Dulles took a leading role in the
proposals of the Federal Council of Churches of Christ in America,
whereas a university contribution was organized through the World Peace
Foundation in Boston. Both the American Federation of Labor and the US
Chamber of Commerce had committees on the subject, as did the Council
on Foreign Relations.

At the Foreign Office in London, planning had begun before the
meeting for the Atlantic Charter, and in Washington the State Department
established an embryonic planning capacity in January 1940. This was
expanded in early 1942 to become the Advisory Committee on Post War
Foreign Policy, with a number of sub-committees. Generally speaking, in
the years 1940–43 both the United States and Britain were leaning towards
a decentralized system that would emphasize regional organizations and
what were, in effect, spheres of influence. However, not all of the governmental thinking was in the United States and Britain, since in June
1941 there was an Inter-Allied Declaration in London formulated by
the European governments in exile and governments of the British
Commonwealth.

In August 1941 Roosevelt and Churchill met and espoused the Atlantic
Charter, with the British leader wishing to establish 'effective international
organization' while the US President was willing only to espouse the
notion of 'a wider and permanent system of general security', since he
was fearful of isolationist sentiments in the USA. The Atlantic Charter
took on greater significance when on 1 January 1942 a United Nations

Declaration was signed not only by Churchill and Roosevelt, but also by Litvinov for the Soviet Union and Soong for China. This was the first major use of the term 'United Nations'; that is, states that were united in the pursuit of the war. However, the Declaration was based on the ideas of the Atlantic Charter which therefore became an ideological and political basis on which the allied powers could not only prosecute the war but also contemplate a post-war world.

Matters really began to take shape in a sustained and serious manner with the Declaration of 30 October 1943 in Moscow of the foreign ministers of the Soviet Union, the UK and the United States, together with the Chinese Ambassador in Moscow, in which there was a clear commitment by the four governments to '. . . recognize the necessity of establishing at the earliest practicable date a general international organization, based on the principle of the sovereign equality of all peace-loving states, and open to membership by all such states, large and small, for the maintenance of international peace and security'.[6] When three of their principals met in Teheran, that is Churchill, Roosevelt and Stalin, the idea was endorsed in general terms in a declaration of 1 December 1943.

At this point a functionalist strategy for the putative United Nations system as a whole began to emerge. The League of Nations had never succeeded in incorporating some of the pre-existing international organizations, dealing with such matters as post and telegraph, into a coherent framework. A major new body, namely the International Labour Organisation, had been founded alongside the League with its own membership, constitution (which was highly innovative for the time and even now), Secretariat and budget. Willy-nilly a decentralized system was created, involving the International Labour Organization and other more specialist organizations which were also continuing. The conference in May 1943 at Hot Springs led to the formation of the Food and Agricultural Organization and, in the same year, the United Nations Relief and Rehabilitation Administration was established. These were followed by a meeting in Chicago in 1944, which led to the International Civil Aviation Organization and the Bretton Woods meeting in July 1944, which gave rise to the foundation of the International Bank for Reconstruction and Development, as well as the International Monetary Fund. Thus, while there was an emerging United Nations Organization coming from the meetings of the Big Three and Four, there was, at the same time, being established a decentralized United Nations system with a range of what were to become specialized agencies.

The stage was now set for a major conference of the Big Three, together with China, which was held in Dumbarton Oaks in the Washington area in the summer and early autumn of 1944. This was a major planning exercise, which resulted in the agreement between Britain, the United

States, the Soviet Union and China on the basic principles that would underlie and infuse the future United Nations Charter. The Dumbarton Oaks meeting was therefore the meeting of the principal sponsors to establish a united front on basic principles, and only then would they be prepared to consider comments and suggestions from the other powers. The Dumbarton Oaks Conversations, as they were called, consisted of two phases, necessitated by the fact that the Soviet Union was not yet at war with Japan. The first phase, involving Britain, the United States and the Soviet Union, was from 21 August until 28 September, and the following day the meetings resumed with the Soviet Union dropping out and China joining Britain and the United States until 7 October 1944. The final document was made available on 9 October 1944 and it was then circulated for comment. At the centre of the whole system was to be a Security Council with five permanent members who would be veto-holding powers. In addition, three other major organs were seen, namely the General Assembly, the Secretariat and an International Court. There was, as yet, no Trusteeship Council, and the Economic and Social Council was deemed to be subsidiary to the General Assembly.

There were, however, a number of unsettled questions. First of all, the Soviet Union proposed a veto for the permanent members on all matters, whereas the others were inclined to be more flexible on the issues the veto would cover. In addition, the Soviet Union suggested informally that all its 16 constituent republics should be members of the organization in the same way that India and the Philippines were, prior to their independence. There was still debate on whether the Permanent Court of International Justice should be continued or whether, formally, a new body should be established. There was also the question of transition from the League of Nations to the United Nations, particularly bearing in mind that the Soviet Union had been expelled from the League of Nations and the United States had never been a member. There was, in addition, a recognition that more work needed to be done on ECOSOC matters.

Some of these matters were resolved at a meeting between Churchill, Roosevelt and Stalin at Yalta on 4–11 February 1945. First, matters concerning the veto were clarified when the Soviet Union agreed that the veto would only apply to substantive questions and could not be used to block a procedural vote. It was also accepted that a party to a dispute would abstain from voting in the Security Council on that question. On the other hand, the USSR would be joined as members of the organization by the Ukraine and Byelorussia, two of the Soviet republics. The date on which the results of the discussions at Dumbarton Oaks and the amendments at Yalta would be taken to the General Conference was set for 25 April 1945 in San Francisco. Both China and France were invited to co-sponsor this conference, an invitation which France declined, but this did not inhibit it from attending the conference as an ordinary member. The question of the Trusteeship system was also agreed upon, but no decision was made, nor would it be made until after the San Francisco conference, as to which countries were to be trustholding powers.

A first reaction to the proposals of Dumbarton Oaks and the results of the Yalta conference came at a meeting of Latin American states in Mexico City from 21 February to 8 March 1945. The Inter-American Conference on Problems of Peace and War in Mexico City evinced considerable dissatisfaction with the way in which matters were unfolding. In particular, the Latin American states wanted a greater stress to be placed on the universality of the United Nations and they wanted a strengthening of both the General Assembly and the International Court, as well as an expanded role for regional organizations. The establishment of UNESCO was foreseen and a marker was placed to ensure that there was adequate representation of Latin America on the Security Council. In the meantime, a Committee of Jurists had been established in March 1945 to draw up a draft statute for a new International Court.

Thus the process that had begun in the early years of the Second World War, and which had quickened considerably from 1943 onwards, was coming to its conclusion. The Big Three and China were now in agreement and it was time to invite the views of others. Already the Inter-America meeting had presaged the reluctance of other states to accept a *Diktat* from the Big Three and China. The question was evident: whose United Nations was the new organization to be? In part that question would be decided in San Francisco, and in part it would be decided in the practice of the organization in subsequent years.

THE SAN FRANCISCO CONFERENCE

Invitations were sent on 5 March 1945 and the conference opened on 25 April. Fifty countries were represented and, in addition, Poland signed the Charter after a dispute about the representativeness of the Lublin government. The conference was serviced by a secretariat of more than a thousand, who were mainly US citizens – a natural consequence of the location of the conference, wartime difficulties in travel and in recognition of the host status of the United States. The Secretary-General of the conference was Alger Hiss of the US State Department. In a departure from usual practice and at Soviet insistence, the presidency of the conference rotated between Britain, the United States, the Soviet Union and China, while the delegations of practically all countries were made up of high quality and prominent delegates. The Chairman of both the Steering Committee and the Executive Committee was the US Secretary of State,

Edward Stettinius. In addition to the Steering Committee and Executive Committee there were four general committees, four commissions and twelve technical committees.

The principal role of the Steering Committee was to consider major policy and procedural questions. The Steering Committee was formed by the heads of all the delegations. The Executive Committee fed recommendations to the Steering Committee and the Executive Committee was formed by the four sponsoring countries and ten others, which included Australia and France. The four commissions dealt respectively with the areas of general provision (such as membership), the General Assembly, the Security Council, and a judicial organization. These were serviced by highly influential technical committees, which fed information, ideas and questions up through the system.

The formal arrangements for the conference were, in effect, a two-way movement, since from the top down there was the agenda that came from the Dumbarton Oaks proposals and any amendments that the participating states proposed. These would be decided on the basis of a two-thirds vote on substantive matters. In the other direction, detailed work was undertaken in the technical committees and fed through the system to the Steering Committee, which was, in effect, a committee of the whole. From a procedural point of view the organization worked very well, since the Charter was ready for signature and ratification in the space of two months. Not, however, before there had been vigorous debate on a range of issues, not the least of which concerned the purpose and functioning of the putative principal organs of the organization.

The general diplomacy of the four sponsoring powers, with whom France was associated, was that they would stand by what they had agreed at Dumbarton Oaks, and they were not prepared to break ranks over any basic issues, particularly those concerning the Security Council and the question of the veto. Indeed, it was made abundantly clear in the course of debate that, in essence, it was either the Dumbarton Oaks United Nations, or no United Nations. Since, in the long run, the organization bade fair to protect and develop the interests of the smaller states in ways that they would find difficult outside the organization, then in the last resort the smaller states were likely to accept the Dumbarton Oaks framework rather than 'leave it', for that indeed was their choice.

The four sponsoring powers had slightly different roles, but try as the small countries might, they could not find any room for manoeuvre on vital issues by playing off one great power against another. The United States, as the host government, had a particularly difficult position, since it could not afford politically to allow San Francisco to fail. Moreover, public opinion in the United States was strongly in favour of the new organization. This meant that the US delegation was caught between the

Senate, whose support for the Charter was a *sine qua non* of ratification, and the demands of the smaller powers for changes in some of the vital provisions for peace and security. However, in this the United States had strong support from Britain and the Soviet Union. The main British concern, besides giving active support for the role of the Big Four, and particularly the preservation of the veto as conceived at Dumbarton Oaks, was to protect its own interests where they might come under scrutiny from the United States, the Soviet Union and the smaller powers. This was especially the case of the Declaration on Non-Self-governing Territories, and also in the question of post-war economic relations where there was strong pressure from the United States to open up the markets of the British Empire and Commonwealth. Thus, on peace and security questions there was solidarity, or at least convergence, between the Big Four, but on the colonial and economic questions the British were under pressure from American economic imperialism and its thrusting anti-colonialism. The USA vied with the Soviet Union as a champion of colonial peoples, with the general support of the non-European members of the conference. Moreover, there were already major movements within dependent territories such as India, Indo-China and the Dutch East Indies, which heightened and gave point to the pressures. France, which had been invited to be a sponsoring power and had declined, was mainly concerned with the domestic problems that followed liberation, and on the whole China was prepared to sit on its hands. The major Soviet requirement was that there should be no significant dilution of the Dumbarton Oaks proposals, particularly where they concerned sovereignty and security. The Soviet delegation knew well that both the United States and the UK needed the membership of the USSR, but in truth there were no real differences between the three on those issues.

With the small powers it was an entirely different matter. In particular, Australia, Belgium, Brazil, Canada and the Netherlands were the leaders, and especially Australia, where the formidable Dr Evatt was a thorn in the side of the sponsoring powers. Evatt was Minister of External Affairs, and San Francisco marks in many ways the beginning of Australia as an independent actor on the world scene.[7] The agenda of the smaller powers had already been outlined at the Mexico City meeting of Latin American countries. It was to strengthen both the General Assembly and the International Court of Justice, and to weaken the veto power in the Security Council. In short, the smaller powers wanted more democracy, more transparency, and a more flexible veto, and to this end they compiled a questionnaire of 22 points in doubt and one addendum which they presented to the four sponsoring powers.

The reply of the Big Four was not to respond to the questions in detail, but to be clear and unambiguous about the veto. A strong veto power for

the permanent members of the Security Council was a *sine qua non*, and
their response on this issue was blunt:

> In view of the primary responsibilities of the permanent members, they
> could not be expected, in the present condition of the world, to assume
> the obligation to act in so serious a matter as the maintenance of
> international peace and security in consequence of a decision in which
> they had not concurred. Therefore, if a majority voting in the Security
> Council is to be made possible, the only practicable method is to provide,
> in respect of non-procedural decisions, for unanimity of the permanent
> members plus the concurring votes of at least two of the non-permanent
> members.[8]

Attempts to enlarge the Security Council in the interest of making it more
representative, and perhaps reducing the relative role of the permanent
members, were defeated, as was the notion that aggression should be
defined, since the permanent members were concerned that any definition
of aggression might bind them in advance to action they might not wish
to take. However, the sponsoring powers did agree to hold a review
conference within ten years of the United Nations coming into operation
if requested by two-thirds of the General Assembly and seven members
of the Security Council. Nevertheless, while there was no veto on calling
such a conference, the veto would be operative in any vote concerning
peace and security questions, including enforcement action.

One area in which the smaller powers did make some progress was
that of the role of regional organizations if the Security Council was not
acting on a question relating to peace and security. The Charter does
permit a role for regional organizations, including enforcement action,
provided that it is within the spirit of the Charter and that the Security
Council authorizes any enforcement action. However, regional organizations are not defined, and in effect this is merely going back to the
possibility of spheres of influence. With the veto on the activities of
regional bodies in peace and security firmly in place, and universalist
sentiments gaining the upper hand in the United States, the major sponsoring powers were able easily to make concessions, since the United
States could envisage a *de facto* Monroe Doctrine, Britain had recently
acted as patron to the founding of the Arab League, and the USSR,
following the Yalta agreement, now had its own sphere of influence in
Eastern Europe.

The role of the other organs was made more specific. Both the Trusteeship Council and the Economic and Social Council were made principal
organs, although both of them were to act within the general ambit of the
General Assembly, with the exception of Strategic Trust Territories. The
jurists who had been meeting privately had resolved their differences and

proposed the establishment of a new court, the International Court of Justice, which, unlike its predecessor, was to be a principal organ of the organization rather than independent from it. There were also some minor changes which reinforced the role and independence of the Secretariat.

On 26 June 1945 the United Nations Charter, in fact a Treaty, was signed in San Francisco. It remained to put it into operation, and with this in mind a Preparatory Commission was appointed, which sat in London, with each of the signatory powers having one member of the commission. The executive secretary was Sir Gladwyn Jebb from the UK Foreign Office, and he worked with an Executive Committee of 14, which was in fact made up of individuals from the same countries that had formed the Executive Committee operating at the San Francisco conference. By the time the Charter had received the necessary ratifications on 24 October 1945, which is now celebrated as United Nations Day, the Executive Committee had already met. The meeting on 16 August established working arrangements and subsidiary bodies, which led to final agreement on 23 December 1945. The General Assembly was therefore able to meet on 10 January 1946 in London, although the decision had already been taken that the permanent seat of the United Nations was to be in the United States. The UN organization had reached 'go'.

CONCLUSIONS

The negotiation of the Charter was an extraordinary achievement. Much of its formulation, and indeed its negotiation, was taking place while the war was still raging. The final outcome of the war in Europe and in Asia, in its political, economic and security terms, was therefore veiled in informed speculation. Moreover, new forces had been released by the war, in particular the undermining of colonialism following the initial defeat by Japan of the major Western powers in Asia – the United States, Britain, France and the Netherlands. Moreover, it was clear that of the Big Three, Britain would find it difficult to sustain its role, and the two superpowers were emerging. Indeed, the term superpower was coined at this time.

Yet through the vicissitudes of the war, with uncertainty regarding the form of its outcome, the Big Three were able, not only to prosecute the war, but also to think of the future. The men who had the wit and imagination to do this had led eventful lives. While they were living a Second World War, many of them had experienced in real terms the First World War and the depression that followed. They did not produce a perfect document, but they were able to lift their eyes above the battlefield and to envisage the possibility of a working future, which would not only aspire to a system of international peace and security, but also develop social and economic ties and promote human rights. The Charter they negotiated is a flawed document. Any competent international lawyer could remove its inconsistencies, close its loopholes and the like in an afternoon, but that is not the point. The Charter is a political document that gives legal expression to the realities of 1945 and the hopes for a better future. It is full of holes, but as we shall see in subsequent chapters, it is a document enabling governments with the will to act to do so if they can command widespread support. In short, it enables but does not prevent, where there is a willing spirit and general support. Rather like the Bible or Shakespeare, you can usually find justification in the Charter for whatever you wish to do or wish to prevent, but such contradictions are both its strength and its weakness, as we shall see as we follow the fortunes of the principal organs in the ensuing years.

NOTES

1. The General Postal Agreement dates from 1875 and the Universal Postal Union was established in 1878, while a conference in Paris in 1865 gave rise to an International Telegraph Bureau in Berne in 1869.
2. The permanent members were Britain, France, Italy, Japan and a place was reserved for the USA, while Belgium, Brazil, Greece and Spain were the initial selected members.
3. The following analysis draws copiously on the excellent article by Leland M. Goodrich entitled 'From League of Nations to United Nations', originally published in the first issue of *International Organization* (1947) and reprinted in David A. Kay (ed.), *The United Nations Political System* (London: John Wiley, 1967).
4. The initial distribution of non-permanent seats was two from Latin America and one from each of the following: the Commonwealth, Eastern Europe, the Middle East and Western Europe. This was later adjusted to reflect the increase in non-permanent members of the Security Council and especially that of members from Africa, Asia, the Pacific and the Caribbean.
5. Inis Claude, *Swords into Plowshares*, 3rd edn (New York: Random House, 1964), p. 51.
6. Quoted in A. LeRoy Bennett, *International Organization*, 2nd edn (Englewood Cliffs: Prentice-Hall, 1980), p. 44.
7. His principal adviser and permanent Head of the Ministry was John Burton, who was later to become an eminent world scholar in the development of the theory of international relations and conflict studies, especially in the 1960s and 1970s.
8. Quoted in Stephen S. Goodspeed, *The Nature and Function of International Organization* (New York: Oxford University Press, 1959), p. 97. This section draws extensively on this source for details of the organization of the conference and the issues as they arose.

CHAPTER 2

THE GENERAL ASSEMBLY: GRANDEUR AND DECADENCE

Marie-Claude Smouts

The forum of states that meets annually to debate in public the planet's most ticklish questions and to define universal standards for what is desirable and what is intolerable has become a routine on the international diplomatic agenda. In assessing these sessions, there is a tendency to see only the immediate results, which are often disappointing. Yet when they are placed in a long-term perspective, it is impossible not to wonder at the extraordinary change in diplomatic practices and international relations they posit. In its early days, the United Nations General Assembly (GA) was a crucial actor in these changes. It gradually became a mere reflection of them and is perhaps today a victim. The history of the General Assembly can actually be viewed in three phases: expansion, stagnation and marginalization. And if it continues to be marginalized, this will probably signify the obsolescence of the entire UN system and its incapacity to make a useful contribution to the establishment of global governance. The General Assembly is, in fact, the locus of co-operation between larger and smaller states. It helps to balance the asymmetrical structure of the international system that is reflected in the very structure of the United Nations: the Security Council alone – and thus the major powers – retains the right to make binding decisions. At the GA, all states are on an equal footing. All sensitivities, ideologies, differences in culture and interests can be expressed there in speech and by votes. The General Assembly is supposed to represent the main currents affecting the planet, and also represent the aspirations of peoples, not only states. Its vocation is to ensure a minimal collaboration from all states in the management of complex interdependencies that are the hallmark of today's international system. The devaluation of the GA at the close of this century is not a good sign. To dismiss it as inconsequential is to disregard the most populated countries, the newest ones, those that will determine the future of the planet.

EFFUSION AND ILLUSION OF A DEMOCRATIC ETHOS

The democratic ideal really permeated multilateral discourse for the first time in history with the League of Nations. President Wilson, the principal architect of the League, was convinced that the best way to eliminate war and the use of force was to build an American-style system with public opinion holding considerable sway over the conduct of political leaders. By ensuring that debates were public and treaties were published, the League was to ring in an era of open diplomacy. In Wilson's mind, all international bargaining would take place in full view of the mass of informed and peace-loving citizens who would punish authoritarian governments and warmongers without hesitation. Moral pressure was supposed to be as effective a wheel in the new institutional machinery as the system of collective security that was to be set up: 'The gentlemen of the League seem to have a great faith in machinery [collective security] for that purpose, a faith I cannot fully share. Personally I count more on the force of organized opinion.'[1] In the new organization, the Assembly was to be on an equal footing with the Council and express the force of international public opinion.

Wilson's idealism was not widely shared. The major European states were not prepared to abandon the old practice of the Concert of major powers in which France and Great Britain set great store. The creation of a universal-minded assembly that would bring states together in complete legal equality was a considerably innovative notion. The European powers endeavoured to make it fit into more traditional frameworks. In the preparatory stages, the Assembly was to be nothing more than a place to 'talk shop', where representatives would get together about every four years to air the 'organized opinion of mankind'. There was talk of sending women, religious figures, trade unionists, in other words, representatives of everyday life, but nothing considered serious at the level of high politics.[2] On the other hand, prime ministers and foreign ministers of the major powers were scheduled to meet yearly, thus perpetuating the old system of diplomatic conferences. In fact, with the first session of the Assembly, it turned out that the delegations were made up not of representatives from 'civil society' but instead of officials, diplomats and political figures. The French representative remarked, with no one to contradict him: 'The Assembly representatives are simply representatives of their respective governments.'[3]

The ethos of egalitarianism

In the minds of the Covenant's authors, the Assembly of the League of Nations was to have so little political weight that the details of its functioning were hardly discussed during the planning stages. They assigned it significant competences without fully measuring the consequences. Each member of the League of Nations was represented by three representatives and had one vote. The Assembly of the League of Nations was 'the epitome of the egalitarian body, the paradise of second-tier states'.[4] It alone was empowered to admit new members (by a two-thirds majority, Article 1, para. 2). It could 'deal at its meetings with any matter within the sphere of action of the League or affecting the peace of the world' (Article 3, para. 3; 11; 15). The debate between the smaller and the larger countries hinged essentially on the role of the Assembly in appointing members that were to make up the Council alongside the Principal Allied and Associated Powers.[5] Lesser powers considered the adoption of paragraph 1 of Article 4 of the Covenant a victory. It provided that four other members could be 'selected by the Assembly from time to time at its discretion'. They were also satisfied with the amendment to paragraph 2 passed in July 1926, introducing the vote by a two-thirds majority to fix 'the rules dealing with the election of the non-permanent members of the Council, and particularly such regulations as relate to their term of office and the conditions of re-eligibility'.

In the spirit of the major European powers, the Assembly of the League of Nations was only supposed to be a temporary body, meeting at rare intervals. It was up to the Council and to its permanent members actually to exercise any power. In fact, the Assembly's actions far exceeded what the architects of the Covenant intended. It established its own rules of procedure and used the Covenant's mechanisms of revision in such a way as to extend its capacities in essential areas and secure three major prerogatives:

1. *Persistence*, first of all. The Covenant provided (Article 3, para. 2) that: 'the Assembly shall meet at stated intervals and from time to time as occasion may require'. The Assembly decided at its very first session to meet every year, the first Monday in September.
2. *Budgetary powers* followed, in 1924, with an amendment to paragraph 5 of Article 6 of the Covenant which provided that 'the expenses of the League shall be borne by the Members of the League in the proportion decided by the Assembly'. In practice, the Assembly controlled all the League's expenses, including those of the International Labour Organization (ILO) and the Permanent Court of International Justice.
3. Last, the *capacity to manage all questions of common interest*. The Assembly

decided to create six committees, with a president and a rapporteur, in which all the delegations had the right to be represented and which naturally engendered as many sub-committees (overlapping and redundancy already loomed on the horizon).[6]

Decisions were made unanimously, which was an impediment to abusively political initiatives, but in general the Assembly of the League of Nations managed to discuss all matters of world interest, formulate important suggestions in all areas, including that of disarmament and security, and encourage international co-operation in all of its technical and functional aspects. It became a normal and recognized institution in international life. There was no marked differentiation either in law or in practice between the Assembly and the Council.

The writing of the Charter: some states more equal than others

The United Nations General Assembly is a child of the Assembly of the League of Nations, but it has never entirely benefited from the inheritance of its predecessor. First, it has never had the glamour of its forerunner, which brought together on the shores of Lake Geneva all that European society had to boast in political dignitaries, artists and scientists of the inter-war period.[7] But above all, the UN General Assembly only partly benefited from the accomplishments of the Assembly of the League of Nations. Certainly the annual meetings, the public debates, the budgetary power and that of establishing 'such subsidiary organs as it deems necessary for the performance of its functions' (Article 22 of the Charter) were maintained. But the distinction between the General Assembly and the Security Council was clearly established by the Charter and everything was designed in such a way that the Assembly could discuss, examine, recommend but not act by the means of binding decisions.

Planning for the creation of a new international organization to replace the League of Nations was mainly undertaken, under United States leadership, by the three major war allies: the USA, Britain and the USSR. The problem was how to incite small and medium-sized powers to join the future Organization while reserving the ascendancy over matters of international security for the major powers. On one hand, the League of Nations had given the smaller states a means of action on the international scene that they had never previously enjoyed and were not prepared to give up. On the other, it was obvious that the responsibility for the future peacekeeping and collective security system had to rest on the major powers, if only because of the USSR's firm position on this point. The USSR never forgave the League of Nations for expelling it in 1939. Its participation in the future Organization was not a foregone conclusion, and it laid down certain conditions. Stalin's agreement to a universal-minded organization was obtained at the Moscow conference in October 1943, then confirmed at the Teheran conference in December of that year. Diminishing the competences of the future General Assembly was the trade-off for this concession to universality. The exact purpose of the United Nations Organization still remained to be defined. This was done at Dumbarton Oaks.[8]

The structure envisaged, based on that of the League of Nations, included a plenary Assembly, a restricted Council and a Secretariat. The Assembly would be composed of all the member states. It would meet once a year, more often if necessary. Each state would have a single vote. But the three major powers agreed that a lack of differentiation between the Assembly and the Council was the League of Nations' main weakness. The League's Council had been distracted by a number of concerns other than having to do with peace and security. The joint responsibility of its two organs for a wide variety of subjects was more a hindrance than an advantage. The USSR concluded thus that the new Organization should deal only with security and leave aside all the economic and technical questions not directly related to this matter. The USA and Britain defended a broader concept of peace that was less exclusively political and military. They insisted that various populations expected the new Organization to help establish a lasting peace, to prevent and repress violence not only through collective security but also through economic and technical cooperation (here we recognize the functionalist approach). To their mind, the solution was not to restrict the Organization's functions but to establish a clear division of roles among its principal organs.[9] The idea of a small Council was put forth. It would have a restricted membership through which the Assembly could pursue its economic and social activities (the future Economic and Social Council – ECOSOC).

One of the thorniest questions was that of membership in the General Assembly, and therefore the United Nations. Not only were the respective competences of the Assembly and the Council with regard to admission (and expulsion) subject to bitter debates that Dumbarton Oaks did not entirely settle,[10] but the question of which states would be invited to be part of the Organization's founding members nearly swamped the entire enterprise. Among the original member states the United States wanted to see not only the 35 signatories of the Declaration by the United Nations on 1 January 1942, but the 'associated' states that had broken off relations with the Axis powers and participated in the United Nations economic conferences (six Latin American states, Egypt, Iceland and the provisional French government) and others viewed with favour such as Denmark, Lebanon, Syria, Saudi Arabia and Turkey. On 28 August 1944, the Soviet

Ambassador literally caused a panic in the West by announcing that the USSR would agree to extend membership to the associated states that had not technically been at war with the Axis but with the condition that the 16 Soviet republics be included among the initial members. Stalin's argument was that most Soviet republics were more important than some so-called independent states such as Liberia or Guatemala.[11] The question was not settled until the Yalta conference in February 1945, after months of intense diplomatic haggling. The USSR ended up being granted two additional seats at the General Assembly, one for Ukraine, the other for Belarus.

In security matters, the four major powers that attended Dumbarton Oaks were in agreement about leaving exclusive responsibility for managing and monitoring the maintenance of international peace and security to the Security Council. The discussion dwelled mainly on whether or not the Assembly should be allowed to make statements on these questions, at what point and in what way. The USSR defended a highly restrictive position: the Assembly could freely discuss problems of peace and security only after they had been examined by the Security Council and with its authorization. In general, the major powers wanted to limit the Assembly's right to discussion to a defined list of specific questions and, especially, to avoid the plenary Assembly from competing with the Security Council and claiming to control its activity.[12] All the organs were 'principal' ones, but the Security Council was more 'principal' than the others! As one might expect, the smaller and medium-sized countries did everything in their power in San Francisco to broaden the General Assembly's prerogatives as much as possible, in this area as well as others. To a certain extent they succeeded.

The compromises agreed in San Francisco gave the General Assembly broad authority accompanied by a significant reserve guaranteeing the Security Council's specific competences: 'While the Security Council is exercising in respect of any dispute or situation the functions assigned to it in the present Charter, the General Assembly shall not make any recommendation with regard to that dispute or situation unless the Security Council so requests' (Article 12). In practice, the General Assembly assumed itself to be competent to discuss and make recommendations on all subjects it cared to, on the basis of Chapter IV of the Charter. It enjoys boundless deliberative powers and deals with a wide variety of areas: 'any matters within the scope of the Charter' (Article 10), in other words, all aspects of international life; those relating to the powers, functions and reports of any organs of the UN, in other words, any matters related to the life of the Organization (Articles 10 and 15); those touching on the 'general principles of cooperation in the maintenance of international peace and security, including disarmament and regulation of armaments' (Article 11), in other words, the whole area of arms control; it 'may call the attention of the Security Council to situations which are likely to endanger international peace and security' (Article 11, para. 3), in other words, it has a power of 'qualification' which allows it weight in setting the international agenda, together with the power 'to recommend measures for the peaceful adjustment of any situation . . . likely to impair the general welfare or friendly relations among nations' (Article 14). The Economic and Social Council (Article 60), as well as the Trusteeship Council (Article 85), was expressly placed under its authority, which gave it a say in economic matters, social development, decolonization and what would later be referred to as North–South relations.

In addition to these expanded functions and political powers, the General Assembly also has administrative competences (it set regulations for nominating staff, Article 101) and financial competences (it considers and approves the United Nations budget and apportions the contributions among members, Article 17). It is also involved in the membership of all United Nations Organization bodies: the election of non-permanent members of the Security Council (Article 23), ECOSOC members (Article 61), the Trusteeship Council (Article 86); it is involved in nominating the Secretary-General (on recommendation of the Security Council, Article 97) and in appointing judges to the International Court of Justice (jointly with the Security Council, Article 8 of the Statute). It can create all the subsidiary organs that it deems necessary (Article 22).

The combination of such diversified competences gives the General Assembly the means to assume the primordial function devolved on the United Nations: to be 'a centre for harmonizing the actions of nations' for the common good, justice, social advancement and peace. It fulfils its role not through binding decisions making states responsible in the eyes of international law – only the Security Council can adopt such resolutions – but through a moral and intellectual authority, due to the fact that it represents, whether one likes it or not, an incarnation of the 'international community'.

Progressing towards universality

The General Assembly's authority is closely linked to its representativeness and therefore to its make-up. But the question of universality, which today is taken for granted, was a lingering problem. Two contrasting conceptions were confronted at the San Francisco conference. For some, particularly the Latin-American states, the United Nations was to represent the international community in its entirety, and any sovereign state that applied ought to be automatically admitted. For others (France especially), candidate states were to demonstrate their attachment to peace and provide guarantees through their institutions and their conduct in the international sphere. Finally, the solution adopted was one of a club of 'peace-loving states' able and willing to carry out the obligations contained in the Charter, without any other specification or reference to democratic institutions that would have been incompatible with the principle of non-interference in domestic affairs. It was agreed, moreover, that new members would be admitted 'by a decision of the General Assembly upon the recommendation of the Security Council' (Article 4, para. 2). This provision led to a series of problems that were to taint the first ten years of the United Nations' activity. Universality was perhaps a goal to pursue, but certainly not a principle to be taken for granted.

Very soon the effects of the Cold War became tangible. The question of admitting new members became a battle for prestige between the East and the West, and more precisely between the two superpowers, the United States and the USSR. In 1946, three candidates considered favourably by the West (Jordan, Portugal and Ireland) were rejected by a Soviet veto; two candidates supported by the USSR did not garner the seven votes necessary to secure a majority in the Security Council. The United States then suggested admitting all the candidate countries at once. The USSR refused. The following year, the USSR offered its own set of 'package proposals' very similar to those the USA had suggested. Meanwhile the latter had reaped the political benefits that came with denouncing the systematically obstructionist policy and the abuse of veto power levied by the USSR. They in turn rejected the simultaneous admission of candidates from both camps. The point was no longer to make progress on the road to UN universality, but to turn admission debates into propaganda operations:

> The United States, attempting to secure the admission of states supported by itself and the rejection of those supported by the USSR, sought a political victory, a demonstration of its primacy in the organization. The Soviet Union, fighting to make certain that its protégés would also gain entrance if the door were opened for Western candidates, sought to avoid a political defeat, a demonstration of its lack of influence in the United Nations.[13]

Between 1946 and 1955, the USSR wielded its veto 47 times against the admission of Western European candidates. The United States, on the other hand, prevented the required majority from coming together to allow entrance to Bulgaria, Hungary and Romania. A few states[14] trickled in until the Korean War (1950) led to a total standstill in the admissions process; 21 applications were rejected.

This 'policy of competitive exclusion' described by Inis Claude could only underscore the General Assembly's weakness and the lack of consideration given to the small and medium-sized countries that constituted the majority. The history of the first decade is also the history of the fruitless efforts made by smaller states to assert the General Assembly's prerogatives before the Security Council in matters of membership. Between 1948 and 1954, each year the General Assembly adopted a resolution which addressed the Security Council, informing it of 'the general feeling in favour of universality',[15] or 'a growing desire for universality'.[16] Two requests for advisory opinions were addressed to the International Court of Justice, one to enquire whether the General Assembly was competent to admit a state as member of the United Nations when the Security Council had not recommended its admission. The Court's opinion was negative, and the Security Council's decisive role in the admission process was clearly stated.[17] In order not to be marginalized entirely, the General Assembly nevertheless created a number of subsidiary organs, special commissions and commissions of good offices with the aim of consulting Security Council members and reconciling prevailing opinions. The evolution that can be noticed in its various resolutions reflects the evolution that was occurring on the diplomatic scene when the end of the Korean War and the death of Stalin modified the climate of East–West relations. The year 1954 was one of intense diplomatic activity. The idea of a 'package deal' was making headway. On 8 December 1955, a General Assembly resolution reversed the prior position by declaring that the practice of studying the merits of each state separately should be abandoned. The Security Council immediately recommended the simultaneous entrance of 16 countries that had applied. On 14 December 1955, the General Assembly admitted those 16 countries.[18]

The question of admitting new members lost its acuteness with the great turning point of the 1955 package deal. Entrance became automatic, with a few exceptions. The case of divided countries, those separated into two blocs by an internal border, long seemed insoluble. Germany was not admitted as two separate countries until 1973. Vietnam was admitted only after its reunification in 1977. The two Koreas did not enter until 1991, when North Korea lifted its opposition to their simultaneous admission which had lasted from 1973. Apart from these particular cases, the trend towards universality made steady progress, the UN admitting new states as they gained independence and made the request, with two high periods: 1960–66, when the new states in sub-Saharan Africa entered; and 1991–93, when new states created in the dismantling of the Soviet empire and collapse of the Yugoslavian federation joined. By 2000, the UN numbered 189 states. The principle of universality has triumphed.

Universality has triumphed so well that the 'capacity' requirement stipulated in Article 4 of the Charter has fallen into oblivion, and several

dozen 'micro-states' are now represented at the United Nations. Their
capacity to assume all the obligations attached to the quality of a sovereign
state, to assume the significant costs in terms of staff and money attendant
upon the participation of the multiple UN bodies, and consequently to
exercise their right to vote in a thought-out and informed manner, can be
seriously questioned. The issue was raised with the admission of the
Maldive Islands in 1965. Naturally committees of experts were formed to
debate the matter. Various plans of association were suggested, micro-
states were advised to federate, and ... the issue was dropped. Too
complicated, too politically hazardous and, anyway, impossible to gain
the assent of a majority of the General Assembly.

The last bastion of sovereign equality

Its universality and its principle of 'one Member, one vote' make the
General Assembly the prime arena to exalt a state's international status,
with its privileges and traditional attributes such as strict conformity to
protocol and diplomatic immunity. It is the living embodiment of the
principle of sovereign equality written in the Charter (Article 2, para. 1):
states represented there are not subjected to any higher authority; they
have the same rights and the same obligations with regard to international
law. Critics like to point out that in defiance of any sort of realism, the
General Assembly confers the quality of state on a number of political
entities that are ill-assured or minuscule in terms of their population and
that it contributes in this way to keeping 'failing states' alive artificially,
though they have no real existence except through their United Nations
status. In truth, the UN's adversaries[19] take exception to the real political
programme contained in the principle of sovereign equality as it has been
interpreted by the majority of the General Assembly. Equal participation
of all in pondering and deciding on subjects of common interest marks a
step in the democratization of international relations that does not suit
everyone. It eliminates any hierarchy among cultures and systems of
political representation by giving everyone, big or small, the right to speak
on a subject that should be brought to the attention of the international
community and how it should be dealt with. Furthermore, in the 1960s
and 1970s, developing states started pulling the principle of sovereign
equality out of its strictly legal framework to use it as a weapon in their
demands with respect to the North to build a New Order that was fairer
and less inegalitarian.[20] We shall see later that today's marginalization of
the General Assembly is to a large extent due to the break-off of the
North–South dialogue and the ensuing shift in negotiations between
industrialized countries and developing countries to other bodies better
controlled by the North.

The delights of parliamentary intrigue

'Decisions of the General Assembly on important questions are made by a two-thirds majority of the members present and voting. On other questions, decisions are made by a majority.' In practice, many resolutions are passed without a vote. Except during the period 1949–54, which marked the height of the Cold War, at least one-third of the resolutions were already adopted unanimously during the first two decades.[21] From 1964,[22] the practice of consensus has tended to prevail, although the countries of the South, a majority in the Assembly, have tried to use the weight of numbers to get resolutions that suited them passed. But the adoption year after year of resolutions that the North did not want and had no intention of implementing gradually turned out to be a fool's game that was just as dangerous as unproductive. The worst illustration of this was the resolution declaring Zionism to be a form of racism, passed in November 1975 thanks to the mechanism of the Assembly majority, without much thought given to what the vote implied. The resolution was annulled 16 years later (December 1991) by the same Assembly.

Since the late 1970s, the proportion of resolutions passed without a vote has continued to increase, now nearing two-thirds of the resolutions. As international institutions cannot resist getting wrapped up in detail, the General Assembly has managed to make a subtle distinction between 'adoption by consensus' and 'adoption without a vote or without objection'. Consensus allegedly means that all delegations were involved in negotiations and all agree with the proposal presented. 'Adoption without a vote or without objection' means that some delegations formally acknowledge a proposal, but they do not want to vote against it, although they do not agree with it. Of course no one outside of the Delegates' Lounge could care less about this sort of subtlety.

Whether passed by consensus or a two-thirds majority, General Assembly resolutions spark off a flurry of backstage activity not unlike parliamentary activity, with its caucuses, permanent groups, *ad hoc* coalitions, clientelism and influence-peddling. Off-the-record meetings, caucus deliberations, rumours, prognostications, dramatization, suspense . . . such are the delegates' delights.[23]

Officially, the General Assembly recognizes the existence of geographic groupings, necessary to ensure an equitable geographical distribution in elections to the various UN bodies. Five groups of states are recognized: African, Asian, Latin American and Caribbean, Eastern European states, and Western European and other states. This categorization in fact only serves to ensure a rotating representation of the various regions of the globe. These geographic groupings rarely constitute an organized bloc representing a coherent political force. All are fairly elastic. Only the members of the European Union form a permanent, united group that tends to speak with one voice. They meet daily to discuss all subjects debated at the General Assembly, and 'European consultation' takes up considerable time on the agenda of delegates from European Union member states. As for the rest, stable coalitions are based not on geographic solidarity but on shared perceptions and a desire to use the weight of numbers despite often divergent immediate interests. The first of these coalitions was the Afro-Asian group, which appeared in 1950 and showed its full force with the Bandung conference in 1955. It displayed seamless solidarity in favour of the emancipation of colonized peoples. It was later eclipsed by the Non-aligned Movement, which itself was often confused with the Group of 77 in the early 1970s. The creation of the United Nations Conference on Trade and Development (UNCTAD) in 1964 in fact led to a *rapprochement* of Latin American countries, which up to then had kept their distance from the initial Third World coalitions. Developing countries regrouped under the Group of 77 (the 77 developing countries that participated in the first UNCTAD). By institutionalizing negotiation by groups, UNCTAD reinforced the group system in the whole UN machinery. Southern countries stacked up their demands by presenting themselves as a single bloc throughout the height of the period of North–South dialogue and the New International Economic Order.[24] Within these large coalitions, the Arab group, the African group (itself divided into French-speaking and English-speaking countries and moderates and radicals), the Latin American states (often competing with and divided on the question of sanctions against Cuba), the members of ASEAN, those of the North Atlantic Treaty Alliance (NATO) constitute a number of more or less closely bound subgroups depending on the time and the topics on the agenda. The practice of 'contact groups' made up of representatives of groups interested in a given subject, and usually known by the name of their president, or 'like-minded countries', helps to establish a link among these informal, short-lived groups, the existence and function of which only those initiated into the arcane reaches of the UN manage to detect and decipher.

Until the mid-1980s, the coalitions were relatively predictable on a wide variety of subjects. The non-aligned countries voted as one against South Africa and Israel's policy in the occupied territories. The same countries, recomposed as the Group of 77, pushed for greater efforts to be made by rich countries in favour of developing countries and for adjustments to be made in the rules governing the trade system, maritime and environmental law that would discriminate in their favour, etc. The general tone was offensive, critical towards the West in general and of United States foreign policy in particular. Several factors helped to change things. The United States offensive against the United Nations system and the big stick policy they implemented from 1986 was one. At the General Assembly, the tone softened, and the game some indulged in of uniting a majority around a 'tough-minded' text, and others of gleaning votes here and there by mobilizing clients and allies to limit the scope of criticism, became less common. The debt crisis and the international public aid crisis was another. The South was divided, the non-aligned no longer had the same interests. Solidarities crumbled. The last factor was the renewal of the Security Council. Since 1986, this is where all the attention has shifted. The end of the Cold War hastened this change. The split that allowed coalitions to form along an East–West axis ceased to exist. The line that separated a divided North and a united South became far less clear. The parliamentary intrigues that made the UN a zero sum game in which every decision seemed like a victory won by one side over the other lost much of its excitement. Coalitions are increasingly formed on an *ad hoc* basis. Discussions are more technical, more austere and less conducive to dramatic gesticulation. Deprived of confrontation and flights of lyricism, the delegates work very hard but are terribly bored.

The functioning of the General Assembly

Delegations

According to the Charter (Article 9), each member shall have not more than five representatives in the GA. The Rules of Procedure adopted by the GA added the possibility of having five alternate representatives, and 'as many advisers, technical advisers, experts and persons of similar status as may be required by the delegation'.

Setting up permanent missions and ambassadors to the United Nations was an innovation with respect to the League of Nations. Though mandatory for the permanent members of the Security Council who must be able to meet at once in an emergency, they were not required of the other members, given that the General Assembly sessions were supposed to be limited in time. Yet since 1948, member states have habitually maintained a permanent mission in New York. The poorest states sometimes combine it with their diplomatic representation in Washington to save money. Permanent mission staff make up the larger part of delegations to the General Assembly. They are 'reinforced' during sessions by functionaries from the various capitals, a horde of experts and a few parliamentarians (Denmark, for instance, is known for having a parliamentary delegation that meets for the entire session, thereby ensuring a close watch over the executive by the legislative). The size, composition and margin of autonomy of a delegation vary considerably from one country to another.[25] Delegations are usually headed by the Foreign Minister. The Head of State or Prime Minister often makes the trip to give a speech during the General Debate.

To understand the role of delegations, it helps to get into the atmosphere of a General Assembly session. It is a huge diplomatic gathering, a constant stream of high level personalities, countless formal and informal meetings to follow daily, not to mention the round of receptions given by states in turn to which it would be improper and politically incorrect not to attend. All this political–social brouhaha makes Assembly sessions the ideal occasion for discreet encounters between protagonists who supposedly are not speaking to one another. Furthermore, the various solidarity, pressure and emotional networks that exist on the planet come together for the General Assembly. NGOs, religious representatives and liberation movements are all present. Observer status, which allows people to participate in the discussions without a right to vote, is freely granted.[26] The role of delegations is therefore multifold. Attendance itself is a primary role. For countries that claim to be present on the world scene, it is important to be there, to show an interest in what is happening on a global scale and reflected at the General Assembly. Expertise is an important role as well: committees work on a daily basis and the subjects are often technical. Above all there is a political role: delegations must be mindful to support projects that might have repercussions on the international order (what Wolfers called 'environment goals') while looking out for the immediate interests of the political entity one represents ('possession goals').

A Credentials Committee, composed of nine members appointed by the General Assembly at each session, examines representatives' credentials and reports to the GA. It is one of the rare Assembly committees to remain constant in its number of members, which tends to indicate its lack of importance. The matter of credentials is, however, not an insignificant one and for this reason they are decided in plenary session. On one hand, the question of accreditation implies a recognition that cannot be taken for granted: one example is the status of China, whose seat was occupied up until 1971 by representatives from Taipei, or the case of Cambodia's representation, which was problematic from 1973 until the Paris Accords of 1985, during which time a variegated coalition unfailingly supported the Khmer Rouge instead of leaving the seat vacant as the USSR suggested. On the other hand, it has happened that the General Assembly rejects representatives' letters of credentials, thereby seeking a de facto expulsion, since it was unable to boot the state out of the UN: this was the case of the South African delegation in 1974 and the Israeli delegation in 1975 (what is known as the Bouteflika doctrine, from the name of the Algerian Foreign Minister, the very influential General Assembly President at that time). The Assembly thus circumvented the

Security Council and its right to veto by transforming a question of substance into a simple matter of procedure.[27]

Sessions

The delegations have all the more work since the sessions have had a tendency to meet for longer and more frequent periods. In fact, there are three types of sessions. There are the **regular annual sessions** that begin each year, barring exceptions, on the third Tuesday in September. Theoretically, they are supposed to end in the third week in December. In practice, they more and more often run into the next year. In 1991, the General Assembly decided that its 46th session would go up until the eve of the opening of the 47th! Since then, the GA has fallen into the habit of meeting frequently between January and September. At the 50th session, for instance, it held 100 plenary meetings from September to December 1995 and 28 meetings (one-quarter of a regular annual session) between February and September 1996.

In addition to the disproportionately long regular sessions there are the **special sessions** authorized by the Charter (Article 20) 'as occasion may require'. Twenty of them were held between 1947 and 1998. Seventeen were called at the General Assembly's request; one was called by the Security Council;[28] two by a member state.[29] Six are scheduled between 1999 and 2001. Finally, since the 'Uniting for Peace' resolution adopted by the GA in 1950, an **emergency special session** can be convened within 24 hours whenever a veto prevents the Security Council from acting. Ten were called between 1956 and 1997, six of which dealt with the Middle East.

If we add to these three types of sessions the General Assembly's habit since the 1970s of calling at least one major Special Conference of the United Nations per year, we can grasp the magnitude of the dizzing diplomatic dance that goes on in the international forum. As the president of the GA pointed out at its 49th session: 'The GA is virtually continuous which clearly poses a number of logistical problems in terms of financial and material resources . . . Many member states also have great difficulty in fully participating in the various meetings, since they are ill-prepared for this new and unexpected trend.'[30]

The making of the agenda

The number of items listed on the agenda of regular annual sessions has been continually inflated over the years: 46 separate agenda items at the first session (1946), 143 at the 39th (1985), 156 at the 52nd (1997–98), 168 at the 53rd (1998), most of which are divided into sub-items. Such inflation can be partly explained by the fact that the Assembly's General Committee (Bureau) never bothers to revise the agenda by removing redundant items or those that give rise to debates and resolutions that have little connection with reality (211 resolutions at the 52nd session, most of which no one will ever read!). The General Assembly has picked up the unfortunate habit of concluding nearly all its resolutions with a note to list the point discussed on the agenda of the following session. Items pile up, weighing down the sessions and lending credence to the opinion of those who believe the GA to be a costly and verbose machine whose activity often amounts to nothing.

Most questions are allocated to GA main committees, which are divided as follows:[31]

First Committee: Disarmament and International Committee
Second Committee: Economic and Financial Committee
Third Committee: Social, Human and Cultural Committee
Fourth Committee: Special Political and Decolonization Committee
Fifth Committee: Administration and Budgetary Committee
Sixth Committee: Legal Committee

These committees are 'committees of the whole', exact reproductions of the plenary Assembly and, consequently, as inflexible as the GA is to conducting genuine negotiations. Committee debates and votes on resolutions provide a means of gauging the strategies and power struggles among members. An intense backstage campaign can sometimes manage to shift votes from the moment a project has been adopted by a committee and the moment it comes up for vote in the plenary Assembly, but this gleans only a few votes and is effective only when the majority promises to be a narrow one.

Often a preliminary battle has already been fought before the General Committee (Bureau),[32] which is charged with 'making recommendations to the General Assembly with regard to each item proposed, concerning its inclusion in the agenda, the rejection of the request for inclusion, or the inclusion of the item in the provisional agenda for a future session' (Article 40 of the Rules of Procedure of the GA). Including an item on the agenda is a highly political and often conflictual procedure. It means, in fact, that a strong coalition, more or less supported by the Secretariat, has decided that there is a breach between the actual state of things and what it should be. This is already a value judgement. At the same time the state of fact is elevated to an 'issue', it must also be 'qualified' so as to decide on the Assembly's competence. This is how, for instance, it was decided that 'discussing' a matter does not mean intervening in this matter.[33] Thus any objection based on Article 2, paragraph 7 was swept away: 'Nothing contained in the present Charter shall authorize the United Nations to intervene in matters which are essentially within the domestic jurisdiction of any state or shall require the Members to submit such matters to settlement under the present Charter.' Never has the invocation of this article prevented the Assembly from dealing with an issue. South Africa and several former colonial powers are well aware of this, particularly France, which fought a long and unsuccessful battle in the 1950s to prevent the Bureau from recommending the Assembly to include the issue of North Africa (Morocco, Tunisia, Algeria) on the agenda. When an issue is brought to the Bureau's attention to be listed on the General Assembly agenda, it means that the international community will be called on to give a political judgement, to bring the matter to the attention of international opinion, even to make recommendations on what ought to be done. Among the items proposed for inclusion in the provisional agenda of the 52nd session were, for instance: 'nuclear-weapon-free southern hemisphere and adjacent areas', 'Israeli practices affecting the human rights of the Palestinian people', 'the question of East Timor', 'net transfer of resources between developing and developed countries', 'situation in the occupied territories of Croatia'. The simple listing of these items gives an idea of the heated debates that were to come and the efforts some would make to dodge them. Many states know that, at all stages of agenda inclusion, they face confrontation at the GA. They try, if not to avoid listing on the agenda, at least to have a say in how the issue will be qualified. There again, debates in the Bureau prefigure those in the plenary Assembly and lift the curtain on the participants' arguments and strategies.

The role of the President

In the spirit of the Charter's authors, the President of the General Assembly should be the incarnation of the United Nations Organization, the chief mediator charged with getting different, even conflictual, partners to work together. This was meant to be a prestigious, global-level function. Its holder was to be a man of experience, a shrewd strategist and diplomat, universally accepted and independent. Because the stakes were so high, the election of the first President (the Belgian politician Paul-Henri Spaak) sparked considerable controversy. It ended up being more a nomination that was the product of a gentlemen's agreement between Western powers and the USSR than an election resulting from the spontaneous vote of the 51 United Nations member states.[34]

The United Nations evolved differently from what was planned because of the unexpected rise of the function of Secretary-General. Dag Hammarskjöld's (1953–61) strong personality made the Secretary-General the main character of the UN, overshadowing all others in the Organization.

Although no other Secretary-General has since equalled him in authority and 'magistracy of influence',[35] Dag Hammarskjöld endowed his function with a dimension that nothing had suggested and which has endured ever since. Anyone who takes an interest in international relations knows the name of the incumbent UN Secretary-General. Who knows the name of the General Assembly President? The means granted to the GA President to fulfil his task are notoriously insufficient. The holders of this position constantly bemoan it and list their 'privations and frustrations', emphasizing that they are mostly dependent on the staff and support granted them by their own government and cannot 'meet the needs of fulfilling basic administrative and official travel expenses and hospitality requirements'.[36]

Yet the President has considerable responsibility in the proper conduct of the Assembly's tasks. He has to see that procedure is respected, manage the floor, suggest means of accelerating cumbersome or backlogged work, help bring the work of the various working groups to a conclusion; in sum, keep the machine running. He is also necessarily involved in a host of informal negotiations to assuage useless dissensions, avert pointless crises and bring points of view into agreement when he can. He also entertains close relations with the other organs within the UN system, especially the Security Council, and of course the Secretariat. To do so he must lend an ear, make himself available, command respect and inspire confidence. It can be said that most of the time, the man elected President of the General Assembly meets these demands and deploys talent in performing a thankless task. Note that out of 52 sessions, only twice was a woman elected President of the General Assembly.[37]

THE EVOLUTION OF THE GENERAL ASSEMBLY

The importance of the General Assembly's role on the international scene and in the UN machinery is closely linked to its capacity to act as a faithful reflection of the actors and stakes in world competition. It is at its height when four conditions are met simultaneously: (1) states are the main actors in the international game as it is currently being played out; (2) the stakes of the competition and the outcomes are on an ideological and symbolic level that is sensitive to the effects of 'world opinion'; (3) the decisions reached within the General Assembly express the actual balance of power in the international system; (4) the 'strategic actors', in other words those upon whom the UN depends for its financing and its functioning, gain some satisfaction during the General Assembly. The variations in the combinations of these four conditions explain the various phases the GA has gone through since its creation.

The General Assembly in world politics: from expansion to marginalization

The rise in power (1945 to early 1960s)

In the first decades following the Second World War, two major clashes tore apart the international scene: the East–West conflict, and colonized peoples' struggle for independence. In both cases, the strategic actors found the General Assembly useful: the United States, which dominated the Organization unchallenged, and the anti-colonialist countries, which benefited from weight in numbers in the plenary Assembly. The East–West conflict soon paralysed the functioning of the Security Council, and the General Assembly became the alternative place to continue to examine political disputes in the realm of peace and security. The decolonization movement found powerful allies in the General Assembly and its various committees (in particular the Fourth Committee: Trusteeship including Non-self-governing Territories). It made the General Assembly, even more than the Trusteeship Council, the instrument of 'collective legitimization' and world pressure in favour of the emancipation of colonized peoples.

In the early years, the General Assembly had a tendency to broaden the scope of its power. It first sought the means to exist in a permanent manner, so as to be able to handle crises that the Security Council found itself incapable of dealing with adequately, without waiting for the regular session to open. The decision to create a 'Little Assembly', called on to meet in the interval between regular sessions (Resolution 111 [II]) was taken in 1947. This interim committee has the same make-up as the General Assembly. It has the power to make a preliminary study on any dispute and any situation for which a request had been made for its inclusion on the agenda. It can conduct enquiries and decide if a situation warrants calling a special session. The 'Little Assembly' was established on a permanent basis in 1949 but, in practice, it soon ceased to function without ever having the opportunity to fulfil its assigned role.[38] Its failure was due largely to the boycott of the Soviet Union and communist bloc, which considered it illegal. In fact, as we have seen earlier, by the combination of special sessions and emergency special sessions, the Assembly quickly became the *de facto* 'standing diplomatic Conference' that the small and medium-sized powers always wanted and which the United States needed at the time to continue to build its case against the communist world.

Beginning in 1947, the Security Council became unable to function as the Charter's authors intended and the UN's centre of gravity gradually shifted towards the Assembly. The General Assembly intervened with increasing frequency in the area of international peace and security. The division of tasks between the Council and the Assembly which the

Charter's designers had attempted to establish became blurred. For instance, in October 1947, the Assembly decided to send a special commission to the Balkans to observe the situation in northern Greece (UNSCOB);[39] in 1948, it appointed a committee of experts to study the monetary problems behind the embargo on Berlin; in April 1947, it met in a special session (at the United Kingdom's request) to create a United Nations Special Commission on Palestine (UNSCOP); on 29 November 1947, it approved the plan for the political partition of Palestine[40] and set the borders of the various states and the Jerusalem sector. In 1948, it devoted another special session to the Israeli–Arab conflict. After the assassination of the mediator (Count Bernadotte) appointed by the Security Council, it appointed a Reconciliation Commission to help interested governments to settle the Palestinian question and adopted a widespread assistance programme to help Arab refugees (which led to the UNRWA, the United Nations Relief and Works Agency). In short, the General Assembly was where all eyes and aspirations turned. At that time, in fact, GA debates were extensively reported in the international press, and major newspapers had a permanent correspondent at the United Nations.

The Korean War accelerated the shift of Security Council power towards the General Assembly. The adoption of Resolution 377 (V), Uniting for Peace, transformed into an established principle what was a *de facto* intrusion into a dimension that had been given by the Charter to the Security Council as a matter of priority. The conditions under which this resolution was adopted are well known. Between 25 June and 31 July 1950, the Security Council adopted several resolutions allowing the UN to intervene militarily to aid the Korean republic. It was actually a question of approving the intervention of American troops already committed to prevent the South Korean forces from being wiped out, and to legitimate this intervention by establishing a unified command (the United Nations Unified Command) placed under the authority of the United States and authorized to use the United Nations flag.[41] This was possible only because the USSR representative had left his seat empty since the beginning of the year to protest against China being represented by officials from Taiwan. When the USSR representative returned to his seat, and at the same time took over the presidency of the Security Council which was rightfully his by an accident of the calendar, on 1 August 1950, the Security Council ended up unable to continue to adopt any measure whatsoever in the Korean affair. Naturally, the General Assembly became the place to pursue action. On 7 October 1950, in accordance with American wishes, it adopted a resolution with enormous political and military consequences by recommending 'all appropriate steps' to be taken to ensure conditions of stability and the establishment of a 'unified government' in Korea.[42] This resolution implicitly authorized the Unified

Command to cross the 38th parallel, despite repeated warnings from China and words of caution from the major Afro-Asian countries who took these warnings very seriously. What came to pass is well known: General MacArthur led the UN troops across the 38th parallel the next day, on 8 October. The UN forces encountered thousands of well-equipped and trained Chinese 'volunteers' and had to beat a retreat. To allow the General Assembly to deal with the Korean issue fully, the United States got another resolution passed on 3 November 1950, introducing a severe modification in the constitutional balance provided for in the Charter, the famous Uniting for Peace.[43] The resolution formally affirmed the responsibility of the GA to deal with international peace and security when the Security Council was unable to act. It asserted its right to make 'appropriate recommendations to Members for collective measures, including in the case of a breach of the peace or act of aggression, the use of armed force when necessary'. In addition, the major provisions of the resolution recommended:

- Establishment of a procedure for calling the GA into 'emergency special session' within 24 hours by a vote of any seven members of the Security Council or upon request of a majority of the members of the Assembly when a lack of unanimity among the permanent members made the Security Council unable to act in the face of a threat to international peace or an act of aggression.
- That all members 'train, organize and equip contingents of their national forces' for prompt availability as UN units. The Secretary-General was authorized to appoint a 'panel of military experts' to advise governments, upon their request, about setting up the earmarked national units to be maintained in readiness for the UN.
- Creation of a 14-member Collective Measures Committee to study and report on further methods of strengthening the ability of the UN to meet breaches of the peace and acts of aggression.
- Creation of a 14-member Peace Observation Commission (POC), including representatives of the five permanent members of the Security Council to be available for immediate assignment as observers and report on the situation in any area where international tensions may threaten peace and security.

The Uniting for Peace plan was conceived as a device for giving the General Assembly a collective security role when conflicts involved the major powers that could not be dealt with by the Security Council; in fact all the high intensity conflicts during the time of the Cold War. In reality, the collective security device never functioned. Of all of its provisions, only the one that allowed the General Assembly to call an emergency meeting and make recommendations on what measures to take was implemented, and this ten times between 1950 and 1997. And member states no more respected the provisions of Article 43 of the Charter[44] than they followed the recommendations that they themselves adopted, starting with the United States. No government was prepared to commit itself beforehand to a doubtful conflict in which the two superpowers were likely to be involved. Never did the General Assembly believe it possible to recommend coercive measures like those provided for in Chapter VII. For a few years the Collective Measures Committee submitted voluminous reports to the General Assembly, none of which was ever put into effect. The POC functioned only once, replacing the UNSCOB along the northern Greek border, and was withdrawn in 1954. When Thailand asked the POC to be sent to its border with Laos and Cambodia, the request was vetoed by the Security Council and was not brought before the General Assembly.

The Uniting for Peace resolution did not function as planned. It did not give the UN the means to operate a permanent collective security system to complement the one provided for in the Charter. The fact that 40 years later B. Boutros-Ghali presented *An Agenda for Peace* reiterating a number of points that had been envisaged in 1950 is a flagrant illustration of this. Yet the adoption of this resolution set off a chain reaction. First of all, it ushered in the enduring preponderance of the Security Council with respect to peacekeeping; in 1998, a former General Assembly president still had this to say: 'I would recommend seeking greater recourse in the General Assembly through the resolution entitled "Uniting for Peace" for those Members who cannot find due justice in the Security Council.'[45] Psychologically and politically it prepared for the launching of peacekeeping operations that were to take place later on. Many of these operations, beginning with the first (UNEF), were deployed on the basis of General Assembly recommendations, at the Secretary-General's initiative, until the moral and financial fiasco of the United Nations operation in the Congo (1960–64) restored greater caution and respect for the Charter's provisions. The Soviet bloc countries, and France (which, nevertheless, was not opposed to the resolution[46]) always felt that Uniting for Peace was illegal. For years they refused to pay the required dues for peacekeeping operations that were not carried out from A to Z by the Security Council (UNEF and ONUC in particular). The UN's financial crisis, recurrent since 1957, dates from that time. Finally, the contempt shown by the United States and their Western allies with regard to warnings from the large Afro-Asian countries throughout the Korean War strongly contributed to the birth of non-alignment ideology.

The move towards decolonization was the other distinctive feature of the UN's early decades, against a backdrop of East–West conflict. The General Assembly tackled the matter vigorously and therein played an historic role that it has never equalled since. Its majority was made up of countries that were themselves the products of major movements of emancipation from colonial domination. Added to these were the socialist countries and Scandinavian countries, stirred by anti-colonial spirit, although for different reasons, and the active support of the two super-powers, the United States and the USSR, they too for different reasons. The confrontation was severe, the tone vehement and the result significant. The General Assembly managed to create a mechanism of control over the situation in the non-self-governing territories as important as the one instituted by the Charter for trust territories. The first step (as early as 1946) was the creation of a GA *ad hoc* committee to examine the information supplied by the administering members. The colonial powers were asked to list the non-self-governing territories under their jurisdiction and to report on the state of economic, social and educational conditions that prevailed there. The status of this Committee on Information from Non-Self-Governing Territories gained influence steadily over the years.

The famous Resolution 1514, 'Declaration on the Granting of Independence to Colonial Countries and People', marked a high point. It legitimated all the anti-colonial struggles and set the objective to be sought by providing that alien domination is contrary to the Charter: all peoples have a right to self-determination; 'inadequacy of political, economic, social, or educational preparedness is no excuse for delaying independence'.[47] At that time, the last strongholds of colonialism were in the Portuguese colonies, South-West Africa, Algeria on the path to self-determination and a few 'patches' of French empire that Paris carefully neglected to put on the list of non-self-governing territories (especially the Comores and New Caledonia). The Fourth Committee was particularly pugnacious, always willing to hear petitions from non-self-governing territories, despite protests from the colonial powers availing themselves of Article 2, paragraph 7. But mainly, the creation of a so-called Committee on Decolonization, known as the Committee of Twenty-Four,[48] gave the General Assembly permanent means of control. The Committee of Twenty-Four took the place of the Committee on Information. It granted itself broad powers: that of making the list of non-self-governing countries itself, of making recommendations to the administering countries, of conducting its own enquiries, of 'condemning', 'disapproving', 'asserting', 'reasserting', in short, defining what was good and what was bad. With its verbal outrages and its radicalization, it was – and potentially still is – the *bête noire* of countries that still have overseas possessions.

No one can measure accurately the role of the General Assembly in gaining independence for colonized countries. It is primarily through their own struggle that they achieved it. But the General Assembly accelerated the process. First, it provided legal and psychological support to national liberation movements. And its intervention increased the moral and

political cost of colonial wars. Condemned by the majority on the international scene, increasingly difficult to justify on the domestic level, these
wars became indefensible for European countries that claimed to be
democratic and prided themselves on respecting human rights. Vulnerable
because more sensitive than others to their image on the international
scene, the Netherlands, Britain, Belgium and France gradually yielded to
pressure. More often criticized than others, it was easy for them to accuse
the Assembly of 'double standards' for being quicker to stigmatize
France's behaviour in North Africa or Belgium's in the Congo than the
USSR's conduct in Hungary, India's in Goa, or Indonesia's in Timor.

Stagnation (1965 to early 1980s)

After two decades of effervescence when the world's eyes were so often
trained on the General Assembly, it entered a second phase characterized
by three major factors. First, the new Third World countries became a
majority. They had the power to set the agenda. They imposed their
concerns. Economic and social problems tended to outweigh problems of
security, with the notable exception of Middle East conflicts and the fight
against apartheid. Second, after the Cuban missile crisis, the international
system entered a phase of loose bipolarism in which the two superpowers
struck up a sort of dialogue regarding disarmament and arms control.
The General Assembly was no longer the closed circle of East–West
ideological confrontation. The major powers took less of an interest in it.
Finally, American hegemony was openly contested, within and outside
the UN, and at all levels: economic (the building of Europe, trade
competition with Germany and Japan), political (de Gaulle's criticism of
the Vietnam War) and intellectual (new development and *dependencia*
theories greatly influenced by the work of the Economic Commission for
Latin America).

In the field of peace and security, the General Assembly had demonstrated that it could not do much when the two superpowers were
involved. In the Cuban missile crisis, the Berlin crisis, the American
military intervention in Vietnam (never put on the GA agenda!), the
General Assembly remained ineffectual. Many local conflicts emerged in
Third World countries that it was no more able to solve: for example the
Western Sahara, Lebanon, Iraq–Iran, Cambodia. These conflicts divided
developing countries and embarrassed them by breaching the façade of
unanimity that was their best asset in multilateral negotiations. During
this period, most of the attention, action and financing was oriented
towards development questions.

The new states had won their political sovereignty with the GA's help.
They now wanted to win their economic sovereignty. Their claim was to

redefine the rules of the economic and trade game which had been defined not only in their absence but, they argued, to their detriment. The decade of the 1960s was proclaimed 'United Nations Development Decade'.[49] The General Assembly thereby inaugurated a long series of 'Strategies', 'Decades' and other events designed to dramatize its efforts. In 1964, developing countries succeeded in having UNCTAD made into a permanent subsidiary organ of the GA. UNCTAD was designed to reflect the needs of developing countries in the face of the GATT which served the interests of rich countries alone. UNCTAD in fact would function as a research organization in the service of developing countries. It helped them to prepare their bargaining positions. It supported their demand for fair prices for raw materials. It drew public attention to the negative effects of widespread free trade on poorer countries. In 1965, the General Assembly made an attempt to rationalize the instruments it had available for technical assistance by combining the Expanded Programme of Technical Assistance (EPTA) and the Special Fund Programme (created in 1949 and 1958 respectively) into a United Nations Development Programme (UNDP). Not only did it create subsidiary organs designed to increase multilateral public development aid, but it sought to change the rules of the game between developing and industrialized countries by, year after year, adopting numerous resolutions all in the same vein, aiming to establish certain basic principles that it felt should be recognized under national and international law. The main ones were those dealing with state sovereignty over natural resources and foreign-owned business activities and those concerning the New International Economic Order (NIEO). The historic 1962 Declaration on Permanent Sovereignty over Natural Resources[50] acknowledges a right of expropriation for public purpose with respect for international law. It would later be quoted in important arbitrating statements.[51] This resolution was followed by increasingly radical resolutions that went from the proclamation of permanent sovereignty on natural resources to sovereignty in economic activity (Resolution 2158, 25 November 1966). The trend led to the construction of a complete New International Economic Order programme, which initiated the so-called North–South dialogue, a focal point throughout the entire decade of the 1970s.

In the early 1970s, tension regarding the price of raw materials ran high. The Club of Rome had just published its alarm bell entitled *Limits to Growth*. The international monetary system had exploded and exchange rates were erratic. In 1974, oil prices quadrupled within a few months. Industrialized countries were worried about the security of their supplies. The whole world economic system seemed in jeopardy. The time was ripe for North–South talks. At the initiative of Algeria, who had taken the lead in the NIEO crusade, the General Assembly met in special sessions two years in a row. The situation was so preoccupying that US Secretary of State Henry Kissinger came in person to utter soothing words. Out of this turmoil came various texts, the most important of which included a Declaration on the Establishment of a NIEO[52] and the Charter of Economic Rights and Duties of States.[53] These texts covered all possible spheres of economic and political activity: international trade, expropriation, commodities, industrialization, technology transfer, international economic cooperation, aid, exploitation of the seabed. The tone was clearly anti-liberal in economics and critical politically of the North. Industrialized countries protested, abstained or voted against the proposals. They pretended to go on with negotiations but had not the slightest intention of implementing a single provision contained in the NIEO programme. The masquerade continued up until 1980 when the thumping failure of the 11th special session on the NIEO brought an end to any illusions. The so-called North–South dialogue turned into a veritable North–South conflict. This time the United States went on the warpath. The General Assembly still has not recovered.

The decline (early 1980s to date)

The General Assembly has been in decline for the past 20 years and is less and less able to satisfy its members. The Third World is disillusioned. The United States is hostile. Competing expressions of universalism are gaining ground.

The misunderstandings of the 1970s durably sapped the prestige and credibility of the General Assembly. Because they had the majority, developing countries thought they had power. They constantly submitted incoherent proposals, offensive resolutions, and allegations that offended Western countries without taking into account their susceptibilities and the reality of the balance of power on the international scene. This lack of realism, it must be said, was encouraged by the policy of benign neglect practised by the United States. Since 1971, the USA have known that they are no longer capable of rallying a two-thirds majority in the General Assembly, even with a vigorous campaign: the conditions under which the General Assembly had decided to recognize mainland China's rights at the UN (by expelling Taiwan) had signalled the end of their ascendancy. What was said at the GA, be it with respect to the collective nature of human rights or the conduct of economic affairs, contradicted the American system of thought. To the United States there was an obvious collusion between non-alignment and Soviet ideology. The General Assembly no longer gave them satisfaction. They stopped fighting and lost interest. And anyway, the things that mattered were taking place elsewhere.

Since 1982, in fact, matters have taken an unfavourable turn for southern hemisphere countries. The price of raw materials has gone down. The debt crisis has destabilized Latin America and Africa. The countries of the South do not frighten anyone any more. The very notion of the South has come apart. Each country tries to negotiate its own case. The major bargaining places are no longer the General Assembly and UNCTAD, which have nothing left to offer but words, but instead the international financial institutions where debt restructuring is negotiated and new lines of credit are opened, at the painful price of Structural Adjustment Programmes. The GA's Second Committee may well pride itself in drawing up resolutions year after year 'with an aim to find a lasting solution to the developing countries problem of foreign debt' or to debate the consequences of the globalization of capital flows on developing countries. But this does not matter in the least. The intellectual content of these resolutions is too barren to compete seriously with the theoretical hegemony of the International Monetary Fund and the World Bank, which are unaware of their existence anyway.[54] This diplomatic posturing is left to diplomats who often have only a very remote relationship with what their country is grappling with and no longer represent much to speak of beyond the shores of the East River. As for the young finance or planning ministers, they go to Washington, London, Paris and Brussels (for countries committed to the Lomé accords), because the game is being played at the IMF, the World Bank, in creditors' clubs (Club of Paris, Club of London) and the major regional development banks.

Not only has the General Assembly been marginalized, but it has also been systematically discredited by the United States administration, and with it all the other bodies where a semblance of North–South dialogue apparently continues: UNESCO, UNCTAD and the FAO. In the mid-1980s, the Heritage Foundation, the very conservative think tank with its offices in the Capitol building, relayed the Reagan administration's offensive to Congress and the media with devastating effectiveness. The General Assembly was accused of being systematically anti-American and anti-Israeli; of legitimating national terrorist liberation movements supported by the Arab League and the USSR; of being in principle hostile to free enterprise, the only effective way to ensure growth and the exercise of human rights; of being a mouthpiece for the USSR and its evil ideology. That the General Assembly had 'strongly deplored' the Soviet invasion of Afghanistan and requested with an overwhelming majority 'the immediate, unconditional and total withdrawal of foreign troops from Afghanistan'[55] did not give it more credit. On the contrary, the GA was criticized for not having 'condemned' the invasion.

In this context of declared hostility, in 1985 the US Congress passed the famous Kassebaum–Solomon Amendment, a direct attack on the General Assembly. This text affirmed that UN budgetary policy did not take the main contributing states enough into account. It asked the US Secretary of State to take steps so that the member states supplying the most financial support could have voting rights with regard to budgetary matters that were in proportion to their financial contribution. Meanwhile, it decided unilaterally to reduce the United States' contribution to the United Nations (from 25 per cent to 20 per cent). The US Congress claimed, on its own, to modify one of the essential provisions of the United Nations Charter: each member of the General Assembly shall have one vote (Article 18).

The financial crisis has yet to be resolved and the political crisis of which it is a symptom endures. The hostility of the United States Congress has not waned despite the noticeable change in tone that has occurred in General Assembly speeches, which no longer contain the blazing diatribes of the past. At the Assembly, exasperation with regard to American ruthlessness and its lack of consideration for the majority is enormous. The United States' refusal to pay their arrears, their refusal to renew B. Boutros-Ghali's mandate, their refusal to expand the Security Council to 24 members, not to mention their unconditional support for Israeli policy, even in its excesses, are all sources of grievance and humiliation. Resentment towards this 'assertive unilateralism' is considerable, but only manages to be vented through minor displays of anger: for example, not electing an American to the Advisory Committee for the Administrative and Budgetary Questions (ACABQ, the all-important budgetary watchdog committee) and the elevation of the PLO's status (see Note 26).

The end of the Cold War and the habit the five permanent members of the Security Council have developed of working together on a continual basis has polished this body's image and contributed to marginalizing the plenary Assembly. The GA no longer manages to capture the public's attention, or even that of the national governments of its member states. It speaks, but no one listens any more.

The General Assembly in the UN system

The General Assembly's loss of credibility has tainted the whole UN system. The Assembly is in fact at the centre of the entire mechanism. It has exclusive competence in budget matters. It is in charge of the Organization's economic and social functions (Article 60). It plays an essential role in devising the prescriptive law furnished by the United Nations. The weakening of the General Assembly has destabilized the entire UN edifice.

Budgetary powers

Following the upheaval created by the Kassebaum–Solomon amendment, a high-level group of intergovernmental experts, known as the Group of

18, was formed to attempt to defuse the crisis by making a number of suggestions to set things right. As its ecumenical composition foreshadowed, the result of its work was a sort of laundry list intended to make everyone happy. A budgetary reform nevertheless followed, of which the high points were a strengthening of the programmatic nature of the budget (which had functioned on a biennial basis since 1974), a better forecasting of expenditures and income, and a mid-term plan of six years for programme previsions.[56] The draft budget is prepared by the Secretary-General. It is submitted to the Programme and Co-ordination Committee (made up of 34 representatives of member states) and the ACABQ (16 individually appointed members) for technical advice. The draft budget is then examined by the Fifth Commission, and afterwards sent for final approval by the plenary Assembly. Until 1986, the Fifth Committee approved the draft budget by simple majority, and the plenary Assembly adopted it by a two-thirds majority in accordance with Article 18, paragraph 2 of the Charter. Since 1986, at the insistent request of the major contributing countries, especially the United States, the draft budget programme is adopted by consensus. The main contributors have thus won a sort of *de facto* veto over the budget. Southern hemisphere countries can only deplore this new violation of the UN's 'basic democratic principles'.[57]

The constituent function

Virtually the entire institutional system set up to deal with economic and social co-operation within the framework of the United Nations is linked in one way or another to the General Assembly. This means that the General Assembly, together with the Economic and Social Council (ECOSOC) placed under its authority (Articles 58 and 60), is in charge of hundreds of permanent committees, agencies, funds and programmes, theoretically to ensure their co-ordination, not to mention the follow-through of increasingly complex relationships with specialized institutions in the UN family and programmes managed jointly with a number of them. The weakness of ECOSOC, unable either to negotiate questions substantively or to ensure a minimum of co-ordination in a tentacular system, is an added burden on the General Assembly. The GA is systematically consulted on all subjects treated by an ECOSOC that itself is transformed into a mini-GA. There is no division of tasks. Total confusion reigns.

By its capacity to create subsidiary organs and its central role in implementing Chapter IX of the Charter,[58] the General Assembly has largely shaped the system as it now exists, described for the past 30 years as 'unmanageable ... becoming slower and more unwieldy, like some prehistoric monster'.[59] The question of restructuring the UN's economic and social sectors has been on the General Assembly's agenda since 1975. It has given rise to a proliferation of special committees, commissions and groups of experts and has produced only minor reforms, taxing the staff considerably without having visible repercussions on the image the system projects.

Paradoxically, it is as if the horde of specialized organs in all fields with which the Assembly and the ECOSOC have endowed themselves so as to fulfil better their functions did not enable them to respond to the major problems facing the world today. Since the 1970s, the General Assembly has been calling UN global conferences, the number and frequency of which have been growing since the 1990s.[60] The success of these giant gatherings, which receive wide media coverage and draw heads of state and of government as well as representatives from civil society, attest to the obsolete nature of the General Assembly as it has been organized traditionally and the need to rethink the classic modes of international cooperation. A great French ambassador once summed up the situation in this way: 'The GA's main utility is to give free tickets for the major global conferences.'[61]

These *ad hoc* conferences enable the UN to recover some of its former shine. People talk about it and pay attention to what is said in its name. The function of collective legitimization that in another era Inis Claude once described so well[62] is no longer satisfied during the Assembly's regular sessions but at these huge happenings where, slowly, common systems of reference and embryos of a global consciousness are being developed.[63] In the best of circumstances, this activity can even result in the building of a legal framework.

The law-making function

The General Assembly's vocation is to help harmonize practices on the international scene. The development and observance of the rule of law being the best way to ensure serene social relations, the Charter entrusted the GA with the mission of 'encouraging the progressive development of international law and its codification' (Article 13). To do so, the Assembly has two instruments at its disposal: the Sixth Committee and the International Law Commission (ILC). The Sixth Committee is charged with examining legal issues that are of concern to the Assembly. It can draft texts of international conventions that will later be submitted for approval to the General Assembly. The ILC, comprised of 34 jurists nominated by UN member states and elected by the General Assembly, has a complex role between 'codifying' existing law and 'progressively developing' the law. In the past it has produced a large number of successful draft instruments: the four 1958 Geneva Conventions on the Law of the Sea, the 1961 Vienna Convention on Diplomatic Relations, the 1969 Vienna Convention on the Law of Treaties and so on.[64] The major traditional subjects of customary law have now been codified, and the Committee seems to have trouble getting its second wind.[65] The ILC is often criticized for being tediously slow. For example, it has been working on state responsibility since 1953. This torpor hardly makes it a suitable organ for building a new body of law adapted to new problems.

The General Assembly is not a world legislature. It has no authority to issue mandatory norms. Except for internal governance, budgetary or membership issues, its resolutions are mere recommendations, without binding authority. The question as to whether the repeated passing of similar resolutions and declarations year after year transformed customary law into 'soft law' preoccupied jurists considerably during the period of North–South dialogue. The debate has gradually become devoid of substance. Political and economic reality has swept away the illusion that a majority of weak states could impose as rule of law declarations that strong states were opposed to but supposed to implement. The General Assembly's contribution to law-making was done in a more subtle manner. By introducing new concepts, such as the common heritage of mankind, the right of future generations and sustainable development, and by legitimating certain principles, such as non-aggression and non-discrimination, it built a sort of common system of reference that can influence states' practices and lead to the emergence of new principles in international law. The GA's law-making role is carried out basically through multilateral norm-creating treaties. Not only are many of such treaties initiated by the GA or by international conferences under its aegis, but on many occasions, the declarations adopted by the General Assembly act as catalysts of the international community consensus. A large number of multilateral treaties have thus grown out of declarations adopted by the General Assembly: the 1967 Outer Space Treaty, the 1968 Treaty on the Nonproliferation of Nuclear Weapons, the 1971 Seabed Arms Control Treaty. Practically all of the international law pertaining to outer space has evolved from resolutions produced by the General Assembly.[66] Major international conventions in the field of human rights have been promoted by General Assembly resolutions. The Universal Declaration on Human Rights was adopted without opposition on 10 December 1948. The International Convenant on Civil and Political Rights and the International Convenant on Economic, Social and Cultural Rights were adopted and opened for signature in 1966. The rights of women, children and minorities, the outlawing of torture, racial discrimination and many other conventions of this sort have made progress on the basis of the General Assembly's work.

The revitalization of the General Assembly

Both useful and ineffectual, indispensable and maligned, the General Assembly must be revitalized. Everyone agrees. 'Reform' is, moreover, the watchword at the United Nations at this turn of the century. But the 'reform' of the General Assembly could occur on three different levels. It could be that the aim is merely to improve the Assembly's operation and rationalize its procedures, without pondering its place in the general configuration of the UN machinery or its functions on the world scene today. In that case reform would be purely technical and procedural. It could be that a redistribution of tasks is envisaged, particularly between the Main Committee of the General Assembly and the Economic and Social Council. This reform is politically sensitive but still fits within the classic framework for multilateralism as it was conceived in 1945. Or, finally, the UN could be rebuilt for the twenty-first century. This would mean taking into account changes in international society. It would mean deciding to meet the challenge of a globalized and interdependent world, where nothing can be durably established without articulating the different levels of 'governance', global and local, public and private. It would involve the invention of new 'cosmopolitan democracy'.

Apparently the General Assembly reform discussed at the UN is reaching no further than the first level. And even then, its achievement remains improbable.

The necessity and difficulty of reform

The UN information department is categorical: the General Assembly has made decisive steps towards reform, witness the fact that: 'In an effort to give coherence and vision to the process of reforming the UN in the post-cold-war period, the General Assembly since 1992 has set up five working groups'! In July 1998, the open-ended Working Group on the Strengthening of the United Nations System completed 'one of the broadest reviews of the functioning of the General Assembly' (not to be confused with the informal open-ended Working Group on the Revitalization of the Work of the General Assembly created by the President of the Assembly in its 47th session and recreated at its 48th session). The Group's assessment of the situation is worth quoting verbatim:

> The working group particularly sought to strengthen the work of the General Assembly. It recognized that the proceedings of the Assembly do not command the attention of member states or the public at large because it has far too much on its agenda for discussion. While all items of interest should be on the agenda, the group concluded, there may be

no need to discuss all of them every year. Agenda items should be grouped, or considered every two years . . .

Other points of agreement:

- The General Assembly should avoid micro-managing the Secretariat;
- General Assembly resolutions should respond to major issues rather than be fragmented;
- Stronger links should be explored between the General Assembly and civil society, particularly non-governmental organizations;
- A uniform four-year term of office, renewable once, for heads of programs, funds and other bodies of ECOSOC and the General Assembly . . .[67]

With so many working groups giving such forceful recommendations, one can see that sweeping reforms are underway!

The question of rationalizing the work of the General Assembly was posed for the first time in 1949! There have been countless special committees charged with making recommendations on General Assembly methods and procedures, and vast numbers of reports have been filed in this regard. It would be cruel to recall the 21 December 1952 resolution creating a Special Committee of Measures (francophones will appreciate this title à la Giraudoux) tending to limit the length of regular GA sessions;[68] the one of 9 November 1970 creating a Special Committee for the Rationalization of Procedures and Organization at the General Assembly;[69] and many others. Since 1992, there has been a shift from 'rationalization' to 'revitalization', but the same questions still crop up: the length of sessions, their opening and closing dates, the duration of speaking turns in the general debate, the reduction of the overall GA workload, the streamlining of its agenda, the reduction in the number of items.

In the package of reforms proposed by the Secretary-General since 1997, several simple and common-sense suggestions apply to the General Assembly.[70] Kofi Annan understands fully that the General Assembly will not recover its credibility unless it pares down its agenda, sets priorities and deals with current events that interest public opinion. He has suggested 'refocusing debates', defining for instance two years ahead of time what major issue will be dealt with. In other words, taking a lesson from the big special conferences, the Secretary-General has suggested that the spirit and main features of these conferences be incorporated into the functioning of the General Assembly. He feels that the General Assembly would do well to encourage its main committees also to orient their work towards a particular theme on which collective substantive study would focus. Furthermore, the Assembly usually asks the Secretary-General to report on the implementation of nearly everything. Secretary-General Kofi Annan has asked the Assembly to concentrate the Secretariat's resources on high-priority areas. That implies that it should rationalize its agenda, which would allow the Secretariat to be less dispersed and the Assembly could finish its work more quickly.

But of all the Secretary-General's suggestions, the one that occupies the little circle of UN functionaries is the 'sunset provision'.[71] It recommends that each initiative involving new organizational structures or major commitment of funds be subjected to time limits. The idea is intended to provide a specific time horizon for mandates, requiring explicit renewal by the General Assembly for their continuation. Activities that would not have continuing relevance and effectiveness could be terminated. Beyond that, the Secretary-General also requests that member states should not adopt new programmes without specifying the anticipated results. This sudden apparition of 'budgeting for results' has provoked quite a commotion. *That* issue is something the Assembly has tackled. As for the rest, time will tell. Six years after the creation of the Revitalization Committee, one year after the Secretary-General's propositions for reform, an initial assessment of recent Assembly sessions shows that not only has the number of items on the agenda not decreased, but that the number of reports requested of the Secretary-General has instead risen: from 283 at the 49th session to 286 at the 51st session.[72]

To rouse the GA out of its inertia and conservatism requires energy. As an institution, the Assembly is too ailing to find the strength to regenerate itself from within, in spite of the efforts deployed by its various presidents. At the same time, no country or group of countries is motivated enough to lead the GA's renewal with all that entails in terms of work and effort. The Nordic countries tried to do it in the early 1990s. Their proposal was probably the best one imaginable, and its advocates had all the necessary credentials. We know what became of it.[73]

Actually, the only reform in which the big powers in the General Assembly are interested is the recomposition of the Security Council and the place that will be given to them. The future of the UN and its role in the twenty-first century are the topic of lofty speeches but remain the least of their concerns. If a reform were to take place, it would instead be fuelled by private initiatives, by 'epistemic communities', major foundations and NGOs. However, nothing can be done unless a state or group of states instils the necessary degree of political will into the machine.

CONCLUSION: A GENERAL ASSEMBLY FOR THE TWENTY-FIRST CENTURY

At the time the General Assembly and the UN were conceived on the model of the League of Nations, communications and transportation were slow. The meeting of representatives from all states in the same place permitted an exchange of information that did not exist by any other means. The Assembly was the locus of one of the most fantastic exchanges of ideas of all times. It shared information on the state of the international system, on the major trends sweeping over the planet, on new cleavages. Voting was the equivalent of an opinion poll on the scale of the globe.

All that has changed. Means of communication have intensified and diversified: there is no longer any need to have a permanent diplomatic conference in order to know what is going on in the world. Above all, international co-operation no longer takes place exclusively through states. The accelerated changes in the international society have expanded the stakes, the actors and the instruments of co-operation. Of all the highly publicized events each winter, the annual meeting of the World Economic Forum in Davos has surpassed New York. The proper functioning of global society no longer depends only on co-ordinating state policies according to generally agreed principles of conduct, which was the very purpose of the General Assembly. An increasingly restive and independent civil society is proving itself capable of resisting government pressures and using specific resources to act alone on the international scene. Finally, the ideology of competition and efficiency that won over all organizations and public services, whether one deplores it or is thrilled about it, will not indefinitely stand on the doorstep of the world organization.

The General Assembly is a closed environment with its 'Your Excellency' and its rites for initiates. It no longer reflects the world at large. The question of how to bring the UN and civil society closer together is becoming more pressing. For a number of reasons, many of which are financial in nature, Kofi Annan has made this his leitmotiv. Among the reforms he put forth, and that the General Assembly agreed on 12 November 1997, are 'initiatives to increase UN consultation and co-operation with civil society – the business community, labour unions, non-governmental organizations and academia'. To restore some of its prestige to the General Assembly, the Secretary-General recommended that the 55th session be designated the Millennium Assembly and that a high-level segment called the Millennium Summit be devoted to deep consideration of the theme 'The UN in the twenty-first century'. At the same time, he suggested that a 'Peoples' Millennium Assembly', a non-governmental millennium forum, be organized around the General Assembly session, in conjunction with the Assembly, to bring together the UN's partners in civil society to deal with future challenges.[74] This landmark solution will be closely followed. It could prefigure the General Assembly of tomorrow or, rather, the day after tomorrow.

Until recently, the idea of 'giving voice to citizens in the world community in an institutional mode parallel to states'[75] was confined to little circles on the edge of international politics. For the past few years it has

been discussed openly. The Report of the Commission on Global Governance, for instance, devoted several pages to it.[76] How can this 'civil society'
be represented in a balanced manner without giving a bonus to already
well-organized interest groups that are well funded but devoid of democratic legitimacy and have to account to no one except unidentified
backers? The system of the NGO forum accredited by the General Assembly does not answer this question.

Several systems are currently being proposed that hinge on the idea of
an 'assembly of the people' as a deliberative body to complement the
General Assembly. They are being discussed in huge conferences led, in
particular, by the Campaign for a More Democratic United Nations
(CAMDUN conferences). The most elaborate proposition remains the one
put forth by Jeffrey Segall and the International Network for a UN Second
Assembly (INFUSA).[77] It recommends a World Parliament that should be
an exclusively consultative body of the General Assembly. In this case,
there is no need to reform the Charter, or to request authorization from
the Security Council: Article 22 is sufficient. For this 'Second Assembly',
the voting system would draw its inspiration from the European Parliament: deputies elected by universal suffrage with a proportional representation reflecting the size of the population with corrections to safeguard
the population of the smallest countries. The proposition is an appealing
one, but it assumes a degree of democratization that is non-existent in
most member states. Moreover, when one is aware of the lack of interest
among European citizens generated by the European Parliament, their
misunderstanding of this institution and the way politicians distort election issues, it is easy to imagine how difficult the enterprise would be. In
any case, civil society's participation in global governance, and especially
its willingness to implement what has been decided in New York, is not
something that can be dictated from on high.

At present, the urgent question is not only how to represent the world's
citizens at the General Assembly in a legitimate fashion, but the way in
which this body can spark their interest and address the problems they
have to face. In the 1960s and 1970s the General Assembly used to play
an important role as an authoritative interpreter of new concepts and
principles relating to international relations. It should be able to play such
a role again in the present transitional period. It still remains at the centre
of the whole UN system – its marginalization would mean the marginalization of the entire UN. But diplomats and citizens have to learn how to
regard it and use it differently from a bureaucratic routine or a narrow
power-oriented machinery.

NOTES

1. Interview with President Wilson on 1 November 1917 by W. E. Rappard, quoted by Paul Alexi Ladame, *L'Assemblée générale des Nations Unies*, doctoral dissertation at the University of Geneva, Institut Universitaire de Hautes Études Internationales, Paris-Montargis, Editions Antares, 1949, p. 15.
2. See David Armstrong, Lorna Lloyd and John Redmond, *From Versailles to Maastricht: International Organization in the Twentieth Century* (New York: St Martin's Press, 1996), pp. 23–4.
3. 24 November 1920, quoted by Paul Alexi Ladame, *op. cit.*, p. 25.
4. Pierre Gerbet, *Le Rêve d'un ordre mondial* (Paris: Imprimerie Nationale, 1996), p. 32.
5. The United States, Great Britain, France, Italy and Japan.
6. The First Committee handled institutional and legal matters; the Second, intellectual co-operation and technical organizations in the League (economic and financial matters, hygiene, communication and transit); the Third, arms reductions; the Fourth, the League's finances and all matters related to the Secretariat; the Fifth, social and humanitarian affairs; the Sixth, political matters and the admission of new members.
7. Albert Cohen, in his famous novel *Belle du seigneur*, gives a fierce description of the strained yet frivolous atmosphere at the time.
8. The United States and British representatives met with their Soviet counterparts from 21 August to 28 September 1944, then with the Chinese from 29 September to 7 October. The USSR was not at war with Japan, it deplored that Roosevelt had imposed China's presence among the great powers and refused to meet in its presence during this preparatory phase.
9. On the history of the planning stages, see Ruth Russell, *A History of the United Nations Charter: The Role of the United States 1940–1945* (Washington DC: The Brookings Institution, 1958).
10. On 31 August, it was agreed that the Assembly should be empowered to admit new members upon recommendation of the Security Council, but the voting procedures in the Security Council had not yet been determined and the scope of these 'recommendations' was not clear.
11. Russell, *op. cit.*, p. 509.
12. See Leland Goodrich, Edvard Hambro, Anne Patricia Simons, *The Charter of the United Nations: Commentary and Documents*, 3rd edn (New York: Columbia University Press, 1969), and Hans Kelsen, *The Law of Nations* (London: Stevens and Sons, 1950).
13. Inis Claude, *Swords into Plowshares*, 3rd edn (New York: Random House, 1964), p. 84.
14. Iceland, Sweden, Afghanistan and Thailand in 1946; Yemen and Pakistan in 1947; Burma in 1948; Israel in 1949; Indonesia in 1950.
15. 8 December 1948, Res. 197 (III).
16. 23 November 1954, Res. 817 (IX).
17. Advisory Opinion on the Competence of the General Assembly for the Admission of a State to the United Nations, 3 March 1950, International Court of Justice, *Reports of Judgments, Advisory Opinions and Orders*, 1950, p. 7.

18. Six Western European countries: Austria, Spain, Finland, Ireland, Italy and Portugal; four Eastern European countries: Albania, Bulgaria, Hungary and Romania; six Afro-Asian countries: Libya, Jordan, Cambodia, Ceylon, Laos and Nepal. Japan and Mongolia were candidates. China was against the admission of Mongolia, which led to the USSR's refusal to allow entrance to Japan. The latter was admitted in 1956, Mongolia not until 1961.

19. In particular the most conservative wing of the Republican Party in the United States Congress and the famous Heritage Foundation.

20. See Marie-Claude Smouts, 'International organizations and inequality among states', *International Social Science Journal*, June 1995, 144, pp. 229–41.

21. See M. J. Peterson, *The General Assembly in World Politics* (Boston, MA.: Unwin Hyman, 1990), ch. 3.

22. Article 19 provides that 'a member of the United Nations which is in arrears in the payment of its financial contributions to the Organization shall have no vote in the General Assembly if the amount of its arrears equals or exceeds the amount of the contributions due from it for the preceding two full years'. The USSR was in this situation in 1964. To avoid raising the question of suspending its right to vote and provoking a general crisis in the UN, the entire 19th session took place without a vote.

23. A French diplomat in our midst compared this activity to American football: the ball disappears beneath the pack of players, there is a chaotic scramble, no one knows what is going on, then the ball reappears somewhere and everyone starts running . . .

24. See Robert Rothstein, *The Weak in the World of Strong: The Developing Countries in the International System* (New York: Columbia University Press, 1977).

25. Regarding delegations, see for instance: Peter Baehr, *The Role of a National Delegation in the General Assembly*, New York, Carnegie Endowment Occasional Paper, no. 9, 1970; Johan Kaufmann, *United Nations Decision-making* (Leyden: Sijthoff, 1980); Marie-Claude Smouts, 'Les délégations à l'Assemblée', CEDIN, *La France aux Nations Unies* (Paris: Montchrestien, 1985), pp. 41–48.

26. The Palestinian Liberation Organization was granted observer status in 1974. It was upgraded by the UN in 1988 when it was designated as 'Palestine' and in 1998, when the GA enhanced the status of the Palestinian observer delegation closer to that of a state. It still cannot vote, but it may co-sponsor resolutions on Palestinian and Middle East issues and speak on non-regional issues after the last registered member state.

27. See Jean-Pierre Cot and Alain Pellet, *La Charte des Nations Unies: Commentaire Article par Article*, 2nd edn (Paris: Economica, 1991), comment on Article 5, pp. 190–4.

28. Palestine, 16 April–14 May 1948.

29. Palestine, 28 April–15 May, 1947, at Britain's request; raw materials and development, 9 April–2 May 1974, at Algeria's request.

30. A/52/856, 17 April 1998.

31. From 1948 to 1993 the General Assembly had two commissions in charge of discussing political matters: the First Commission and the Special Political Committee, which made seven main committees. It is in these bodies that major crises are discussed, in particular the Middle East conflicts. Representation to it is usually at the highest level: ambassador or deputy. On 17 August 1993 (AG/117), the General Assembly decided to rationalize the structure of

these major committees and merge its Special Political Committee and the Decolonization Committee.

32. The General Committee is made up of 28 members: the president and 21 vice-presidents of the Assembly and the chairmen of the six main committees. According to the GA Rules of Procedure (Article 38), 'no two members shall be members of the same delegation and it shall be so constituted as to ensure its representative character'. Among the vice-presidents, the five major regions are represented, as well as the five permanent members of the Security Council.

33. See Cot and Pellet, *op. cit.*, comment on Article 2, para. 7.

34. Trygve Lie, *In the Cause of Peace* (New York: Macmillan, 1954).

35. The expression is Michel Virally's.

36. Note of the president of the 46th session (A/52/969), seconded by the Presidents of the 49th, 50th and 51st sessions (A/52/856, 17 April 1998). In this document can be found an interesting viewpoint from Mr Razali Ismail (51st session) on the definition of the President's functions and how to assess them.

37. Vijaya Lakshmi Pandit from India in 1953; in 1969, Miss Angela Brooks of Liberia.

38. See Sydney D. Bailey, *The General Assembly of the United Nations* (New York: Praeger, 1964).

39. The Greek government at the time was fighting communist guerrillas abetted by the bordering communist states.

40. Resolution 181 (II) adopted by 33 votes to 13 and 10 abstentions.

41. The famous photograph in which the Secretary-General, Trygve Lie, handed the UN flag to US General MacArthur is one of the most shocking there is in the annals of the UN. J. Pérez de Cuéllar was careful not to commit the same mistake during the Gulf War in 1991.

42. Resolution 376 (V), adopted by 45 votes to 5 (the Soviet bloc) with 7 abstentions: Yugoslavia, India, Saudi Arabia, Yemen, Syria, Lebanon, and Indonesia not participating.

43. Resolution 377 (V), 52 votes to 5 (the Soviet bloc) with 2 abstentions (Argentina and India).

44. Article 43: 'All Members of the United Nations . . . undertake to make available to the Security Council, on its call in accordance with a special agreement or agreements, armed forces, assistance and facilities. . . . Such agreement or agreements shall govern the numbers and types of forces, their degree of readiness and general location, and the nature of the facilities and assistance to be provided. The agreement or agreements shall be negotiated as soon as possible.'

45. Razali Ismail, 20 January 1998, A/52/856, p. 6.

46. See Marie-Claude Smouts, *La France à l'ONU* (Paris: Presses de la Fondation nationale des sciences politiques, 1979), pp. 206–8.

47. Resolution 1514 (XV), 14 December 1960.

48. Special Committee on the Situation with Regard to the Implementation of the Declaration on the Granting of Independence to Colonial Countries and Peoples, created in 1961, made up of 17 members, then expanded in 1963. The Committee of Twenty-Four is made up of 12 African countries, 4 Eastern European countries, 3 from Latin American and 5 'others'.

49. Resolution 1710, 19 December 1961.

50. Resolution 1803 (XVII), adopted by 82 votes to 2 with 12 abstentions.

51. See Stephen Zamora, 'Economic relations and development', in Christopher C. Joyner, *The United Nations and International Law* (Washington, DC: American Society of International Law/Cambridge: Cambridge University Press, 1997), p. 259.
52. Resolution 3201, 4 May 1974.
53. Resolution 3281, 12 December 1974.
54. Verified by the author in the course of interviews conducted in New York and Washington in 1987.
55. Resolution ES/6/2, 14 January 1980, adopted by 104 for, 18 against and 8 abstentions.
56. Resolution 41/213, of 16 December 1986.
57. See South Centre, *For a Strong and Democratic United Nations: A South Perspective on UN Reform* (Geneva: the South Centre, 1996), pp. 67–70.
58. Chapter IX: International Economic and Social Co-operation.
59. Sir Robert Jackson, *A Study of the Capacity of the United Nations' Development System* (Geneva: 1970), known as the Jackson Report. See also Maurice Bertrand, *Reporting to the Economic and Social Council* (Geneva: Joint Inspection Unit, JIU/REP.84/7, 1984), known as the Bertrand Report.
60. On this phenomenon see Paul Taylor, 'The origins and institutional setting of the UN special conferences', in Paul Taylor and A. J. R. Groom, *Global Issues in the United Nations' Framework* (London: Macmillan, 1989), pp. 7–34; Jacques Fomerand, 'UN conferences: media events or genuine diplomacy?', *Global Governance*, vol. 2, 3, September–December 1996, pp. 361–75.
61. Private interview with the author.
62. Inis Claude, *The Changing United Nations* (New York: Random House, 1967), ch. 4.
63. See Marie-Claude Smouts, 'La construction équivoque d'une "opinion mondiale"', *Revue Tiers Monde*, 151, July–September 1997, pp. 679–93.
64. See Christopher C. Joyner, 'The United Nations as international law-giver', in Christopher C. Joyner, *The United Nations and International Law, op. cit.,* pp. 442–43.
65. See Oscar Schachter, 'The UN legal order: An overview', in Christopher C. Joyner, *op. cit.,* pp. 6–8.
66. For these examples and many others, see Joyner, *op. cit.,* pp. 443–6.
67. www.un.org/reform/focus/.html, 5 June 1998.
68. Resolution 689 A (VII).
69. Resolution 2632 (XXV).
70. A/51/950, 14 July 1997.
71. Document A/52/851/Corr.1.
72. A/52/856.
73. It was discussed and quickly forgotten.
74. Document A/52/850.
75. Daniele Archibugi, 'From the UN to cosmopolitan democracy', in Daniele Archibugi and David Held (eds), *Cosmopolitan Democracy* (Cambridge: Polity Press, 1995), p. 137.
76. *Our Global Neighborhood* (Oxford/New York: Oxford University Press, 1995), pp. 257–63.
77. J. Segall, 'A UN Second Assembly', in F. Barnaby (ed.), *Building a More Democratic United Nations* (London: Frank Cass, 1991), pp. 93–109.

CHAPTER 3

THE SECURITY COUNCIL

Juergen Dedring

INTRODUCTION

The end of the Cold War and the defusing of the East–West conflict gave
rise to the unexpected chance to review the functioning of the United
Nations in general, and of its Security Council in particular, under
conditions approximating to the supposedly harmonious atmosphere of
co-operation between the wartime Allies at the end of the Second World
War and during the San Francisco conference of spring 1945, at which the
Charter of the United Nations was adopted and the Organization was
formally established. After more than 40 years of warlike tension and
hostility, which weakened the newly established world Organization and
negated the high expectations placed on the Security Council (the key
instrument of the Charter for the maintenance of peace and security), the
newly found amity and mutual understanding between the Soviet and US
leadership had a direct and immediate impact on the workings of the
principal organ in the UN system. Numerous breakthroughs in several
protracted regional conflicts in the late 1980s documented for the international community the significant benefits of the changed international
situation and awakened hopes for another opportunity to create a global
order of peace for mankind.

The central question for the policy-maker and for the analytical observer
has been whether the aura of friendship and unanimity in the Security
Council and in other international bodies has begun to revive the initial
vision enshrined in the text of the UN Charter and to translate the norms
of international co-operation into the day-to-day political practice of global
governance. A full decade of the Council's work under these near-ideal
conditions is now available for critical examination and should enable the
policy-maker and academic observer to arrive at a more balanced empiri-
cally based judgement about the viability of the Council's role in the
search for world peace in the next millennium.

In this chapter an attempt is made to review the Charter's conception
and the practical record of the Security Council over more than 50 years
of its existence. How does it stand up to thorough examination and
rigorous criticism? How are its resolutions and decisions assessed in the

light of the many international crises and conflicts in the last half of the twentieth century? What are the criteria of effectiveness that can be fairly applied to this intergovernmental organ charged with the burdensome task of maintaining international peace and security? Finally, is the harsh sentence of failure justified as regards the Security Council's efforts in the first 40 years of its existence when it was crippled by the destructive effects of the Cold War dividing its members? These questions will inform the following pages of description and evaluation, in the end enabling the sympathetic critic to reconsider the important basic query whether this Council, as constituted in the Charter and matured in more than 50 years of practical experience, is suited to deal with the unforeseeable but undoubtedly difficult challenges in the coming decades of global growth and development, or whether another more appropriate tool or mechanism must be designed to handle the exigencies of worldwide turbulence.[1]

THE ORIGINS AND MAIN FEATURES OF THE CHARTER'S PEACE AND SECURITY PROVISIONS

Much has been written about the antecedents and developments during the last four years of the Second World War and the first few months after the unconditional surrender of Nazi Germany in May 1945 that brought about the crucial decision at San Francisco in June 1945 to establish for the second time in the twentieth century a general and universal international organization for the purpose of assuring a stable peace order and averting the recurrence of global armed conflict.[2] These important movements began even prior to the Japanese surprise attack on Pearl Harbor and the entry of the United States into the Second World War.

Memoirs and critical historical writings provide conclusive evidence that the main sponsor and conceptualizer of the new proposal for a global security organization was President Franklin D. Roosevelt and his third administration. This does not mean that the principal allies of the United States, that is the United Kingdom and the Soviet Union, and their respective leaders were either inactive or excluded in regard to these far-reaching reflections. Nevertheless, the leading role of the US President and his immediate advisers throughout the whole gestation and birth of the United Nations must be emphasized.

The first step on this path of designing the post-war world order was taken in connection with what is commonly referred to as the 'Atlantic Charter', which was formulated during a meeting of President Roosevelt and Prime Minister Winston Churchill off Newfoundland on 14 August 1941, at a time when the United States was still officially a neutral party in the war. As part of a brief but weighty statement of common aims, the two leaders issued the following eighth principal point:

> Eighth, they believe that all of the nations of the world, for realistic as well as spiritual reasons must come to the abandonment of the use of force. Since no future peace can be maintained if land, sea or air armaments continue to be employed by nations which threaten, or may threaten, aggression outside of their frontiers, they believe, *pending the establishment of a wider and permanent system of general security*, that the disarmament of such nations is essential. (Emphasis added)

The highlighted phrase reveals a most cautious indirect endorsement of some formal arrangement for a security system to ensure the peaceful conduct of interstate relations. Ruth Russell, in her magisterial extensive study of the history of the United Nations Charter, reports that President Roosevelt did not accept an explicit reference, as advocated by Churchill, to an 'effective international organization' because he was concerned about possible opposition and suspicions in the United States to such an objective.[3] This cautious attitude of the American President reveals very early on the given or assumed limitations to the political conception of a new global peace and security organization. Even under the best of circumstances it was certain that the actual framework for international co-operation would fall short of the hopes and dreams of visionary idealists who had earlier embraced the fervent language of Wilsonianism.

As the war ran its course, the process of searching for building-blocks of a post-war international order intensified. The next input into the cross-Atlantic dialogue came from the British government in early 1943. The UK suggested that the heart of the new organizational arrangements should be the continued co-operation of the four great powers in the maintenance of world peace. A key aim would, of course, be the full and permanent demilitarization of Germany. In case the Big Four should have a falling out, the remaining great powers, together with smaller states, could seek to protect global peace.

Churchill was confident that there was complete accord with the United States on this general outlook. In a radio address he launched his own conception in which the Great Three – the US, the UK and the USSR – were to lead some world institution under which would be placed a Council of Europe and a Council of Asia; other similar regional councils could be added, if necessary. The British proposal coming from the highest levels led to the US side clarifying its own viewpoint and insisting on the idea of a global body in which China would be included among the great powers. In a countermove, Churchill now offered a modified model with a Supreme World Council – the Big Four and other Powers – at the top, whose main mandate would be the prevention of future German aggression; under this highest organ, three regional councils were to be established.[4]

With these still-imprecise formulations emanating from the British and US capitals, the US State Department started drafting two agreements, one between the Big Four, and the other bringing in all the members of the war alliance of the 'United Nations'. These two drafts contained as the core component the American pledge to co-operate in setting up a permanent international organization for the maintenance of peace and security, based on the principle of sovereign equality of nations.[5]

The British government, in its *aide-mémoire* of 14 July 1943, proposed the establishment of a United Nations Commission for Europe to deal with German disarmament and political and related other aspects of the maintenance of peace.[6] In response, the United States issued a memorandum on 9 August 1943, which presented a very detailed counterproposal for a comprehensive global agency to deal with the post-war peace settlements and to prepare plans for handling various long-range problems.[7] The fourth paragraph of a 'Tentative Draft of a Joint Four-Power Declaration' reads as follows: 'That they recognize the necessity of establishing at the earliest practicable date a general international organization based on the principle of sovereign equality of all nations and open to membership by all nations, large and small, for the maintenance of international peace and security.'[8] This exchange resulted in a total redrafting of this text. In the end, the idea of a Transitional UN Agency for the War and Post-War Periods was agreed upon; among its envisaged tasks was the formulation of a plan for a permanent international organization for peace and general welfare.[9] The two sides had reached full agreement on this proposal.

The number of participants in these declarations and exchanges grew to three and then four, as the Soviet leadership and thereafter the Chinese authorities were included. The occasion for a more formal articulation of the evolving notion of some post-war peace and security organization presented itself at the Moscow conference from 19 to 30 October 1943, at which the foreign ministers of the Big Three reviewed a significant number of pending military and political issues and resolved many of the outstanding differences. As part of the final communiqué from the Moscow conference, a Joint Four-Nation Declaration was published in which, in its fourth paragraph, the four governments recognized 'the necessity of establishing at the earliest practicable date a general international organization, based on the principle of the sovereign equality of all peace-loving states, and open to membership by all such states, large and small, for the maintenance of international peace and security'.[10]

This official declaration of intent, with China joining in, constituted a solid platform on which Secretary of State Hull and President Roosevelt could start to erect the intellectual and operational foundations for the global organization to be created. A first detailed draft statute was prepared in the US State Department and, following its formal endorsement by President Roosevelt, Secretary Hull proposed a formal exchange of related documents on the nature and functions of the planned international organization among the principal powers of the Alliance.[11]

The following months until June 1944 brought serious misgivings in the Congress and more widely in the American public on two important aspects of the future international organization: for one, would the new body amount to the great powers imposing order in the international community, and, second, could the organization become a superstate over and above the existing sovereign nation–states? These two questions were significant enough to cause some delay and change of direction in the Roosevelt administration. The President responded to these worries in a statement of 15 June 1944 in which he emphasized that maintaining peace and security was a task of all peace-loving nations and that no superstate was in the making, but that the new organization would involve the search for effective agreements and arrangements among the nations. With this firm rejection of imperialistic and supranational characteristics for the new peace and security organization, the road was clear to finalize the principles undergirding the emerging edifice of the postwar order.[12]

This critical advance was planned for the four-power consultations at Dumbarton Oaks, which lasted from 21 August to 28 September 1944 (for the United Kingdom and the Soviet Union), and from 29 September to 7 October 1944 (for the Chinese government). It must be stressed that the Roosevelt administration, especially the State Department under Secretary Hull, had not been idle in the previous 18 months and had come up with a complete draft Charter for the new organization, which was officially submitted to the allied partners barely one month before the opening of the Dumbarton Oaks meeting.

At this juncture, it appears opportune to consider in greater depth and detail the original springs from which the fully fledged American position was fed. Secretary of State Hull favoured a general international organization, similar to the League of Nations, but with more authority and power to maintain the peace. Roosevelt himself was inclined initially towards a highly centralized, small peace-enforcement organization, surrounded by much looser decentralized organizations dealing with functional issues. But the President's views evolved, in the end embracing the idea of a single world organization charged with enforcement and other functions. The ideas on international organization of the Roosevelt administration were opposed, on the one hand, by isolationists and, on the other, by advocates of world government and a supranational federation of states. The State Department confined its proposals to an international organization of sovereign states and was clearly unwilling to entertain thoughts of reforming the League, as it was surrounded by an aura of failure.[13]

The basic principle as espoused by the State Department, that the new international organization would under no circumstances derogate from national sovereignty, shaped the letter and spirit of the Charter drafts that eventually became the final carefully revised and rewritten integral text that was shared with the allied powers before the critical Dumbarton Oaks discussions. The two key innovations in the draft Charter of 1944 were the arrangements for the collective use of force and the introduction of the great power veto. It was envisaged that the decision to use force needed the consent of the great powers, but that they would act within the international organization framework rather than alone in the framework of a continuing military alliance. This second option was quickly abandoned due to the outcry of the other states against notions such as the 'Four Policemen', as proposed earlier by President Roosevelt. For the purpose of collective security and of other action for peaceful settlement, an Executive Committee (consisting of the Big Four) within the structure of an 11-member Council would become active, while the General Conference (later the General Assembly) would merely be given a supporting role. This conception required concurrence among the Four, but did not call for unanimity in the Council. However, the enforcement decisions were to be binding on all states.[14]

While the Soviet Government, in its first comment of 12 August 1944, reiterated its support for a restricted security enforcement organization, with separate organizations for other issues, in the end it did join the other allies in endorsing the idea of a general multi-functional international organization. The consultations at Dumbarton Oaks encountered a roadblock over two issues: (a) the voting system in the new Security Council; and (b) the demand for separate membership of USSR republics in the new international organization. Both these matters required top-level discussion, without which the conference to write and adopt the new Charter could not be convened.[15]

The argument over the veto right in the Council was of critical significance. All great powers were in full agreement about the introduction of their veto power. The disagreement erupted over the extent of this privilege in the Council's anticipated business. The Soviet party demanded that it extend to all votes, substantive and procedural; but this excessive interpretation was rejected by the partners. The US and the UK saw the veto restricted to substantive matters, and they argued that the veto should not be applicable if a great power was a party to a dispute before the Council. This aspect, too, was not acceptable to the Soviet representatives at Dumbarton Oaks. It took the Yalta meeting in February 1945 to remove this specific veto problem from the agenda of the forthcoming San Francisco conference.[16]

A consultation on the side between the United States and the Latin American countries casts a fascinating light on the US position on the effect of majority decisions in respect of the use of force. When the Latin American countries submitted a unified draft resolution that would commit all members of the Pan-American system – to which the USA belonged – to the use of force if an absolute majority of the members so decided, the United States articulated the strongest opposition to any arrangement that would oblige the US Government to join in an action against a transgressor that would put US troops under foreign command. Such a forceful rejection of a proposal that was fully within the spirit of the UN Charter revealed strikingly the absolute claim to national sovereignty insisted upon by the US authorities and their strict opposition to abiding by a majority decision and to placing American troops under a non-American commander.[17] This argument from early 1945 foreshadows the unresolved policy posture of the United States in more than 50 years of the Security Council's work.

In preparing the US delegation to the San Francisco conference, the State Department paid special attention to the provisions on peaceful settlement and the specific role of the Security Council in the relevant procedure. The US position was very restrictive in that it held that the Council could take jurisdiction over any dispute likely to threaten the peace, but that it could not settle disputes on their merits. Its function was to be limited to the investigation of a dispute or situation in order to determine whether it was indeed likely to become a threat to international peace and security. Thus the US interpretation of the meaning of the Chapter on Peaceful Settlement was narrowly restricted to a procedural role for the new Council.[18] Only at San Francisco did the USA give in to the British wish that the Council should be enabled to recommend terms of settlement under Chapter VI.[19] The US internal debate makes very clear that as far as the US authorities were concerned, the authority of the Council as guardian of international peace was defined in a very narrow and feeble manner. Nothing was to be allowed to diminish the sovereign rights of the USA as leader of the anti-Hitler alliance and as a rising global power.

At the United Nations Conference on International Organization at San Francisco from 25 April to 26 June 1945, bringing together 50 states united in their struggle against fascism, the stage was set for a speedy acceptance of the slightly amended Dumbarton Oaks document that reflected foremost the pragmatic extraction from nearly two years of intensive and argumentative discussions and drafting within the US government. The conference revealed quickly and unmistakably the dominant political will of the USA in stamping its own seal of approval on what was presented to the official representatives at the San Francisco conference. Nevertheless, the clash between the Big Four (and then Five) and the other states was dramatic and harsh, exposing the adamant and nearly ruthless determination of the great powers and testifying to the anger and deep disappointment of the overwhelming majority of the small and weak partners at the launch of the new world organization.

The main bone of contention giving rise to lengthy and animated debates was the introduction of the veto right for the great powers, setting them up as a privileged elite in this association of sovereign states. A large group of middle and small powers attacked the whole notion of the veto and the unanimity of the Big Five, and insisted that the organization would be more harmonious and productive if the equality of its members were not so blatantly violated. Much of the fury and annoyance was directed against the rigid claim of the Soviet representatives that the veto was to be applicable in all cases, including the decision to discuss the case. Here, the other great powers agreed that the decision to discuss a matter in the Council was a procedural vote and therefore not subject to the exercise of the veto.

Another grave aspect of the veto debate was the question as to whether it should be applicable in Chapter VI (peaceful settlement) cases. The middle and small powers rallied together and pressed the Big Five at least to accept the exclusion of this part of the Council's mandate from the unfair application of the veto right. The representatives, led by the Australian Foreign Minister, argued quite persuasively that the delicate task of dispute settlement required sensitivity and peace-making skills rather than the crude application of the veto under the guise of great power unanimity.[20]

Both matters were finally decided, allowing the successful conclusion of the conference. Settlement of the question of whether the decision to discuss a matter was merely a procedural vote, or would fall under the category of non-procedural or substantive which thus permitted the veto, took a special US mission to Moscow to extract Stalin's concession and the abandonment of the extreme Soviet position.[21]

The request to exempt Chapter VI matters from the requirement of the unanimity of the permanent members and thereby exclude this important realm from the application of the veto was presented as a formal amendment by Australia and co-sponsored by several other small and middle powers and at their insistence was formally voted upon. The vote for the Australian proposal was 10 for, 20 against, 15 abstentions and 5 absent. It can be assumed that the abstentions and absences came from representatives favouring the Australian *démarche*. In the light of this vote one can indeed speak of the disenchantment and resentment of that group representing the large majority at the founding conference with the form and substance of the proceedings at San Francisco.[22]

In the end, the alignment of the middle and small powers was compelled to surrender to the ultimatum of the great powers, who were totally united in their response to the complaints of the non-privileged co-signatories of the UN Charter: it was either the Charter with the veto right or no Charter. The threat of the Big Five was credible, in particular through the dramatic gesture of US Senator Tom Connally tearing up the copy of the Charter in his hand and throwing the pieces of paper on the conference table as he was getting up.[23] While the uncompromising attitude of the Soviet government was especially resented and criticized, it needs to be underlined that the USA was the actual leader in the great power club insisting upon the privileged position and harshly rebuking the charges and demands of the lesser partners prior to and during the eight weeks of the San Francisco conference.

This brief survey of the movements leading to the decision to establish a global multifunctional organization and to adopt its Charter as its programmatic guideline brings out the sober and unenthusiastic mood with which the participants at San Francisco concluded their task and launched the new organization, primarily as a tool of political control in the hands of the newly designated permanent members. As the necessary steps were taken to obtain the required ratifications of the Charter and to begin implementing the provisions of the new Charter, the idealism and euphoria of the believers in world peace and world government were inappropriate and misplaced. The emerging characteristics of the international system after the collapse of Nazi Germany, and in particular the looming spectre of a new division of the world, contributed to the rapid shedding of illusions and even hopes among the political and intellectual elites throughout the Western world. The chance for effective global governance was lost even before the first meetings of the UN were called to order.

FROM COLD WAR TO DECOLONIZATION: THE FIRST 25 YEARS

The already contentious relationship among the key members of the victorious anti-Hitler alliance affected the functioning of the Security Council from the beginning, as has been reported by eye-witnesses and other contemporary observers.[24] The tension between the Soviet Union and the United States became apparent in the Council's consideration of the Iranian complaint against the USSR. In a letter dated 19 January 1946, Iran accused the Soviet Union of interference in its internal affairs, claimed that efforts to negotiate a mutually satisfactory solution had been in vain, and asked the Council to investigate the situation and recommend appropriate terms of settlement. The Soviet government replied on 24 January 1946 that the matters raised by Iran should be settled by means of bilateral negotiations, denied that the USSR had interfered in Iran's internal affairs and, in view of these baseless charges by the Iranian party, expressed categorical opposition to the Council's consideration of the Iranian appeal.

This dispute involving one of the permanent members of the Council was included on the agenda of the second meeting of the Security Council on 25 January 1946. The constellation of the dispute involving the continued presence of Soviet troops on Iranian territory offered a perfect test for the viability of the Charter provisions for peaceful settlement and for the critical ingredient of the close co-operation of the permanent members entrusted with special responsibility for the maintenance of international peace and security. While the Soviet side was clearly opposed to the Iranian allegations, it is noteworthy that the USSR delegation did not seek to block the Council's consideration of the issue and accepted the inclusion of the Iranian question on procedural grounds, i.e. for the purpose of an initial discussion of the case.

In the opening debate, the Iranian representative urged the Council to recommend that, pending the completion of the withdrawal of Soviet forces, the Soviet authorities should cease to interfere in the internal affairs of Iran. The Soviet delegate pointed out that negotiations had taken place between the Iranian and USSR Governments in November 1945 and had produced satisfactory results. He therefore concluded that there were no grounds for considering the substance of the Iranian statement, and suggested that the two parties should be given the opportunity to settle the matter on their own.

Following consideration of the matter at the third and fifth meetings of the Council on 28 and 30 January 1946, the debate was concluded with the unanimous adoption of a British draft resolution, which requested the parties to inform the Council of any results achieved in their bilateral negotiations, while the Council retained the right to seek information at any time on the progress of the negotiations. The unanimous decision of the Council was assured after the British sponsor had agreed to withdraw the suggested clause that the Council would retain the matter on its agenda.[25]

Up to this point in the treatment of the Iranian question, as it was impartially labelled, the fundamental unanimity of the Big Five was preserved, although with significant difficulties. Two key questions raised by the Soviet delegation during the deliberations regarding the first substantive question under Chapter VI of the Charter revealed the conditions that had to be satisfied to maintain the good faith of the USSR and its readiness to co-operate in the post-war peace directorate of the great powers. The first one related to the strictly preliminary reason for the inclusion of a so-called dispute in the Council's agenda: it was essential for the Soviet partner that the 'false' charges by the Iranian government would not appear validated by the Council's procedural move. The second question was even more decisive. By the deletion of the British draft provision for the retention of the Iranian question on the Council's agenda, the Soviet Union felt confirmed in its principal argument that a matter that was effectively dealt with by the two parties did not require or merit retention in the Council's agenda. At this early moment in the Security Council's history, one can identify a persistent feature throughout its more than 50 years of functioning, namely the careful and knowledgeable manner with which Soviet delegates have usually interpreted Charter and Rules of Procedure provisions and often succeeded in making a case for their viewpoint in the Council's proceedings – a quality they have shared with many French representatives.

The outcome of the second time the Iranian question came before the Security Council was radically different and set the stage for the more than 40 years of severely hampered work for international peace under the heavy burden of the Cold War. In this connection, it should also be noted that between the first and second Council consideration of the Soviet–Iranian dispute fell the momentous 'Iron Curtain' speech of former Prime Minister Churchill at Fulton, Missouri, when he visited President Truman in the latter's hometown on 5 March 1946. This and other events became milestones on the way to the total collapse of the alliance of the victors of the Second World War.

The Iranian representative sent a letter dated 18 March 1946, in which he informed the Security Council that a new dispute had arisen between Iran and the USSR as a result of the continued presence of Soviet troops on Iranian soil after 2 March 1946, contrary to the provisions of the Tripartite Treaty of Alliance of 29 March 1942. In a second letter dated 20 March 1946, the representative of Iran added that Soviet–Iranian negotiations pursuant to the Council resolution of 30 January 1946 had failed. At the 26th meeting on 26 March 1946, the Council included the question in the agenda and considered it at the 26th to the 30th, 32nd, 33rd, 36th, 40th and 43rd meetings between 26 March and 22 May 1946.[26]

The Soviet strategy against the renewed Iranian accusations was very direct and consistent. At the 26th meeting on 26 March 1946, the Soviet representative proposed that the question raised by Iran should not be included on the agenda since an understanding had been reached in the negotiations between the two governments and therefore no reason existed for taking up the matter in the Council. In the subsequent discussion, the USSR representative elaborated his explanation and suggested that the Iranian question was not fraught with complications that would lead to a violation of international peace and security. He cautioned the other Council members to guard against the admission of unwarranted or frivolous communications for consideration by the Council. At the same meeting, the Soviet proposal, which was handled as an amendment to the provisional agenda and was voted on separately, was rejected by two votes (USSR and Poland) in favour and nine against.[27] The rejection of the Soviet argumentation, which was a reasonable reading of the legal basis of the Council's involvement, could not have been clearer. One wonders whether the solid majority front was acting on constitutional or political grounds.

In a second more forceful démarche, the Soviet delegation, having lost the first procedural vote, launched another proposal at the 26th meeting, seeking to postpone consideration of the Iranian communication until 10 April 1946. After extended discussion of this motion at the 26th and 27th meetings, the proposal was rejected at the 27th meeting. Thereupon the Soviet representative stated that he was not in a position to take part in a discussion of the Iranian question after the defeat of his motion, and left the Council chamber. The USSR delegation did not return to the consideration of the Iranian question until the 32nd meeting on 15 April 1946.[28]

There can be no doubt that the choice of this crude instrument of a Soviet boycott of the Council's deliberations came about as a result of the Soviet realization that the new fronts of the post-war estrangement between the US and its allies on one hand and the Soviet Union on the other were of a more permanent nature, and that the earlier hopes for a lasting amity between the East and the West had to be shelved for good, or at least for the time being. Of course, it strikes the neutral analyst as odd that the boycott tool, which turned out to be a capital mistake in the Iranian case, was again – and unwisely – used during the time of the outbreak of the Korean War (albeit over the question of the Chinese seat). It was an extraordinary measure of protest that was calculated to express to the other powers the depth of alienation and isolation felt by the leaders and representatives of the Soviet regime. In light of this early rapid decline in the quality of international relations, it remains a suitable subject for academic study to explain the survival of the UN organization and functioning over the period of more than half a century.

The remainder of the story of the Council's consideration of the Iranian question, while interesting in itself, does not add much to the description of the political and diplomatic point of departure for the UN and its Security Council. The Iranian complaint finally became immaterial, in that over time the Soviet troops completed their total withdrawal from Iranian territory and thus the Iranian–Soviet friction ended. The cold and uncooperative atmosphere in the Council was, however, clearly demonstrated in that the United States and its friends insisted, during the 43rd meeting on 22 May 1946, on retaining the Iranian question on the Council agenda. This was despite a notification dated 15 April 1946 by the representative of Iran, withdrawing its complaint from the Security Council, and a directly related effort at the 33rd meeting of the Council on 16 April 1946, by the representative of France to remove the matter from the Council's agenda, as the underlying case had been fully resolved.[29]

The Iranian case illustrates as well as any other early political conflict how quickly the prospects for a co-operative and effective Security Council had deteriorated to this low point of bleak disillusionment. Important elements of the authority of the Council in crucial peace and security matters became quickly inoperable and were basically cast aside; for example, the Military Staff Committee and key aspects of the Charter's collective security system, in particular the implementation of the central Article 43. Other larger concerns such as the nuclear arms race and the formation of military blocs, as well as the ambitious targets in collective action that logically belonged on the menu of the world's peace and security organ, were neglected or dropped completely. The Korean War, and the one-sided involvement of the Western world in fighting this unexpected aggression, removed the last doubts as to the complete failure of the vision underlying the erection of the edifice of the UN. It forced the member states and the committed citizens of the post-war world to reconfigure the viable elements of the crumbling world organization and to use the remnants for much more modest duties in the divided world of the Cold War.

With the UN losing its first Secretary-General as a casualty of the bitterly fought East–West confrontation, new hope began to spring from a totally unexpected quarter, namely the fortuitous choice of the charismatic and visionary Dag Hammarskjöld as Lie's successor. As the Security Council suffered terribly under the blows of the rivalry, it was clear that any possibility of innovation had to come from outside the UN's principal organ. In the first ten to fifteen years, the Council itself was safely in the hands of the Western superpower, and the Soviet reply to the 'pax Americana' was the frequent use of the veto power whenever it felt pushed to the wall, with no other way out without losing face. Little good could come from this futile competition amounting to hardly more than provocation and denial. After early 'defining moments' such as the Iranian question taking place in the Soviet sphere of interest or in its immediate backyard, or the Korean War renewing the danger of a global conflagration between the democratic West and the communist East, it was understood on all sides that issues of direct concern to either of the two superpowers would simply not be taken up by the Security Council, regardless of the danger that such deliberate neglect could constitute for world peace. If these were taken up, it was usually to serve polemical purposes by embarrassing the ideological adversary and to score rhetorical triumphs on the international battlefield. This stalemated role of the Council could not be transformed into a proactive force on the world stage.

Hammarskjöld was catapulted into the hot seat of Secretary-General at a time when the Organization was being criticized from many sides, and when its future role and even survival were under sharp attack from the anti-communist frenzy of US Senator McCarthy and his fanatical followers. It was due to Hammarskjöld's belief in the significance of the UN Charter and the usefulness of the existing Organization, and his political acumen as well as administrative skill, that at a time when the Security Council was largely paralysed and ineffective, the organizational centre shifted to the Secretary-General and allowed for a considerable recovery for the UN and its organs. It also brought about a revival of the political importance of the Council for many international issues brought to the Council's attention, either by member states or occasionally by the popular and visible Secretary-General.[30] In this way, the most severe losses in the Council's actual position in international relations could at least be mitigated and sometimes even reversed, as the Suez Canal crisis and the Congo crisis amply document. These changes were also facilitated by an easing of the East–West conflict and periods of *détente* among the superpowers.

Despite the severe narrowing of the Council's political agenda under the conditions of the Cold War, and its consequent inability to carry out the assigned task of maintaining global peace and security, the list of items on the Council's agenda and of its resolutions and decisions grew longer and more relevant in terms of the needs of a growing and ever more complex world community. Following the inevitable acceptance of the unfortunate effects of the Cold War, and of the fateful presence of the nuclear balance of terror, most peoples and governments decided to make the best of a bad thing and utilize the Security Council in as much as the political realities would allow it. The Council's records in the 1950s and 1960s reveal to the unprejudiced student a picture of limited engagement. Increasingly it involved governments and situations in countries that were newly decolonized and independent and seeking the attention of the Security Council as a neutral forum where their grievances and disputes would be given a fair hearing. While the number of these cases increased with the immense wave of decolonization beginning in the 1950s and extending into the early 1970s, the major innovation of peacekeeping, a unique achievement in the annals of the UN, emerged into the limelight of public awareness. The catalytic role of Hammarskjöld must be emphasized in this connection, but the quick and full embrace of this new peace technique by the Security Council is a major aspect of the aforementioned recovery and rise of the Council in matters of international peace and security. The main examples of this new UN involvement in conflict zones are the operations on the Suez Canal, in the Congo and in Cyprus. The seeds of this innovative UN presence were sown early in 1948 in the Middle East and on the Indian subcontinent in the form of observer missions, but the full scope of the peacekeeping function became visible only in the large-scale deployments in the Suez Canal area and in the newly independent Congo.

Another major impetus for the continued evolution of the Security Council in the 1960s and 1970s was the rush of decolonization and the subsequent admission to UN membership of a large number of newly independent states mostly from Africa, but also from other parts of the developing world. The widening gap between the small size of the original Security Council (11 members) and the enormous increase in member states as represented in the expanding General Assembly led to demands for increasing the number of non-permanent members of the Council. The expansion from 11 to 15 members was decided by the Assembly, accepted by the Council, ratified by the required number of member states and entered into force in 1965. Herewith the non-permanent group grew to two-thirds of the total membership, making it much more difficult for the permanent members to impose their individual or collective will and more costly to exercise their right to cast a negative vote thereby defeating the wishes of a clear or overwhelming majority. The repercussions of the new seat and vote distribution were far-reaching and soon led to a radical change in the Council's informal consultations in search of a generally acceptable methodology of arriving at resolutions and decisions.

One should begin from the harsh fact that the overwhelming majority of 14 out of 15 Council members could be defied and defeated by the casting of a single veto, a situation the representatives had experienced far too often ever to forget it. Disregarding the specific norms of the Charter and the Provisional Rules of Procedure, the Council members focused on the basic necessity to avert the use of the veto. This could only be achieved if the members searched through informal consultations in the corridors and rooms near the Council chamber for the consensus obviating the need for the veto or for voting altogether. If such a consensus position were to emerge, the Council could proceed into the formal meeting and briefly adopt what had emerged as a result of the consultations. If no consensus was achievable, despite lengthy and complex consultations, the matter could be abandoned before the Council needed to enter into the public phase of its diplomatic activity. What was still debated and negotiated in public during the Council's adoption of Resolution 242 in 1967 following the six-day war in the Middle East, was no longer handled openly by the early 1970s. While the general public may be deprived of an impressive diplomatic spectacle like that of 1967, the Council has improved its record of positive decisions and has learned to get around the burdensome effects of the veto.

As sketched out by insiders and experts, the fully developed scheme of consultations consisted of three components. Once a request for a meeting of the Council on a particular dispute or situation was received by the Council President, he (or she) would initiate bilateral consultations with the individual members of the Council, with the parties to the dispute or critical situation and with other interested parties. If the general sense of these bilateral consultations was to proceed with the request, the President would enter the second round of consultations dealing with groups of states in and around the Council; this would include in particular the non-aligned group which had begun to play a more important role in the enlarged Council, but also the Soviet bloc and the Western group among others. Regional groups in the area of tension and *ad hoc* groups were also occasionally drawn into this phase of the consultative process. If the general sentiment favoured pursuing the matter further, the President would engage in the third and most important phase of these consult-ations, the consultation of the whole, convening the Council members under the chairmanship of the President, but behind closed doors and informally. This third round became the occasion where all pending procedural as well as substantive aspects of the particular issue or dispute were taken up and resolved. By the time this collective consultation was finished, the members would have before them in nearly all cases the agreed draft resolution or statement of the President, and the firm arrangements on procedural items, such as adoption of the agenda item, invitations under Articles 31 and 32 and Rule 39 and other details. Since the consultation of the whole deals with many and complicated issues, the informal meeting could be interrupted and, if need be, postponed to another day. But the business at hand had to be completed before a purely procedural official meeting lasting usually just a few minutes was con-vened and held. For the student of the Security Council it is both fascinating and frustrating to realize that with the insertion of the consult-ation procedure into the decision-making process, the records of these minimal meetings at the end of a lengthy track of informal exchanges and drafting sessions have become documents that reveal little, if anything, about the earlier political exchanges and understandings.[31]

The gain in discretion and effectiveness that accrued to the Council as a result of the elaborate and refined consultation procedure has, of course, brought about a loss in openness and transparency, thereby further removing the organ devoted to the maintenance of international peace and security from the public view and intensifying the misperception of the Council returning to the traditional practices of secret diplomacy. This discomfort and alarm have been voiced by the wider membership of the UN shut out from the dealings in the Council's informal processes, and by the educated and interested public, which continues to be guided by Woodrow Wilson's ideal of public diplomacy publicly arrived at. Still, examining the basic dilemma of the Council's role between publicity and relevance, many detached analysts will decide in favour of political weight and importance at the expense of openness and representation.

FROM DECOLONIZATION TO THE END OF THE COLD WAR

With the completion of the decolonization process, not only had the size of the membership expanded tremendously, but also its political orientation began to undergo significant change. The initial purpose of the great power guardianship had been to avert another large-scale global war and to maintain a stable international system. The first 15 years had turned out to be a period of US predominance in the world and in the UN system. But by the late 1960s and early 1970s, the growing group of non-aligned developing countries started to take possession of the stage provided by the main organs of the UN, and paid special attention to a fair and equitable role in affecting the bearing and decision-making of the Security Council, the pinnacle of the construct of the world organization.

During the same years, the United States noticed the widening gap between its views and goals and the principles and policies espoused by the spokesmen of the Third World and the leaders in the Non-aligned Movement. The central focal points of the non-aligned agenda were the fight against apartheid and racism, the campaign for a 'New International Economic Order', and the support for national liberation movements; in this connection the Third World took up the South African and Palestinian causes and declared their solidarity with the suffering civilian populations and their revolutionary leaders. These battles were carried into the meeting rooms of the United Nations and quickly led to the alienation of the US representatives and authorities. The distancing between North and South, between the conservatism of the highly developed industrialized countries and the progressive goals of the developing countries, occurred rapidly and made itself noticed quite abruptly in the political debates and positions taken in formal meetings, as well as informal gatherings and encounters. This contentious climate in the 1970s worsened markedly with the arrival of the Thatcherite and Reaganite conservatives in the corridors of the UN Organization.

The four years of a basically pro-UN policy of the US administration under President Carter offered a brief respite between Moynihan's polemics against the Third World and Reagan's renewal of the Cold War. Between 1977 and 1981, important diplomatic advances were achieved regarding southern Rhodesia, Namibia and the Middle East, based on a co-operative attitude and a gentle form of leadership by the United States. The bipolar tension in the Security Council was not too overt, and the impression prevailed that patience and goodwill could move multi-lateral policy-making in the Council. Nevertheless, Third World challenges on the new international economic and information orders, and increasing public clamour for the Palestinian cause, undermined the remaining pillars of support for the UN in the United States. The turn-around after the inauguration of President Reagan was swift and blunt. The role of the Council was not the main target of the Reagan adminis-tration, but in no time, the new US team had turned the Council into a main battlefield in the ideological campaign against Communism and multilateralism.

Fortunately, the Cold War skirmishes in the Security Council were conducted in camera, away from the glaring lights of television and the media. There were, of course, exceptions, as the occasion of the shooting down of Korean airliner KAL 007 by Soviet fighter planes demonstrated. In this case, the US representative called for an official public meeting of the Council and brought her government's charges against the USSR, accusing the Soviet leaders of deliberately shooting down a civilian plane and killing several hundred innocent passengers, supporting her accu-sations by the playback of a sound-track of intercepted in-flight communi-cations. The Council was misused for the purpose of hostile propaganda intent on exposing and hurting the 'evil regime' and its agents. This gloomy spectacle was totally opposite to the goals and assets of the Council as a peacemaker and peacekeeper. Could anybody be surprised that after this staged denunciation the other side in the global struggle was not interested in moderate language and mutual accommodation, but vied eagerly to retaliate as soon and as much as possible? As the East–West struggle heated up, and as the nuclear arms race escalated in the 1980s, the impact of bipolarity was devastating for the collegial search for a meaningful consensus to bring to bear on the many pressing global problems. These years lowered the number of formal or informal Council meetings and reduced the instances when a united Council was able to take a decision and recommend some measure to promote a peaceful settlement. This sobering experience showed most clearly how much the Council's fruitful immersion in international crises depended on the preservation of an atmosphere of openness, tolerance and co-operation. By the resurgence of the Cold War the world's leading powers paralysed and marginalized the Charter's peace and security organ and wasted the opportunity to approach the so-called 'regional conflicts' in a collaborative fashion within the realm of the Council's assigned mandate. It actually increased the danger of a global war arising from one or other of the regional conflicts that the two superpowers reserved for themselves, regardless of the eventual outcome on the people affected or the global situation.

Still, in this dismal world under the black clouds of the second Cold War, there were fleeting moments where the highly complex international reality drew the ideological warriors out of their fortified encampment and coaxed them into dealing with the problem at hand pragmatically and in harmony with other members of the UN. A case in point occurred early on in the first year of Reagan's presidency. Israeli military planes had destroyed the Iraqi nuclear reactor on 7 June 1981, and the international reaction was very angry. The action involved a clear violation of international law. The question for the US government was clear-cut: did it wish to stand by the side of Israel, to which the US has long been bound by principle and interest, or would it try to find some working compromise with the other Council members censuring Israel, but without imposing a concrete penalty? With this choice before the US administration and its UN representative, it deserves emphasizing that the US ambassador got directly involved in the back and forth of political dealing and, in a private meeting with the Iraqi Foreign Minister Hammadi, struck a deal with the Arab side; the compromise consisted of the US supporting the resolution naming Israel as the guilty party and the Arabs, primarily Iraq, dropping the demand for an arms embargo against Israel. Inevitably, Mrs Kirkpatrick was sharply attacked for her role in multilateral diplomacy by the Republican Right in America and by the Israeli government and media.[32]

Such bright spots were the rare exception. But one could still detect that the Council's informal consultative process remained available and suitable throughout the 1980s. This quality can be demonstrated in the instance of the decision of the Security Council to recommend Pérez de Cuéllar as next Secretary-General in December 1981. This followed a prolonged and agonizing race between Waldheim seeking a third term – and supported by four out of five permanent members in this personal ambition – and Salim Salim, former Foreign Minister of Tanzania and former President of the UN General Assembly, hoping to win the post for an African whom the US opposed strongly. Security Council President Olara Otunnu, then Uganda's UN Ambassador, benefited cleverly from the informal quality of the Council's proceedings to persuade both main candidates to step aside for one informal straw ballot before resuming their active candidacy. This device, which could not have been tried in a formal setting, was sufficient to break the deadlock and establish very quickly the overwhelming backing for Pérez de Cuéllar who had not declared himself a candidate and was away on vacation in Peru at the time of the Council's exercise of its Charter duty.[33]

As the new Secretary-General faced the task of preparing his first Annual Report to the General Assembly on the work of the Organization in summer 1982, he determined to break with tradition and try something new in order to enliven the conduct of the whole Organization and to reactivate in particular the Security Council. In the report that he presented at the end of August 1982, his main lament and plea related to the inordinate delays incurred in efforts by the Security Council and the Secretary-General to respond in a timely fashion to newly emerging and incipient crises: 'Unfortunately, there has been a tendency to avoid bringing critical problems to the Security Council, or to do so too late for the Council to have any serious influence on their development.' He also deplored the inability of the Secretariat to provide the Council with up-to-date reliable information on global developments and to warn the Council members early on about those matters that might in due course turn into international disputes entailing the use of military force. While the Secretary-General put much of the blame for the information deficit on the Secretariat, he appealed to the Security Council to play a more active and forceful role in defusing international tensions and in preventing dangerous confrontations.[34]

In response to the eloquent testimony and appeal by the Secretary-General, the Council members decided, after further consideration of his suggestions, to pay close attention to the views and recommendations of the Secretary-General and to hold closed consultations of the whole at irregular intervals, fitting these meetings into the regular schedule of the Council's work.

From early 1983 until late 1987, the Council held a number of these informal consultations and devoted considerable time to the topics raised by the Secretary-General, especially the timely topic of the UN role in conflict prevention. On several occasions during these few years, very general brief summary reports were issued by the respective presidents. From these brief reports, it appeared that the representatives strongly reaffirmed the existing principles and instruments of the Charter and recommended *inter alia* early resort to the Council, informal consideration of pending issues with the parties, periodic or occasional reports by the Secretary-General on potential conflict situations, resort to Article 99, good offices missions and quiet diplomacy; engaging retired senior statesmen or retired UN ambassadors to visit and report about trouble spots, and the establishment of a UN system for monitoring developments on a global scale to aid the preventive role of the Council.[35]

These topical consultations took place in the harshest Cold War climate of the early 1980s. The relationship between the two superpowers was very bitter, and the margin for exchange and understanding between them was minimal. By the time these consultations ended quietly in 1987, it could be stated that the room for improvements, as far as the UN fulfilling its challenging peace mandate was concerned, was considerably wider than was believed by the rivals in the new Cold War. In that sense, the focus on strengthening the management and policy role of the Council proved to be quite relevant and productive, and constituted an early link to the resurgence of the UN in the post-Cold War era.

THE SECURITY COUNCIL IN THE POST-COLD WAR ERA

Realizing the ruinous economic consequences of the bitter political confrontation and nuclear arms race the Reagan administration had launched in 1981, the Soviet leadership under Gorbachev decided in the mid-1980s radically to change the direction of the USSR government's policies and seek an accommodation on all fronts with the United States, enabling the two superpowers and their allies to turn their urgent attention to clearly identifiable global issues and use the limited budgetary resources for the mastering of these challenges. Within a few years the revamping of world politics brought about the end of the East–West conflict and of the Cold War and soon thereafter the disappearance of the ideological divide between capitalism and Communism.

It goes without saying that the impact on the Security Council was swift and massive, and resulted in a quick succession of major breakthroughs in nearly all 'regional conflicts'. This list includes the Iran–Iraq War, and the crises in Afghanistan, Central America, Namibia, Cambodia and, a few years later, South Africa. Suddenly it appeared as if there were no problem that could not be solved in the new spirit of goodwill, harmony and common security. The prospects for a revitalized resurgent UN were bright indeed, and the Council members prepared finally to implement the Charter vision as it had been conceived and codified in 1945.

The enmity of the US and the USSR had been the decisive impediment to the Council's effective role in peace and security. The removal of that obstacle opened up a window of opportunity as far as testing the effect of unanimity and close collaboration among the permanent members was concerned. For the first time in UN history, the core condition of the peace system as spelled out in the Charter was fulfilled. Complemented by a new sentiment of global harmony among members of the United Nations, and specifically among the 15 members of the Council, the impressive successes of the late 1980s and early 1990s created a sense of unlimited possibilities for the reformed and strengthened Security Council in the resurgent UN system.

Built around the basic accord and unanimity of the permanent members, the Council's impressive accomplishments between 1988 and 1993 provided a breakthrough in global governance that validated the usefulness of the 1945 constitutional arrangements and affirmed the suitability of the Charter at the edge of a new world order. It also managed to survive the radical changes in the Soviet realm resulting in the democratization of the former satellites in Eastern Europe and in the break-up of the Soviet Union itself. The quiet acquiescence in the UN to the transition from the Charter member USSR to the reborn Russian Federation and its discreet seating in the Security Council testifies to the extraordinary nature of that moment in recent history. The demise of the Soviet Union and of the spectre of Communism profoundly affected the world political stage with unexpected consequences for the position and attitude of the United States as the only superpower and its relationship with the United Nations.

At the high point of the multilateral euphoria, Saddam Hussein's surprise attack on, and annexation of, neighbouring Kuwait in the summer of 1990 forced the international community and foremost the Security Council to acknowledge the fact that in the post-Cold War era global or regional peace could not be taken for granted, and that the new international situation might give rise to unexpected and highly destabilizing challenges with unforeseeable consequences for the world community. In order to understand more clearly the extraordinary character of the UN response to the aggression against Kuwait, one should consider the composition of the Council in 1990. In addition to the five permanent members, the other ten members were Canada, Colombia, Côte d'Ivoire, Cuba, Ethiopia, Finland, Malaysia, Romania, Yemen, and Zaire. This list shows a highly diverse group, reflecting different ideological, economic, political and cultural characteristics. It is indeed a marvel that under these conditions the Security Council reacted in as strong and as united a fashion as it did. It condemned the brazen act of aggression and imposed under Chapter VII of the Charter the most comprehensive non-military sanctions ever imposed by the United Nations to force the aggressor to release its prey and restore the independence and sovereignty of Kuwait. With this decisive action, the Council deliberately invoked the framework and provisions of the collective security system contained in Chapter VII and acted under Articles 39 and 41 of the Charter.

The strength and resilience of the underlying agreement among the Council members throughout the collective action against the aggressive Iraqi regime can best be measured by identifying the very few dissenting or abstaining votes with regard to the relevant resolutions. Resolution 660 (1990) of 2 August 1990, which called the Iraqi invasion of Kuwait a breach of the peace under Article 39 and demanded the immediate withdrawal of the Iraqi troops, was adopted by 14 votes to none, with Yemen not participating in the vote. That meant that the Arab member preferred to stay completely out of the decision, since neither a negative vote nor an abstention appeared appropriate or prudent to the Yemeni government. Resolution 661 (1990) of 6 August 1990, imposing wide-ranging non-military sanctions, was adopted by 13 votes to none, with Cuba and Yemen abstaining. These abstentions could not have surprised the experienced analyst of the international situation. Of the next nine resolutions adopted on this item between 9 August and 28 November 1990, all tightening sanctions against the Iraqi regime, five were adopted unanimously, one was opposed by Cuba and Yemen, another one just by Cuba, and two received abstentions by Cuba and Yemen. The voting pattern changed slightly for the important Resolution 678, based on a US draft, which was adopted on 29 November 1990, when the US Secretary of State occupied the President's chair in the Security Council, by 12 votes to 2 (Cuba and Yemen), with 1 abstention (China), acting under Chapter VII of the Charter, authorizing member states to use 'all necessary means' to expel Iraq from Kuwait unless Iraq, on or before 15 January 1991, complied with the resolutions of the Security Council. It can only be described as astounding that the most unusual authorization to a coalition of states outside the legal or organizational boundaries of the UN to use military force against Iraq found such overwhelming endorsement in the Council as constituted. The Chinese statement following the adoption of Resolution 678 sheds considerable light on the careful argumentation underlying its abstention in this critical vote.[36]

The Iraq–Kuwait crisis is a most appropriate test case for the *ex post facto* evaluation of this second attempt to practise collective security within the confines of the UN's existing capacities. Due to the fact that the Charter was never fully implemented, and that especially Chapter VII provisions fell victim to the negative force of the Cold War, the weaknesses of the UN approach to Iraq's aggression are easily exposed. The near-unanimous Council at a most propitious moment in the Organization's history displayed the legal and political clout right from the beginning of this difficult confrontation. The comprehensive sanctions under Resolution 661 (1960), amplified by the provisions of Resolution 687 (1991) of 3 April 1991, imposed on vanquished Iraq after the US-led military strike brought about the aggressor's defeat and the restoration of Kuwait, also showed the pain this collective instrument is able to inflict. But when it came to the consideration of the collective use of armed force under Article 42 of the Charter, the members of the UN drew the inevitable conclusion that the world Organization was not equipped to carry out such a military operation. Moreover, many member states from the Non-aligned Movement asked themselves and the other partners in the Organization whether, at the end of the twentieth century, the UN, designed to maintain peace and security, should 'make war' and engage in overt military action against an aggressor. Furthermore, the United States and other major powers aired the view that the UN lacked the military and logistical capacity effectively to carry out Article 42 operations. A related predicament noticed in the Iraqi crisis was the lack of any progress regarding Article 43 agreements that could eventually make military contingents available for collective purposes. Once again, the burden of responsibility for this massive shortcoming had to be borne by the leading members of the UN system. For these and other reasons the adoption of Resolution 678 constituted a declaration of impotence and surrender before the overwhelming military strength of the United States and other leading powers.

Instead of the celebration of its renaissance and the realization of its full peacemaking potential, the Council members had to admit their current inability to enforce their collective will and stand aside while the high-tech 'blitzkrieg' was started and ended by the US President as Commander-in-Chief of the US armed forces without formally reporting to the UN Security Council as the authorizing organ. The fact that the US forces were fighting under the American flag is symptomatic of the wide gap between the military aspect of the Iraqi crisis and the UN involvement. Still, the matter was restored to the custody of the Council after the military phase, and the Council was suitably engaged to adopt the legal instrument of Resolution 687 (1991), adopted on 3 April 1991 with 12 votes to 1 (Cuba), with 2 abstentions (Ecuador and Yemen), setting out in great detail the multifaceted punitive regime which at the time of this writing is still in place, as the Iraqi state and regime has not yet fulfilled the manifold requirements of that mammoth resolution. The question that has recently assumed growing significance addresses the relationship between the collective will, as expressed by the Security Council, and the individual policy guiding the US in this unending punishment of the Iraqi leader and his coterie of aides and followers.

The strongest asset and centrepiece of the Charter, the collective security provisions of Chapter VII, which would indeed equip the Council with the tools of global authority, turned out to be incomplete and falling short in the political reality of the UN in the post-Cold War era.[37] Its implementation in the years to come would help strengthen the foundations of true global governance. But the most recent instances of stagnation and failure provide little encouragement that such a far-sighted decision will be taken in the near future. Therefore, the question must be raised again and reconsidered: in the current international atmosphere, can the UN Security Council fulfil its global peace and security mandate, or will it remain inferior and therefore subject to the will and whim of leading states or coalitions and alignments of states whose political and military standing allows them to disregard the principles and decisions of the highest organ in the global Organization? This basic issue requires further reflection.

The beginning of the year 1992 saw the UN and its Security Council experience one of its finest moments, a time when the Organization was in demand everywhere in the world and when the impact of the UN and its principal organs seemed limitless and all-pervasive. Had the era of multilateralism started, and would the international community pull together and live and act in harmony? In order to commemorate this auspicious turn in the right manner, the British government suggested that the Security Council meet at UN Headquarters on 31 January 1992 for the first time at the level of heads of state and government and consider, within the framework of their commitment to the UN Charter, 'the responsibility of the Security Council in the maintenance of inter-national peace and security'. At the end of the meeting that was attended by presidents, kings and prime ministers, the members of the Council authorized the President of the Council, the UK Prime Minister, to make a statement on their behalf.[38] This statement was as revolutionary as the Communist Manifesto of 1848.

The Council members considered their exceptional meeting 'a timely recognition of the fact that there are new favorable international circum-stances under which the Security Council has begun to fulfill more effectively its primary responsibility for the maintenance of international peace and security'. The statement then referred to the time of momentous change and mentioned the advances towards democracy, the dismantling of apartheid, and positive trends in the area of human rights and personal freedoms. UN efforts at conflict resolution and its many peacekeeping operations were especially lauded. The Council acknowledged the new challenges in the search for peace and stated the joint commitment to increase the effectiveness of the UN. Furthermore, the Council made reference to the need to pay attention, in addition to war and military conflicts, to so-called non-military sources of instability in the economic, social, humanitarian and ecological fields, as well as to international terrorism, and urged the UN to give highest priority to the solution of these matters. The Council members recommitted themselves to the collective security system of the UN, praised continuing peacemaking and peacekeeping activities in the UN, asked for a comprehensive report from Secretary-General Boutros-Ghali, and identified major themes in disarma-ment, arms control and weapons of mass destruction as relevant for the Council under its Charter mandate. In conclusion, the Council agreed that the world had the best chance of achieving international peace and security, and recognized that 'peace and prosperity are indivisible and that lasting peace and stability require effective international cooperation for the eradication of poverty and the promotion of a better life for all in larger freedom'.

In response to the specific request to him that was included in this exciting and dynamic political manifesto by the Council, the Secretary-General submitted on 17 June 1992 his report entitled *An Agenda for Peace*,[39] offering an 'analysis and recommendations on ways of strengthening and making more efficient within the framework and provisions of the Charter the capacity of the United Nations for preventive diplomacy, for peacemaking and for peacekeeping'. Its reception among the member states was enthusiastic, but the content of the analytic study did not focus much on the place of the Security Council in the widening peace operations scene and mentioned only in passing the more active role of the Council in peacemaking efforts. More relevant and controversial was the Secretary-General's separate discussion of collective security and peace enforcement following the unusual proceedings in regard to the Iraq–Kuwait situation and some lessons from the Gulf War. The integral importance of Article 43 agreements was raised in connection with collective security, and the Secretary-General suggested for the Council's consideration the idea of the UN deploying so-called 'peace enforcement units' under Article 40 at the decision of the Council or as suggested by the Secretary-General, with the Council's agreement.

Reflecting the appreciation of the Council for the Secretary-General's *An Agenda for Peace*, the 15 members decided to 'examine in depth and with due priority' his recommendations.[40] This careful review was carried out in monthly consultation meetings followed by consensus statements of the President, which were presented in official meetings of the Council. Altogether, the Council held substantive consultations and issued presidential statements on eight occasions, beginning on 29 October 1992 and ending on 28 May 1993.[41] Each of the sessions and statements was prepared by an informal working group that the Council had set up in the summer of 1992 for this purpose. The topics taken up by the Council ran the gamut of key issues of the 'new' United Nations that the Council's 31 January 1992 declaration and the Agenda for Peace had formulated and publicized. Other than peacekeeping issues, to which the Council devoted very special attention and much time, fact-finding, humanitarian assistance, field personnel safety, post-conflict peace-building, Article 50 economic sanctions' effects, and co-operation with regional organizations were separately debated, and agreed positions were then included in the presidential statements.

The concluding statement of 28 May 1993[42] contained not only a brief summary evaluation of the significance of the *An Agenda for Peace* recommendations, but also, marking the Council's preoccupation and operational priority, offered a detailed policy statement and guidelines for the much enlarged UN peacekeeping and complex field operations on all continents. In succinct language, the Council went on record stressing the importance of precise mandates, periodic review of these mandates, prior agreement of the government and the parties concerned, impartiality in carrying out the mandates, the authority of the Council to authorize all means necessary for UN forces to carry out their mandate, the exercise, if necessary, by UN forces of the inherent right of self-defence, and the urgent need for political settlement and the avoidance of indefinite peacekeeping operations. This emphasis was further made clear in that the Council requested a subsequent report on the priority problems of the then UN capacity for these kinds of complex operations and ways and means to strengthen the Organization's capabilities in that regard.

Reviewing the visionary drive of the high-level Security Council statement of 31 January 1992, and the dynamic and forward-directed message of *An Agenda for Peace*, the thoughtful and receptive response of a co-operative Council and its eagerness to endow itself with the foresight, circumspection and authority required to handle the many political, military and legal challenges of the new era, it must puzzle the partisan believer and the impartial analyst why and how the same forces that welcomed the new world order so enthusiastically, turned in such a rush away from multilateralism and abandoned, dismayed and disappointed, the proven and reformable instruments of global governance. A few weeks after the concluding Council statement of 28 May 1993, the Somalia operation ran into major trouble, leading to blame and misunderstandings between the US leadership and the UN diplomats and officials.[43] This dramatic turnaround was followed by sharp criticism of the performance of the UN and by either stubborn self-righteousness or nagging self-doubt on the part of diplomats and Secretariat personnel. The new situation immediately affected the atmosphere and work of the Security Council, undoing to a large degree that which had so far been gained in the post-Cold War years.

While the new crisis of multilateralism cast a dark shadow on many areas and activities of the sprawling UN system, leading to distortions of the record of the Organization as a whole and of its constituent parts, the dissatisfaction with the Security Council in particular found an outlet and expression in the continuing debate about the reform of the Council. One should recall that ten non-aligned countries (Algeria, Argentina, Bangladesh, Bhutan, Guyana, India, Maldives, Nepal, Nigeria and Sri Lanka) had proposed to inscribe on the agenda of the 34th session of the General Assembly in 1979 an item entitled 'Question of equitable representation on and increase in the membership of the Security Council'. By the late 1980s, with the newly found unanimity and influence of the Council at the end of the Cold War, a further effort was launched to generate a wider debate on the closed character of the Council's proceedings, and to demand more democracy and openness to make its confidential debates and decisions accessible to all member states.

At its 47th session in 1992, the General Assembly requested the Secretary-General to invite member states to submit written comments on a possible review of the membership of the Council, and to submit to the Assembly at its 48th session a report containing these comments. In July 1993, the Secretary-General submitted this report containing comments made by 79 member states and three regional groups on this subject. This enormous response has given rise to continuing debates at meetings of the General Assembly over several sessions. At the 48th session, the General Assembly established a working group open to all governments to 'consider all aspects of the question of increase in membership of the Security Council and other related matters' and to report back to the 49th session in autumn 1994. Reports of the working group were submitted, as requested, to the 49th and subsequent sessions, informing the Assembly of the continuing discussions of the group, indicating the thrust of its deliberations, the issue areas covered, and any solutions or formulas reached. These mostly procedural progress reports have continued to be put before the Assembly, revealing the unresolved nature of the main bottlenecks in the reform debate.[44]

The issues before the working group, well known and hotly debated by many parties and individuals surrounding this great debate, are grouped in two clusters: the first one deals with the size and composition of the Security Council, under which is included the veto question and the suggestion of a periodic review of the Council's structure; the second part is labelled 'working methods of the Security Council, transparency of its work as well as its decision-making process' and contains mostly housekeeping and other easier matters. The deadlock is totally unbroken as far as the first cluster is concerned, whereas a good number of small but efficient improvements, such as more frequent public Council meetings, daily presidential briefings, and better and more informative reports to the Assembly, have found much acclaim and are already implemented in part. Thus, important wishes of the smaller member states that have little chance of ever being elected to the Council on a non-permanent basis, are met, leading to a more cordial overall atmosphere in the meeting rooms and corridors of the UN.

Still, the reform discussion focuses on the important obstacles, and the duration of the working group dialogue emits a loud message about the stalemate over size and veto right. There is general agreement that the Council should be enlarged as the dichotomy between the UN membership of 185 states and the peace and security organ of 15 members could not be wider. The pertinent issue, however, is first of all: how many members can the Council have before its size slows down the speed of its decision-making and its effectiveness? Distinguished Council members and several secretaries-general of the UN have commented on this critical link between size and decision-making capacity.[45] Based on past performance, and in particular on the condition of closeness and personal relations among the representatives, it would not be prudent to go much beyond 20 members, an argument that has also been made by the US government in the reform debate. Anything beyond 25 members would destroy the cordial relationship and intimate atmosphere without which the intense consultation and interaction among delegations would no longer be possible. Various Third World governments and groups have advanced proposals enlarging the Council to between 30 and 35 regular members. The danger of reducing the Security Council to a mirror image of the Economic and Social Council is too grave to be ignored. In this sense, the numbers game matters greatly.

The second and even more difficult complex question relates to the idea of adding additional permanent members 'with all rights and responsibilities', as worded by the representatives of Germany and Japan at earlier occasions at the UN. As has been pointed out by numerous experts and analysts, the designation of specific countries for such seats would mean that they would obtain the same status as the present five permanent members. It has become clear that the African, Asian and Latin American groups cannot agree on a single candidate for the respective permanent regional seats under consideration. Although support for Japan as a new permanent member continues to be quite solid, the German candidacy is forcefully opposed by the Italian government and has not only suffered delay, but also lost some support for its elevation to the club of permanent members. Demands for additional African or non-aligned permanent seats have further complicated the whole affair.

The sticky problem is, of course, epitomized by the veto right, the distinguishing mark in the political system of the UN. A very large number of countries, mostly non-aligned or developing, view the veto as undemocratic and outdated, and would prefer its elimination in the Council of the new millennium. Everybody knows, of course, that the five permanent members, without whom the Charter cannot be amended, have voiced their joint position that a Charter revision can only be achieved with their veto privilege in place and undiminished. The dictate of 1995 is as unbending as the dictate of 1945. The other members acquiesce because they do not want to destroy the UN, which is more significant for them than for one or the other among the privileged Five. Combining the realistic acceptance of the current veto privilege with the principled rejection of such an unequal arrangement is difficult enough for the non-aligned. Conceiving of further veto powers and thereby exacerbating the split between the haves and the have-nots in the organ for world peace must be anathema to all governments and delegations resenting the veto and fighting for its reduction and limitation, as its cancellation is not an option. At this point in the futile and redundant debate, it is inconceivable that an accord can be engineered that would satisfy the ambitions of the status-seekers in the race for permanent seats in an enlarged Council.

Will permanence of membership be an acceptable substitute in lieu of the veto? This essentially political question is not insignificant as the long-standing proposal to add a certain number of permanent members of a lesser rank, i.e. possibly without the veto, to the restructured Council is still before the working group and on the minds of a lot of delegates and their governments. If certain regional members serving a long term of office were to be added to the enlarged body, the traditional division between the permanent Five and the non-permanent members would be replaced by a much more stratified organ, consisting of four categories of membership. This scenario has been maintained in the reform discussion, but it is unlikely to obtain the required majority in the General Assembly if the suggestion were to reach that juncture in the Charter amendment process. Moreover, these far-fetched reflections still encounter the practical difficulty that the regional groups have proved unable to agree on unified nominations for new permanent seats or so-called special regional seats, although the African group let the other members of the UN know that they would come up with a single nomination, on the basis of the rotation principle, if and when the time came for their recommendation. Would Japan or Germany agree to a veto-less permanent seat and accept a lower rank in the new Security Council? The answer to that pertinent question is still outstanding. All this proves that the four-tier proposition is fraught with enormous theoretical and practical difficulties assuring, if nothing else, prolonged inconclusive reform discussions in the foreseeable future.

Let us return to the key question in the reform debate – the need for a larger Council to make it more representative in the complexity and disorder of the emerging international system. The non-aligned and developing countries that are most directly affected by the turbulence of today's world politics and have a large stake in the global capacity for effective governance, require much better representation to improve their share in the maintenance of peace and security in an uncertain future. Starting from the fundamental requisite of the Council's continued or strengthened effectiveness, it needs repeating that its future size must be carefully calibrated at no more than 20 members. Cutting the seats to be added to a low number of five to seven shrinks the room for negotiation and trading for the interested governments. Much of the recent academic discussion on the size question affirms that the available decision choices are not too enticing for the main groups and the leading contenders in the current phase of the debate.

One variant in the long-drawn debate has not received much attention, but it might gain in popularity as more far-reaching and ambitious schemes fail to obtain the required support or agreement from the membership at large or from the permanent Five. This suggestion involves merely the deletion of the last sentence of Article 23, paragraph 2 ('A retiring member [of the Security Council] shall not be eligible for immediate re-election'). This small change could have important consequences. Deserving countries winning a non-permanent seat and proving their value as responsible and impartial Council members and respected spokespersons of their own region could stand for re-election after each two-year period and be rewarded for good behaviour or suffer the punishment of not being re-elected for unrepresentative or disloyal conduct. It would also help to lighten the burden of the veto privilege in the new and slightly enlarged Council because the permanent Five, together or individually, would have to work much harder co-operating with the non-permanent members in the elaboration and adoption of the joint decision – usually in form of the consensus – instead of wielding their greater power in the Council's deliberations. Non-permanent members gaining in constancy of belonging to the Council would enhance their standing with their colleagues on the Council and with the other representatives outside the Council.

Furthermore, such a Charter revision would not detract from the original vision and wisdom of the basic constitution and would instead strengthen fundamental norms such as democracy, representation and accountability in the workings of the UN and its main organs. It might also assist in furthering current efforts to reduce the exercise or application of the veto on the basis of informal understandings between the veto powers and the other members. This would have to rely on non-binding compromises worked out in confidential exchanges. But it might eventually offer an opportunity to resubmit the 1945 Australian submission at the San Francisco conference, formally proposing the exemption of Chapter VI decisions from the exercise of the veto. It is quite revealing that the long-forgotten grievance about a flaw in the legal construct of the Charter has resurfaced in connection with the current reform debate. The lingering regret and dismay about such undemocratic and inequitable components of global constitutional law may be perceived as yet another good reason for the non-aligned and sympathetic middle and small states to sustain their absolute rejection of various proposals to add new veto powers to the current composition.

When all is said and done on the Council reform discussion – and that moment is still far removed and highly uncertain – the world will see one

major change: the increase in the size of the Council by an as yet
undefined number. This would replicate the precedent of 1963–65, when
the original Council of 11 was enlarged to 15. Since everybody agrees to a
similar decision to enlarge, there is little doubt that after the dust of the
current battles has settled, a bigger Council will emerge, with the required
ratifications by the member states delaying the realization of the amendment to enlarge. The small gain produced by years of intense and testy
arguing at the UN will disappoint both believers and friends and incite
the foes of the world Organization to disparage the global instrument and
those who are working very hard to make it viable.

To mitigate the negative reaction to the often unattractive underside of
the UN machinery and procedures, the close observer of the reform
debate ought to emphasize the remarkable gains in the working methods
of the Security Council referred to above. Such improvements and innovations as have been made should be put into the wider context of the
heavy workload of the Council, necessitating daily informal consultations
searching for provisional steps or long-term solutions on a wide front of
pressing global situations and of continuing UN operations which the
Council is mandated to monitor and direct. The careful and far-sighted
manner with which the Council followed up on several major themes of
An Agenda for Peace has given new insight into the inner workings of the
post-Cold War Council and its busy schedule.

As a result of the new spirit and the new proactive outlook, Council
members have started to reach out to outside viewpoints and influences
in order to connect the reclusive Council to the forces that help shape the
political environment in which its members must take action. This outreach
movement has been tried through the development of the so-called 'Arria
formula', under which Council members, away from the Council chambers,
hold informal frank sessions with eminent international personalities on
issues of relevance to the Council and its members. Only Council members
are allowed to request such exchanges, and if such a session is held, it is
not regarded as an informal consultation of the Council members. A
variation of the Arria formula is the so-called 'Somavia formula', under
which Council members would meet in a similar arrangement to hear
statements by international or non-governmental organizations. This practice has not yet materialized. Both these developments are reflective of the
growing desire of Council members to be connected to individuals and
NGOs above and beyond the confines of the Council's procedural constraints and its constitutional duties. These breaches of the high wall of
protocol and decorum document that, in small and unofficial ways, the
post-Cold War Council has initiated steps towards its evolution in order
to equip itself for the novel and untried challenges of the new millennium.[46]
Throughout this chapter, the role of the United States as major actor in

the UN system has been mentioned prominently. After everything has been said and done, everybody must realize that after more than 50 years of US predominance and leadership in the world Organization, the attitude of the US government has become the most decisive factor for the future of the UN in years to come. The huge burden under which the UN has been labouring since 1993, when the US left the path of 'assertive multilateralism' and resumed the earlier posture of an unwilling and indecisive player in the game of global governance, is that the membership does not know and cannot decipher what the US is willing to contribute to the commonweal, and how much it is disposed to commit in financial and political support for the functioning of the global instrument of positive peace.

President Roosevelt talked of the four Allies of the Second World War as the 'four policemen' of the 1945 post-war world. In past decades various US governments have invariably turned down requests in the world for the United States to be the world's policeman ensuring law and order everywhere. But after the collapse of the Soviet empire, the United States rose to the rank of 'the only superpower' during Krauthammer's 'unilateral moment'[47] and began to appreciate its ability to carry out global operations without the restrictions and limitations intrinsic in the membership and interaction in global or regional intergovernmental organizations, primarily the UN and its Security Council. Since that unfortunate mishap of early autumn 1993, the arch-enemies on the American Right have heated up their rhetorical struggle against the so-called intrusions of the UN seeking to become a 'world government' and to 'enslave' America's free citizens. The withholding of huge sums of owed arrears has helped to weaken the global instrument and may very well bring about its eventual ruin if no relief is provided soon. How will the fight between unilateralism and multilateralism end?

There is general agreement that the US does not need the UN to play its role as hegemon and superpower at the turn of the century. The use of the UN instrument as a tool of US foreign policy is quite limited. The basic dilemma, however, is not that the benefits accruing to the United States from using the UN are insignificant, but that the multilateral tool, if ill-used or neglected, cannot serve as an effective enhancer of the world order objective shared by the US as well as by the UN community. Put differently, the chance for the fulfilment of the UN's peace potential under the US-sponsored Charter of 1945 would be enormously improved and advanced if the US decided to become *primus inter pares*. If all members in the UN system, foremost among them the US delegation, acted unanimously and with determination and circumspection, the Security Council would flourish and grow as the democratic and representative authority designed in the 1945 programme for a world in peace.

The cardinal problem for the Security Council at the threshold of the new millennium is the choice between achieving its potential within and beyond the UN Charter or declining to a dismal mediocrity and political impotence. The years of American suspense and indecision have widened the gap between the current superpower and the rest of the UN membership. The policy of constraining proactive Council initiatives and blocking innovative decisions (e.g. some preventive military deployment around Burundi in recent years, or the extension of the multilateral team on Haiti, or – worse still – refusing the financing of these and other measures) defeats the commitment of diplomats and international staff. It increases the doubts about the utility of global processes for their daily needs among those who expect much from the global Organization and pin their hopes on active support from UN agencies. One would hope that sooner rather than later the member states would get together and confront the reticent superpower and demand a clear answer on the future of the UN and its role in it. Otherwise, many governments may start to look for other organizations and governance structures to handle their numerous common concerns, pushing the UN aside. It has been reported that the African countries are quite disappointed about the recent retrenchment in the UN system and the loss in political and economic benefits for the African continent. Other regions can be assumed to look similarly sceptically at what the last few years have wrought and to scout around for viable alternatives.

Thus the fear that the reform debate may turn out to be an exercise in futility and reflect nothing other than the selfishness and hypocrisy of the major powers might at last provoke an honest dialogue. Should the existing UN system, in particular its Security Council, be effectively used and further improved for the forthcoming decades of global co-operation and progress, or should the Organization and what it stands for be disbanded and abolished? Do states and peoples see the need for global governance in future centuries and believe that common dialogue and agreement are the best way to address the global and regional challenges? In the end the will of the clear majority should prevail. It would be a nasty surprise and a blunt shock if after ten years of multilateral action based on consultation and consensus in the post-Cold War era the tested machinery of the UN were to be cast aside. Governments will perceive the clear political and financial benefit of keeping it intact compared to the very low cost of maintaining the basic structures.

If one state or another were to decide not to join the world community in the next decade, it would be worthwhile testing the capacity of the Security Council to play a meaningful role under these new conditions. Since the enforcement provisions of the Charter – with the exception of non-military sanctions under Article 41 – have proved to be the least used, untested and unlikely to be applied frequently, one could expect far more activity under the articles of Chapter VI on peaceful settlement. These more subtle and less intrusive tools are especially helpful in the case of internal, largely ethnic or communal, conflicts involving a government under siege and a rebellious faction or insurgent group. Using these instruments together with an imaginative application of more than 50 years of UN peacekeeping would empower the Council to deal promptly and probably quite effectively with these new types of disputes and situations endangering the wider peace. This core function of the Council could safely be carried over into the uncharted waters of an uncertain global future. But it would inspire hope and confidence for an enduring peace and harmony in the evolving world community.

CONCLUSION

The main conclusions of this chapter can be summarized in the following points:

1. The historical–political analysis of the events and processes leading to the adoption of the UN Charter at San Francisco proves conclusively that idealistic expectations about world peace through federation and integration were totally unfounded and that the emerging international Organization was based on, and subject to, the sovereign will of the states and their governments constituting the membership. The Charter affirmed the supremacy of state sovereignty, especially in relation to the mandate and functioning of the Security Council.
2. The political practice of the UN was immediately curtailed by the onset of the Cold War so that even the limited aims of the Charter could not be fully realized. Instead, an *ad hoc* manner of conducting meetings and adopting resolutions and decisions resulting from prior informal consultations developed in permanent adjustment to the changing policies of major and minor members of the Council and of the Organization at large. Important achievements of the UN, in particular peacekeeping, were born out of the practical necessity of the moment. Decolonization happened as a result of the fundamental effects of the Second World War, but the partially paralysed UN system was deeply shaken up, with large-scale consequences for the role and work of the UN Security Council. As a result, the Council became better than its reputation and on many occasions defeated the odds of the deadening impact of the Cold War.
3. The post-Cold War era offered a dual opportunity: it enabled the Council to practise the Charter as it was drafted in 1945 and as it was

expected to be applied. It further gave the Council members, for the first time in agreement about the basic principles of international peace and security, a chance to undertake forceful action on behalf of the community of states and employ new approaches to promote peaceful settlement and even to help heal division and strife in many internal conflict situations. While the UN was underequipped and overstretched in some of these complex operations, the Council members acted knowledgeably and responsibly, in full recognition of the novel circumstances that were encountered in the field. In this role, the Council began to emerge as the guardian of world peace and the voice of legal and moral authority.

4. At the most promising turn in its development, a further crisis of confidence has put this newly acquired relevance and effectiveness of the UN in question. It can be argued that the UN stands ready to tackle the challenges and problems of a turbulent and complicated world community, and that the Council's work during the first decade of the post-Cold War era instils international confidence in its continued and increased viability in years and decades to come. However, two problems must be resolved: the Council must become more democratic and more representative without losing its capacity to make quick and effective decisions. The second problem relates to the erratic policy of the US, the only superpower, towards the Security Council: will it cast aside this collective instrument, or will it serve in it, and lead it, as the first among equals, thereby strengthening the multilateral instrument of a co-operative peace and security policy? The answers to these two questions will be decisive for the basic issue, namely the Council's suitability for the promotion and maintenance of peace and security in the next millennium.

NOTES

1. Since the focus of this chapter is mostly on the recent past and the short- and medium-term future, the survey must inevitably be incomplete and somewhat superficial. More detailed research and careful analysis are planned for a longer follow-up study. This chapter is partially inspired by the theory of consociationalism and endorses its basic assumptions and conclusions fully. See Paul Taylor, *International Organisation in the Modern World* (London: Pinter, 1993).

2. This section closely follows the outstanding and most careful account by Ruth B. Russell, *A History of the United Nations Charter: The Role of the United States 1940–1945* (Washington, DC: The Brookings Institution, 1958).

3. See Russell, *op. cit.*, p. 38 *et passim*.

4. *Ibid.*, pp. 104–6.

5. *Ibid.*, pp. 110–11.
6. *Ibid.*, p. 114.
7. *Ibid.*, pp. 116–19.
8. *Ibid.*, p. 120.
9. See *ibid.*, p. 121 *et passim.*
10. See *ibid.*, p. 134. For the text of the Joint Four-Nation Declaration, see Henry Steele Commager (ed.), *Documents of American History*, 7th edition (New York: Appleton-Century-Crofts, 1963), vol. II, pp. 477–78.
11. See Russell, *op. cit.*, p. 166 *et passim.*
12. For this internal US debate, see *ibid.*, pp. 193–99.
13. See here *ibid.*, pp. 206–12.
14. See *ibid.*, pp. 220–31 for details about the preparatory work for Dumbarton Oaks.
15. See *ibid.*, pp. 392–411 for Russell's most detailed account.
16. See *ibid.*, pp. 443–49, 533 *et passim.*
17. For this fascinating insight into US policy, see *ibid.*, p. 563.
18. See *ibid.*, pp. 600–2.
19. See *ibid.*, p. 664.
20. For the painstaking description and analysis of the veto debate at San Francisco, see *ibid.*, especially pp. 713–18 *et passim.*
21. See *ibid.*, pp. 734–35.
22. See *ibid.*, pp. 718, 738.
23. This story is vividly retold in *ibid.*, p. 713 *et passim.*
24. From among the many memoirs and documentary accounts of the beginnings of the UN in 1945–46, two more recent publications should be listed for this section: Brian Urquhart, *A Life in Peace and War* (New York: Harper & Row, 1987), especially chapters 7 and 8; and Stanley Meisler, *United Nations: The First Fifty Years* (New York: Grove/Atlantic, 1995), especially chapters 1 and 2.
25. For the basic procedural history of the Iranian question (I), see the *Repertoire of the Practice of the Security Council, 1946–1951* (New York: United Nations, 1954), pp. 300–1. See also *ibid.*, chapter II (Agenda), p. 75 (case 27).
26. The Iranian question (II) is presented *ibid.*, pp. 303–8 in the same fashion, providing the basic procedural history of the Council's consideration of the issue and relevant documentation.
27. For this particular procedural matter, see *ibid.*, chapter II (Agenda), p. 71 (case 16).
28. See *ibid.*, p. 303.
29. See *ibid.*, pp. 305–6.
30. Urquhart's unequalled evaluation of Hammarskjöld as Secretary-General is found in his *A Life in Peace and War*, especially chapters 9–13, and his definitive biography *Hammarskjöld* (New York: Knopf, 1973).
31. For some preliminary sketches outlining these and related procedural advances and changes see Davidson Nicol (ed.), *Paths to Peace: The UN Security Council and Its Presidency* (Elmsford, New York: Pergamon Press, 1981), in particular part I, with contributions by Davidson Nicol, Sydney D. Bailey and F. Y. Chai. See also J. Dedring, 'Towards greater effectiveness of the Security Council', *UNITAR Newsletter*, vol. 1(2), November/December 1989.
32. This process took place safely hidden behind the screen of informal consultations and quiet diplomacy. A brief reference to this episode is found in Urquhart, *A Life in Peace and War, op. cit.*, p. 329.

33. See *ibid.*, p. 332 for Urquhart's story and judgement. See also Meisler, *op. cit.*, ch. 14 *passim*.

34. See especially Urquhart, *A Life in Peace and War*, p. 348 covering also his direct participation in drafting this seminal report.

35. For brief notes see the Reports of the Security Council to the General Assembly, 1983–1987, under 'Other Matters Considered by the Security Council: Consideration of the Report of the Secretary-General on the Work of the Organization'.

36. For the full procedural account of the Council's treatment of 'The Situation Between Iraq and Kuwait' during 1990–91, see Report of the Security Council to the General Assembly, *Official Records of the General Assembly, Forty-sixth Session, Supplement No. 2* (A/46/2), 29 November 1991, ch. 4.

37. For a comprehensive look at the collective security question see Thomas G. Weiss (ed.), *Collective Security in a Changing World* (Boulder, Colorado: Rienner, 1993), with contributions by Bloomfield, Gordenker, Schachter, Ayoob, E. B. Haas, Sutterlin, Mackinlay, Farer, and Weiss. See also 'The Use of Force by the Security Council for Enforcement and Deterrence Purposes', a Conference Report edited by David Cox (The Canadian Centre for Arms Control and Disarmament, Ottawa), December 1990, including a contribution by Dedring, 'Collective Security Revisited: The Utilization of Military Force by the United Nations'.

38. Security Council document S/23500, dated 31 January 1992.

39. Document A/47/277//S/24111, dated 17 June 1992.

40. This was contained in the presidential statement S/24210 of 30 June 1992.

41. The presidential statements were issued under the following document numbers: S/24728, S/24872, S/25036, S/25184, S/25344, S/25493, S/25696 and S/25859.

42. Issued as S/25859 on 28 May 1993.

43. For an outstanding critical account of the earlier phases of the Somali débâcle, see Jeffrey Clark, 'Débâcle in Somalia: failure of the collective response', in: Lori Fisher Damrosh (ed.), *Enforcing Restraint: Collective Intervention in Internal Conflicts* (New York: Council on Foreign Relations, 1993), pp. 205–39.

44. A comprehensive and clear report on the progression of the diplomatic debate on Security Council reform is contained in General Assembly document A/50/47, dated 13 September 1996, *Official Records of the General Assembly, Fiftieth Session*, Supplement No. 47 (Report of the Open-Ended Working Group on the Question of Equitable Representation on and Increase in the Membership of the Security Council and Other Matters Related to the Security Council).

45. In the recent past, Pérez de Cuéllar and Boutros-Ghali have been quoted to favour a small Security Council.

46. The question of Security Council reform has engaged many policy-makers and academics. From the recent crop of very perceptive writings a few should be mentioned: Jose E. Alvarez, 'Provocations: the once and future Security Council', *Washington Quarterly*, vol. 18, no. 2, Spring 1995, pp. 5–20; Paul Kennedy and Bruce Russett, 'Reforming the United Nations', *Foreign Affairs*, vol. 74, no. 5, September/October 1995, pp. 56–71; Patrick A. McCarthy, 'Positionality, tension, and instability in the UN Security Council', *Global Governance*, vol. 3, no. 2, May–August 1997, pp. 147–69; Bruce Russett, Barry O'Neill and James

Sutterlin, 'Breaking the Security Council restructuring logjam', *Global Governance*, vol. 2, no. 1, January–April 1996, pp. 65–80; Modesto Seara-Vasquez, 'The UN Security Council at fifty: midlife crisis or terminal illness?', *Global Governance*, vol. 1, no. 3, September–December 1995, pp. 285–96; James S. Sutterlin, 'United Nations decision-making: future initiatives for the Security Council and the Secretary-General', in Thomas G. Weiss (ed.), *Collective Security in a Changing World* (note 37 above), pp. 121–38; and Peter Wallensteen, 'Representing the world: a Security Council for the 21st century', in Paul F. Diehl (ed.), *The Politics of Global Governance: International Organizations in an Interdependent World* (Boulder, Colorado: Rienner, 199), pp. 103–15.

47. Charles Krauthammer, 'The unipolar moment', *Foreign Affairs: America and the World 1990/91*, vol. 70, no. 1, 1991, pp. 23–33.

CHAPTER 4

MANAGING THE ECONOMIC AND SOCIAL ACTIVITIES OF THE UNITED NATIONS SYSTEM: DEVELOPING THE ROLE OF ECOSOC

Paul Taylor

INTRODUCTION

In this chapter the evolution of the mechanisms for managing the economic and social work of the United Nations system is considered. The Secretariat and the General Assembly had functions, alongside another institution in the central system – the Economic and Social Council (ECOSOC) – for overseeing the activities of a large number of other international institutions which formed what came to be called the *United Nations system*. In addition to the central system the latter was made up of two main kinds of institutions, namely the specialized agencies and the funds and programmes. The former included such well-known institutions as the World Health Organization (WHO), the International Labour Organization (ILO), and the Food and Agriculture Organization (FAO), which had their own constitutions, regularly assessed budgets, executive heads and assemblies of state representatives. They were self-contained constitutionally, financially and politically, and not subject to direct UN control. The funds and programmes were much closer to the central system in the sense that their management arrangements were subject to direct General Assembly supervision, and could be modified by Assembly resolution, and, most importantly, were largely funded on a voluntary basis. Overall, they were a response to the failure to co-ordinate social and economic activities that did not fall clearly into the sphere of responsibility of any one of the agencies, and therefore they emerged because of changes in global economic and social circumstances after the setting up of the agencies. The most important were the United Nations Development Programme (UNDP), the United Nations Fund for Population Activities (UNFPA), the World Food Programme (WFP), and the United Nations International Children's Emergency Fund (UNICEF).

The founders of the Charter had tried to improve on the mechanisms of the League for overseeing the economic and social institutions. The League had attributed responsibility for this to its Assembly, but the founders of the UN agreed to establish a smaller body, ECOSOC (now 54 members), to carry out this more specialized function. This body was appointed by, and responsible to, the General Assembly. These changes in the UN, compared with the League, were a consequence of thinking in more functionalist terms, but they did not give ECOSOC the necessary powers to manage effectively.[1] It was only empowered under Articles 61–66 of the Charter to issue recommendations to the agencies, and to receive reports from them. In consequence, the history of the UN's economic and social organizations was one of searching for ways of achieving effective management. The United Nations system, therefore, became multicentred and constantly concerned with the problems of co-ordination, as it was made up of a large number of constitutionally distinct institutions, which had a strong urge to go their separate ways.[2]

This chapter discusses these problems and how they were approached after the Second World War up to the millennium. The discussion moves from a concern with a functional approach to the new arrangements in the early days – setting up institutions to deal with the economic and social problems of the international community as they emerged – through a developmental approach, in which the main stress seemed to be on adapting the system to the promotion of economic development in new countries, through to the most recent period of what this author calls entrenched multilateralism. The latter is characterized by a widening of the agenda, and an increasing difficulty of participants in avoiding emerging rules of behaviour.

THE ORIGINS OF THE SYSTEM[3]

The League of Nations' work on economic, social and technical matters was essentially centralized, although each technical organization enjoyed some scope for independent action. Their executive committees reported to the League of Nations, and were served by members of the League Secretariat and work was financed from the League's budget. That budget also financed the work of the International Labour Organization (ILO), which had been established in accordance with Chapter 13 of the Treaty of Versailles, 'at the seat of the League of Nations as part of the organization of the League'.

In August 1939 the Special Committee of the League of Nations on the Development of International Co-operation in Economic and Social Affairs (the Bruce Committee) proposed setting up a new Central Committee for

Economic and Social Questions to manage those areas. It would be made up of government representatives with expertise in the various more functional areas, in which non-members of the League could also participate on a basis of equality with members. The Central Committee was to take over 'direction and control' of all the League's economic and social activities, with the exception of that of the ILO, which remained largely autonomous. The proposals were approved by the League's Assembly in December 1939, but because of the outbreak of the Second World War they could not be carried into effect.

Chapters IX and X of the UN Charter, which concerned the management of economic and social activities, and, in particular, the establishment of the Economic and Social Council (ECOSOC), drew heavily on the League's experience, including the Bruce Report's proposals. There was, however, another important difference in the new arrangements compared with those of the League: the new constitutional arrangements were highly decentralized on a functional basis, autonomous international organizations being entrusted, under a somewhat vague co-ordinating authority of the United Nations, with functions corresponding roughly to those of the traditional national government departments: finance, agriculture, labour, health, education, etc. The broad reasons for this change are not difficult to identify and understand. By the time the San Francisco conference met, several essential parts of the new international economic and social organization already existed, or were in the process of being established, as autonomous international entities. The International Labour Organization, which throughout the inter-war years had chafed under its at least nominal subordination to the League of Nations, emerged from the Second World War strengthened by the Philadelphia Declaration of 1944 and supported not only by Ministries of Labour but by organized labour and management throughout the world. Its independence was assured by its history. While it might have been just possible to bring the newly established Food and Agriculture Organization of the United Nations more closely within the United Nations framework, there had never been any question of more than a very loose relationship between the United Nations and the International Monetary Fund and the World Bank, which had likewise resulted from wartime decisions of the United Nations allies to create the elements of a new international system in time to act when peace returned.

There were not many voices raised in favour of centralization.[4] Much was made of the argument that it would be safer to establish in each essential functional area international organizations that could stand on their own feet and survive if the United Nations Organization itself did not come into being, or was torn by political conflicts, like the League. Other reasons were that this was the only way the United Nations could cope with a task of the magnitude and scope envisaged in Chapter IX of the Charter, and that successful international action in the various fields of economic and social policy depended on the active participation of, and complementary action by, the national authorities in each field which had close associations with their international counterparts. Such considerations could have been satisfied under varying degrees and forms of decentralization, and experience of the problems of co-ordination over the years has shown that it was a pity that the most influential governments, and in particular those of the USA and the UK, did not press for a stronger central authority.

Governments also did not press for this because international action in economic, social, humanitarian and related fields was envisaged largely in terms of what the League of Nations and the ILO had achieved. There would, it was thought, be more, much more, of the same. Some operational activities of the type carried out by the United Nations Relief and Rehabilitation Administration (UNRRA), of which there had also been examples in League days, might continue to be needed in respect, for example, of refugees or particular devastated areas, but they thought this kind of operational work was likely to be rather marginal. Essentially, the work would, as in the past, be concerned with the setting of standards, the conclusion of conventions, the interchange of experience, expert studies, consultations aimed at the harmonization of policies, and the development and refinement of statistical and other data required for the formulation of policy. Before the war, most of this work had been within sectors sufficiently self-contained to be handled by a single agency or organ. They were essentially forum organizations without large operational programmes and corresponding budgets and numbers of personnel. In the future, a rational division of work and arrangements for co-ordination would, it seemed, be needed rather than unified action or central direction of operations in the field.

The bringing into relationship with the United Nations of 'the various Specialized Agencies, established by intergovernmental agreement and having wide international responsibilities . . . in economic, social, cultural, educational, health and related fields' was provided for in Article 57 of the Charter; co-ordination was directly provided for in Articles 58 and 63, and implicit in the broad responsibility for the promotion of the economic and social objectives of the United Nations given to ECOSOC, under the authority of the General Assembly, in Article 60; it was implicit, furthermore, in the specific authorization given to ECOSOC by Articles 62 and 68 to 'initiate studies and reports, make recommendations, call international conferences and set up commissions on matters within its competence'. The United Nations was, in effect, given a central role and a universal competence in the field of economic and social co-operation. At the same time – as is clear not only from the Charter provisions and the relationship agreements subsequently concluded, but also from the texts of the constituent instruments of many of the agencies – it was intended that the agencies should participate, and consider themselves as participating, in promoting the purposes of the Charter as a whole.

Relationship agreements were negotiated by ECOSOC between 1946 and 1951 with the major existing intergovernmental institutions (ILO, FAO, the United Nations Educational, Scientific and Cultural Organization (UNESCO), the International Bank for Reconstruction and Development (IBRD), the International Monetary Fund (IMF) and the International Civil Aviation Organization (ICAO)), certain smaller agencies (the Universal Postal Union (UPU), the International Telecommunication Union (ITU) and the World Meteorological Organization (WMO) – all three dating from the nineteenth century, the first two as international bureaux, the third as a non-governmental organization of meteorological services), and three organizations that were created through the instrumentality of the United Nations itself (the World Health Organization (WHO), the International Relief Organization (IRO) and the Inter-Governmental Maritime Consultative Organization (IMCO)). The charter of a fourth agency with a very wide mandate (the International Trade Organization (ITO)), drawn up at the Havana conference of 1947–48 called by the United Nations, never came into force, the convention not having been ratified by the USA. This failure had a big effect on the later development of international organization – more particularly the conclusion of the General Agreement on Tariffs and Trade in 1948 among many of the major trading countries and ultimately the establishment of the UN Conference on Trade and Development (UNCTAD) in 1964. It was not until the 1990s that a new formal trade organization was established, the World Trade Organization (WTO). Some of the other proposed functions for ITO were taken on by UNIDO in 1966.

The first agreement was concluded between the United Nations and the ILO and constituted the model on which most of the others were based, subject to considerable modification in the case of IMF and the Bank Group and simplification in the case of the smallest agencies. It was also the model for the agreement concluded by the General Assembly in 1957 with the International Atomic Energy Agency (IAEA), which because of the nature of its responsibilities and its obligation to report directly to the General Assembly, was established as an agency 'under the aegis of the United Nations' and not as a specialized agency under the terms of Article 57 of the Charter. Agreements, usually of a more limited character, have been concluded by a number of specialized agencies and the IAEA with one another.

Apart from extensions of the United Nations–IBRD agreement in 1957 to include the International Finance Corporation (IFC) and in 1961 the International Development Association (IDA) (now known collectively as the World Bank Group), no move to increase the number of specialized agencies was taken by ECOSOC between 1951, when WMO entered the fold, and 1973, when ECOSOC decided that it was desirable that the World Intellectual Property Organization, which had recently been restructured and expanded and was co-operating actively with several United Nations bodies, be 'brought into relationship with the United Nations and that the ECOSOC should enter into negotiations with a view to achieving that end, in accordance with Articles 57 and 63 of the Charter of the United Nations'.[5] In the intervening years, many new and important institutions including the United Nations Development Programme (UNDP), the United Nations Conference on Trade and Development (UNCTAD), the United Nations Industrial Development Organization (UNIDO) and the United Nations Environment Programme (UNEP) were created as subsidiary organs of the General Assembly; different degrees and forms of relationship, including reciprocal representation at meetings, were established with non-United Nations regional and other organizations, while working agreements providing for co-operation and co-ordination, but not conferring specialized agency status, were concluded with a number of organizations such as the International Union of Official Travel Organizations (IUOTO) (in anticipation of its being transformed into the World Tourism Organization) and the International Criminal Police Organization (INTERPOL).

The system of weighted voting adopted by the Bretton Woods institutions always distinguished them sharply from the agencies, and the relationship the United Nations established with them, after considerable difficulty, was much less close and was hedged about by reservations to prevent possible interference by the United Nations that they might find embarrassing or prejudicial. The first article of the agreement with each of these organizations contains the statement:'By reason of the nature of its international responsibilities and the terms of its Articles of Agreement, the Bank [Fund] is, and is required to function as, an independent international organization.' Both agreements also contain the following statement: 'The United Nations agrees that, in the interpretation of paragraph 3 of Article 17 of the United Nations Charter it will take into consideration that the Bank [Fund] does not rely for its annual budget upon contributions from its members, and that the appropriate authorities of the Bank [Fund] enjoy full autonomy in deciding the form and content of such budget.'[6]

The other United Nations–specialized agency agreements generally began with the United Nations' recognition of the agency's authority in its field and proceeded to provide for reciprocal representation at meetings, reciprocal right to propose items for the agenda of the main organs, the treatment to be given by the agency to formal recommendations of the United Nations, the exchange of information and documents, assistance to United Nations organs, and co-operation in regard to personnel arrangements, statistical services, administrative and technical services and budgetary and financial arrangements.

Problems also arose from the geographical dispersal of the organizations, which was to have costs in terms of efficiency, budget and difficulties of co-ordination. A strong bid was made in 1950 to locate FAO, which had started in Washington, with the United Nations in New York, but it was lost by a narrow margin to Rome, the seat of the old International Institute of Agriculture, whose assets and liabilities had passed to FAO. Among the factors influencing the choice were the very tempting terms, including a fine headquarters office building and diplomatic privileges for the entire non-Italian staff, offered by the Italian government. There was never any question that ILO would leave its permanent headquarters in Geneva, to which it had returned after its sojourn in Montreal during the war, that the Bank and the Fund would be elsewhere than Washington, or, for that matter, that UNESCO would be other than in Paris. Ministries of Health showed no desire to place WHO's headquarters in New York, while available accommodation in the Palais des Nations and the existence of the archives and a few remaining officials of the League's Health Service provided sufficient arguments in favour of Geneva. Among the old international bureaux originally located in Berne, the Universal Postal Union (UPU) stayed where it was, while the International Telecommunication Union (ITU) moved to Geneva in 1948, and the United International Bureaux for the Protection of Intellectual Property (BIRPI) (later transformed into the World Intellectual Property Organization) in 1961. The IAEA was located in Vienna in 1957 as part of the arrangement among the principal nuclear powers, while Vienna, with the help of strong pressure from the Austrian government, became the seat of the United Nations Industrial Development Organization (UNIDO) in 1966, after a hot contest with Paris, which had been generally favoured on professional and administrative grounds.

THE EVOLUTION OF THE SYSTEM AND EARLY PROBLEMS

Problems of co-ordination were apparent at an early stage. Even in 1949, the General Assembly in Resolution 310 (IV), complained of 'the proliferation of activities and the multiplicity of programmes', and went on to observe that 'the resulting excessive numbers of sessions and meetings as well as the creation of subsidiary organs' were placing a severe burden on the technical and personnel resources of member states. It drew attention to a resolution adopted earlier the same year by ECOSOC (Resolution 259 (IX)) calling for 'a greater concentration of efforts and available resources'. Reconciling respect for the autonomy and technical competence of the agencies with the more general responsibilities of the United Nations was already a major problem. From an early stage a limiting factor was the difficulty of getting ECOSOC, on which the whole system hinged, to work as it should. More than 50 years ago, its then President was complaining that 'the ECOSOC must exercise a high degree of leadership, and I submit that few can be fully satisfied with the role it has thus far played'.[7]

Another 'built-in' problem was how to bring about – even assuming much consultation and co-operation – a coherent international programme, or to obtain something approaching an agreed conceptual framework, from a variety of independently conceived programmes, each with its own objectives and administration. Of fundamental importance were the overlaps in the range of activities of different organizations sanctioned by their respective constitutions and desired by their national counterparts. The ILO illustrated the problem. Its main fields of activity were employment promotion, vocational guidance, social security, safety and health, labour laws and labour relations, labour administration, workers' education, co-operatives, rural and related institutions. But most of these fields contained 'grey areas' where other agencies were also much concerned. Furthermore, the ILO was empowered by the Philadelphia Declaration of 1944 to undertake, if it wished, a considerably broader range of international economic and social responsibilities. Small wonder then that not a few cases of overlap and proliferation of machinery occurred. For example, the improvement of living conditions involved the ILO in aspects of rural development generally, including land reform (FAO) and the conditions of indigenous populations; training was closely linked to education (UNESCO); manpower to questions of small industries (FAO and UNIDO); workers' health standards with health standards generally (WHO). Such situations of overlapping mandate constantly produced resource-consuming special co-ordination devices.

The United Nations Educational, Scientific and Cultural Organization (UNESCO) provided other illustrations. UNESCO had a general responsibility in matters of science, education and culture which entitled it to contribute to almost every field of international endeavour. To take the field of science, UNESCO had a direct responsibility for the development, dissemination and teaching of science in general, the establishment of scientific cadres in developing countries, etc. It followed and co-operated in the scientific activities of other organizations such as the United Nations itself, WHO, WMO, ITU, IMCO, IAEA, which, however, retained responsibility for scientific work in their own spheres. Since UNESCO interpreted the term 'science' to include social as well as natural sciences, it was concerned from time to time with such subjects of major concern to the United Nations as development theory, the peaceful settlement of disputes, and the reduction of 'tensions'. On the basis of its scientific mandate, it established an International Oceanographic Commission, while FAO (Fishery), IMCO (Marine Pollution), IAEA (Pollution through Atomic Wastes) and, of course, the United Nations itself also developed their own machinery and programmes in closely related aspects of ocean-ography. In the field of science in general, the United Nations had the task of mobilizing the efforts of all concerned agencies in connection with the application of science and technology to development and the peaceful uses of atomic energy.

An underlying and pervasive problem was the absence of co-ordination at the national level in regard to international policies and programmes. The weakness and rareness of such policy co-ordination in many govern-ments led not only to divergent positions being taken by the representa-tives of the same country in different organizations, but also not infrequently – as in the case of UNCTAD and GATT as well as of UNIDO and the ILO – to divergent decisions actually being reached. Despite repeated resolutions of the General Assembly and ECOSOC urging better co-ordination of policies at the national level, as well as studies by the United Nations Secretariat and by UNESCO of measures taken in some countries to this end,[8] improvement in the situation was patchy, even in key countries like Britain. Most countries still lacked systematic arrange-ments even for keeping the activities of international organizations under central review, let alone for developing co-ordinated positions on issues coming before them. One could not expect anything approaching full coherence and co-ordination in the United Nations system so long as this situation prevailed. At the same time, differences of view among delegates from the same country were influenced by differences within the inter-national organizations they participated in, so every step towards harmo-nizing the attitude of those organizations should improve the situation.

Difficulties of co-ordination in respect of international activities in certain cases often reflected difficulties of co-ordination on those subjects at the national level. Proliferation and the overlapping of programme activities arose because in so many broad fields different ministries and divisions were involved in different countries, and initiatives varying slightly in approach but having very similar objectives could well be launched and carried through simultaneously in two or more international agencies. For example, the United Nations' regional and community development programme was closely related to UNESCO's work on functional literacy, FAO's agricultural extension work, aspects of the public health work of WHO and aspects of the ILO programme on handicrafts and cottage industries. UNESCO's early work on fundamental education and that of the United Nations on community development, each with its separate antecedents, were found to be so similar in aim and content that they were eventually merged under arrangements proposed by the secretariats concerned.

Increase in scope and interdependence of international activities

After the emergence of the new system in the post-war period, a number of changes occurred which, if anything, made the inherent problems of co-ordination worse. First, there had been a vast increase in the scope of international economic and social activities after the mid-1940s, accompanied by a constant broadening of the programmes and an ever-greater interdependence of the activities of different agencies. Second, and no less fundamental, was the advent and rapid growth of field activities, especially technical assistance, through international organizations, which had become the disbursers of considerable public funds and the purveyors of extensive advisory services direct to their member governments. This development called for major changes in the internal structure and staffing of most of the organizations concerned, which, with the notable exception of WHO, were geared to non-operational activities, as the League of Nations and the pre-war ILO had been.

This new concern with operational field activities led to the setting up of new overarching mechanisms to attempt co-ordination in their areas which, if anything, further obscured the path of ECOSOC responsibility. The first of these was the Expanded Programme of Technical Assistance (EPTA) which distributed its funds among the United Nations and the various specialized agencies, first on a basis somewhat arbitrarily determined by itself, then in accordance with decisions reached through the inter-agency Technical Assistance Board. The EPTA worked under the authority of ECOSOC and the Administrative Committee on co-ordination (ACC), both the Technical Assistance Committee and the Technical Assistance Board reporting to ECOSOC (the second through ACC). The position was altered, however, in the cases of the Special Fund, which was added to the armoury in 1958, and the United Nations Development Programme (UNDP), which resulted from the merger of EPTA and the Special Fund as from January 1966. For UNDP, following the pattern of the Special Fund, special co-ordinating arrangements were made by ECOSOC and the General Assembly, providing at the staff level for a co-ordinating body (the Inter-Agency Consultative Board (IACB)), advisory to the administrator and having no formal contacts with ACC, and, at the intergovernmental level for a governing body which reported to ECOSOC. It is hardly surprising that in this morass of byzantine administrative structure ECOSOC failed to assert itself in respect of this large and vital part of the work of the United Nations.

The first of the big reports on the reform of these arrangements dates from the late 1960s. In 1967, the governing body of UNDP called for a study of the capacity of the United Nations' development system which led to the remarkable report published in 1969, often referred to as the Capacity Report, or, after its main author, Sir Robert Jackson, the Jackson Report. A consensus on certain steps to be taken in the light of that study was reached in the governing body of UNDP in 1970 and endorsed by ECOSOC and the General Assembly. Neither the Capacity Study itself, nor the implications of the Consensus for the United Nations System as a whole, was considered by ACC – or for that matter, except in the most general terms, by ECOSOC.

A third development affecting United Nations–agency relations was the growth of activities at the regional level. Problems, which were enlarged and aggravated in later years, began to appear with the creation by the United Nations in 1947 – primarily for the purpose of helping to meet reconstruction problems of war-devastated areas – of two regional economic commissions, the Economic Commission for Europe (ECE) and the Economic Commission for Asia and the Far East (ECAFE). These and the regional economic commissions subsequently established had, like the General Assembly and ECOSOC, a broad responsibility for economic and (since the 1950s) social development, and this responsibility covered the sectoral areas of many specialized agencies, to which, as well as to governments, they were authorized to make recommendations direct. From the outset, the attitude of some of the agencies towards the regional commissions was somewhat guarded because of the danger of overlapping, and several of the major agencies set up their own regional networks. The guarded attitude tended to be reciprocated by the regional commissions, which were often critical of the agencies' sectoral approach to the problems of their region and its individual countries. Nor was the work of the commissions' staff and of the Department of Economic and Social Affairs (ESA) at Headquarters easy to co-ordinate. Year by year, for example, regional economic surveys were published by the commissions' economists, with the minimum of consultation with the staff responsible for preparing the annual World Economic Survey at UN Headquarters. Elaborate measures – including the establishment of joint divisions of certain agencies and the commissions, the posting of agency representatives at the commissions' headquarters, and frequent arrangements for jointly sponsored meetings and conferences – were taken to forestall difficulties between the commissions and the agencies and promote co-operation. Such measures proved useful though by no means fully effective, and the price was rather high in terms of staff and budget.

Though the commissions had no explicit co-ordinating authority, their special role was recognized by ECOSOC at its 54th session in the spring of 1973. It reaffirmed that 'the regional economic commissions, in their respective regions, are the main general economic and social development centres within the United Nations system', and called upon 'all the organizations and Agencies in the system to work closely with [them] to achieve the overall economic and social development objectives at the regional level'.[9] In accordance with its Constitution, WHO at an early stage established a highly decentralized regional structure. UNICEF, working closely with WHO, followed suit. Some years later, FAO and UNESCO developed extensive regional activities and still later the ILO initiated the same process. While the seats of the regional economic commissions attracted a number of agency offices, the agency centres and subcentres were spread over every region; and in the case of each agency the powers and functions of these offices differed. The resultant 'jungle' – in the words of the Capacity Study – was naturally a further cause of co-ordination difficulties, both for international organizations and for governments.

A fourth development that caused problems was the effect on the structure, efficiency and co-ordination of international organizations of the increase in their membership and the determination of the new members, mostly poor developing countries, to maximize the development assistance provided to them through those organizations. The new members, furthermore, wished to exercise maximum influence in, and control over, the central policy organs concerned with economic and social development. Until it began to be realized that good co-ordination might result in more and more effective assistance and that the lack of it might contribute to drying up the source of funds, co-ordination had little appeal for such countries. This attitude was strengthened by the attempts made by a number of donor countries, especially as the financial stringency in the United Nations became acute, in the 1960s because of the Congo crisis, and in the 1980s with the US withholding of funds, to use the organs concerned with administrative and budgetary co-ordination to check or delay the expansion of United Nations and agency budgets for economic and social programmes.

The absence of a clear mandate for ECOSOC *vis-à-vis* the General Assembly also became a factor of importance. It was natural and fully understood that the General Assembly should take the lead in securing action or consideration by the different organizations in respect of questions of a political character such as decolonization, or on questions extending beyond ECOSOC's normal sphere, such as the establishment in 1966 of the Enlarged Committee for Programme and co-ordination for the purpose of enhancing the contribution of the United Nations system to economic and social development. But it became more and more common for ECOSOC to be by-passed in respect of initiatives that the developing countries wanted to be launched or supported by the superior and more prestigious body.

The failure of ECOSOC to reflect the changed political balance in the United Nations or the new concepts of justice and economic co-operation that were emerging in the Third World contributed much to the fragmentation of United Nations economic machinery that occurred in the mid-1960s: namely, the establishment by the General Assembly, under strong pressure from the developing and 'non-aligned' countries (and despite resistance from some of the developed countries), of important new organizations within the United Nations in the fields of trade and development (UNCTAD) and industrial development (UNIDO). These organizations were not placed under ECOSOC and their Secretariats were made independent of the Department of Economic and Social Affairs in the Secretariat. The form they were given – that of 'an organ of the General Assembly' (UNCTAD) or an 'autonomous organization within the United Nations' (UNIDO), and not of specialized agencies – was influenced largely by the General Assembly's desire to exercise control, but also by considerations of economy and doubts as to the efficacy of the arrangements between the United Nations and the specialized agencies for ensuring co-ordination.

The new organizations, whose creation represented a significant re-orientation of United Nations action, as well as an enlargement of its scale and scope, were given certain co-ordinating functions in their respective fields; UNCTAD was 'to review and facilitate the co-ordination of activities of other institutions within the United Nations system', but to 'cooperate with the General Assembly and the ECOSOC with respect to the performance of their responsibilities for co-ordination under the Charter of the United Nations'. UNIDO was to 'play the central role in and be responsible for reviewing and promoting the coordination of all activities of the United Nations system in the field of industrial development'. Both organizations were to report to the General Assembly through ECOSOC; this meant, in effect, that ECOSOC could comment, but that decisions could only be taken by the General Assembly: as in the case of UNDP, it was ECOSOC's practice to send on their reports without significant comments. Given the circumstances in which they were established, considerations of good administrative order were perhaps bound to be secondary, but the then Secretary-General felt it necessary to observe that:

> The creation of autonomous units within the Secretariat, and therefore under my jurisdiction as Chief Administrative Officer, raises serious questions of organizational authority and responsibility. Moreover, such

a trend is not altogether consistent with the concept of a unified secretariat working as a team towards the accomplishment of the main goals
of the Organization. On the contrary, it may tend to have the adverse
effect of pitting one segment of the Secretariat against another in competition for the necessary financial and political support for its own work
programmes.[10]

The position was complicated, in the case of UNCTAD and ECOSOC, by
the absence of a clear conceptual distinction between their respective roles
as regards development. Arrangements on a pragmatic basis for the
distribution of Secretariat responsibilities were in most cases eventually
worked out, while a series of decisions at the intergovernmental level
further eased the position. For example, ECOSOC at its 55th session (1973)
decided to transfer to UNCTAD for consideration documents relating to
the transfer of operative technology, while an annual ESA publication on
financial flows to developing countries was discontinued and replaced by
an annual UNCTAD publication dealing with the same subject. A *modus
vivendi*, but no firm agreement, emerged between UNCTAD and FAO as
regards trade in agricultural commodities and between UNIDO and FAO
as regards the pulp and paper industry, with which FAO continued to
deal. In a number of other areas also, including shipping, uncertainties as
to competence remained.

UNCTAD also represented a direct challenge to GATT, which, apart
from its traditional work on tariffs, quickly embarked on a number of
the activities that were assigned to UNCTAD by the General Assembly
after the first UN Conference on Trade and Development in December
1964. In February 1965, the contracting parties to GATT added a Fourth
Part, on Trade and Development, to the General Agreement, giving
GATT a mandate – as well as subsidiary bodies – on subjects falling
directly within UNCTAD's domain. Two great intergovernmental institutions with largely overlapping membership were thus, by deliberate
decision of their governing organs, engaged in open duplication. Despite
representations by their chief executive officers – Mr Raul Prebisch for
UNCTAD and Mr (later Sir) Eric Wyndham White for GATT – neither
the new GATT committee nor the UNCTAD Trade and Development
Board (37 of whose 55 members were also parties to, or associated with,
GATT), nor even the New Delhi conference of UNCTAD in 1967, would
discuss the overlap, let alone take any decision to correct it, but confined
themselves to calling for intersecretariat co-ordination and for the
governments to be kept informed 'so that they may give such directives
as may appear necessary'. Co-operation in several areas (for example, the
establishment in 1967 of the joint UNCTAD–GATT Trade Centre) and a
provisional *modus vivendi* were worked out between the staffs of the two

organizations. Such arrangements were, however, no substitute for inter-governmental decisions and no solution for structural shortcomings. The Secretary-General of UNCTAD stated in 1974, 'The consequences of this omission to provide intergovernmental guidance . . . include the negation of an integrated approach to trade and development problems, the dupli-cation of efforts by governments as well as by the secretariats concerned, and the prospect of inconsistent or conflicting actions in the two bodies which work in separate compartments without adequate cooperation or coordination.'[11]

The process of institutional fragmentation, including in some cases the assignment of co-ordinating authority to new organs, did not, of course, begin or end with the creation of UNCTAD and UNIDO. While those organizations were financed by the regular budget of the United Nations, the process had become increasingly associated with reliance on voluntary contributions rather than assessed contributions to finance new economic and social activities. As early as 1946 the General Assembly had decided that the then United Nations International Children's Emergency Fund (UNICEF), which it set up for the purpose of meeting in part some of the most pressing emergency needs that the wartime United Nations Refugee and Rehabilitation Administration (UNRRA) had covered, should be financed entirely from extra-budgetary sources. The Expanded Pro-gramme of Technical Assistance (EPTA) was likewise financed by volun-tary contributions. The Special United Nations Fund for Economic Development (SUNFED), which appeared in 1958 to assist developing countries in pre-investment projects, was also voluntarily financed. The joint UN–FAO World Food Programme, which was to become the inter-national institutions' primary provider of logistical support for humanitar-ian relief, was established in 1962; UNITAR, also financed exclusively by voluntary contributions, came into being in 1963. When the General Assembly merged EPTA with the Special Fund to form the single United Nations Development Programme (UNDP) in 1966, that too was volun-tarily funded. The UN Fund for Population Activities (UNFPA) began as a very independent trust fund under the Secretary-General in 1967 and retained a great measure of autonomy. One might mention, finally, the United Nations Environment Programme (UNEP), set up by the United Nations General Assembly in 1972, following the Stockholm conference. While UNEP's administrative expenses were to be borne by the regular budget of the United Nations, a voluntary fund was established to provide for additional financing of environmental programmes. The general trend was towards voluntary financing and this tended if anything to promote further fragmentation as funds were contributed more whimsically for governments' favoured projects.

By the time UNEP was set up, something at least had been learned.

Great emphasis was placed on its co-ordinating and promotional role. The General Assembly decided among other things that the Executive Director should 'co-ordinate, under the guidance of ECOSOC, environmental programmes within the United Nations, keep their implementation under review and . . . assess their effectiveness', and that an Environment Coordination Board, under the chairmanship of the Executive Director, should be established under the auspices and within the framework of the Administrative Committee on Coordination. The language used to protect the overall co-ordinating role of ECOSOC was more specific than in the case of UNCTAD and UNIDO. The Governing Council 'shall report annually to the General Assembly through the Economic and Social Council, which will transmit to the Assembly such comments on the report as it may deem necessary, particularly with regard to questions of co-ordination and to the relationship of environment policies and programmes within the United Nations system to overall economic and social policies and priorities'. But many organizations had direct responsibilities relating to the environment, and dangers of overlaps and costly additional procedures for co-ordination had already appeared. For instance the General Assembly, when deciding at its 28th session on the recommendation of the UNEP Council to call a Conference–Exhibition on Human Settlements in 1976, thought it should set up, in addition to a large Intergovernmental Preparatory Committee, a special Secretariat under a Conference Secretary-General.

Special problems of readjustment for the UN system were posed by organizations such as UNEP, UNDP and UNFPA. At the outset, each part of the United Nations system was conceived of as covering one or more economic or social sectors – for example, food and agriculture; health; education; science and culture; labour. Likewise, UNCTAD and UNIDO each covered a broad economic sector. Some organs and agencies, however, were created on the basis of other criteria: for example, UNICEF and UNHCR dealt with special groups, UNRWA with a special group in a particular area, while the UNEP *et al.*, like ECOSOC itself, were largely concerned with the pursuit of objectives that were within the functional competence of a number of other organizations.

PROBLEMS AS THE MILLENNIUM APPROACHED

The Economic and Social Council had, of course, been intended to manage the system, but, as has been indicated, it failed to live up to the expectations of the founders. This failure was seen by Gunnar Myrdal as early as 1960 as 'almost scandalous in view of the declared purposes of the Charter'.[12] This judgement still seemed to apply in the early 1990s and is one measure of the difficulty of bringing about any useful reform in the organization. A further weakness was that the General Assembly lacked the authority to instruct the agencies, though it could give them advice and address recommendations to them. It tended not to consult the agencies very closely when it considered economic and social proposals – an omission that might be considered extraordinary – and it lacked the means of effectively monitoring the performance of the agencies. For instance, it lacked a way of checking the relationship between the agencies' budgets and their programmes; it was said that the General Assembly checked budgets in a vacuum.[13] Its main watchdogs over the agencies, the Advisory Committee on Administrative and Budgetary Questions (ACABQ) and the Joint Inspection Unit (JIU), though capable of providing good, hard-hitting reports, were essentially advisory. The ACC, the agencies' main administrative co-ordinator, which also, however, had a potential for developing a role in generating overall policy, and an ambition to do so, became a framework within which agencies' heads defended their interests while discussing ways of implementing UN programmes: its members were as much involved in justifying positions adopted within each agency as in co-ordinating their activities in striving for a common purpose. Ameri concluded that 'towards the coordination of overall policy it cannot be claimed that the ACC has made more than a minor and intermittent contribution'.[14]

Another route to effective management and policy co-ordination was sought when in the 1977 Resolution it was recommended that a new Director General for Development and International Economic co-operation should be appointed within the Secretariat to ensure 'the coherence, co-ordination and efficient management of all activities in the economic and social fields financed by the regular budget or by extra budgetary resources'.[15] The references to both regular budget and extra-budgetary resources seems to imply that the new officer was to supervise the activities not only of the United Nations' own organizations – the funds and programmes – but also the specialized agencies. The post was established and was held first by Kenneth Dadzie, and later by Michael Ripert, but again it was largely unsuccessful with respect to its major goals.

These various characteristics and deficiencies illustrate the lack of any overall coherent management at the start of the twentieth century's last decade, either in terms of administration, or in terms of policy initiatives and monitoring. Proposals for reform in the making of coherent overall policy and achieving effective direction focused upon ways of improving the supervisory function of the General Assembly, and upon reorganizing the work of the Economic and Social Council and upgrading the status of its members. The latter was stressed in both the 1975 report and the 1977 resolution: the 1975 report identified the central problem when it argued that the

> revitalisation of the Economic and Social Council, through far-reaching changes in its functioning and methods of work [is] one of the conditions for strengthening the central structure of the system and enabling it to play an effective role in world economic affairs ... if the United Nations system is to contribute effectively to the solution of international economic problems there must be a central organ within the system where the inputs from the various United Nations bodies can be shaped into coherent policies for development and international economic co-operation, and where there can be a central review of the mutual consistency of actions taken sectorally, particularly of the interdependence of decisions on trade, monetary reform and the development of financing, and of decisions taken in the field of agriculture, industrialisation and other areas.[16]

The question addressed in what follows is that of how far ECOSOC has been able to take on this role in more recent years.

The past failure of ECOSOC in these respects was one reason for setting up those institutions in the United Nations that are called funds or programmes, and which were often initiated at special conferences. One experienced United Nations diplomat even argued in discussion with the present writer that had ECOSOC been more effective, there would have been no call for a New International Economic Order in the 1970s, and UNCTAD would not have been created. Though this may be an exaggeration, the general thrust of the argument is valid.

Once they existed, however, the funds and programmes created new difficulties in the way of achieving agreed policies and central direction over and above those arising from the status of the agencies. They were not subject to ECOSOC supervision in contrast to the agencies, which were at least required to report to ECOSOC under the terms of Article 64. Furthermore, as their name indicates, they were financed out of funds to which governments directly contributed and therefore felt better able to control. Although a United Nations Pledging Conference was established as a way of raising finance, states were not subject to the same long-term financial commitment that they incurred with regard to the agencies, which were financed out of a regular budget. The failure of the older system and in particular the visible self-interest of the agencies, was likely to lead to resistance on the part of some states to the closer incorporation of funds and programmes in the larger system as part of a process of reform. In some cases it was particularly apparent that they were creatures of a coalition of states – UNCTAD and UNIDO, for instance, were dominated by developing countries – and subjecting them to a general manager would have weakened the coalition's influence.

Proposals to strengthen central direction also immediately raised the delicate issue of the membership of the common framework: ECOSOC had 54 members and was dominated by the richer states. Though it had been accepted that all UN members could attend and speak, only the 54 could vote. If it were to be strengthened, the developing states argued, it would also have to be representative, a view that was resisted by the developed states. It was also the case, of course, that simply increasing the range of independent agencies, each with interests of its own, was likely to make the task of creating a stronger ECOSOC more difficult: indeed some of the funds/programmes, in particular UNDP and UNC-TAD, became major rivals of ECOSOC as candidates for the role of policy-maker and co-ordinator for the system. For these reasons the funds and programmes should be seen not only as part of a process of adaptation within the UN system: they were also a result of the failure of internal management within the United Nations system, and one of the causes of that failure.

The views of the 1975 report of the group of experts were reflected closely in the 1977 General Resolution 32/197. The General Assembly reasserted the need to give the ECOSOC greater authority, by strengthening it in two major respects.[17] First, it was felt necessary to strengthen its monitoring function: better procedures were needed by which it could be informed of what was going on, and of what needed to be done. A new office was set up in the Secretariat, the Office for Programme Planning and Co-ordination, which was to produce improved reports for ECOSOC. One version of these was called Cross Organizational Programme Analyses (COPAs) which were on a range of programmes involving several agencies and funds, and were addressed to the ECOSOC's Committee for Programme and Co-ordination (CPC).[18] They were to be an 'analysis of the actual state of co-ordination'.[19] The CPC insisted that it should evaluate the programmes and indicate where greater efforts should be made. This was, however, only one element in an effort to increase the range of information available to ECOSOC in a form that would allow an effective response to new problems.

The second goal was that of increasing ECOSOC's capacity for generating programme initiatives in the light of changing circumstances. It was enjoined to disband most of its subsidiary committees, and instead to deal with their work in the Council itself in 'shorter but more frequent subject-orientated sessions spread throughout the year'.[20] The idea was that such meetings should be designed to make it easier to involve higher level specialists, whose views would naturally carry more weight. In addition, following along the same lines of argument, it was recommended that the

Council should, when necessary, hold special sessions to deal with emerging problems meriting special or urgent international attention; it would also hold 'periodic meetings at the ministerial or other sufficiently high level to review major issues in the world economic and social situation'.[21] The General Assembly's intention that the Council should bring conferences more directly under its wing was also indicated in its injunction that the Council should assume 'direct responsibility for carrying out the preparatory work for ad hoc conferences convened by the Council itself, and as appropriate by the General Assembly, without prejudice to arrangements already agreed upon for conferences currently under preparation'.[22] The clear implication was that arrangements outside the Council's framework were to be phased out.

The various changes were intended to create an improved mechanism for monitoring economic and social developments and the progress of programmes already established, and in the light of this to initiate appropriate policies, and necessary institutional amendments and additions according to a comprehensive strategy. The absence of such procedures was one reason for the system's minimalist response to new problems, and the tendency for them to be considered in special conferences.

The various reports and recommendations on the reform of the United Nations system are themselves a measure of its failings. There was the Capacity Report of 1969 and Resolution 32/197 of 1977, mentioned above. The most prominent in the 1980s was that produced in December 1985 by the Joint Inspection Unit, a searching analysis and critique of current arrangements, written by Maurice Bertrand, reflecting in many ways the same old problems and the system's continuing failure to adapt.[23] The main themes were that the range of information on the system's success in pursuing its chosen goals was still deficient, although the extent of the description of its activities had been much expanded in the 1970s and 1980s (the literature still did not permit a well-founded estimate of attainment in comparison with defined goals); the procedures for co-ordinating the activities of the wide range of organizations involved in work on projects in particular countries – about 15 of them in a country receiving aid[24] – were deficient. A COPA reported in 1984 that in Barbados there had been three organizations concerned with human settlements, 'but none reports cooperation'.[25] The system lacked a common controlling brain that could choose a strategy, for instance, in 'joint planning', and adjust it to circumstances; and the relationship between judgements about need and the provision of resources was remote. Although the specific context of the reports is that of development, the complaints certainly applied to the UN's work in general in the economic and social field, and this point is made explicit in the various reports.

These indications of the system's failings helped to explain Bertrand's scathing comment that 'the notion of an integrated approach to develop- ment, although adopted by the General Assembly of the United Nations and ritually repeated at each General Assembly, has remained for the United Nations an empty formula';[26] the various alterations in the struc- ture and procedures of the previous 15 years had been a 'useless effort at coordination', and the system showed 'lack of intellectual preparation for work of programming, inadequate analysis of the role assigned to the United Nations system in the general scheme of technical assistance requirements of the various countries, absence of a unified concept of development, lack of satisfactory machinery at the centre of local levels to ensure the preliminary work of coordination of contributions of the various Agencies, lack of a common methodology for defining types of projects'.[27] In other words, the United Nations' economic and social arrangements remained unmanaged, unfocused and essentially irrational.

APPROACHES TO REFORM IN THE 1990s

An important part of the background to the following discussion was inevitably that a number of changes had taken place in the context of reform over the previous decade or so which reinforced determination to get something done. There had been a number of global conferences called to discuss the pressing problems of the age: in the first part of the 1990s these included environmental questions in Rio de Janeiro (1992), human rights in Vienna (1993), women's questions in Beijing (1995) and popula- tion questions in Cairo (1994). These conferences had each spawned a commission (discussed later) to carry forward the programme agreed at the conference itself. Such conferences represented a growing sense of the interdependence of the globe, and stimulated a renewed interest in translating such concerns – called by some a collective intentionality[28] – into more specific and more manageable programmes. Were the reforms likely to be successful in doing this? This is the question that is discussed in what follows. But there was also a more realist consideration, namely that the shortage of funds that resulted from the increasing parsimony of states was especially reflected in the reluctance of the US to pay its dues. This placed the barons of the big agencies under a lot of pressure to undertake reforms and to get their acts together, literally and metaphori- cally, in a way that had not been true earlier. The ending of the Cold War also created an attention space previously occupied by the threat of nuclear war between the superpowers. The economic and social work of the United Nations system had always been important, but it now moved up the agenda, especially as the increasing number of failing states threatened new kinds of international disorder.

Although work on the improvement of the machinery was given a new impetus in the 1990s, the European Union states remained of the view in October 1996 that 'many UN Programmes and operations in the field were too often undermined by lack of adequate coordination, overlapping responsibilities and fragmentation of activities'.[29] One of the reasons for the new energy behind the reform process, however, was the emergence, relatively recently, of the EU as a force prepared to push this agenda. It had been agreed in the Maastricht Treaty that the states would act together in the economic and social areas in the United Nations: these were areas where the EU had competence which until the early 1990s it had lacked.

In the mid-1990s there were three conceivable approaches to the reform of the economic and social arrangements of the UN system. One was to adopt a more supranational or managerial approach, by appointing a central manager such as the Director General for Development and International Economic Cooperation (DGDIEC), as had been proposed by A/32/197 in the late 1970s. This was not a promising route.[30] It had proved impossible to give such a manager the authority required to supervise the agencies, and any efforts to introduce major changes into the Charter, in order to redistribute powers in favour of that officer, or a central organization like the General Assembly or ECOSOC, risked being protracted and bruising. The system's multicentred character had to be one of the givens of the situation.

A second proposal was that the UN system's operations should be considerably scaled down, turned into research institutes with no operational capacity.[31] The money that went to them should then be transferred to the World Bank, which had a reputation for being more efficient, and, happily for those who held this view, was more generally disposed to favour right-wing economic principles. The problem with this approach was that it was not likely to appeal to the developing states themselves, which generally suspected the Bretton Woods institutions, regarding them as being in the pockets of the developed states. It was highly unlikely that agreement about such radical changes would be found among the various constituencies of states. Another cost was that it involved scaling down the presence of the UN actors in the developing states, which could reduce the attention given by outsiders to their internal problems. Indeed, such a system would make it easier for funds to be syphoned off by beneficiary governments for illegitimate purposes.

The third way was the one identified and supported in this chapter: entrenched multilateralism. This would involve the strengthening of system norms within the existing structures, so that they were more likely to impose upon the participating actors. The relationship between the existing actors was to be altered within the present system so that the weight of the injunctions on their behaviour to conform with system rules was strengthened. The question of how the changes proposed in the 1990s could lead to this quiet revolution is now to be discussed.

The meaning of entrenched multilateralism is given in the interlinked ideas of *regime theory*, and of *global governance*. The first of these postulates that there is a hierarchy of 'injunctions on behaviour, of greater or lesser specificity',[32] ranging from 'principles' and 'norms', which are less specific, through to 'formal institutions', which embody precisely defined decision-making procedures. 'Rules' come somewhere in between, but they are of particular importance because they are the point in the hierarchy at which general impulses are translated into explicit constraints on behaviour. They are the specific instruments for realizing common purposes in a society of legal individuals – persons or institutions – and can be applied without further interpretation or enactment. Principles and norms lack this specificity. Global governance involves 'sets of rules that guide the behavior of participants engaged in identifiable social practices',[33] and can be distinguished from 'government', which requires formal institutions capable of authoritative allocation of values. 'Governance', then, as a form of rule-dominated, ordered society, is appropriate to a multicentric system, such as the UN system of states and organizations in which 'government' is of necessity excluded. Rules, however, may be generated through multilateral diplomacy even in the absence of government. They require adhesion by governments to a set of specific injunctions on behaviour which require no further interpretation, and which need no further enactment by courts or by other authorities. So 'entrenched multilateralism' arises when multilateral diplomacy is effective in generating rules.

Rules may be developed as a result of particular contingencies that arise in the process of multilateral diplomacy, including fixing the agenda, building supportive interests and empowering them, establishing epistemic communities,[34] or, generally, the creation of circumstances during negotiation in which participants perceive that to opt out is more costly than to opt in. They generate a powerful, self-fulfilling prophecy, such as that which frightened Eurosceptics in the British government with regard to Monetary Union in the EU in the mid to late 1990s. When multilateral diplomacy takes place in circumstances like these, it becomes entrenched in the sense used in this chapter. Negotiation has its own dynamic and tends to create commitments that give rise to a sort of self-fulfilling prophecy, especially when there is a rule of consensus, as applied in the EU and in decisions on UN reform issues.

The question examined in this chapter, discussed directly in the final section, is that of how far the diplomacy which has been going on over the reform of the economic and social arrangements of the UN system had come to resemble this process by the last decade of the twentieth century. The first stage of decisions was to be in the negotiations because of the pattern of interests concerned (as when the British government decided that the national interest dictated that it had to be involved in negotiations over European Monetary Union, even though it was uncommitted to the goal), and the second was of progressively entrenching multilateralism as a consequence of the negotiation process itself so that the specific goal was accepted.

THE REFORM PROCESS IN THE UNITED NATIONS

In the 1990s the attempt to reform the UN's economic and social arrangements concentrated on two levels: first, those at the general or headquarters level, especially as regards the role of ECOSOC; and, second, those concerned with operations in the field within the developing countries. In both cases the reforms were included in a series of key resolutions approved by the General Assembly between 1992 and 1996, namely A/47/199, A/48/162, A/50/120 and A/50/227. The origins of the new phase of reform may be traced further back to the Secretary-General's report on economic and social matters in 1990 (A/45/714), which followed the failure of the special commission in 1987 and 1988.[35]

Country level

A key feature of the reforms at the field level was the adoption of Country Strategy Notes.[36] These were statements about the development process tailored to the specific needs of individual countries, which were evolved on the basis of discussions between the agencies, funds and programmes, donors and the host country. They were described in 1996 as a *tour de table* of the plans of the various involved institutions and governments,[37] but had the potential for development into something closer to indicative planning. The UNDP played a key role in instigating the process of formulating such a Note. They were identified as being the property of the host country, and had the obvious merit of setting out targets, roles and priorities.

The role of the UNDP resident co-ordinator as the responsible officer at the country level was also to be reinforced, with greater care to be taken about the selection of officers, and providing any necessary training for them. This was another feature of the reform process: increased concern with professionalizing the way in which services were provided in this area, as in the area of humanitarian crisis responses, and the management of peacekeeping. The pace of change with regard to such reforms had accelerated remarkably quickly since the end of the Cold War in 1989. In the 1990s major steps away from the earnest amateurism of the earlier generation had been taken. There was an increasing professionalization of international organizational service providers which involved the agreeing and monitoring of standards of performance. In this the continuing complaints of NGOs about poor IGO performance in the field had often been a powerful stimulus for reform.[38] Though they themselves had not always been wholly committed to co-ordination, NGOs became increasingly so, and in any case in the last decades of the millennium became major players in the system. They had henceforth to be taken into account.

It was recognized that UNDP officers in the past had often not been good performers: they did not have a very favourable press either within or outside the system. The conclusion was that at field level it was necessary for there to be a central co-ordinating figure, and the route of putting right deficiencies in the existing system was chosen (A/47/199, paras 36–38). But the actors were now subject to a wider range of pressures to conform with system norms than earlier: the UNDP resident would not now be faced with horses that were freely running in all directions, but rather a posse that was more disposed to hunt as one. For instance, field-level agency and fund officers were to be given enhanced authority, so that decisions could be taken at that level about the redeployment of funds within a programme without reference to headquarters (A/47/199, especially para. 25); a further attempt to introduce common information sharing and communication facilities was to be made; the activities of the various involved UN organizations were to be located in a single premises, which would bring officers from different UN organizations together on a daily basis and facilitate improvements in inter-agency communication: the development of inter-agency collegiality was to be encouraged (more on this below!). The money saved by this would be redirected to the development process. It was also stipulated that the approach was to be an integrated programmes approach, rather than an approach through distinct projects organized by the various agencies, often in blissful ignorance of each other's presence in the same country. Technical improvements, such as changes in information technology, made it more likely that 'stand alone' projects would in the future not be the norm (see below).

There was also a decision to measure achievement through impact and sustainability rather than through the level of inputs of resources, technology or personnel. The Advisory Committee on Coordination (ACC) also co-operated with the Secretariat in setting up a number of task forces to promote more effective inter-agency co-ordination at the country level. Task force members were chosen from the agencies concerned with the programme selected, of which four had been identified by 1996. The ACC was pushed away from its traditional reluctance to get close to ECOSOC, the Secretariat, or to the major co-ordination committees of the Assembly such as the CPC. Furthermore, the states were to allocate funds to these task forces in response to approved plans and programmes, which was itself an incentive to accept the need to fit into the system at the country level.

Because of these changes it looked as though by the mid-1990s the task of the UNDP resident co-ordinator of promoting enhanced co-ordination between participating actors in countries had been made much easier than it had been earlier. This was combined with better selection procedures and training for the officers themselves. Certainly their reputation was higher than in the past. There were numerous illustrations of the results of this: the UNDP resident in Palestine had become a major channel for funding into the area, and the UNDP Capital Development Fund had been used by the World Bank as the pilot for larger-scale investment; in Ghana a UNDP-administered $50,000 project in local development had led to a well-reported large-scale tourism development programme. It was agreed, however, that UNDP needed to be involved operationally only to the extent necessary to get larger programmes off the ground. Some thought this should be the model for the rest of the UN system!

Headquarters level

Nevertheless, this was only part of the story. Supporting changes were also required at the general or headquarters level if the role at the country level was to be effective. At the global level attempts were focused upon the reorganization and rationalization of the work of the Economic and Social Council (A/50/227, section IV). The Council was to hold a single substantive session each year in New York, and Geneva in alternate years. It was to be divided into four primary segments, or parts of the overall meeting, called General, High Level, Co-ordination, and Operational, which were to meet over a period of four to five weeks (A/45/264). A Humanitarian segment was added later. The High Level segment of four days was to discuss general questions of policy and it was expected that the shorter sessions would facilitate attendance by more senior government representatives and agency heads, who would have authority to commit their governments and institutions to action in the chosen areas. The conclusions were in the form of 'agreed conclusions' and resulted from discussions at the ministerial level. There remained, however, a suspicion that the way topics were chosen for High Level segment discussion needed further consideration: there was scope for states and agencies to indulge in political manipulation in the preparatory meetings to choose topics that they found less awkward. It was reported that the 1996 segment on narcotics had been a success. It was also pointed out that the increasing public awareness of global problems, which had been stimulated by the global conferences, made it more difficult for governments to ignore such meetings. The climate of opinion had changed (more of this below).

The meetings of the Co-ordination segment were to look at cross-sectoral and common themes in the work of so-called functional commissions. These were themes that cut across, or were common in, the sectors of work of global conferences. Each of the global conferences, which had become a routine feature of international society since the 1970s (though with an increasing number in the 1980s and 1990s) – population in Cairo, women's interests in Beijing, human rights in Vienna, environment and development in Rio de Janeiro, etc. – had led to the setting up of a new, or the upgrading of an existing, functional commission.[39] In July 1996 there were nine such commissions, the members of which were chosen by the plenary meeting of ECOSOC to represent the various self-identified groupings of states. There were usually 53 members of the commissions.

The Co-ordination segment based its efforts on the multi-annual programmes of work of the functional commissions, which in turn derived from the agreed conclusions of the global conferences: themes were identified and related to specific proposals for action. The work of the commissions also helped to identify issues to be considered at the review conferences that were to be held in relation to each of the major global conferences, usually five years after the first meeting. A series of working groups was also set up to pursue more co-ordinated strategies in specific areas of work, such as the AIDS Programme. In 1996 attention was focused upon the further rationalization of the relationship between the General Assembly, the functional commissions and ECOSOC. It was agreed that the functional commissions should concentrate upon their particular specialized sectors of activity, but that attention should be given to eliminating any overlap or duplication in their areas of concern. The General Assembly was 'to consider and establish the broad policy framework, the Council was to integrate the work of its functional commissions, to provide guidance to the UN system on coordination issues, and to support the General Assembly in its policy role'.[40] How was the Council to realize this laudable, if vague, ambition?

The question of whether the commissions had adopted agreed programmes of work was important in promoting the rationalization of ECOSOC's role. It was realized that the Council could carry out its functions with regard to the commissions much more effectively if it was able to relate their agreed programmes to each other in advance and identify cross-cutting or common themes. A document produced in July

1996 identified such items and suggested programmes on that basis for the ECOSOC Co-ordination segment meetings over the next five years.[41] The Council's role was most definitely not to duplicate the work of the commissions, though it had a duty to oversee their operations, and eliminate duplication and waste. Rather, its role was to identify issues that arose in the relationships between their areas of work. Thus commissions should adopt programmes of work for the next four or five years to follow up the conclusions of UN conferences, though human rights, which hitherto had its own agenda, was an exception: this was the basis on which the ECOSOC could generate proposals that reflected cross-sector concerns, as it allowed proper preparation of studies and documents in advance, as well as ensuring the relevance of the work of ECOSOC to the work of the commissions. It was reported that the work of this segment in 1996 had been marred by inadequate document preparation. In July 1996 four of the commissions had a programme of work agreed up to the year 2000.[42] These were the Commission on Sustainable Development, the Commission on the Status of Women, the Commission on Population and Development and the Commission for Social Development. The Commissions on Human Rights, Statistics, Crime Prevention and Criminal Justice, and Narcotic Drugs had not produced such an agreed programme of work (E/1996/CRP.4), and it was proposed that they should now do so.

Various decisions were taken about the relationship between the segments and other institutions linked with ECOSOC. The role of the substantive meeting was enhanced at the expense of the subordinate committees, which were subsumed in the plenary as of 1994 (Clause 17 48/162), and the relationship between ECOSOC and the General Assembly was made more specific. There were strict injunctions about not repeating discussions in the various fora, about the need for the plenary meetings to reach firm conclusions, and about avoiding overlapping mandates. In Clause 2.12 2 (A/48/162) 'agreed conclusions containing specific recommendations to various parts of the UN system for their implementation . . . were to be agreed' in the High Level segment which had quasi-legal status. The Secretary-General was to inform the Council of steps taken to implement recommendations: the language here was much closer to an assertion of the authority of ECOSOC than had been usual hitherto, which was itself a remarkable development.

This picture was reinforced by the requirement 2.15 (A/48/162) that the Operational segment was to ensure that General Assembly policies were appropriately implemented on a 'system wide basis' and the outcomes of this segment were to be 'reflected in the adoption of *decisions and resolutions* [author's italics]'. This was further reinforced with the injunction in A/50/227, paragraph 37, that 'The Council should fully implement its authority to take final decisions on the activities of its subsidiary bodies and on other matters relating to its system-wide coordination and overall guidance functions in the economic, social and related fields, as appropriate'; and by paragraph 44, which asserted that 'Resolutions, *decisions and agreed conclusions* [my italics] should be implemented and followed up fully by all relevant parts of the United Nations System'. This may be compared with the very modest powers attributed to the General Assembly and ECOSOC in the Charter, which were only asked to issue recommendations and receive reports, which in practice were usually uninformative and banal. Inter-agency working groups were set up in the Operational segment to pursue more co-ordinated programmes in their allotted sectors. The Operational segment was also to monitor the division of labour between the funds and programmes and make recommendations on this as required to the General Assembly.

The theme of ECOSOC's greater assertiveness was also reflected in a new way of agreeing the respective agendas of ECOSOC and the General Assembly, which was so devised that the Assembly would not repeat work done by ECOSOC, and the executive responsibility of ECOSOC in a framework of overall General Assembly policy supervision would be respected. Annexe 2 of 48/162 established a procedure for agreeing a draft programme of work of the General Assembly's Second Committee with the assistance of the bureau of the Council, and once agreed, this *'should be changed only in extreme circumstances* [my italics]'. This effort to rationalize the agendas of the General Assembly's committees in relation to ECOSOC was taken further when it was agreed in paragraphs 21–24 and Annexe 11 of A/50/227 that the agendas of the Second and Third Committees of the General Assembly should have 'greater coherence and complementarity', a goal supported by the agreement that issues of a procedural nature should be taken by *decision* rather than resolution. This was evidence of an attempt to achieve a more rational and effective relationship between ECOSOC, the Assembly, and its committees. ECOSOC had significantly increased its power over the agendas of the Second and indirectly of the Third Committees of the Assembly. The language used in 48/162 and 50/127 was altogether more positive and authoritative than that in earlier resolutions, and, indeed, in the Charter. ECOSOC's leading role in the co-ordination of the system was asserted and it was correspondingly more assertive. There was evidence by the autumn of 1996 of a rapid increase in the number of conclusions in the form of decisions taken by ECOSOC which were more often linked with more concrete proposals. An official reported that the change in this direction had begun in 1994.

The European Union and the United States also pressed for adjustments in the divisions of the Secretariat concerned with economic and social work. These were proposed by the G7 meeting at the Lyons summit in

June 1996. They proposed the merger of the three existing divisions, Sustainable Development, Economic and Social Information and Analysis, and Development Support and Management Services. They also argued for placing this work in the charge of a new Under-Secretary-General who would act as Executive Secretary of ECOSOC, and thus strengthen the Council's policy formulation and co-ordination role. The new officer would also pursue the reform process in collaboration with the heads of agencies, reducing overlap in mandates, abolishing redundant organizations, and generally enhancing effectiveness and efficiency. The outcome was the appointment of a new Deputy-Secretary in 1998 (see below). The appointment would also 'advance the rationalization of UN economic analysis and reporting and maintain a clear oversight in respect of UN funds, Programmes and Agencies while respecting autonomies and competencies'.[43] The Union also backed the proposal made in 50/227 of 1 July 1996 to review the 'mandates, composition, functions and working methods of the Functional Commissions and expert groups and bodies with a view to ensuring more effective and coordinated discussions and outcomes of their work'.

The boards of the funds and programmes were also reformed so that their effectiveness with regard to day-to-day management was enhanced. According to 3.21 A/48/162 they were to be transformed into executive boards, under the authority of the Council. They were to meet more often for shorter periods, to be more professionally staffed with individuals selected for their managerial and technical skills rather than politicians, and were to be smaller. They were turned into boards of management in a practical sense, rather than being remote committees of semi-detached figures, and were required to 'take into account the need for the effective conduct of the work of each Board'. At the same time it was made easier for ECOSOC to evaluate the relationship between them and to approve specific countries' programmes under their aegis. They were made more directly subject to ECOSOC, to which they were accountable, and by which they could be instructed.

TAKING THE REFORMS FORWARD IN THE FUNDS AND PROGRAMMES: THE TRACK II PROCESS IN THE LATE 1990s

In 1997 these reforms were taken forward when the big four funds and programmes, UNICEF, UNDP, UNFPA and WFP, were combined to set up a joint UN Development Group (UNDG), made up of the representatives of the four and a small number of other officers, 15 in all, to produce the so-called United Nations Development Assistance Frameworks (UNDAFs). These developments followed from the new Secretary-

General's Report of July 1997, in which he promised to seek further savings by an additional thinning of the UN's administration – by losing up to a thousand jobs – and to use the money saved for development purposes. Indeed Kofi Annan, compared with previous secretaries-general, treated reform of the economic and social mechanisms as a matter of first importance. Such reforms had largely been a side issue for his predecessors.

The General Assembly approved implementing legislation in September 1997 in A/52/12 a & b. The package became known as the Track II process, though the exact meaning of this term – what in specific terms it included and excluded – was hard to determine. Future reforms and increased system-wide co-ordination were to be considered by the office of a new Deputy Secretary-General, Louise Frechette. A new Strategic Planning section, with John Ruggie in charge, was to advise Frechette and the Secretary-General on specific proposals to improve institutions and programmes. The reforms were in essence a parallel route to the ways of working located above in ECOSOC and could replace or supplement them in the future.

They were to be followed by an ambitious programme of further reform in the organization proposed by the Secretary-General for the approval of member governments in future Assembly resolutions. This package included proposals for a Millennium Assembly to consider other aspects of development; a people's assembly for NGOs; a ministerial commission to consider the constitutions of the specialized agencies, with a view to making them more system-sensitive; and the Secretary-General proposed to convert the Trusteeship Council into a Global Commons Council. He also envisaged a revolving credit fund to cover the UN's short-term debts. The dominant sentiment in the UN in the late 1990s was that this ambitious range of proposals was unlikely to attract enough support from UN members.

The one exception was the development process work of the funds and programmes about which the judgement was generally favourable, and where extensive changes could be made by the Secretary-General under his own authority, as these were formally extensions of the Secretariat. The new process was driven by the energetic head of UNDP, Gus Speth, who had been imaginative enough to allow the other organizations onto the turf previously commanded exclusively by UNDP. For instance, the resident co-ordinators in developing countries, previously exclusively from UNDP, could now be from one of the other partner organizations (in 1998 UNICEF officers had become resident co-ordinators in five countries). And the offices of the funds and programmes were now to be brought together in the target countries in what became known as UN houses. Sixty or so had been set up by March 1998. This was an old idea, which, as already argued, had important implications for promoting savings and better, more co-ordinated, management.

Under Speth UNDP remained in charge of the grand strategy and determined the allocation of posts in the joint arrangements – it retained what was called a godfather role – and UNDP chaired UNDG, and the executive committee. But the concessions made to the other funds and programmes to achieve greater efficiency obviously ran the risk of a declining UNDP role in the future.

The principal members of the new partnership were all within the jurisdiction of the United Nations central system and the new arrangements were a carrying forward of the proposals made in A/48/162 to reform the executive boards of this group of organizations. The idea was that the work of the funds and programmes would be more tightly integrated through UNDG and that indeed their executive committees would hold frequent joint meetings; this happened for the first time in January 1998. This move in some ways looked back to the League system, when the main economic and social actors had been closely linked with the central system. The changes stopped short, however, of fusing them into a single entity, a course favoured by the members of the European Union and the Nordic countries. A joint Secretariat was, however, set up with secondees from the participating organizations, a remarkable development in view of the earlier resistance to even modest integration. It was reckoned that working together on joint plans in this Secretariat, and in the UN houses in the beneficiary countries, would help to develop agreement between the partner organizations. They could command the development strategy of the United Nations through UNDG, and create a common evaluation of what the system could provide in relation to the target countries.

One view was that the resulting country plans, the UNDAFs, amounted to a supply-side view of development, whereas the Country Strategy Notes represented the demand side. In March 1998 such frameworks had been agreed for 11 countries and the goal was to produce plans for all developing countries. The target states were then invited to accept the plans, not on a take-it-or-leave-it basis, but obviously in a context of pressure. The new plans were more specific with regard to policies and finance than the Country Strategy Notes: they were a further step towards more specific planning within the overarching framework of the Country Strategy Notes.

As with the ECOSOC Co-ordination/Operational segments the new plans also drew on the work of the global conferences through the functional commissions, and aimed at agreeing cross-sector programmes in consultation with field-level officials who worked in such mechanisms as the agency task forces. The analysis applied above to the ECOSOC arrangements was also relevant to the UNDG/UNDAF system. The latter was also likely to be considered by the Operational and Co-ordination segments of ECOSOC and through this to help shape future Country Strategy Notes. Channels were likely to open up in this way, which would reinforce the influence of the UNDG/UNDAF process on the agencies and the member states. But very few agencies had agreed to join by the time of writing at the turn of the millennium. At that date the cohort of the latter was limited to UNIDO, though there was pressure on the other agencies from the Secretary-General and others to join. In late March 1998 a meeting of the agencies' main co-ordination committee, the ACC, was to discuss their involvement, and it was hoped that there would be a move in that direction. The hope was that this would contribute to the development of a collective sense of best development practice, drawing upon the global conference agendas and the related cross-sector pro-grammes, which would become system wide to include funds and pro-grammes, agencies, donors and beneficiaries. One official argued that the way in which a collective view about population policy had emerged was the model: 'tremendous things are happening'.

The new development frameworks also reflected the new policy of linking development with a wider agenda of creating an enabling environ-ment within which private investment in the developing countries would be encouraged. Like an increasing range of international organizational arrangements in the late 1990s, especially in the UN system and the EU, the new development plans included proposals for creating supporting infrastructures in the economic, social and political contexts. The range of these was wide and startlingly frank in its commitment to liberal pluralist arrangements. It encompassed the elements of a well-founded civil society and democratization, as well as such changes as improved credit and insurance arrangements. The significance of this should not be underesti-mated: for the first time in the history of the United Nations the organiz-ation was directly addressing core structures in the state and some argued that even in the difficult continent (Africa) illiberal practices were increas-ingly delegitimized. The head of UNDP stated that 40 per cent of the resources of his organization now went on governance improving activi-ties, which was a remarkable alteration in stress. UNICEF's strategy had also been reconsecrated: the new approach was to be 'rights based', meaning that it was to be derived from the Rights of the Child Conven-tion. In the late 1990s another wind of change seemed to be blowing in the UN system. There was increasing perception of the need to give priority to a *strategy* of change in many areas – including human rights and development – rather than a policy of dealing with immediate pressing problems in ways that put the chances of long-term improvement at risk. But it was arguable that another change was also underway: a change of ideology. The new changes were increasingly backed by the power of the liberal states in pursuit of freer markets, and more liberal, pluralist arrangements. There was a weakening of the view among the lead states that the UN system could only achieve change on the basis of an inter-ideological consensus.

For two years or so the donor countries had indicated their preparedness to work within the new framework of OECD's Development Assistance Committee (DAC). The World Bank, a primary channel of influence for the donor countries, was also willing to link its own development planning process with that of the DAFs. The World Bank and UNDG had worked together in developing the assistance strategy for Mali and Vietnam, and the practice was likely to be repeated elsewhere. But predictably there was some uncertainty in the attitudes of both the target countries and multilateral companies. The former went along with the new approach reluctantly, seeing it as the only realistic option in the post-Cold War period. The latter were reluctant to see multiple conditionality get in the way of their untrammelled freedom to invest, which was implied in such texts as the recently agreed multilateral investment agreement, but were usually reluctant to come out publicly in favour of protecting social and political underdevelopment. The companies also found the shift in the ideology of development congenial: that one of the purposes of multilateral action was to facilitate enhanced private investment.

The UNDAFs were really enabling instruments, pushing democratization and an improved economic infrastructure, but hoping through this to encourage private business to fill the gaps left by the retreat in the 1990s of official overseas development assistance, even of the more well-disposed countries, such as those of Scandinavia. In the longer term, improvements in the target states could make it more politically acceptable in the richer states to return to higher levels of official bilateral aid, and to achieve the targets indicated in the UN Development Decade agreements. It would also make it more likely that the developing states would be able to help themselves.

In the debate to approve the new course in the General Assembly in December 1997 the G77 had shown much unease. But the new instruments rested on a powerful coalition – the funds and programmes acting together with donor country support were hard to resist – and this was enough to convince a number of actors, including the main beneficiaries, that they needed to concur, despite considerable initial opposition. The emerging arrangements reflected an increasing preparedness on the part of the developed world to put pressure on those in the developing world to put their house in order. But this fracture led to a much clearer identification of another: it had become evident by the late 1990s that the developing world, often referred to collectively as the G77, was itself divided between the more developed and the least developed. When the former insisted upon the unity of the whole they got in the way of special efforts to help the latter: there could be a beneficial fracturing of the G77 to make it easier for the richer to help the poorest states.

THE LOGIC OF REFORM: RELATING GLOBAL INTENTIONS TO COUNTRY PROGRAMMES

By the late 1990s the three overlapping groups of actors in the system were under increasing pressure to increase their internal co-ordination: the agencies, funds and programmes and states formed the macro-group, which was involved with the Country Strategy Notes; the funds and programmes were a sub-group, now more tightly organized and involved with the Development Assistance Frameworks; and in another sub-group the states were now under increased pressure to fit their bilateral efforts into the emerging multilateral plans. This section considers the pressures to co-ordinate in the macro-group, which was the larger concern of ECOSOC, though similar pressures could be identified within the two sub-groups.

The structure of the segments of ECOSOC was of the greatest importance with regard to entrenching the informal pressures to increase co-ordination. Within them the heads of agencies were brought into close consultation with the main donors and beneficiaries about the programmes for action, which were now increasingly derived from the global conferences, and carried forward by the respective global commissions. In the co-ordination segments the donors, the heads of the agencies and the ACC, as well as the Secretary-General, the members of the Committee and Programme and Co-ordination (CPC) and the beneficiaries were present. This meant that decisions about money were now to be taken in the context of decisions about policy. Agencies were made more aware of a need for good performance with regard to collectively approved programmes. And they were also made more clearly subject to inspection and monitoring by the bodies that took the initial decisions about money and policy. Though difficulties remained in the form of the agencies' inclination to remain as aloof as possible – as was shown in the Secretary-General's Report of June 1997 – they were now under much greater pressure to fit into the system, if only to maintain budgetary provision. The new arrangements had the effect of making it politically in the interest of the agencies to become system oriented. In this way the multilateral system was adapted to enhance actor compliance.

The essence of the problem was to relate global *intentions*, which were increasingly defined in global conferences with regard to a particular sector of problems, to *programmes*, which were trans- or cross-sectoral, and were the functional application of the global intentions in the field. Three developments were necessary to achieve this transfer of intentions to programmes. First was a reasonably unobstructed transmission belt transferring one to the other through linked organizations. Second was a mechanism by which the sectoral intentions could be translated into cross- or trans-sectoral plans. Third was a place where the operational agencies could be subjected to pressures that bound them to the intentions, and that also committed them to pursuing the cross- or trans-sectoral plans. The logic of the process judged in these terms, as it had evolved by the late 1990s, was as follows:

1. Since the late 1980s the number of global conferences had been greatly increased, and they had been accepted as one of the routine events of international society. The conferences involved massive amounts of preparation, were a focus of heroic effort by non-governmental organizations throughout the world, and promoted intense interaction between the members of participating governments. The mandate they produced reflected compromises that were not always satisfactory, but they did add something new to multilateral diplomacy: the identification of a core of agreed values and purposes, which formed the basis of special actions and programmes over a very wide range of human interests and needs. They were a remarkable contribution to the strengthening among diverse groups of human beings of a sense of common destiny.

2. The conferences spawned two further institutions: the functional commissions, and follow-up conferences, normally five years after the first event. The commissions were intended to work out the implications of the conference conclusions and produce specific plans and costs. One of the features of the conferences in the 1990s compared with those of earlier periods was that their documentation and concluding statements more frequently included specific targets, timings and policy proposals. A major feature of the Population Conferences of 1974 and 1984 was the determination of the developing states to water down and render less precise the initial World Population Plan of Action. This was a less common inclination in the 1990s, with conclusions more often pinned to specifics.

3. The ECOSOC was now to oversee the work of the commissions, to inspect and alter their mandates so that efficiency and effectiveness were enhanced, and to identify cross-cutting and overlapping themes. *In this process the Council undertook a key task: to translate plans evolved in particular sectors of activity, which was the nature of the work of the*

commissions, into proposals that were relevant to cross-sectoral programmes.
The creation of such programmes was now recognized as an essential
feature of effective development, and that there was now an organizational mechanism for establishing them was one of the two key
innovations of the reforms.

4. The next major link between intentions and programmes was estab-
    lished in the second key innovation. The ECOSOC clearly had to find
    better ways of dealing with the agencies, funds and programmes if
    there was to be a more effective translation of intentions into field-level
    programmes. The innovation (contained in 48/162 and 50/227), was to
    bring the heads of the agencies and relevant officers into work centred
    in ECOSOC. They were now under greater pressure to commit them-
    selves to the specifics of programme activities, and fit their own plans
    into a common framework. Mandates were shaped with them in the
    presence of the representatives of those countries that might be
    expected to foot the bill. Officers from the countries were also to be
    brought into the centre, where they could observe the behaviour of
    their executive masters more closely. This was another element in a
    cluster of pressures upon agencies to be much more system oriented
    than before. But it was also in their political and financial interests to
    be so.

5. There was a further set of interactions generating practical responses to
    broad intentions in the evolving relationship between the central mech-
    anisms and field activities. Task forces, which were inter-agency,
    received a mandate informed by the cross-sector decisions of the Co-
    ordination segment of ECOSOC. At the same time the Country Strategy
    Notes, and the greatly enhanced position of the UNDP resident co-
    ordinator on the ground, provided a machinery through which the
    programme-related cross-sector and common themes could be specified
    and operationalized. A number of developments reinforced this tend-
    ency: the introduction of unified United Nations premises, which,
    though by no means universal, were now intended to be common, and
    the parallel reforms in the arrangements of the funds and programmes
    encouraged the development of more co-ordinated cross-sector activi-
    ties. In consequence, as already noted, in 1996 the number of 'stand-
    alone' projects had been halved compared with 1991. (These were
    projects undertaken by agencies acting alone.)

  In sum, overall reorganization meant that the two poles of the system
– the end where *intentions* were formulated, and that where *programmes*
were implemented – had been, in a sense, stretched further apart, while
also being more rationally related. Operations at the programme end,
the field level, had been integrated to a greater extent than in the past,
and field officers had been given enhanced discretion. *At the other pole,*

the greater number of global conferences encouraged a greater degree of agreement about what should be done; and the reform of ECOSOC sharpened its capacity to shape these globally defined intentions, or broad aims, into cross-sectoral programmes with well-defined objectives. At the same time ECOSOC had acquired greater capacity to act as a conduit through which the results of field-level monitoring could be conveyed upwards to the permanent representations of the global conferences, namely the commissions, which then became more capable of formulating well-informed proposals for the consideration of the five-yearly review meetings, and the successor conferences.

6. The development of entrenched multilateralism had various advantages. Procedures had been introduced which strengthened mutual obligations and respect for common rules with regard to the work of the agencies. At the same time it had become more difficult for both agencies and states to opt out, because the system worked in such a way that the benefits of compliance and the costs of non-compliance were continuously upgraded and there was no supranational challenge or rival pole of action to react against. The system had become a forum of obligation.

One source of pressure upon states to conform with plans for multilateral action could be the new plans for development action which included the Country Strategy Notes, which by 1998 subsumed UNDAFs. If such plans acquired substance, in that they included specific targets and programmes, it would become increasingly difficult for states contemplating bilateral measures to act in opposition. They were formally required to respect them. But the plans would become part of the intellectual environment that had to be taken into account when states determined their own plans; the alternative would be a greater exposure to accusations of deliberately undermining the agreed approach to the development problems of particular states. The plans were multilateral and backed by a consensus of operators, donors and the host country government.

States that flouted the rules of the regime ran the risk of being identified as cheats, and incurring the associated costs. The General Assembly reflected this in 50/227 when it concluded that 'Developing countries are responsible for their development processes and operational activities for development are a joint responsibility of all countries. *Partnership between developed and developing countries should be based on agreed mandates, principles and priorities of the United Nations system in the development field.* All countries should demonstrate their commitment to the Funds and Programmes.'[44] It was further reinforced in paragraph 63 A/50/227, with the invitation to 'national officials directly involved in the implementation of national development strategies in recipient countries, as well as field-

level representatives of the United Nations' to participate in the work of
the operational segment.

The new process had the effect of strengthening the norms of a
multilateral system, and did not attempt reform by setting up some kind
of supranational manager, or by destroying multilateralism with regard
to intentions by transferring money to the Bretton Woods institutions. The
reform of the budgetary process in the UN and agencies of the 1980s was
an illustration of the method. Major responsibility for agreeing the budget
was given to the Committee for Programme and Co-ordination, which
had a limited membership, usually including the main donors and the
representatives of the Group of 77. The agreement that the budget should
be approved by consensus in this committee, taken in December 1986,
was the key step in creating a system in which the budget was unlikely to
be radically altered in favour of the recipient countries by the General
Assembly's Fifth Committee.[45] This was easier in the smaller forum
because being co-opted into it and involved in the details of creating the
budget enhanced the sense of being in the inner circle for the representatives of the G77, and the requirement of agreeing by consensus to a
detailed budget in this setting reinforced their commitment to it.

CONCLUSIONS

The agencies and the developing countries concurred, though each were
in some ways under pressure, that strengthening the co-ordination mechanisms – the route of co-operation – was the preferable course. It could
lead to an increase in the level of funding, and at worst could help slow
down the reduction in development resources. They expected to be worse
off if such mechanisms were not introduced, or if they stayed outside the
new system – hence the wan acceptance by the G77 of the proposed
changes. The backlash at the meeting of the World Trade Organization in
Seattle in 1999 was in part a protest against these pressures. The donors
for their part had an interest in the mechanisms because they promised
greater efficiency in the use of development resources, and could weaken
the case for a significant increase in development provision. For them
opting out was likely to be the more costly option in terms of development, but also because of the other important agendas, especially
democratization.

The new mechanisms created two new kinds of rules emanating from
negotiations. First were the progressively defined rules embodied in the
new working arrangements; and, second, the working decisions produced
with regard to policy, programmes and finance in the new system.
Entrenching multilateralism meant that sub-system actors' behaviour was

more likely to be subject to system-level rules, i.e. rules in the two senses outlined, as determined in the UN's reformed economic and social arrangements, because:

- finance was a reward for compliance with the new rules for agencies, developing countries and funds and programmes;
- a number of actors had been set up or empowered by the reforms which were system supporters, such as the task forces, the functional commissions, the Co-ordination segment of ECOSOC, the UNDG, and the agency and fund and programme officials who were engaged at the country level in UN premises, and (increasingly!) were linked by new communication systems: the weight of system-focused activity generated by this increased range of actors was more difficult to resist;
- actors within the developing states were likely to become system supporters, like the national courts in the EU, because they were empowered in the new arrangements through finance and function. Taking more decisions about the content and financing of programmes within local mechanisms, including national governmental and inter- and non-governmental organizations, created a system clientele. Democratization reinforced system orientation, but also enhanced loyalty to extra-state system actors;
- bilateral providers were also now more likely to be system responsive, as they were required to take note of the Country Strategy Notes. They were also together in the key ECOSOC committees and exposed to socialization into system norms. Officials in provider ministries, like the ODA in Britain, were likely to be pushed to support system orientations, as there had been open commitment to support for the concept of the reforms; the alternative would imply a flat contradiction of the concept. Behaving badly remained an option but would be a more public transgression;
- the juxtaposition of three functions in a single unit – ECOSOC – created a powerful instrument. The three functions were the translation of sector proposals into integrated programmes that were more easily related to country plans; the allocation of resources for programme implementation within countries; and the monitoring of operational performance under the scrutiny of the main providers and programme formulators. Doing these three things in the same forum had a multiplier effect on pressure towards system-oriented behaviour for policy formulators, resource contributors, and programme implementers alike. Contributors, implementers and formulators were locked into a way of working which supported system rules.

In sum, once a pattern of interrelated interests existed, ensuing negotiations could lead to developments that trapped cautious and willing actors alike. They were pushed to compliance with system rules by: a fear of losing benefits by exclusion; an unwillingness to weaken a related existing regime that was regarded as beneficial; the creating and empowerment of new or existing actors that favoured co-operation; specifying sets of rules about co-operation, like the Country Strategy Notes, which could be evaded only by appearing to abandon the agreed concept, i.e. abandoning co-operation; and being involved in a forum where the only alternative to system compliance was marginalization.

NOTES

1. For an interpretation of functionalism see Inis Claude Jr, *Swords into Plowshares*, 5th edition (New York: Random House, 1971) and A. J. R. Groom and Paul Taylor (eds), *Functionalism* (London: University of London Press, 1973).
2. See Paul Taylor, *International Organization in the Modern World* (London: Pinter, 1995).
3. The following two sections of this chapter draw heavily on the work of the late Martin Hill in his book *The United Nations System: Co-ordinating its Economic and Social Work* (Cambridge: Cambridge University Press and UNITAR, 1978), especially pp. 11–34. I am grateful for permission given to use this material as the basis for this section, but accept full responsibility for it and for the updating and textual alterations I have added.
4. C. Wilfred Jenks, *The International Labour Organization in the UN Family* (UNITAR Lecture Series, 3, 1971), p. 45.
5. Official Records of the Economic and Social Council, Fifty-fifth Session, Supplement No. 1 (E.5400), 'Decisions', p. 33.
6. For a discussion of these agreements see Edward S. Mason and Robert E. Asher, *The World Bank Since Bretton Woods* (Washington, DC: The Brookings Institut, 1973), pp. 54–60.
7. Official Records of the General Assembly, Seventh Session, Supplement No. 3 (A/2172), Introduction, p. x.
8. See E/3107 and E/4844.
9. Council Resolution 1756 (LIV), para. 2.
10. Official Records of the General Assembly, Twenty-First Session, Supplement No. 5 (A/6305), Foreword by the Secretary-General, para. 20.
11. 'Question of the establishment of a comprehensive international trade organization', Report of the Secretary-General of UNCTAD, Document TD/B/535 of 30 December 1974.
12. Quoted in John P. Renninger, *ECOSOC: Options for Reform* (New York: UNITAR, 1981), p. 5.
13. Martin Hill, *op. cit.*, p. 44.
14. Housang Ameri, *Politics and Process in the Specialized Agencies of the United Nations* (Aldershot: Gower, 1982), p. 93.
15. A/32/197, *op. cit.*, p. 127, para. 64.
16. Group of Experts Report, loc. cit., fn. 12, p. 13, para. 42.
17. A/32/197, loc. cit., section II.

18. COPAs were instituted in 1977 by the ECOSOC in EC/2098/LXIII.
19. *Reporting to the Economic and Social Council*, prepared by Maurice Bertrand, Joint Inspection Unit, JIU/REP/8417, Geneva, 1984, p. 16.
20. A/32/197, p. 122, para. 7.
21. *Ibid.*, para. 9.
22. *Ibid.*, para.11(d).
23. Joint Inspection Unti, *Some Reflections on Reform of the United Nations*, prepared by Maurice Bertrand, JIU/REP/85/9, Geneva, 1985. Referred to as the Bertrand Report.
24. *Ibid.*, p. 7, para. 18.
25. Cross Organizational Programme Analysis of the Activities of the United Nations System in Human Settlements, E/AC.51/1984/5, 4 April 1984, p. 43, para. 97.
26. The Bertrand Report, p. 10, para. 29.
27. *Ibid.*, p. 10, paras 29 and 30.
28. See John Ruggie, *Constructing the World Polity* (London: Routledge, 1998), p. 21.
29. European Union presidency letter to the Secretary-General, Permanent Mission of Ireland to the United Nations, 16 October 1996, para. 12.
30. See a comment on this in Paul Taylor and A. J. R. Groom (eds.), *Global Issues in the United Nations Framework* (London: Macmillan, 1989), ch. 1.
31. This is the approach recommended by Rosemary Righter in her *Utopia Lost: The United Nations and World Order* (New York: Twentieth Century Fund Press, 1995).
32. Robert O. Keohane, *After Hegemony: Co-operation and Discord in the World Political Economy* (Princeton: Princeton University Press, 1984), p. 57.
33. Oran Young, *International Governance: Protecting the Environment in a Stateless Society* (Ithaca, New York: Cornell University Press, 1994).
34. An epistemic community is a group of people who share an area of knowledge or expertise, and who might belong to common professional associations or work together on common problems over a period of time. They may include people from a number of countries and therefore they may lead to transnational alliances.
35. See Paul Taylor, *International Organization in the Modern World*, *op. cit.*, ch. 5.
36. Set out in A/47/199, para. 9, and frequently alluded to in the later resolutions.
37. By an official Danish mission to the UN, September 1996.
38. See Paul Taylor, 'Options for the reform of the international system for humanitarian assistance', in John Harriss (ed.), *The Politics of Humanitarian Intervention* (London: Pinter and Save the Children, 1995).
39. Commissions were first created in the 1940s; they were only later attached explicitly to global conferences and their number then increased.
40. Economic and Social Council, General Segment, Background paper on the harmonization and co-ordination of the agendas and multi-year programmes of work of functional commissions of ECOSOC, E/1996/CRP.4, 10 July 1996, para. 6.
41. *Ibid.*
42. E/1996/CRP.4, July 1996, paras. 8–10.
43. EU presidency letter, *loc. cit.*, p. 5.
44. A/50/227: annexe 1, clause 7.
45. For an account of the reforms in budgetary arrangements see Paul Taylor, *International Organization in the Modern World*, *op. cit.*, ch. 5.

CHAPTER 5

THE TRUSTEESHIP COUNCIL: A SUCCESSFUL DEMISE

A. J. R. Groom

INTRODUCTION

The Trusteeship Council has been a considerable success. At its opening session on 26 March 1947 the first Secretary-General of the United Nations, Trygve Lie, stated that the Trusteeship Council was to work for its own demise in that the 'ultimate goal is to give the Trust territories full statehood'. But the Trusteeship Council was not only to deal with those entities placed under its guidance, it was also to be an exemplar. As Mr Lie pointed out: 'A successful Trusteeship System will afford a reassuring demonstration that there is a peaceful and orderly means of achieving the difficult transition from backward and subject status to self-government or independence, to political and economic self-reliance.'[1] In the narrow sense, this goal was achieved when all 11 territories placed under the Trusteeship Council achieved their independence. In 1994, with the termination of the Trusteeship Agreement for the Trust Territory of the Pacific Islands by Security Council Resolution 956 and Palau's admission to the UN, there remained no more territories under the aegis of the Trusteeship Council, although theoretically colonial territories could still be placed under the Council's auspices. In a larger sense the Trusteeship system was also a great success in its benign influence on the coming to independence of practically all colonial territories, although some difficult cases still remain, such as the Falklands/Malvinas, Gibraltar and Western Sahara.

The League of Nations' Mandate system and its successor, the Trusteeship system, reflected both the spirit and parameters of colonial empires and a growing awareness of the need to change them. While colonialism at its worst involved the cruellest form of exploitation and indeed the extermination of indigenous peoples, it did in other instances give some evidence of enlightened ameliorative policies. It was rather like the proverbial curate's egg; that is to say, it was good in parts, but the good parts far from determined the nature of the whole. The Trusteeship Council was part of a wider movement, both within and beyond the

United Nations, to make formal colonialism a relic of history, and this has occurred with a speed that was unimagined at the time the Trusteeship Council was established. For example, the British Empire in 1946 governed more than a quarter of humanity, whereas British dependent territories now have a total population of a few thousand. In 1946, if the reports of the British Colonial Office are to be believed, the general anticipation was that colonial territories, particularly in Africa, the Pacific and the Caribbean, were only likely to become self-governing or possibly independent after several decades, yet in less than two decades colonialism was effectively dead.

The Trusteeship Council and the system that it represented were not the cause of this remarkable transformation, but it did play a role therein and particularly when, in the early days of the UN, together with the Chapter on Non-self-governing Territories, it served as an exemplar. One of the successes of the UN system as a whole has been to stimulate aspirations while at the same time easing the process of decolonization, bloody though that has been at times. Moreover, the UN system has provided a framework for post-independence assistance through such programmes as the UN Development Programme and the work of the specialized agencies, albeit an inadequate one when faced by the magnitude of the tasks to be confronted. The Trusteeship system did not constitute an innovation but rather a development of trends and tendencies that had been evident not only in the Mandate system of the League of Nations but also in the growth of the idea of international responsibility in the nineteenth century.

HISTORICAL BACKGROUND

The phrase 'a sacred trust' is one frequently associated with the notion of Mandates and Trust Territories, but as long ago as the eighteenth century Edmund Burke had used the phrase as a guiding principle for the governance of colonies. The concept of 'a sacred trust' could be applied to a single administering power or as a general principle to which a group of powers, individually and collectively, would adhere. In the nineteenth century there are several examples of this, although it was painfully evident that the 'trust' was far more likely to benefit those governing than those being governed. Yet it must be acknowledged that the slave trade was abolished, and so eventually was slavery too. While the Congress of Berlin in 1885 was an unseemly scramble for Africa, nevertheless it did at the same time bring the weight of informed opinion to ensure that some limited minimum standards were set out and aspirations for their implementation were elicited, notably in the case of the Congo. Again, there were instances of international regimes, often to impose a system of financial regulation, to control piracy or to collect debts. Thus some general standards of civilized behaviour began to emerge and came, hesitantly, to be applied as an exercise in collective colonial governance.[2] Within that framework, a notion of international responsibility could grow. The principles of responsibility, accountability and supervision, as opposed to an occasional co-ordination of colonialism, received their formal acceptance in the Covenant of the League of Nations.

The League of Nations was open to a rather wider membership than the United Nations, in that Article 1.2 states that 'any fully self-governing State, Dominion or Colony ... may become a Member of the League if its admission is agreed to by two-thirds of the Assembly, provided that it shall give effective guarantees of its sincere intention to observe its international obligations, and shall accept such regulations as may be prescribed by the League in regard to its military, naval and air forces and armaments'. The aspiration was, therefore, clearly one of universality. However, that universality was prejudiced by the fatal exclusion of Germany and the Soviet Union at the beginning and, to a lesser extent, by the self-exclusion of the United States. There were, however, other entities and territories in the international system. There were the colonial territories that were not fully self-governing in which, in Article 23(b), members of the League undertook 'to secure just treatment of the native inhabitants of territories under their control'. This still left the territories of the Austro-Hungarian and Ottoman Empires and the colonies of Germany. While the territories of the Austro-Hungarian Empire became fully independent states, only Turkey had such a status following the collapse of the Ottoman Empire. Finally there remained the Mandates that were thus formed by parts of the former Ottoman Empire and the former colonies of Germany. Article 22 stipulated their status and the way in which they were to be administered. It constitutes a major attempt at political engineering, and a formidable exemplar for the colonial powers, since they had to administer the Mandates under the principles of responsibility, accountability and supervision, which was likely to rub off on the administration of their own colonies that were not placed under the protection of the League of Nations other than under Article 23(b).

Article 22.1 states quaintly but clearly: 'To those colonies and territories which as a consequence of the late war have ceased to be under the sovereignty of the States which formerly governed them and which are inhabited by peoples not yet able to stand by themselves under the strenuous conditions of the modern world, there should be applied the principle that the well-being and development of such peoples form a sacred trust of civilisation and that securities for the performance of this trust should be embodied in this Covenant.' Article 22.2 states further: 'The best method of giving practical effect to this principle is that the tutelage of such peoples should be entrusted to advanced nations who, by reason of their resources, their experience or their geographical position, can best undertake this responsibility, and who are willing to accept it, and that this tutelage should be exercised by them as Mandatories on behalf of the League.' Article 22 then goes on to differentiate between territories according 'to the stage of the development of the people, the geographical situation of the territory, its economic conditions and other similar circumstances'. Thus, 'Certain communities belonging formally to the Turkish Empire have reached a stage of development where their existence as independent nations can be provisionally recognised subject to the rendering of administrative advice and assistance by a Mandatory until such time as they are able to stand alone.' This was not the case for 'other peoples, especially those of central Africa . . .'. South-West Africa and certain South Pacific islands, on the other hand, 'can be best adminis- tered under the laws of the Mandatory as integral portions of its terri- tory . . .'. Mandatory powers were obliged to submit an Annual Report to the League Council regarding the territory committed to their charge, and a Permanent Commission was set up to receive and examine these Annual Reports and to advise the League Council 'on all matters relating to the observance of the mandates'.

The negotiation of the Mandates was no easy matter. Some countries found it difficult to resist old-fashioned attitudes to the spoils of war. New Zealand, Australia and South Africa were certainly not averse to the annexation of former German colonial territory, and in Europe there were territorial claims by the victorious powers, notably Italy. Moreover, intense rivalries between Britain, France, the United States and Italy, together with Greece, over the territories of the Ottoman Empire reflected wartime promises and betrayals, issues of enlightened principle tempered by naked self-interest, control on the ground and old-fashioned colonial rivalries. The net result was that the initial vision of a strong Mandate system became an almost empty shell, but thereafter, through the assidu- ous work of the Mandates Commission to which reports were sent, a body of practice and precedent was established, which rehabilitated the shell. Moreover, by 1946 when the League was formally wound up, only one Class A Mandate, namely Palestine, had not become an independent state. The work of the Commission and the Mandates section of the League Secretariat, which took a very proactive and broad interpretation of its functions, met with a high degree of success, at least initially. Although some Mandatory powers applied political pressure and others dragged their feet in providing adequate reports, nevertheless the genie of international accountability could not be put back into the bottle of untrammelled colonial possession, either for the Mandates themselves or, to a lesser degree, for all colonial territories.[3]

The Mandate system was a harbinger of the *pêle-mêle* process of decolonization that was such a characteristic of the first two decades after the Second World War. Like any harbinger it grew out of the dominant mindset of the past, in this case that of nineteenth-century colonialism. Its revolutionary potential was not only concerned with improving standards of colonial rule by setting an example in the mandated territories, but it had implicit in its underlying philosophy the notion that colonialism was not a stable end in itself but a way-stage to a different status of at least full self-government. The Mandates and the Mandate system were the cuckoo in the colonial nest.

The Mandate system had grown out of liberal thought in Britain, which had advocated a policy of no annexations in 1917, and the ideas of Woodrow Wilson, which stressed a notion of some form of international responsibility. When the United States took no direct part in the League, and in the end did not accept or insist upon being a Mandatory power (although President Wilson was ready to accept a US Mandate over Armenia, and the United States had trading privileges in the Mandates), then the pace was set by a dialogue between the principal administrators, namely Britain and France, the secondary administrators, namely South Africa, Australia, New Zealand and Belgium, some of whom had annexationist ideas, and the League Secretariat. However, the idea of a Mandate system was, by the time of the Second World War, well rooted in international thought, and therefore when planning began for a post-war world organization, the notion of no annexation and a code of conduct for colonial powers had taken root. These ideas need to be seen in context.

THE IMPACT OF THE SECOND WORLD WAR

The United States, both wittingly and unwittingly, sought to be a world leader. However, there is no one United States, but many, and the policies of different powerful groupings within the American political system can be at variance with each other. Generally speaking, there was an ideological and axiomatic dislike of colonialism, except where US interests were at stake, as in what became the Strategic Trust Territories, or where US possessions or spheres of influence were concerned, such as the Panama Canal zone. The United States had done extremely well economically in the Second World War, as it had in the First World War. It had asset-stripped British global economic power, especially in South America, and for a while Britain was faced by an attack on two flanks: by Germany and Italy on the political and military flank in Europe, and by the United

States on the financial and commercial flank globally. It was only when Britain was on its knees that the United States then relented its pressure. Some of this was due to strong anti-British feelings in parts of the United States, including the Congress. It was also due to normal commercial ruthlessness, and partly it was a reaction to imperial preference whereby, following the Ottawa Agreement in 1932, the British Empire had built extensive commercial barriers around itself to the detriment of US interests. The only area in which the 'special relationship' could genuinely be said to have existed, was in that of military intelligence. Otherwise matters were decided principally on the crude basis of comparative strength and importance. The relationship was very different from that which pertains now between member states of the European Union, or has in the past pertained between members of the Commonwealth. The United States was, therefore, politically and economically pressing the colonial powers, and Britain as the largest colonial power took the brunt of this crusade.

In this the United States had the support of the Soviet Union, which shared the American ideological conviction of the evils of other peoples' colonialism. Moreover, like the United States, the Soviet Union was more than ready to chip away at areas of British hegemonial influence in Greece and Turkey, in Iran and in Afghanistan. There were still elements of the 'great game' in Central Asia to be played, but there were also other actors – the colonial peoples themselves.

While for a time colonialism in its various forms may have had a degree of legitimacy in the eyes of indigenous peoples, this was no longer the case during the period of the Second World War and its immediate aftermath. The myth of the superiority of the European (including Americans) had been shattered by the impressive initial victories of Japan over the four major European powers in Asia, namely the UK, France, the Netherlands and the United States. The fall of Singapore was symbolic of this, when the Japanese made British officers sweep the streets in front of the local population the day after they took control of the island colony. This was no victory by an Asian power over a European power that was weak and operating far from its major sources of strength, as in the case of the Japanese victory over the Russians in 1905, but rather a fearsome campaign against the major European powers in Asia, fought with all the might that they could bring to bear to secure the outcome, and the Europeans, including the United States, had lost. Not only had the Europeans lost the war, but in some cases they had also lost the will to be colonial powers. The growth of socialism, democracy and a welfare state at home rested uneasily with a non-democratic, indeed autocratic, administration abroad that was looking more to the interests of those governing than those governed. Moreover, the military strength of the colonial powers, such as it was, also rested on the use of indigenous military forces to a far greater extent than had been the case in the First World War. Those who were deemed fit to die for a colonial power also began to feel themselves fit to be free from that colonial power. They now had a leadership, as the development of major colonial territories led to the rise of a national indigenous middle class which began to demand independence, and not merely self-government or even good government. In other words, by the time the United Nations was being negotiated, colonialism was under attack from without by the United States and the Soviet Union, and from within by changing values in the colonial powers themselves and by subject peoples.

From the United States there was a demand by pressure groups concerned with colonial questions that the new United Nations to be formed should become an agency for the emancipation of colonial peoples, as well as a forum for an international control of colonial policy. Thus, in the United States and Britain there were those who chose to emphasize the Atlantic Charter in which both the United States and Britain had acknowledged a willingness to 'respect the right of all peoples to choose the form of government under which they will live'. On the other hand, a very powerful pressure group, namely the United States Navy, was in no mood to relinquish its hard-won control over the Pacific Islands, for security reasons. In this context, the notion of trusteeship played a mediating function. Moreover, Britain was careful to stipulate that it preferred self-government to independence as the objective for any Trust areas. Thus, the discussions that took place in the formulating conferences leading to the San Francisco conference in 1945 were subject to buffeting in different directions from pressure groups and governments. There were differences of principle and of emphasis, and disagreements about who should control which territory and on what basis. In this it was widely recognized that the former Mandates and any new Trust Territories would be subject to tighter international control than existing colonies. Nevertheless, Churchill had made it clear that he had not become His Majesty's Prime Minister to preside over the liquidation of the British Empire. However, the British Empire was subject to the changing *Zeitgeist*. Moreover, since the war was still raging, the question of international peace and security in the context of Mandates and Trusts was an important one, as well as economic openness in such territories, human rights and the prospect of self-determination or independence. There was also a policy of tit-for-tat in that the Soviet Union, which gave powerful support to the notion of the Trusteeship principle, also signalled its interest in obtaining a trusteeship over Libya to compensate for the United States Navy's determination to retain military control of the Pacific Islands.

As the war in Europe came to an end, Churchill's national administration in Britain gave way to a Labour government with a large majority in the House of Commons. While Churchill was an imperialist in the grand style, the Labour Party was imbued with very different ideas. Its colonial policy statement in 1943 called for the development of political self-government 'and the attainment of political rights not less than those enjoyed or claimed by those of British democracy', to be accompanied by 'the application of Socialist policy in the economic organization of the colonies and the acceptance of the principle of international supervision and accountability'. In 1944 the Annual Conference of the party urged the 'preparation for self-government without delay' of the colonies and stated; 'There must be a sincere determination on the part of those responsible for colonial administration to put native interests first in the priorities they organize ... with a view to making the interests of the colonial peoples primary beyond all doubt.'[4] However, not all the colonial powers exhibited such progressive views.

After France had suffered the humiliation of the Armistice and subsequent occupation, the Free French were able not only to repair to London as their principal base but also to parts of the French Empire, where they sought to preserve the honour of France and prepare for the eventual liberation of the Hexagon. Thus, the French government and political elite were in no mood to dispense with an empire that had enabled them to regroup and from which they were able to participate in the restoration of France to its rightful place in Europe and the world. While the material position of France was in political, economic and social terms much inferior to that of Britain, nevertheless its structural position in world politics was the same, and it was for this reason that Churchill insisted that France should be able to play a role as one of the Big Five.

With this background, the French had little truck with the notion of self-government or independence as a goal for the Trusteeship system, still less for colonial possessions as a whole, advocating no more than the 'progressive development of political institutions' which would be limited to Mandates and enemy colonies. The Netherlands, too, while accepting the Trusteeship principle for enemy areas, shared with the British and French a frank dislike of the term 'independence'. In this they were joined by South Africa. Britain, France and the Netherlands, and for that matter Portugal too, all looked towards a political development of their colonies within a framework and context that would maintain links with a metropolitan power, whereas South Africa wished merely to annex South-West Africa. The British were looking for a Trusteeship Council that would function under the Economic and Social Council and not be a principal organ of the United Nations. They had restrictive views about the rights of petition and visit which would be applicable only to former Mandates and new Trust Territories and not to colonies.[5]

The differences of opinion and strength of conviction both within and between countries, as well as other pressing matters, meant that the question of the future of Mandates and other potential Trust Territories was not finally decided until the San Francisco conference. This was because it formed part of a major debate about the future of colonialism and notions of international governance, responsibility and transparence. It is thus to San Francisco that we now turn to see how these fraught questions were resolved.

THE CHARTER

The Yalta Agreement established that there was to be a Trusteeship system into which the existing Mandates of the League of Nations could be incorporated, as well as territories detached from the enemy as a result of the Second World War, together with any other territories that might be voluntarily placed under trusteeship. However, the powers at Yalta decided that there would be no division of the spoils in San Francisco since the allocation of specific territories that might become part of the Trusteeship system would be left for later.

The Charter, as agreed in San Francisco, is shot through with elements that apply to Trust Territories and, indeed, to dependent territories more generally. This is hardly surprising since although the Charter was, in effect, a document negotiated by the United States, Britain and the Soviet Union, and is a document in which the structural power of the five permanent members of the Security Council is firmly protected, nevertheless it is also a document that contributes to furthering the interests of the small powers and dependent territories of all sorts. In short, any document that sets limits to the power of the strong is likely to be to the benefit of the weak. Thus, the principles that govern any Trusteeship system, apart from those concerned with sovereign authority, are likely to be of interest to many members of the United Nations system, since they protect rights and further development. This can be seen from the very beginning of the Charter, where not only is the scourge of war deplored in the preamble, but there is also a reaffirmation of faith in fundamental human rights, a desire to establish conditions under which justice and international law can be maintained, and a commitment 'to promote social progress and better standards of life in larger freedom'. To this end the signatories of the Charter undertook 'to employ international machinery for the promotion of the economic and social advancement of all peoples'. Yet at the same time the Charter is essentially a political document with let-out clauses primarily, but not exclusively, for the great powers. One such let-out clause is Article 2.7, which states: 'Nothing contained in the present

Charter shall authorise the United Nations to intervene in matters which are essentially within the domestic jurisdiction of any state or shall require the Members to submit such matters to settlement under the present Charter. . . .' Full use was made of this clause by South Africa in regard to its Mandate over South-West Africa, as we shall see below.

The United Nations has six principal organs, of which the Trusteeship Council is one, and such organs may establish such subsidiary bodies as may be found necessary. However, these principal organs are not equal, and in particular the Trusteeship Council is subject to the general oversight of the General Assembly and, insofar as Strategic Trust Territories are concerned, the Security Council. Indeed, this specific principle is also set out in general terms in Article 10, which states: 'The General Assembly may discuss any questions or any matters within the scope of the present Charter, and . . . may make recommendations. . . .' This includes, in Article 13.1(b), matters that pertain particularly to Trust Territories such as 'promoting international co-operation in the economic, social, cultural, educational, and health fields, and assisting in the realisation of human rights and fundamental freedoms for all without distinction as to race, sex, language, or religion'. Decisions relating to Trusteeship matters taken by the General Assembly are made on the basis of a two-thirds majority of the members present and voting, including the election of members to the Trusteeship Council.

Article 55, dealing with international economic and social co-operation, argues that the 'creation of conditions of stability and well-being which are necessary for peaceful and friendly relations among nations based on the respect for the principle of equal rights and self-determination of peoples . . .' requires the promotion of higher standards of living, full employment, the solution of international economic and other problems, as well as a universal respect for, and observance of, human rights and fundamental freedoms. While all member states pledged themselves to work in that sense, those that accepted the obligations of administering a Trust Territory incurred the obligation of some international supervision to ensure that they were carrying out their duties in an effective manner.

To a lesser extent, so did those who were responsible for non-self-governing territories. Their specific obligations were set out in the Declaration Regarding Non-Self-Governing Territories, which is Chapter XI of the Charter. Article 73 refers to 'the administration of territories whose peoples have not yet attained a full measure of self-government' in which those responsible for such territories 'recognise the principle that the interests of the inhabitants of these territories are paramount, and accept as a sacred trust the obligation to promote to the utmost, within the system of international peace and security established by the present Charter, the well-being of the inhabitants of these territories . . .'. These include the need to ensure 'due respect for the culture of the peoples concerned' and various forms of advancement, their just treatment and their protection against abuses. Significantly, they also include the obligation 'to develop self-government, to take due account of the political aspirations of the peoples, and to assist them in the progressive development of their free political institutions, according to the particular circumstances of each territory and its peoples and their varying stages of advancement . . .'. This also includes the obligation 'to transmit regularly to the Secretary-General for information purposes . . . statistical and other information of a technical nature relating to economic, social and educational conditions . . .', with the caveat that this is subject to limitation on security and constitutional grounds. Article 74 then goes on to stress 'the general principle of good neighbourliness, due account being taken of the interests and well-being of the rest of the world, in social, economic, and commercial matters', this being a potential but largely unused (and unneeded) lever for the United States to gain economic access to the markets of colonial territories.

Chapter XII deals with the international Trusteeship system. It is the high point of the Charter, insofar as international control of dependent territories is concerned. Article 76 states the basic objectives of the Trusteeship system as the furtherance of international peace and security and the promotion of the political, economic, social and educational advancement of the inhabitants of the Trust Territories. It refers further to 'their progressive development towards self-government or independence as may be appropriate to the particular circumstances of each territory and its peoples and the freely expressed wishes of the peoples concerned'. The use of the term 'self-government or independence' reflects on the one hand the philosophies of the colonial powers, who preferred self-government, and on the other the United States, the Soviet Union and, later, newly independent countries, who stressed the notion of independence. It is significant that the word 'independence' is included in Chapter XII dealing with the international Trusteeship system, whereas it is not referred to in Chapter XI which deals with the Declaration Regarding Non-Self-Governing Territories. Again, as might be expected, there is the obligation to encourage respect for human rights and also 'to ensure equal treatment in social, economic, and commercial matters for all Members of the United Nations, and their nationals'.

The territories that might form part of the Trusteeship system fell under three categories as set out in Article 77:

(a) territories now held under mandate;
(b) territories which may be detached from enemy states as a result of the Second World War; and

(c) territories voluntarily placed under the system by states responsible for their administration.

Article 77.2 states: 'It will be a matter for subsequent agreement as to which territories in the foregoing categories will be brought under the Trusteeship system and upon what terms.' This implies that not all territories in the first two categories need necessarily be placed in the Trusteeship system. Moreover, Article 78 states that the Trusteeship system shall not apply to territories that become members of the United Nations, a clause which is of some contemporary significance.

The terms of the Trusteeship as set out in Article 79 'shall be agreed upon by the states directly concerned, including the mandatory power in the case of territories held under mandate by a Member of the United Nations'. In the meantime, Article 80 reassures states that 'nothing in this Chapter shall be construed in or of itself to alter in any manner the rights whatsoever of any states or any peoples or the terms of existing international instruments to which Members of the United Nations may respectively be parties'. But the Article then adds that this 'shall not be interpreted as giving grounds for delay or postponement of the negotiation and conclusion of agreements'. It did, however, give the whip hand to those who had control on the ground.

Those who are to administer a Trust Territory 'may be one or more states or the Organisation itself' (Article 81), and the following Article states: 'There may be designated in any Trusteeship agreement, a strategic area or areas, which may include part or all of the Trust territory', and the approval of these terms, their alteration or amendment, were within the remit of the Security Council. However, Article 83 goes on to state that in political, economic, social and educational matters in the strategic areas, the Trusteeship Council shall provide assistance to the Security Council.

An innovation from the norms that prevailed in Mandates is contained in Article 84 in that in order to ensure that 'the Trust territory shall play its part in the maintenance of international peace and security . . . the administering authority may make use of volunteer forces, facilities, and assistance from the Trust territory in carrying out the obligation towards the Security Council . . . as well as for local defence and the maintenance of law and order within the Trust territory'. Article 85 states formally that 'the Trusteeship Council, operating under the authority of the General Assembly, shall assist the General Assembly in carrying out these functions', except for those matters directly pertaining to the Security Council through Strategic Trust Territories.

Chapter XIII establishes the Trusteeship Council, the membership of which is set out in Article 86 as follows:

(a) those Members administering trust territories;
(b) such of those Members mentioned by name in Article 23 as are not administering trust territories; and
(c) as many other members elected for three-year terms by the General Assembly as may be necessary to ensure that the total number of members of the Trusteeship Council is equally divided between those Members of the United Nations which administer trust territories and those which do not.

The members mentioned by name in Article 23 are the five permanent members of the Security Council. This proved to be awkward in later years when the number of administering powers declined, following the independence of a growing number of territories.

The functions and powers of the Trusteeship Council are held by the General Assembly but normally exercised under its authority by the Trusteeship Council, and they are stated in Article 87 as being the consideration of reports on territories submitted by their administering authority, the acceptance of petitions and their examination and consultation with the administering authority, the undertaking of periodic visits to the Trust Territories at times agreed upon with the administering authority and, as set out in Article 88, the formulation of a questionnaire on the political, economic, social and educational advancement of the inhabitants of each Trust Territory, which shall form the basis of an Annual Report to the General Assembly. The remaining three Articles of the Chapter established that each member of the Trusteeship Council has one vote and that decisions are taken by a majority of members present and voting. The Council decides its own rules of procedure and meets as required in accordance with the request of the majority of its members. It also has the right to call upon the assistance of the Economic and Social Council and of the specialized agencies.

The UN system was in part a development of the League of Nations' Mandate system, but it was also a great leap forward. In terms of developing from League practice, the League Council had relied on the Mandates Commission, which had been formed of individual experts. In addition, the League Assembly had taken a strong interest in the question of Mandates and this was in some sense reflected in the new arrangements. The Mandate Commission was the forerunner of the Trusteeship Council which was linked to the General Assembly and, for Strategic Trust Territories, to the Security Council. However, there is a difference in that the Trusteeship Council is made up of governments. The role of the individual was eliminated, which left a greater potential for a politicization of the process by governments. Such a politicization is potentially enhanced by the right of the Council to send missions to territories, a right which was not available to the League of Nations, and to send a questionnaire and debate its response. However, the great leap forward lies not in the Trusteeship system but in the Chapter on Non-Self-governing Territories. This was fully recognized by Field Marshal Smuts when he remarked: 'This scheme diverts in scope very largely from that old Covenant scheme. The principle of trusteeship is now applied generally. It applies to all dependent peoples in all dependent territories. It covers all of them, and therefore an extension has been given to the principle of the very far-reaching and important character.'[6] It was for this reason that the colonial powers emphasized at San Francisco, in the words of the United Kingdom delegate, 'a distinction between the *principle* of trusteeship which should guide Colonial Powers in the administration of their dependent territories (and should therefore be of universal application) and the creation of a special system of international *machinery*, to apply to certain specific territories'.[7] The potential battle lines were already being drawn. Nevertheless, it is evident that a serious attempt had been made to create colonialism with a human face. To what extent was this aspiration met, and to which territories was it applied? If the aspiration was met in the Trust Territories, would this hinder or hasten the wider and more fundamental process of decolonization that was already underway? While the Mandate system was undoubtedly progressive in its day in its effects on the process of the emancipation of colonial peoples, could the Trusteeship system be anything other than a convenient solution for a specific problem of former enemy territories, while the transformation of the global political structure took place elsewhere?

TRUST TERRITORIES: ACTUAL AND POTENTIAL

The Charter states that there are three categories of candidate for Trust Territories. Two of these can be dispensed with quickly in that all the Mandates from the League of Nations, except for two, were transferred relatively smoothly to the Trusteeship Council and no colonial territories have been placed voluntarily under the aegis of the Council. The two League Mandates that were not transferred to the Council were that for South-West Africa held by South Africa and that for Palestine held by the UK.

South Africa had resisted transfer and this gave rise to a considerable debate, to which we shall return later. In the case of Palestine, it was clear that the situation was extremely difficult. A reluctant Britain under heavy military pressure in Palestine itself was being virtually persecuted by the United States while trying to maintain a semblance of protection for the indigenous inhabitants of Palestine. At the same time, Britain was under intense pressure from world Jewry and many governments to permit uncontrolled Jewish immigration, which was understandable in the context of the Nazi policy of genocide and its aftermath, notwithstanding the implications for the indigenous people. The Trusteeship Council had little to do with Palestine and where the UN played a role it was in the General Assembly, with such proposals as the partition of Palestine. In the event, the British threw in the sponge and the matter was decided, at least in the interim, on the battlefield. It was therefore the greatest failure of the League Mandate system and one in which no actor appears in a particularly favourable light. Indeed, the reverse was more often the case.

The possibility of placing existing colonies under the auspices of the Trusteeship Council was for a time considered to be a very real one. However, it was quickly eschewed, although the option remains and might be appropriate even now for certain territories, as we shall discuss below. Perhaps the most obvious likelihood of making use of this provision was where a Trust Territory could be managed better in conjunction with an existing colony of a Trustee power, whereby the existing colony would be made a Trust Territory and the two jointly managed under the aegis of the Trusteeship Council. However, this did not occur. Indeed, the integration of the Trust Territory with a neighbouring colony for administrative purposes was a more frequent occurrence. It is also instructive to note that no serious demand within colonies was made for a transfer of a colony to the Trusteeship Council. Rather, those who wished for change did not look to the Trusteeship Council as an interim solution but wanted a policy of independence directly and this demand was made on the colonial power, often using other parts of the UN system to buttress the demand.

There remains then the third category of territory, which is those territories to be removed from enemy states at the end of the war. This did not concern Germany since Germany had lost such territories at the end of the First World War and the prime candidates were therefore those territories controlled by Japan and Italy.

In the discussions that took place at the end of the Second World War, there was a substantial range of possibilities for a number of Japanese territories, but in the event only one ended with the Trusteeship Council and then only in part since it was a Strategic Trust Territory. The territories concerned were Korea, Formosa, the Kurile Islands, Okinawa and the Pacific Island Mandate. There was some discussion about whether Korea could be a joint Trusteeship of the United States, the Soviet Union, the UK and China for a period of not more than five years prior to independence.[8] However, the military occupation of the Korean peninsula by the Soviet Union in the north and the United States in the south hardened in the context of the emerging Cold War and the idea of trusteeship was no longer on the agenda. The island of Formosa (Taiwan) had a different ethnic character from continental China. However, given that China was a permanent member of the Security Council and both the nationalists and Communists agreed that Formosa was an integral part of China, there was little or no discussion that Formosa should become a Trust Territory, eventually to have a choice between self-government and independence. The policy was clearly one of restitution to China rather than self-determination. The Kurile Islands, which were occupied by the Soviet Union at the end of the Second World War, might have become a Strategic Trust Territory rather than being incorporated into the Soviet Union. Okinawa, like Formosa, is ethnically different from its 'mainland', i.e. Japan. Indeed the islands were under United States control for a considerable period after the Second World War, but eventually the policy of restitution, rather than a Strategic Trust followed by self-determination, was the one that was followed.

The Pacific Islands were a different matter. They had been placed under Japanese control as a Mandated territory after the First World War, after Japanese military occupation had detached them from German administration. They were under the control of the United States Navy at the end of the Second World War and the US Navy was determined not to relinquish this control because of strategic considerations and the bitter fighting that had preceded their capture. In the collective mind of the US Navy of the time, the Washington Naval Treaty of 1921 had given Japan effective control over its Pacific region, which then enabled it to launch the attack on Pearl Harbor in 1941. The US Navy was in no mood to permit any such possibility in the future. However, in the long run annexation was not possible for the United States, since the United States had been strongly instrumental in seeking the adoption of a non-annexation policy, and therefore the outcome was a compromise whereby the Pacific Islands became a Strategic Trust Territory under the control primarily of the Security Council, but for non-strategic questions supervised by the Trusteeship Council.

The Italian case concerned Italian Somaliland, Libya, Ethiopia and Eritrea. Italian Somaliland, became, in 1950, a Trust Territory under the administration of Italy and, together with British Somaliland became independent in 1960. The transition to independence was relatively smooth, although probably premature since its future turned out to be sombre.[9] The question of Ethiopia was not a real one since, as a member of the League of Nations invaded by Italy, it had been liberated by British-led troops. The East African military campaign in the Second World War

led to British occupation of the Italian colony of Eritrea, as well as of
Ethiopia, and for some years Eritrea was under British control (1941–52).
However, Ethiopia had been the victim of Italian aggression and a cause
of guilty conscience, about which many former members of the League
felt a sense of shame. It was also a leader of the newly independent
African countries, and made no bones about its view that Eritrea formed
part of Ethiopia. However, it was also clear that this was not necessarily
the wish of the indigenous inhabitants of Eritrea. Nevertheless, for the
contextual reasons set out above, the United Nations first of all decided
Eritrea should be federated with Ethiopia as an autonomous unit on a
federal basis under the Ethiopian Crown in 1952, and then turned a blind
eye when in 1962 the colony was incorporated fully into Ethiopia. The
consequences, however, were not happy, either for Eritrea or for Ethiopia,
and a long and bitter war of Eritrean independence ensued which
included the demise of Haile Selassie's regime and his subsequent death,
major incursions by the superpowers, terrible famine and even to this day
a border conflict.

The Italian possessions were the object of much complicated bargaining
and the shifting of positions. Libya was the most controversial issue at the
time. There were a number of proposals which included an Italian
trusteeship, and a division into the provinces of Tripolitania and Cyrena-
ica, with the Soviet Union to administer the former and Britain the latter,
with France incorporating part of the south of Libya into Chad. The
policies of the United States, the Soviet Union, Britain and France veered
between various alternatives.[10] At one point, as the politicking went on,
the USA favoured the placing of Italian colonies under a direct (collective)
UN trusteeship as envisaged under Article 81 while the Soviet Union
suggested individual trusteeships for each territory. Later the positions
were reversed. The United States' position was very much influenced by
the ethnic Italian vote in the 1948 presidential elections and also by the
elections in Italy where the Communists were in a strong position. This
led to the idea of one state being in control, and that should be Italy,
while British military bases would remain in the country, as did those of
the United States. The Cold War ensured that the Soviet Union was kept
out of the Mediterranean, and the role of Italy as the brief administrator
(but not under the Trusteeship Council) garnered the ethnic Italian vote
for President Truman, Christian Democratic dominance in Italy and also
that Libya would come quickly to independence, which in fact it did,
joining the UN in 1955. It should be noted that, although a former enemy
state, Italy was considered and actually did become an administering
power in the case of Italian Somaliland. However, as a former enemy
state, Italy was not at that time a member of the United Nations and
therefore while Italy took part in discussions in the Trusteeship Council

until it became a member of the United Nations in 1955, it did so without a vote.

The net result of all these possibilities for the Trusteeship Council was meagre. The Japanese-mandated Pacific Islands became a Strategic Trust Territory, the administration of which was only partly under the auspices of the Trusteeship Council, and Italy's status changed from having been a colonial power to being an administering power in Italian Somaliland under the auspices of the Trusteeship Council. However, the debates were not yet over since it was necessary to make agreements for the transfer of mandated territories to the Trusteeship Council.

The Charter is not as clear as it might be about the method of transferring territories to the Trusteeship system. It refers to 'the states directly concerned', but it was not evident whether this was simply the members of the League of Nations Council, or all members of the League of Nations, or all members of the United Nations, or merely those states that were in actual control of the territories. In the end, despite significant Soviet objections, possession proved to be the determining factor. The Soviet Union considered that the relevant parties to negotiate a Strategic Trust Agreement were the five permanent members of the Trusteeship Council. Nevertheless, the existing mandatory powers or those in control of former enemy territory were in a position to exercise great influence since they were the ones with whom the United Nations had to make an agreement for a Trust Territory. Without such an agreement, the status quo would continue. This was all the more so with the Strategic Trust Territory since its relationship would be with the Security Council where the United States, which was the occupying power, also had a veto. There were in fact no other Strategic Trust Territories, even though President Roosevelt had at one time considered Gibraltar, Hong Kong and Panama to be candidates for Strategic Trust Territories because of their strategic position, and there were often suggestions such as Berlin, Jerusalem and Trieste. It would be unfair to imply that the Mandatory powers used their position of actual control in a negative way or in some sense to feather their own nests, but, on the other hand, the name of the game was clear. Nowhere was this more so than the designation of the former Japanese Mandate of the Pacific Islands as a Strategic Trust Territory. Moreover, the Trusteeship agreements, with one exception, did not include a pre-determined date of termination. Only the agreement for Somalia had a termination date of ten years after the signing of the agreement (1960). Nevertheless, all of the Trust Territories have now become independent and the last to do so was the Strategic Trust Territory of the Pacific Islands.

These 2,141 islands have a small population and are divided into four separate political entities: the Northern Mariana Islands, the Federated

States of Micronesia, the Marshall Islands and Palau. The Northern
Marianas voted eventually to become the United States Commonwealth
territory and the UN held plebiscites in the other three jurisdictions, with
Micronesia and the Marshall Islands ultimately becoming independent
with defence responsibilities remaining with the United States. This was
not, however, possible for Palau, since the constitutional requirement to
have a plebiscite with a 75 per cent majority was not attained. In 1992 the
constitutional requirement was reduced to a 50 per cent approval[11] so that
in 1994, following a plebiscite, Palau became independent and the 185th
member of the United Nations.

THE TRUSTEESHIP COUNCIL AT WORK

The Trusteeship Council began its work in 1947 with ten members.
Generally speaking, the work of the Council was smooth. It was perturbed
twice when the Soviet Union boycotted it, on the first occasion in 1947
over the issue of which states were directly concerned, as specified in the
Charter, to draw up the agreements, and, the second, over the issue of the
representation of China in the Trusteeship Council in 1950. Each member
of the Council has one vote, and there is no veto, so that decisions are
normally arrived at by a majority vote in open session. The Council
functioned through standing committees and *ad hoc* committees whenever
necessary.

The Standing Committee on Administrative Unions was established in
1950 and consisted of four members elected by the Council to deal with
the sometimes fractious issue of unions between Trust Territories and
adjacent territories. Although these administrative unions were included
in the draft agreements and were accepted by the General Assembly,
nevertheless, they were viewed with a certain amount of suspicion as a
potential form of back-door annexation, although in hindsight this was
hardly warranted. The second standing committee was on petitions and was
created in 1952. It had three administering and three non-administering
members of the Council who served for one session and the period
between sessions. Petitions were an important part of the Council's work
and could be received from within the Trust Territories or from outside,
and they could be presented in writing or orally – the latter usually being
in support of a written submission. Literally thousands of petitions were
presented and, together with visits, questionnaires and the reports to the
General Assembly, they provided the staple fare of the Council. On the
whole, the Council was not the theatre of great political debate. It
exercised oversight of the administrative powers concerned with questions
of peace and security, economic development and the prevention of abuse,

Table 5.1 Territories placed under United Nations Trusteeship

Territory	Previous Status	Administering Authority	Duration of Trusteeship
Cameroons (British)	Class B Mandate (UK)	United Kingdom	1946–61
Cameroons (French)	Class B Mandate (France)	France	1946–60
Nauru	Class C Mandate (Australia)	Australia (on behalf of Australia, New Zealand and UK)	1947–68
New Guinea	Class C Mandate (Australia)	Australia	1946–75
Ruanda-Urundi	Class B Mandate (Belgium)	Belgium	1946–62
Somaliland (Italian)	Italian Protectorate	Italy	1950–60
Tanganyika	Class B Mandate (UK)	United Kingdom	1946–61
Togoland (British)	Class B Mandate (UK)	United Kingdom	1946–57
Togoland (French)	Class B Mandate (France)	France	1946–60
Trust Territory of the Pacific Islands	Class C Mandate (Japan)	United States	1947–94 (Palau)
Western Samoa	Class C Mandate (New Zealand)	New Zealand	1946–62

Source: amended from A. LeRoy Bennett, *International Organization*, 2nd edn (Englewood Cliffs: Prentice-Hall, 1980), p. 350.

so that the Trust Territories became independent in fairly short order, which also suggests that politically it kept pace with the times. Nevertheless, the Trusteeship Council was essentially a lowly and docile body since it was dominated by the veto-holding powers and the administering powers. The great debates on colonialism took place elsewhere, chiefly in the General Assembly and in its committees.

Inis Claude remarks that the Trusteeship Council 'did not modify the principle that *international influence,* rather than *control,* should be the distinctive mark of Trusteeship'.[12] Nevertheless, the Charter did contain fora for fierce debates about colonialism, even though none of the three Chapters of the Charter – XI, XII and XIII – specifically mentions the principle of self-determination, while the Trusteeship Council was limited to a relatively small number of Trust Territories. The Fourth Committee of the General Assembly dealt not only with trusteeship matters but also with non-self-governing territories in general. However, it was not until 1961 that this was buttressed by the Special Committee of the General Assembly on the Situation with Regard to the Implementation of the Declaration of the Granting of Independence to Colonial Countries and Peoples, which was further strengthened by the Special Committee of the General Assembly against apartheid and the UN bodies dealing with Namibia (South-West Africa). In this framework the anti-colonial coalition had a majority and used it to noisy effect. One way in which it did this was, through the General Assembly Special Committee, to grant observer status and the like and to permit petitions, even from Trust Territories, despite the fact that the Trusteeship Council made ample provision for the presenting of petitions. There was therefore the possibility of shopping around for the most congenial forum for anti-colonial rhetoric and press-ure, which was usually not the Trusteeship Council but rather the Fourth Committee of the General Assembly. The most likely petitions to go to the General Assembly rather than the Trusteeship Council were those that were more political in nature, given the anti-colonial majority in the Fourth Committee and other General Assembly bodies. The Trusteeship Council dealt with administration rather than high politics. It was amelio-rative rather than a vehicle in the quest for structural change in global politics.

The United States' administration of its Strategic Trust Territory gave rise to political comment. This is in some ways to be expected since any Strategic Trust Territory, by virtue of being strategic, is likely to be so because of its military and political implications. However, the criticisms were not in essence due to the strategic position of the Pacific Islands but related to the use of them made by the United States. For example, in 1954 the United States conducted nuclear testing in the area and both the Bikini and Eniwotok regions were closed to visiting missions. Not only were the nuclear tests of no interest to the indigenous inhabitants of the region, they also prejudiced their safety. Moreover, the inhabitants were uprooted against their will and removed from their ancestral homes in the area where the testing took place. This was clearly an abuse of the rights of the inhabitants and the United States was strongly criticized in the Trusteeship Council for its behaviour. Article 76(d) of the Charter guarantees equal treatment for all members of the United Nations in regard to Trust Territories in social, economic and commercial matters. However, despite strong general support from the United States for this provision, when it came to the Strategic Trust Territory of the Pacific Islands the 'U.S. Agreement relating to the Pacific Islands alone of the trusteeship agreements does not provide for this but substitutes most favoured nation treatment amongst all UN members *other than* the administering authority; the U.S.A. can, therefore, arrogate to itself a preferential treatment by provision of doubtful legality'.[13]

To be sure, the struggle to end colonialism led to some nasty colonial conflicts involving Britain, France, the Netherlands, Portugal and South Africa, but in historical context the independence of the Indian subcontinent, followed by that of Ghana ten years later, indicated that fundamentally the principle of decolonization was no longer a generally contentious issue, although it was in particular instances. Prime Minister Nehru of India shocked many Africans when he stated that colonialism was dead when the Non-aligned Movement first met in the early 1960s. But Harold Macmillan, the British Prime Minister, in his 'Winds of Change' speech to the South African Parliament in 1960, and General de Gaulle in sometimes forcing independence on reluctant African territories in 1960 and in signing the Evian Agreements for the independence of the Algerian *départements* of France in 1962, were plainly in agreement. In this process, the United Nations was able, for the most part, to smooth the way, particularly through peacekeeping operations, which Dag Hammarskjöld and Lester Pearson clearly envisaged in the 1950s should operate wherever possible as a means of trying to separate the two great global issues of the 1950s and 1960s, namely the Cold War and the process of decolonization. The latter was an area in which the UN could and in fact did play a role, whereas the former was not.

Yet, despite clashes that were both dramatic and bloody at times, the process was well underway and had been from the inter-war period. The former colonial territories won a pyrrhic victory because although formal colonialism is dead, global structural exploitation is alive and well. The world's centre does not need colonialism in order to exploit its periphery. The colonial powers gradually realized that colonies were not an economic advantage and that they could obtain what they wanted by other means. Market forces in the process of globalization strengthened the centre of North America, Western Europe and Japan at the expense of the periphery. Even major semi-periphery powers such as Brazil, Korea, Taiwan, Hong Kong, Singapore and Nigeria are buffeted mercilessly by global economic forces. The United Nations' programmes of the specialized agencies and UNDP, and the activities of the International Monetary Fund and the World Bank are at best palliatives or at worst a vehicle for exploitation. All too often they exacerbate rather than ameliorate the situation. Put crudely, the former colonial powers, including the United States, are smug in their superiority, but whether they are wise to be so is beyond the scope of this chapter. Our concern now is with hard cases and analogous activities.

HARD CASES AND ANALOGOUS CASES

There is but one hard case, that of South-West Africa, but there are a number of analogous cases where the United Nations has undertaken Trusteeship-type activities, such as West Irian, Kosovo, Cambodia, Congo and, to a lesser degree, several other peacekeeping operations. In all of these analogous cases the Trusteeship Council has not had a role to play but rather it has been a matter for the Security Council or the General Assembly. The case of South-West Africa, however, was central to the work of the Trusteeship Council, at least in its early stages, since it was clearly a Mandate of the League of Nations in the C Category, which permitted its administration as an integral part of the territory of the administering state. Other C Category territories were transferred to the Trusteeship Council. South Africa refused to place the Mandate under the Trusteeship Council and instead proposed to incorporate South-West Africa fully into its own territory.[14] The case of South-West Africa gave rise to four advisory opinions and one judgment from the International Court of Justice, and as South-West Africa moved towards becoming Namibia the legal and political battle became enveloped in the Cold War until a solution was only found in that context. The first part of this process, namely the battle over whether or not South-West Africa should be transformed into a United Nations Trust Territory, concerns us directly since it relates to a Charter implication regarding transfer of the territory to the Trusteeship Council. As the issue became a wider one of decolonization linked to the question of apartheid and the Cold War as it developed in Southern Africa, then the Trusteeship Council became of lesser relevance.

The first opinion of the Court was given in 1950 at the request of the General Assembly. This opinion stated that South Africa's rights over the territory arose from Article 22 of the Covenant and the Mandate itself and therefore South Africa could not modify the international status of South-West Africa unilaterally. Thus, although the territory could be administered under the rules of a C Mandate, as part of its own territory, it could not be legally incorporated into the Union of South Africa. Moreover, the Court advised that it was not compulsory to place a Mandate under the Trusteeship Council and that this could only be done with the agreement of the Mandatory power. Clearly South Africa was unwilling to make such an agreement. Therefore, the territory remained under Mandate but the Court advised that the supervisory functions should now be passed to the General Assembly of the United Nations, although they should not exceed those pertaining in the Mandate system and should conform as far as practicable to the procedure of the Council of the League. However, in a further advisory opinion in 1955, the Court favoured the procedure of the General Assembly where reports and petitions required a two-thirds majority for their acceptance rather than the League Council's unanimity, and the following year the Court gave yet another opinion that the General Assembly's Committee on South-West Africa could grant oral hearings to petitioners on the grounds that although the League Council had never exercised this practice, the right had existed.

The legal battle continued when Liberia and Ethiopia alleged that South Africa had breached Articles 2 and 22 of the Mandate through the practice of apartheid and its attendant economic, political and social policies. Initially South Africa contested the jurisdiction of the Court, but this was rejected in a judgment of December 1962, but then in July 1966 the Court reversed its earlier judgment and found that it had no jurisdiction in the case and therefore did not broach the substance of the issue. Thereupon the General Assembly expressed its own outrage at the judgment of the Court, one which was shared by many legal authorities, and stated that in its view there had been a breach of the Mandate, of the UN Charter and of the Declaration on Human Rights. It therefore terminated the Mandate and established an *ad hoc* committee to consider the administration of the territory which resulted through Resolution 2248 of May 1967 in the establishment of a UN Council for South-West Africa with a UN Commissioner to administer the territory which, by a further resolution, was to be called Namibia. Neither the Commissioner nor the Council was able to visit the territory which the Assembly considered no longer to be under mandate but held illegally by South Africa. Sovereignty was regarded as being in suspense and the administration of the territory was under the direct control of the United Nations, even though it could not be exercised. In 1970, the Security Council requested an advisory opinion of the Court in the light of the Security Council resolution which had reaffirmed the General Assembly's termination of the Mandate and declared the continued presence of South Africa in Namibia to be illegal. The Court then advised that South Africa's presence in Namibia was illegal and that member states were bound to recognize it as such and to refrain from any acts or dealings that could be interpreted as sustaining South Africa's claim.

South-West Africa was therefore the case of 'the one that got away'. As soon as South Africa refused to make an agreement with the United Nations, then in effect the Trusteeship Council was irrelevant and the question became first a legal one and then a political one, which only had its final dénouement as the Cold War waned in Southern Africa. However, Namibia did provide a great success for the United Nations in the way that power was transferred under the auspices of the UN but within the political framework provided by agreements between the Western Contact Group, and especially the United States, the Soviet Union, Cuba, Angola and South Africa. In the end, the people of Namibia were able to go through the exercise of self-determination and, with the dismantling of the structures of apartheid in the territory, they were freed from abnormal abuse. In short, after a tortuous route, Namiba was finally able to achieve independence, helped by the action of the United Nations.

If the case of Namibia is one of a Trust Territory *manqué*, that of West Irian, West New Guinea or Dutch New Guinea, as the territory has been variously called, is perhaps the closest analogy to a Trust Territory since it involved the United Nations acting as an executive authority ostensibly with the interests of the indigenous population in mind. The history of West Irian was an unhappy one.

The cataclysmic effect on Western legitimacy in Asia of the defeat of the United States, Britain, France and the Netherlands by Japan has been alluded to earlier. The Japanese surrender on 15 August 1945 was followed by the proclamation of the independence of Indonesia two days later, a proclamation the Netherlands refused to accept. This led to a period of armed struggle and negotiation which culminated in the Charter of Transfer of Sovereignty of 27 December 1949. However, the status of Western New Guinea was exempted from this transfer and the status quo was maintained with a stipulation that within a year from the date of transfer of sovereignty to Indonesia the question of the political status of New Guinea would be determined by bilateral negotiations between Indonesia and the Netherlands. This led to a series of protracted negotiations that produced no agreement and a classic argument developed between the Indonesians arguing restitution of the former territory of the Dutch East Indies and the Dutch arguing in favour of self-determination, with the United Nations acting as the forum. There was no provision in the Charter of Transfer of Sovereignty which would decide the outcome if there was an absence of agreement between the Netherlands and Indonesia.

Although the Indonesians initially had a good deal of support in the United Nations General Assembly for their position over West Irian, this support gradually withered when the Indonesians insisted on the restitution of what they considered to be a divided entity. For example, in 1960 the Malaysians proposed the creation of a trusteeship for the territory, with the Netherlands, Australia and Malaysia sharing the trusteeship role.

The Dutch accepted this provided that the UN was not given the right to pronounce on the question of sovereignty, whereas Indonesia demurred because, as Luard put it, 'the logical end of UN Trusteeship was independence'.[15] However, the Netherlands had done itself no great service by being dilatory in establishing some form of representative assembly. There was thus a very weak indigenous voice. The following year, Australia, which had been very vigorous in its diplomacy led by Herb Evatt and John Burton in support of Indonesian independence and which was the Trustee power in the other part of the island of New Guinea, proposed a final outcome which should be the process of self-determination by the people of the entire island. At the same time, the General Assembly was moving towards a similar view of self-determination, rather than restitution, in the passing in 1960 of General Assembly Resolution 1514 on the Declaration of the Granting of Independence to Colonial Countries and Peoples. The Netherlands government then took the bull by the horns and proposed the setting up of a UN Commission for Netherlands New Guinea to assess the opinion of the people, consider a plebiscite under UN supervision and to examine the desirability of an interim administration by the United Nations. The Netherlands signalled that it was willing to terminate its sovereignty if the right to self-determination was properly safeguarded. Moreover, if the UN established an interim administration, the Netherlands would continue its economic support and co-operate fully with the administration.

This proposal led to strong opposition from Indonesia for whom the only question was the orderly transfer of authority while the role of the UN was to facilitate this transfer. In the General Assembly, the Netherlands won the vote, but not by a two-thirds majority. Unfortunately, this was the high point of the process insofar as the interests of the indigenous people were concerned because of two developments. First, the United States intervened on the side of Indonesia since it considered that Indonesia was a powerful actor in South-East Asia and beyond and therefore it was in the interests of the United States that Indonesia should support Western policies in a turbulent Asia and, in particular, with the growing conflict of Vietnam in mind. The second change was a virtual invasion of New Guinea by the Indonesian military.

US diplomacy was in fact crude pressure on the Dutch to make all the concessions necessary to appease the Indonesians. It was conducted by Ellsworth Bunker who acted as a less-than-honest broker. Bunker's initial proposals were that the Netherlands would transfer administrative authority to a temporary executive authority under the UN Secretary-General, who would appoint a neutral administrator. This arrangement would continue for a period of between one and two years and would prepare for an act of self-determination. In the first year, the international administration would run the territory, but in the second year UN staff would be replaced progressively by Indonesians who would have completed the take-over by the end of the year. The date of the act of self-determination was not specified but was clearly crucial. If it occurred while the international administration was still in place, then it was reasonable to presume that it was a genuine act of self-determination, whereas if the Indonesian administration was in place, then, given the past armed struggle it was likely that doubt would be cast on the validity of the outcome.

When these proposals were discussed by the parties, pressure was put on the Dutch to make further concessions. The period of international administration was reduced to seven months, while the act of self-determination was put back until 1969, i.e. six years after the Indonesian take-over. The territory would be under the control of a UN Temporary Executive Authority (UNTEA) from 1 October 1962 until 1 May the following year, whereupon Indonesian administration would begin, while the plebiscite in 1969 was to determine whether the population wished to remain part of rather than become part of Indonesia. Moreover, the arrangements for the plebiscite were the responsibility of Indonesia, with a representative of the UN Secretary-General in a role of advising, assisting and participating in the arrangements.

Even during the period of the UNTEA, only the top level of administration was genuinely international and Indonesians were engaged for the middle and junior posts almost from the start of the TEA. Similarly, on the military side, although there was a Pakistani force of 1500 men it was also necessary to make use of Indonesian armed forces which had been sent to the country to fight the Dutch. Thus in both civil and military terms the Indonesians were, in effect, running the territory on the ground, and UN officials acted in a way to avoid giving offence to Indonesia and discouraged public expression of anti-Indonesian or pro-independence views. In short, the UN could hardly conceal its anxiety to leave the Indonesians in control as soon as possible.

When in 1969 the question of a free choice arose as to whether the territory should remain in Indonesia, the Indonesian government decided not to act through a system of one-man one-vote, but to seek the will of the population through consultative assemblies formed in each regency or administrative region in West Irian. In these assemblies, decision-making was through a process in which debate took place until a unanimous decision was reached. Members of each consultative assembly included regional representatives elected by the people, organizational or functional representatives of political, social and cultural organizations including religious ones, being chosen by their respective organizations, and finally traditional representatives consisting of tribal chiefs to be chosen by the local councils. At the same time, the Indonesians banned any political organization in favour of rejecting ties within Indonesia on the basis that only those political groups that existed legally could be represented in the consultative assemblies. The outcome was that all eight consultative assemblies decided unanimously that West Irian should remain part of Indonesia. This view was endorsed by the UN General Assembly with only a single vote in opposition.

The whole story makes a very sad tale. First of all, a superpower bullies a small ally to act against its better judgement; second, a major regional power uses military force in conjunction with the pressure from the superpower; and third, the United Nations connives at a process of restitution in which the will of the local people is not given a reasonable chance to be ascertained and freely expressed. The whole sorry business also set a precedent for East Timor when Portuguese power collapsed. Restitution without consultation is a recipe for tears, and the United States and the United Nations have more than a little to answer for in this sordid affair.

In the case of West Irian the idea of trusteeship was mentioned, but was rejected by one of the parties, although presumably the Netherlands could have acted unilaterally at the risk of further embittering a deteriorating situation. It would also have raised an interesting issue about whether the Trusteeship Council was obliged to accept a territory to be placed in trust or whether it could refuse to do so. However, this was a genuine possibility in the sense that the Netherlands New Guinea was a dependent territory. The other two analogous cases are Cambodia and Kosovo, which are more analogous to Class A Mandates in the League System than UN Trust Territories in that they are both sovereign but for a time not fully independent, although as in the case of Class A Mandates, full independence was expected in short order. This clearly took place in the case of Cambodia in that the UN's role was envisaged for a finite period and where, on the whole, it was remarkably successful in extremely difficult circumstances in allowing the Cambodian people a new opportunity for self-determination. However, there is no evident time limit to the likely involvement of the UN administration (UNMIK) in Kosovo, the nature of which seems a recipe for tears.[16] In still other cases the United Nations has been involved in various aspects of administration in collapsed states such as the Congo with mixed results. In none of these instances has the Trusteeship Council been involved and the control mechanisms for UN activity have normally been through the Security Council and the General Assembly and their subsidiary bodies.

PRINCIPLES AND POLICIES

The Trusteeship Council (and the ideas behind it) take further an idea that
was rooted in the nineteenth century but which first received cogent
institutional expression in the League of Nations and was further developed in the Charter of the United Nations; that is the notion of responsibility of the administering powers for the governance of the territories
they control, whether they be colonial territories or more specifically
Mandates or Trust Territories. The Trusteeship Council, in its practice,
became a standard-setting body, and if a colonial power in its non-Trust
Territories wished to accrue international legitimacy, then it had to adopt
the standards that pertained in the Trusteeship Council and its practices.
Any governing power that did not meet these standards could hardly
claim to have a policy of good governance and thereby to have an
accolade of some degree of international legitimacy. Perhaps the most
important standard was that colonialism was not a permanent state of
affairs, and thus the Trusteeship Council embodied the idea that not only
must Trust Territories eventually be given the opportunity for self-
government or independence but that so too should other dependent
territories. Thus the Trusteeship Council's underlying philosophy was, in
essence, anti-colonial. Until 1960 it was perhaps the lead agency in the
UN system in developing this philosophy, but following the independence
of a large number of states in Africa, the Caribbean and the Pacific,
beginning with Ghana in 1957, the cutting edge of the anti-colonial thrust
in the UN system moved from the Trusteeship Council to the General
Assembly and its subsidiary bodies. Thereafter, the Trusteeship Council
was in the business of closing shop as the Trust Territories each came to
independence.

   The Charter does not designate independence as the sole final goal for
dependent territories, but does indicate that self-government would be as
appropriate. Nevertheless, as the process of decolonization moved to a
rapid conclusion, with few exceptions, such as the Cook Islands, the idea
of self-government as a final goal received little support. In part this was
because the colonial powers (and the United States) could secure their
ends of economic access and political influence without having the tram-
mels of full administration, at less cost, and possibly more effectively,
than with a policy of enforced political administration. Thus there was no
opposition to the notion of independence as a norm.

   There was a swing, too, between the ideas of restitution notionally
to restore a supposed violated territorial integrity and those of self-
determination. Restitution is based on the argument that colonialism had
forcibly driven apart peoples who had formerly been or were naturally

together. The principle of restitution has been applied effectively and peaceably to Hong Kong and China, and forcibly by India in Goa and by Indonesia in West Irian and East Timor. Spain, in the case of Gibraltar, and Argentina in the case of the Falkland Islands/Malvinas both argue from the point of view of restitution and territorial integrity, but this view is vigorously contested by the local populations of the two colonies. Moreover, Africa has for the most part rejected the idea of restitution since the OAU accepted the validity of imposed colonial boundaries no matter what nonsense they made of pre-existing and contemporary patterns of economic, social and cultural development. In the UN system, the dominant view has therefore become that of self-determination rather than restitution. The case of West Irian is an interesting one, since it was at the cusp of where attitudes were changing between ideas of restitution and ideas of self-determination, principally under the impact of the new African members of the UN system. Indeed, one of the major policies of the United Nations now in the context of collapsed states is that those peoples should be helped into a position whereby they can once again go through an act of self-determination. This was the underlying justification for the UN intervention in Cambodia, although the idea of self-determination in the case of the UN administration in Kosovo is fraught with difficulties for the major sponsoring powers who are providing the political backing for the UN in Kosovo.

There is a great debate in the UN system and beyond on the relative importance of the idea of domestic jurisdiction as safeguarded in Article 2.7 and the notion of the universality of human rights. Clearly, ideas have changed on this subject and in some instances a situation of the abuse of human rights can lead to the United Nations acting collectively to override the notion of the supremacy of domestic jurisdiction. A prime example of this is the UN's activities against apartheid, but it should not be forgotten that the Trusteeship Council was in the early years of the UN at the forefront of this debate, like the League's Mandate system before it. It emphasized the protection of indigenous peoples from abuse and the development of their political, social and economic capacities leading to a possibility of self-determination, either internally through self-government or externally as well through independence. Moreover, it was able to buttress this with the sending of missions, by the requirement of reports and by their public debate and appraisal. In particular, it pioneered the idea of petitions not only from indigenous people but from outsiders. Administering powers could therefore be taken to task in the UN system by individuals and this was a powerful exemplar and harbinger of current debates. Moreover, the emphasis in the Trust Territories on the importance of questions of peace and security does foreshadow the notion of abuses of human rights as threats to international peace and security which may bring forth action under Chapter VII of the Charter. Security Council Resolution 688 regarding Northern Iraq makes such allusions and the intervention in Northern Iraq is under the shadow of Chapter VII. The intervention of NATO in Serbia, Kosovo and Montenegro regrettably did not have, initially in its military phase, clear backing from Security Council or General Assembly resolutions, even though its ostensible justification was one of the abuse of human rights. However, the point is that the Trusteeship Council helped to point the way for more dramatic developments in the Security Council and the General Assembly which are, in any case, its parent bodies.

FUTURE USES?

Article 78 of the Charter places restrictions on the territories that may be placed under the Trusteeship Council in that 'the trusteeship system shall not apply to territories which have become Members of the United Nations, relationship among which shall be based on respect for the principle of sovereign equality'. *Ipso facto* no member state, even a collapsed state, can therefore be placed under the Trusteeship Council and whereas the notion of respect for the principle of sovereign equality might be fudged, this would be more difficult with the status of membership of the United Nations. Thus, without an amendment to the Charter, the Trusteeship Council is severely limited. However, it is not without the possibility of some future tasks, whether as a dumping ground for remaining dependent territories or as a means of governance for elements of the global commons. Where collapsed states are concerned, the more likely fora are subsidiary bodies of the Security Council or the General Assembly, or regional bodies. However, these could act in the manner of the Trusteeship Council by following its philosophy and procedures after suitable adaptation to the new circumstances.

There would be little to be gained for the administering authorities of most of the remaining dependent territories for them to be placed under the Trusteeship Council. Standards of governance are now high and there is little evidence of abuse or the lack of development in any domain in most dependent territories. It might, therefore, be considered wasteful to revive the Trusteeship Council in such non-controversial cases. However, the remaining colonial possessions do provide some instances of controversy, and in particular the cases of Gibraltar and the Falklands/Malvinas whereby the administering power, Britain, insists that it will not act against the wishes of the local population, whereas the claimant powers argue in favour of restitution. Indeed, in the case of Gibraltar, the Treaty of Utrecht states specifically that if the British Crown is to relinquish its control over the colony, then in the first instance, if it is so wished by Spain, the territory would revert to the Spanish Crown. Only if either Spain or Argentina wished effectively to abandon their claim to the respective territories would the Trusteeship Council be useful. It would clearly be a major change of policy on their part, but the Trusteeship Council could then act as a face-saving device, since if Britain placed the territories under the Trusteeship Council and Spain or Argentina were also a member of the Trusteeship Council, then the powers concerned could claim that they were acceding to an act of self-determination under neutral auspices. If Britain were to place the territories under the Trustee-ship Council without the agreement of the powers requiring restitution, then this would raise the issue of whether the UN had to accept a trusteeship status for the territories concerned and would clearly be viewed as an unfriendly act by Britain from the point of view of Spain or Argentina. Again, could Britain place the colonies under the Trusteeship Council against the clear wishes of the local inhabitants? Moreover, as a face-saving device, the Trusteeship Council might not be the most obvious solution.

What, then, does the future hold for the Trusteeship Council? Following the independence of Palau and its admission to the UN, Trusteeship Council Resolution 2200 (1994) became operational and henceforth the Council will meet as and when occasion may require. Moreover, in the same year, the Secretary-General recommended in his Annual Report that the General Assembly should proceed to steps to eliminate the organ in accordance with Article 108 of the Charter. This, however, has not occurred, and some thought has been given to other potential uses for the Council. The Report of the Special Committee on the Charter of the United Nations and on the Strengthening of the Role of the Organization to the Sixth Committee of the General Assembly mentioned the consideration of proposals concerning the Trusteeship Council in the light of the Secretary-General's suggestion.

The government of Malta was particularly active in circulating an *aide-mémoire* in which it sought to redirect the Trusteeship Council into new domains that would benefit from the Trusteeship Council's 'essential attribute as depository of the principle of trust'.[17] The Maltese argued that the 'principle of trust through common responsibility proved to be a prototype of preventive diplomacy. It forestalled the conflict potential of differing claims of possession and ensured progressive development towards self-government or independence. . . .' The *aide-mémoire* then argued that this notion of trust and common responsibility had led to 'the recognition of such concepts as common heritage, global commons and global concerns. Trust is their common denominator. The body most appropriate to co-ordinate these intertwined activities of trust is the

Trusteeship Council.' The Maltese document recognized that 'existing agencies and bodies are and should remain the backbone and nervous system of worthy advance and rational implementation'. However, 'The distinct assignment of these bodies ... needs a co-ordinating core ... this co-ordinated approach is still lacking.' The Maltese argued that the Trusteeship Council 'is the focal point for such co-ordination'. The Maltese contribution led to some discussion in the Special Committee on the Charter. There were those who argued that bodies other than the Trustee-ship Council were better suited to carry out such tasks as becoming a trustee of the common heritage of mankind. Indeed, the view was expressed that the Trusteeship Council should be abolished although this would require an amendment of the Charter, but not all delegations accepted this view. Some noted that the Council employed no staff, held no regular meetings and did not make any call on the resources of the UN, but 'the possibility that its services might be called upon again in the future could not be entirely ruled out. Moreover, any amendment to the Charter was a very complex exercise and should not be undertaken for the mere intellectual satisfaction of removing texts pertaining to a non-working organ. Such an amendment might carry profound political and legal ramifications and might endanger the delicate balance between the various organs of the Organisation.' However, in regard to the Maltese argument, it was noted that for the Trusteeship Council to act in this manner constitutionally would in itself require significant amendments to the Charter, although the idea had 'many merits and deserved the most attentive consideration'.[18] A similar debate took place the following year when there was a particular concern expressed that a conversion of the Trusteeship Council 'would lead to a duplication of the work of other bodies, such as the International Seabed Authority, the Commission on Sustainable Development and the United Nations Environment Pro-gramme'. It was also emphasized that there was still potentiality for use of the Trusteeship Council in its traditional mode as has been suggested earlier.[19]

However, the Maltese suggestion did cause the Secretary-General to issue a note entitled *A New Concept of Trusteeship*.[20] Indeed, the Secretary-General proposed that the Trusteeship Council 'be reconstituted as a form through which Member States exercise their collective Trusteeship for the integrity of the global environment and common areas such as the oceans, atmosphere and outer space, and that the Trusteeship Council served to link the United Nations and Civil Society in addressing those areas of global concern, which require the active contribution of public, private and voluntary sectors'. The Secretary-General noted that 'while a number of inter-governmental bodies and legal instruments have been put in place ... there is no high-level deliberative form that could take a comprehensive, strategic and long-term view of global trends and provide policy guidance in those areas to the world community. A new high-level council with a well-defined mandate, that does not create overlaps or conflicts with existing inter-governmental bodies, could serve this purpose.' The Secretary-General then noted that a task force had been set up to prepare proposals on environmental and human settlement areas and this would be an appropriate body to consider this new concept of trusteeship. Thus, the Trusteeship Council is comatose but not yet quite dead.

Its contribution has clearly been to raise standards of administration and to act as an exemplar. It has also played its role in quickening the pace of independence and doing so in a peaceful manner. Moreover, the wheel is turning full circle, since in Kosovo we are in the process of inventing once again Class A Mandates, as in the League of Nations, where sovereignty exists but not independence. Such is the nature of a 'Strategic Trust' that has been created in Kosovo. It is to be hoped that activities analogous to those of the Trusteeship Council will lead to a growing point of civilization and a strengthening of civil society. It is no easy task and the Trusteeship Council has a record, albeit of modest achievement, of which it can be proud.

NOTES

1. Quoted in Benjamin Rivlin, 'Self-determination and dependent areas', *International Conciliation*, January 1955, no. 501, p. 221.
2. It is important, however, not to be overly sanguine. I am grateful to Ben Rivlin for reminding me of John Hobson's stricture in his classic *Imperialism: A Study* (London: Unwin Hyman, 1988), published originally in 1905, in which Hobson writes, 'The claim of a "trust" is nothing else than an impudent act of self-assertion' (p. 237).
3. I am grateful to Anique van Ginneken of the University of Utrecht, Department of History of International Relations for an English summary of her PhD thesis 'The League of Nations as a Guardian' (1992).
4. Quoted in Ernst B. Haas, 'The attempt to terminate colonialism: acceptance of United Nations Trusteeship System', in David A. Kay (ed.), *The United Nations Political System* (London: John Wiley, 1967), p. 293.
5. For an interesting analysis of these debates see *ibid*.
6. Quoted in Rivlin, *op. cit.*, p. 239.
7. *Ibid*.
8. For a discussion of views at the time, see the chapter on the Trusteeship system in Andrew Boyd, *The UNO Handbook* (London: Pilot Press, 1946). This is a semi-official publication.
9. See Lawrence Finkelstein, *Somaliland Under Italian Administration: A Case Study in United Nations Trusteeship* (New York: Woodrow Wilson Foundation, 1955).
10. I am grateful to Ben Rivlin for giving me help with these intricacies.

11. See Robert E. Riggs and Jack C. Plano: *The United Nations*, 2nd edn (Belmont, CA: Wadsworth, 1994), p. 191.
12. Inis Claude, *Swords into Plowshares*, 3rd edn (New York: Random House, 1964), p. 328.
13. D. W. Barrett, *The Law of International Institutions*, 4th edn (London: Stevens, 1982), p. 79.
14. The analysis that follows is closely based on *ibid.*, pp. 73–75.
15. Evan Luard, *A History of the United Nations* (London: Macmillan, 1989), vol. 2, p. 332. Luard's chapter on West Irian is a helpful and concise analysis of the case.
16. See A. J. R. Groom and Paul Taylor: 'The role of the UN in Kosovo', in Albrecht Schnabel and Ramesh Thakur (eds), *Kosovo and the Challenge of Humanitarian Intervention* (Tokyo: United Nations University Press, 2000).
17. *Aide-Mémoire*: The government of Malta on the Review of the Role of the United Nations Trusteeship Council, circulated in the spring of 1996.
18. Report of the Special Committee on the Charter of the United Nations and on the Strengthening of the Role of the Organization, General Assembly Official Records 51st session, Supplement no. 33(a/52/33).
19. Report of the Special Committee on the Charter of the United Nations and on the Strengthening of the Role of the Organization, General Assembly Official Records 52nd session, Supplement no. 33 (a/52/33).
20. General Assembly 52nd session, Agenda item 157 A/52/849, 31 March 1998.

CHAPTER 6

THE INTERNATIONAL COURT OF JUSTICE

B. G. Ramcharan

INTRODUCTION

An assessment of the International Court of Justice at the turn of the century requires one to recall that it was a hundred years ago that the Hague Peace Conference convened in 1899 with the express objectives of beginning the process of systematization and consolidation of international law and of promoting the peaceful settlement of disputes through arbitration and judicial settlement. The Hague Peace Conferences of 1899 and 1907 gave birth to the Permanent Court of Arbitration. The Covenant of the League of Nations, a decade later, gave life to the Permanent Court of International Justice and the Committee for the Progressive Codification of International Law. These two institutions became, under the Charter of the United Nations, the International Court of Justice – sometimes referred to as the World Court[1] – and the International Law Commission. The Permanent Court of Arbitration continues to make its services available to governments wishing to avail themselves of them.

Seen from this perspective one must be grateful that the International Court of Justice, building on the work of the Permanent Court of International Justice, has given the international community three-quarters of a century of experience with international adjudication. Keeping the concept alive and viable is already an important contribution. On top of that, one can say that the International Court of Justice has contributed in a significant way to the process of systematizing, consolidating, codifying and progressively developing international law. The century closes with a much clearer idea of the basic rules of international law than when it began. Between them, the Permanent Court of International Justice and the International Court of Justice have helped in no small measure in clarifying the relevant rules of international law. They have also added important principles of public international law. Examples in point are the imperative principles of international order, *jus cogens*, as they are termed in technical parlance; elements of international constitutional law, insofar as they touch on the competence of international institutions; and foundation principles of international relations.

The Court is far from having a stellar record. The unwillingness of states to submit themselves to compulsory adjudication has been one of the crosses it has had to bear. While the Court has counted among its numbers some of the finest international lawyers of its time, its benches have also been occupied by politico-legal entrepreneurs who have attracted harsh criticism.[2] On its benches have sat some who have trampled on human rights at home and then gone on to champion the principles of justice from its precincts.

In the South-West Africa cases of 1966 the Court lost touch with the pulse of the international community and with the aspirations of peoples of the world for justice against the then apartheid system. The Court has not yet been able to place international law in the position of undergirding the emerging international public order – particularly when it comes to co-operation between the political and legal organs of the United Nations in addressing the maintenance of international peace and security. It has, for the most part, not been a central player, and has served mainly by rendering technical opinions and decisions on those matters that governments were prepared to submit to it. Seen from the perspective of keeping the concept of international adjudication alive, historians might argue that the Court was wise in the circumstances in striking a balance between law and power. There have, however, been instances, such as its decisions in the Nicaragua case, when the Court held forth courageously in upholding the law against the most powerful country in the world.

In this chapter on the International Court of Justice we shall seek to discuss the Court's experience from the perspectives of its contribution to the facilitation of international co-operation and to the establishment of the legal underpinnings of the evolving international society. In a work on international co-operation published in 1971, Paul Taylor looked at international institutions, diplomacy and international law through three sets of theoretical lenses (gradualist, pessimistic, optimistic) and concluded: 'The more optimistic views seem to me to give a clearer impression of the progress which has been made; in achieving at least the beginnings of an international constitutionalism, international institutions have increased the level of international co-operation.'[3]

We shall retain as one of the topics for examination, the role of the Court in the development of international constitutionalism. We shall have in view the question Taylor posed about international law: '. . . is international law also acquiring an increasing strength? Are sanctions behind the law becoming stronger? Are we, in other words, moving towards a time when we will be able to speak of an international authority?'[4]

We shall also have in view a set of guidelines adopted in 1998 at a Colloquium on Parliamentary Supremacy and Judicial Interdependence which advanced, among others, the propositions that:

- Courts should have the power to declare legislation unconstitutional and of no legal effect. However, there may be circumstances where the appropriate remedy would be for the court to declare the incompatibility of a statute with the Constitution, leaving it to the legislature to take remedial legislative measures.
- Judges should adopt a generous and purposive approach in interpreting a Bill of Rights. This is particularly important in countries that are in the process of building democratic traditions. Judges have a vital part to play in developing and maintaining a vibrant human rights environment.
- While a dialogue between the judiciary and the government may be desirable or appropriate, in no circumstances should such dialogue compromise judicial independence.[5]

We think that guidelines such as these should be applicable in assessing the International Court of Justice and in looking to its future evolution. To begin with, we shall look at the hopes of the founders of the United Nations and of the drafters of the Statute of the Court. We shall then consider the Court's contribution to the peaceful settlement of disputes. We shall thereafter look at the Court's contribution to the development of international constitutionalism, its position regarding the principle of legality, its place in efforts for conflict prevention, and its contribution to the protection of human rights.

THE HOPES OF THE FOUNDERS

At the San Francisco conference on 25 June 1945, the rapporteur of Commission IV, that worked on the Statute of the International Court of Justice, told the assembled delegates:

I shall only mention here my firm conviction that the International Court of Justice resulting from our discussions in San Francisco will fatefully carry on the heritage of noble traditions established by the World Court at the Hague, which has functioned with such excellent results for more than twenty years, and that the just and impartial decisions which it will hand down will indicate a continued progress in the evolution of a judicial structure for the peaceful settlement of international disputes. Allow me to reaffirm here my faith in the triumph of right as the criterion of international relations of which the Court will be both the symbol and the expounder, and the hope that its powers shall extend progressively and unrestrictedly to all the members of the organization and to the states which may be permitted in the future to adhere to the Statute.[6]

The San Francisco conference unanimously recommended that members of the United Nations proceed as soon as possible to 'make declarations recognizing the obligatory jurisdiction' of the Court. Thereafter the United Nations General Assembly urged on members, in 1947, the 'desirability of the greatest possible number of states accepting this jurisdiction with as few reservations as possible'.[7]

It would be fair to say that none of these expectations of the drafters of the Statute of the International Court of Justice has yet been fulfilled. As far as acceptances of the compulsory jurisdiction of the Court is concerned, the number of states that have done so still stood at the end of 1999 at only 59. To date, the Court has delivered 60 judgments and rendered 21 advisory opinions. As to the hope of the rapporteur of Commission IV for 'the triumph of right as the criterion of international relations', it can be said that the Court tries to be 'the symbol and the expounder' but that the world is far from having attained such a level of maturity in the relations among states.

A distinguished former President of the Court, Sir Robert Jennings, in a thoughtful presentation at a commemorative meeting on the fiftieth anniversary of the Court, cautioned that 'It is important to appreciate that there are large and important areas of international relations where what is wanted is not a decision based upon the law, but a decision based upon political wisdom, or even expediency, and the lessons of political or administrative experience'.[8] He therefore counselled:

> The first thing I want to say about the International Court of Justice is that it needs to be envisaged not in isolation, but as one major partner in a general complex of different kinds of decision-making under the rule of law ... Judicial decision-making and political decision-making are very different from each other, and sometimes it may be necessary to choose between them in respect of a particular problem; but they are also complementary and can be used together to great effect. This ought to be the basic consideration when examining the relations of the Security Council and the International Court of Justice. Their functions are not rival but complementary.[9]

Sir Robert emphasized 'that any working society needs, besides the decisions of courts applying rules of law, decisions made for political reasons, even including reasons of political expediency'.[10] It is important to keep these observations in mind because they are relevant to an assessment of the balance between political and judicial decision-making and to a realistic understanding of what can be expected from the Court.

THE PEACEFUL SETTLEMENT OF DISPUTES

The Court has indeed made a useful contribution to the peaceful settlement of disputes. Since its establishment it has rendered decisions in 68 cases and 24 advisory opinions. It has rendered decisions in 12 applications for the indication of interim measures of protection.[11] As at 31 December 1999, 59 states had made declarations accepting its compulsory jurisdiction.

A perusal of the kinds of issues that have come before the Court in the exercise of its contentious jurisdiction shows that governments have been prepared to bring to it matters such as the use of international waterways; fishing rights; the protection of nationals; asylum; the interpretation of judgments; nationality issues; the expropriation of property; maritime boundaries; property rights; treatment of aircraft and crew; aerial incidents; territorial rights; right of passage over territory; application or interpretation of conventions; sovereignty over frontier lands; interpretation of arbitral awards; compensation for expropriation; the right to self-determination; delimitation of maritime boundaries; fisheries jurisdiction; nuclear tests; trial of prisoners of war; jurisdiction over the continental shelf; the treatment of diplomatic and consular staff; frontier disputes; the activities of military and paramilitary groups against a sovereign state; border and trans-border armed actions.

As to requests for advisory opinions, they have touched on questions such as admission to membership in the United Nations; reparation for injuries suffered in the service of the United Nations; interpretation of peace treaties; competence of the General Assembly with regard to the admission of a state in the United Nations; the international status of a non-self-governing territory; reservations to multilateral treaties; effects of awards made by a tribunal; voting procedures; interpretation of judgments of an international tribunal; admissibility of the hearing of petitioners; interpretation of the constitution of a specialized agency; obligations of members of the United Nations to contribute to its expenses; the legal consequences for states of a resolution of the Security Council; application for review of judgment of an administrative tribunal; the status of Western Sahara; interpretation of an international agreement; interpretation of the United Nations headquarters agreement; applicability of an international convention; legality of the use by a state of nuclear weapons in armed conflict; and legality of the threat or use of nuclear weapons.

Well-wishers and supporters of the Court naturally tend to play up the importance of the cases it considers. Belief in the Court leads to a desire to cast it in the most favourable light. Justice Bedjaoui, a distinguished former President of the Court, for example, has written:

In spite of what some scholars have been wont to advocate or predict, the Court is not currently seised of minor matters, neither is it seised merely of disputes of only moderate importance. It is seised of considerable, and even crucial issues, such as, for example, those raised by the requests for advisory opinions on the legality of the use of nuclear weapons ... No less important are, for example, the questions constituting the subject matter of the case concerning the *Application of the Convention on the Prevention and Punishment of the Crime of Genocide*. There can be no doubt that contentious proceedings have a significantly pacifying effect. On a number of occasions, the decisions of the Court on the merits, as in incidental proceedings, have made a decisive contribution not only to the settlement of disputes of very different kinds, but also, directly, to the maintenance or restoration of peace between the parties.[12]

While there is certainly truth in this assessment, the fact remains, as noted by another distinguished former President, Sir Robert Jennings, that, in respect of contentious cases submitted by states:

the dominant kind of case in the list comprises those over land boundaries and territory or over maritime limits. This kind of case is, of course, the legal dispute *par excellence*. The question at issue is one of legal entitlement.... [T]hey tend to involve, like real property claims in domestic law, the need to investigate claimed roots of title going back a long way into history.... [A]nother kind of dispute to which settlement by adjudication appears to have proved very suitable ... [is] the more obdurate disputes that have defied other attempts at settlement, often over a very long period of time.[13]

For the most part, governents still prefer to resort to political methods for the settlement of disputes, particularly the method of negotiation. Governments wish to maintain some control over the outcome they are prepared to accept. In my view, a fair assessment of the Court would be that of an institution which has rendered useful service in the contentious and advisory cases it has considered (in all about a hundred in half a century – an average of two per year), which is laying some foundations for a more central role it hopes will come in the future, which wavers between dynamism and timidity, between judicial independence and political sensitivity, and which is waiting for its time to come.

THE DEVELOPMENT OF INTERNATIONAL CONSTITUTIONALISM

Justice Bedjaoui, a wise and learned long-serving judge on the Court – cited earlier – has commented thus on the Court's handling of the Charter and its provisions: 'Discretion, measure, modesty, restraint, caution, some-times even humility, such appears to be the general keynote of the Court's conclusions when it has had occasion to deal with the interpretation of the Charter or to review the legality of the acts of organs.'[14] In all instances, he added, it has performed its office with a discretion that some may consider excessive.[15]

In reflecting on this assessment it needs to be borne in mind that for four out of its five decades the Court had to wrestle with the phenomenon of the Cold War and had to keep the concept of international adjudication alive. Wisdom and discretion were therefore to be applauded. Even in its fifth decade a cautious approach could be justified. Notwithstanding proclamations of the emergence of a 'new world order', major powers show no inclination to submit to the authority of international organiza-tions, not even the International Court of Justice.

Notwithstanding the arid conditions in which it has had to exist, the Court has nevertheless made some important contributions to the devel-opment of international constitutionalism. Some examples of this are given below.

Duties of a state towards the international community as a whole

In the Barcelona Traction case, 1970, the Court introduced an important concept of legal obligations owed towards the international community as a whole. The Court considered that an essential distinction should be drawn between the obligations of a state towards the international com-munity as a whole, and those arising *vis-à-vis* another state in the field of diplomatic protection. By their very nature the former are the concern of all states. In view of the importance of the rights involved, all states can be held to have a legal interest in their protection; they are obligations *erga omnes*.

Such obligations derive, for example, in contemporary international law, from the outlawing of acts of aggression and genocide, and also from the principles and rules concerning basic rights of the human person including protection from slavery and racial discrimination. Some of the corresponding rights of protection have entered into the body of general international law; others are conferred by international instruments of a universal or quasi-universal character.[16]

Elementary considerations of humanity

Earlier, in the Corfu Channel case, 1949, the Court had also laid an import-ant constitutional building-block in grounding duties based on 'elementary consideration of humanity'. The Court held that the obligations incumbent

upon the Albanian authorities consisted in notifying, for the benefit of
shipping in general, the existence of a minefield in Albanian territorial
waters and in warning the approaching British warships of the imminent
danger to which the minefield exposed them. Such obligations were based,
not on the Hague Convention of 1907, No. VIII, which was applicable in
time of war, but on 'certain general and well-recognized principles, namely:
elementary considerations of humanity, even more exacting in peace than
in war'; the principle of the freedom of maritime communication; and
every state's obligation not to allow knowingly its territory to be used for
acts contrary to the rights of other states.[17]

Key principles of international relations: sovereignty, non-use of force, and non-intervention

In an early case brought before it, the Corfu Channel case, 1949, the Court
struck out on a laudable course of judicial independence and it made
pivotal findings crucial to the post-1945 international order and to the
international constitutional order of the future. The United Kingdom had
sought to argue in that case that it could intervene to secure possession of
evidence in the territory of another state, Albania, in order to submit the
evidence to an international tribunal and thus facilitate its task. Treating
this as a new and special application of the theory of intervention, the
Court held in forthright terms that it could not accept such a line of
defence:

> The Court can only regard the alleged right of intervention as the
> manifestation of a policy of force, such as has, in the past, given rise to
> most serious abuses and such as cannot, whatever be the present defects
> in international organization, find a place in international law. Interven-
> tion is perhaps still less admissible in the particular form it would take
> here; for, from the nature of things, it would be reserved for the most
> powerful States, and might easily lead to perverting the administration
> of international justice itself.[18]

The Court would return to these issues nearly 40 years later in the
Nicaragua case (Merits), 1986.[19] In that case the Court rejected the justification of collective self-defence asserted by the United States of America
in connection with military and paramilitary activities in and against
Nicaragua. It found that by training, arming, equipping, financing and
supplying the Contra forces, or otherwise encouraging, supporting and
aiding military and paramilitary activities in and against Nicaragua, the
United States of America had acted, against Nicaragua, in breach of its
obligations under customary international law not to intervene in the
affairs of another state.

The Court further decided that the United States of America, by certain attacks in Nicaraguan territory in 1983–84 and further by acts of intervention that involved the use of force, had acted against Nicaragua in breach of its obligation under international law not to use force against another state. In addition, the United States of America, by directing or authorizing overflights of Nicaraguan territory, and by acts imputable to the United States, had acted against Nicaragua in breach of its obligation under customary international law not to violate the sovereignty of another state.

By laying mines in the internal or territorial waters of Nicaragua, the Court further held, the United States of America had acted against Nicaragua in breach of its obligations under customary international law not to use force against another state, not to intervene in its affairs, not to violate its sovereignty, and not to interrupt peaceful maritime commerce. The United States of America, by failing to make known the existence and location of the mines laid by it, had acted in breach of its obligations under customary international law. Furthermore, the United States of America, by producing in 1983 a manual on psychological guerrilla warfare and disseminating it to Contra forces, had encouraged the commission by them of acts contrary to general principles of humanitarian law. The Court went on to hold that the United States of America, by attacks on Nicaraguan territory and by declaring a general embargo on trade with Nicaragua, had acted in breach of bilateral treaties between the two countries.

Having regard to the contemporary debate on the principle of humanitarian intervention being advocated by the current Secretary-General of the United Nations, Kofi Annan, the Court pertinently held in the Nicaragua case just referred to:

> The principle of non-intervention involves the right of every sovereign State to conduct its affairs without outside interference; though examples of trespass against this principle are not infrequent, the Court considers that it is part and parcel of customary international law. As the Court has observed in the *Corfu Channel Case*: 'Between independent States, respect for territorial sovereignty is an essential foundation of international relations' ... and international law requires political integrity also to be respected. The principle (of non-intervention) is not, as such, spelt out in the Charter. But it was never intended that the Charter should embody written confirmation of every essential principle of international law in force. The existence in the *opinio juris* of States of the principle of non-intervention is backed by established and substantial practice.[20]

The Court went on, in the case, to elucidate the principle of non-intervention. It noted that in view of the generally accepted formulations, the principle forbids all states or groups of states to intervene directly or indirectly in the internal or external affairs of other states. A prohibited intervention must accordingly be one bearing on matters in which each state is permitted, by the principle of state sovereignty, to decide freely. One of these is the choice of political, economic, social and cultural system, and the formulation of foreign policy. Intervention is wrongful when it uses methods of coercion in regard to such choices, which must remain free ones. The element of coercion, which defines and indeed forms the very essence of prohibited intervention, is particularly obvious in the case of an intervention that uses force, either in the direct form of military action, or in the indirect form of support for subversive or terrorist armed activities within another state.[21]

In an important passage in paragraph 241 of its decision, the Court stated:

> The Court considers that in international law, if one State, with a view to the coercion of another State, supports and assists armed bands in that State whose purpose is to overthrow the government of that State, that amounts to an intervention by the one State in the internal affairs of the other, whether or not the political objective of the State giving such support and assistance is equally far-reaching.

There are several contemporary situations in which this pronouncement would be particularly pertinent.

Legality of the threat or use of nuclear weapons

In this case the Court was asked for its advisory opinion on the legality of the threat or use of nuclear weapons. The Court held unanimously that: 'A threat or use of force by means of nuclear weapons that is contrary to Article 2, paragraph 4, of the United Nations Charter and that fails to meet all the requirements of Article 51, is unlawful.'[22]

By seven votes to seven, and by the President's casting vote, the Court held:

> It follows from the above mentioned requirements that the threat or use of nuclear weapons would generally be contrary to the rules of international law applicable in armed conflict, and in particular the principles and rules of humanitarian law.
>
> However, in view of the current state of international law, and of the elements of fact at its disposal, the Court cannot conclude definitively whether the threat or use of nuclear weapons would be lawful or unlawful in an extreme circumstance of self-defence, in which the very survival of the State would be at stake.[23]

The Court had an important pronouncement to make on the duty of states to protect the environment. It recognized

> that the environment is under daily threat and that the use of nuclear weapons could constitute a catastrophe for the environment. The Court also recognizes that the environment is not an abstraction but represents the living space, the quality of life and the very health of human beings, including generations unborn. The existence of the general obligation of States to ensure that activities within their jurisdiction and control respect the environment of other States or of areas beyond national control is now part of the corpus of international law relating to the environment.[24]

The Court held unanimously that 'there exists an obligation to pursue in good faith and bring to a conclusion negotiations leading to nuclear disarmament in all its aspects under strict and effective control'.[25]

The role of international organizations

In this case the Court had to grapple with issues involving the legal personality and the powers of international organizations. Analysing the United Nations Charter, the Court recalled that the purposes of the United Nations were set forth in Article 1 of the Charter. While those purposes were broad indeed, neither they nor the powers conferred to effectuate them were unlimited. Save as they had entrusted the Organization with the attainment of common ends, the member states retained their freedom of action. But when the Organization took action that warranted the assertion that it was appropriate for the fulfilment of one of the stated purposes of the United Nations, the presumption was that such an action was not *ultra vires* the Organization:

> If it is agreed that the action in question is within the scope of the function of the Organisation but it is alleged that it has been initiated or carried out in a manner not in conformity with the division of functions among the several organs which the Charter prescribes, one moves to the internal plane, to the internal structure of the Organisation. If the action was taken by the wrong organ, it was irregular as a matter of that internal structure, but this would not necessarily mean that the expense incurred was not an expense of the Organisation. Both national and international law contemplate cases in which the body corporate or politic may be bound, as to third parties, by an *ultra vires* act of an agent.
>
> In the legal systems of States, there is often some procedure for determining the validity of even a legislative or governmental act, but no analogous procedure is to be found in the structure of the United Nations. Proposals made during the drafting of the Charter to place the ultimate authority to interpret the Charter in the International Court of Justice

were not accepted; the opinion which the Court is in course of rendering is an *advisory* opinion. As anticipated in 1945, therefore, each organ must, in the first place at least, determine its own jurisdiction. If the Security Council, for example, adopts a resolution purportedly for the maintenance of international peace and security and if, in accordance with a mandate or authorisation in such resolution, the Secretary-General incurs financial obligations, these amounts must be presumed to constitute 'expenses of the Organisation'.[26]

THE PRINCIPLE OF LEGALITY

At the time of the drafting of the Charter in San Francisco explicit choices were made to renounce setting up a specific mechanism for interpreting the provisions of the Charter; to recognize that each organ would interpret from day to day those provisions of the Charter concerning its activities; to invite the Organization and states to consider themselves legally bound by any 'generally accepted' interpretation; and to leave the question of an authoritative interpretation of the Charter open for the time being.[27]

In 1949, in the reparations case, the Court laudably held that it had the powers to interpret the Charter of the United Nations although no such power had been expressly conferred upon it in either the United Nations Charter, its own Statute, or Rules of Court.[28] Unfortunately, however, in its advisory opinion of 1971 on Namibia the Court took the view that it lacked powers of review over the actions of organs of the United Nations. In that case the Court had been faced with a challenge to the legal validity and effect of General Assembly Resolution 2145 (XXI) and Security Council Resolution 276 (1970) whose legal consequences it had been asked to advise upon. The Court took the view that it did not possess powers of judicial review or appeal in relation to these United Nations organs. Nor did the validity of the two resolutions form the subject of the request for its advisory opinion. This position of the Court was trenchantly criticized by Judges Fitzmaurice, Gros and Onyeama. As Judge Onyeama pointed out: 'I do not conceive it as compatible with the Judicial function that the Court will proceed to state the consequences of acts whose validity is assumed without itself testing the lawfulness of the origin of those acts.'[29] Aspects of legality in its own composition also arose in this case. The participation of some members of the Court in this case was criticized on the ground that they had been associated with actions or views on matters that the Court had been called to pronounce upon. In particular, the participation of its own President had been challenged on the ground that he had played a part before he came to the Court in drafting a relevant UN resolution on Namibia. Dr Rosalyn Higgins, now a member of the

Court, commented: 'I myself feel that one Judge who played a part before he came to the Court, in drafting a relevant resolution on Namibia, should have stood down.'[30] In the Lockerbie case,[31] Libya, on 3 March 1992, referred to the Court what it considered a legal issue concerning the interpretation and application of the Montreal Convention. It sought a decision as to whether it was its duty under international law to extradite two of its nationals, accused of the destruction of a Pan Am aircraft in flight, and hand them over to the United States and British judicial authorities. Libya had been called upon to so do by the Security Council, to which the matter had previously been referred by the United States, the United Kingdom and France.

On 14 April 1992, the Court decided that it was not in the circumstances required to indicate provisional measures as requested by Libya but that this did not mean that the Court considered the case to have been taken out of its hands, despite the fact that the Security Council, for its part, had already adopted Resolution 748 of 31 March 1992 emphasizing that Libya must extradite its nationals or face sanctions. This decision has been severely criticized as an abdication of authority by the Court. It has been forcefully argued that the Court should be willing to consider legal issues properly referred to it, even in respect of matters that are simultaneously the subject of consideration in the Security Council. This point is of some importance at a time of great power imbalance in the relations among states. The International Court of Justice can play a role as a legal bulwark in upholding the principles and provisions of the United Nations Charter.

Justice Bedjaoui has commented on this issue: '[T]he Court's organic and functional autonomy is a logical necessity, since it would be absurd to allow states freedom to seize the Court as well as the Council if the Court were obliged to bow to the other organ. What would be the point of any concurrent referral to the Court if the Council were hierarchically able to place any restraint upon its [the Court's] action?'[32]

CONFLICT PREVENTION

At the start of the twenty-first century the earnest search for the peaceful settlement of disputes is on conflict prevention. In the past decade or so secretaries-general of the United Nations have sought to push an agenda of conflict prevention. As part of this process Secretary-General Pérez de Cuéllar established an office to help detect and prevent conflicts. This task is now being carried out by the Department of Political Affairs. The emphasis on conflict prevention was given a big push in Secretary-General Boutros Boutros-Ghali's *An Agenda for Peace* (1992). The current

Secretary-General, Mr Kofi Annan, and successive declarations of the Security Council have sought to emphasize the importance of conflict prevention.

The foreign ministers of the G8 countries met in Berlin on 16 and 17 December 1999 to make conflict prevention a priority in their political agenda for the years to come. In a press communiqué issued on this occasion they remarked that recent regional conflicts and their history, in particular, had demonstrated time and again that there was not a lack of 'early warning' but 'early decision', and long-term, concrete and sustainable strategies of prevention. The foreign ministers, recalling the mandate of the United Nations for the maintenance of international peace and security, 'reaffirmed that a reformed and effective UN remained central to our vision to this end'.[33]

With this kind of importance being accorded to conflict prevention it is reasonable to ask what has been or should be the role of the principal judicial organ of the United Nations in this sphere. The record does not show much of a role for the Court in this area. Supporters of the Court nevertheless strive to cast it in a positive light. In the words of a respected current member of the International Court of Justice, Mr Weeramantry, 'over the past fifty years, the court has provided a focal point for the peaceful resolution of international disputes, for radiating through the entire global community a consciousness of the international rule of law, for injecting an authoritative legal element into the processes of preventive diplomacy, and for developing international law to serve the needs of a rapidly changing world'.[34] Another eminent member, Justice Bedjaoui, then President of the Court, has claimed that 'the advisory procedure . . . appears to be at least an instrument of "preventive diplomacy", a privileged means, whereby the Court can defuse tensions and prevent conflicts by hearing and determining cases'.[35]

One can understand these submissions but it would nevertheless be accurate to say that, as matters stand at present, the Court rarely contributes to preventive action as such. For this to change there should be more of a willingness on the part of the Security Council to refer legal issues to the Court for its advice. It would also be helpful if the Secretary-General of the United Nations were granted the power to refer legal issues to the Court. This has been proposed by different secretaries-general but has not so far been viewed with favour by leading governments. Discussing the Court 'as an instrument of world governance' Professor Georges Abi-Saab, while noting that 'preventive diplomacy' as a strategy for the maintenance of peace and security usually refers primarily to activities of the political organs of the UN, pointed out, however, that 'the Court, as the "principal judicial organ of the UN", can play a much more active role in conjunction with these organs to that end'.[36] Seen from this perspective the Court's decision in the Lockerbie case not to take up a matter that was being addressed by the Security Council, came as a great disappointment to many.[37]

THE PROTECTION OF HUMAN RIGHTS[38]

The Court has not so far been given a significant role when it comes to the protection of human rights. There are human rights treaties such as the Convention against Genocide that provide for referral of issues to the Court with regard to applicability or interpretation, but these have remained largely unused. It was only recently that a referral was made to the Court under the Genocide Convention. When the International Covenants on Human Rights were being drafted, proposals were made to give substantive roles to the Court in the scheme of implementation of the Covenants but, in the Cold War environment then prevailing, these did not find favour.

Issues of human rights have come up in the Court insofar as it has had to address situations involving the principle of self-determination, situations involving the issue of non-discrimination, and issues pertaining to the Genocide Convention and the right to life. On the issue of self-determination, the Court, in its Namibia advisory opinion of 1971, noted the development of international law in regard to non-self-governing territories, in the Charter of the United Nations, which, it observed, 'made the principle of self-determination applicable to all of them'.[39] In the Western Sahara case, the Court confirmed and emphasized 'that the application of the right of self-determination requires a free and genuine expression of the will of the peoples concerned'.[40]

On human rights and non-discrimination, the Court, in the Namibia advisory opinion, referred to South Africa's violations of its obligations under, *inter alia*, the Universal Declaration of Human Rights and underscored the importance of the principle of non-discrimination stated.

In the case involving the Legality of the Threat or Use of Nuclear Weapons, the Court had to deal with the contention that the use of nuclear weapons would violate the right to life as guaranteed in Article 6 of the International Covenant on Civil and Political Rights, as well as in certain regional instruments for the protection of human rights. Article 6, paragraph 1, of the International Covenant states: 'Every human being has the inherent right to life. This right shall be protected by law. No one shall be arbitrarily deprived of his life.'

The Court made important pronouncements on the meaning and scope of this provision:

The Court observes that the protection of the International Covenant of Civil and Political Rights does not cease in times of war, except by operation of Article 4 of the Covenant whereby certain provisions may be derogated from in a time of national emergency. Respect for the right to life is not, however, such a provision. In principle, the right not arbitrarily to be deprived of one's life applies also in hostilities. The test of what is an arbitrary deprivation of life, however, then falls to be determined by the applicable *lex specialis*, namely, the law applicable in armed conflict which is designed to regulate the conduct of hostilities. Thus whether a particular loss of life, through the use of a certain weapon in warfare is to be considered an arbitrary deprivation of life contrary to Article 6 of the Covenant, can only be decided by reference to the law applicable in armed conflict and not deduced from the terms of the Covenant itself.[41]

CONCLUDING OBSERVATIONS

A commemorative volume on the occasion of the fiftieth anniversary of the Court set forth what the Secretary-General of the United Nations and leading members of the Court considered its landmark achievements. It would be useful in concluding this chapter to present some of their assessments before offering a few personal concluding observations. For the Secretary-General of the United Nations the jurisprudence of the Court has been more than a mere continuation of that of its predecessor, the Permanent Court of International Justice, since many of the Court's decisions have had a profound impact on the structure of different domains of international law and upon the very foundations of the international legal system and the modern order of international relations. In his assessment the Court has dealt successfully with some of the most difficult international disputes of our time. He also considers that the advisory opinions which it has given have been of fundamental importance to the functioning of the United Nations and to the stability of its constitutional order: 'They have been instrumental, too, in maintaining a uniform interpretation of the Organization's law.'[42]

The United Nations' Legal Counsel paid 'tribute to the contribution which the Court has made to the further development of international law'.[43] In his view, the Court has made a substantial contribution to the development of international law, in particular the law of international organizations and the doctrine of their international personality.[44]

One of the foremost authorities on the Court, Shabtai Rosenne, has offered the assessment that 'in its first fifty years the Court has brought out a series of quite unsuspected possibilities for the judicial settlement of international disputes, lying embedded in the Statute. One cannot point to any single topic of international law and say that there is the principal contribution of the International Court to its development. The work of the Court has become pervasive in virtually every branch of the law.'[45] It is an impressive record that, in the words of Sir Robert Jennings, 'it is not easy to find a decision of the present Court which has not either been complied with fully or has had at least an important effect'.[46]

A quarter of a century ago, around the twenty-fifth anniversary of the Court, Ian Brownlie suggested in an assessment of the Court that the following factors, among others, explained the reluctance of states to resort to the Court: the political fact that hauling another state before the Court is often regarded as an unfriendly act; the greater suitability of other tribunals and other methods of review for both regional and technical matters; the general conditions of international relations; preference for the flexibility of arbitration in comparison with a compulsory jurisdiction. His evaluation was that, given the conditions of its existence, the Court had made a reasonable contribution to the maintenance of civilized methods of settling disputes, but that it had

> not been at all prominent in the business of keeping the peace; indeed, the provisions of the United Nations Charter do not place emphasis on the role of the Court. In certain respects, however, the Court has been influential, viz., in the development of international law as a whole as a result of its jurisprudence and in the giving of advisory opinions on the interpretation of the United Nations Charter and other aspects of the law of International Organizations.[47]

This, in our submission, remains a valid assessment of the Court at the start of the twenty-first century.

We would, overall, maintain the assessment of the Court offered earlier: that of an institution which has rendered useful service in the contentious and advisory cases it has considered, which is laying some foundations for a more central role it hopes will come in the future, which wavers between dynamism and timidity, between judicial independence and political bending, and which is waiting for its time to come. As we have sought to demonstrate, it has contributed some important pillars to the constitutional architecture of future world society.

NOTES

1. See Georges Abi-Saab, 'The International Court as World Court', in V. Lowe and M. Fitzmaurice (eds), *Fifty Years of the International Court of Justice* (Cambridge: Cambridge University Press, 1996), pp. 3–16.

2. Professor G. Abi-Saab has pointed out that 'Article 2 of the Statute does not provide for another alternative cursus or curriculum, though a third breed is becoming increasingly more visible: neither the pure scholar – jurisconsult – nor the pure legal practitioner – judge, but the "legal diplomat". He or she has studied law and international law without, however, necessarily or usually attaining the status of jurisconsult; and he or she practices it, not, however, through the bar and the courts of his or her country but in Ministries of Foreign Affairs and the fora of multilateral diplomacy.' in C. Peck and R. S. Lee, (eds), *Increasing the Effectiveness of the International Court of Justice: Proceedings of ICJ/UNITAR Colloquium to Celebrate the 50th Aniversary of the Court* (Geneva: United Nations Publications, 1997), pp. 167–68.
3. Paul Taylor, *International Co-operation Today: The European and the Universal Pattern* (London: Elek, 1971), p. 102.
4. *Ibid.*, p. vii.
5. See J. Hatchard and P. Slinn (eds), *Parliamentary Supremacy of Judicial Independence: A Commonwealth Approach* (London: Cavendish Publishing Ltd, 1999), pp. 18–19.
6. UNCIO, Vol. 1, DOC 1210 (English), p. 626.
7. L. M. Goodrich, E. Hambro and A. P. Simons, *Charter of the United Nations: Commentary and Documents*, 3rd revised edition (New York: Columbia University Press, 1969), p. 551.
8. Peck and Lee, *op. cit.*, p. 78.
9. *Ibid.*, pp. 79–80.
10. *Ibid.*, p. 85.
11. The corresponding figures for the Permanent Court of International Justice for the period 1922–46 were: contentious cases: 33; advisory opinions: 28; decisions on applications for interim measures: 6.
12. In Peck and Lee, *op. cit.*, p. 22.
13. *Ibid.*, p. 84.
14. M. Bedjaoui, *The New World Order and the Security Council: Testing the Legality of its Acts* (The Hague: Kluwer Law International, 1994), p. 22.
15. *Ibid.*
16. Barcelona Traction: Light and Power Co. Case, *ICJ Reports* 1970, p. 3, para. 33.
17. *ICJ Reports* 1949, p. 4 at p. 22.
18. Corfu Channel (Merits), UK v. Albania, *ICJ Reports* 1949, p. 4 at pp. 34–35.
19. *ICJ Reports* 1986, p. 14.
20. *ICJ Reports* 1986, p. 14, para. 202.
21. *Ibid.*, para. 205.
22. *Ibid.*, para. 105 C.
23. *Ibid.*, para. 105 E.
24. 'Legality of the threat or use of nuclear weapons, Advisory Opinion of 8 July 1996', *ICJ Reports* 1996, p. 226, para. 29.
25. *Ibid.*, para. 105 F.
26. *Certain Expenses of The United Nations*, Advisory Opinion of 20 July 1962: International Count of Justice, Reports 1962, p. 151 at p. 168.
27. See the records of Committees II/2 and IV/2, Doc. 664, IV/233, 29 May 1945. See also M. Bedjaoui, *op. cit.* in note 14 above, p. 10.
28. 'Reparation for injuries suffered in the service of the United Nations', *ICJ Reports* 1949, p. 174.

29. 'Legal consequences for states of the continued presence of South Africa in Namibia', *ICJ Reports* 1971, p. 16 at p. 144.
30. *The Times*, 29 June 1971.
31. 'Questions of interpretation and application of the 1971 Montreal Convention arising from the aerial incident at Lockerbie (Libyan Arab Jamahiriya v. United Kingdom); (Libyan Arab Jamahiriya v. United States of America), Provisional Measures, Orders of 14 April 1992', *ICJ Reports* 1992, pp. 3 and 114.
32. See M. Bedjaoui, *op. cit.*, p. 67.
33. Press release, 17/12/99: G8 Foreign Ministers' Meeting in Berlin, 16–17 December 1999.
34. In Peck and Lee, *op. cit.*, p. 1.
35. *Ibid.*, p. 23.
36. Georges Abi-Saab, 'The International Court as World Court', *op. cit.*, p. 13.
37. See M. Bedjaoui, *op. cit.*.
38. See V. Gowlland, 'Judicial insights into fundamental values and interests of the international community', *Leiden Journal of International Law – The International Court of Justice: Its Future Role after Fifty Years (1997)*, pp. 327–66.
39. *ICJ Reports* 1971, p. 16, at p. 31.
40. *ICJ Reports* 1975, p. 32.
41. Legality of the threat or use of nuclear weapons, Advisory Opinion of 8 July 1996', *ICJ Reports* 1996, p. 226, para. 25.
42. In Peck and Lee, *op. cit.*, pp. 5–6.
43. *Ibid.*, p. 6.
44. *Ibid.*, p. 12.
45. *Ibid.*, p. 470.
46. *Ibid.*, p. 81.
47. I. Brownlie, *Principles of Public International Law*, 2nd edition (Oxford: Clarendon Press, 1973), pp. 708–9.

CHAPTER 7

THE UNITED NATIONS SECRETARIAT: REFORM IN PROGRESS

Yves Beigbeder[1]

One of the principal organs of the United Nations (UN), its Secretariat,[2] is (as a national administration *vis-à-vis* its government and parliament) the necessary and essential basis for preparing and implementing the decisions and resolutions of the UN governing bodies (General Assembly, Economic and Social Council, Security Council, Trusteeship Council). Its permanency provides these bodies with an indispensable institutional memory, research capacity, a tool for the collection and dissemination of information, for diplomatic action with member states and other organizations. The UN Secretariat has legal and political expertise, linguistic versatility, and maintains relations with member states' representatives, other intergovernmental organizations (IGOs), non-governmental organizations (NGOs) and foundations, private sector business leaders, academics, the media and the public at large.

The head of the Secretariat, the UN Secretary-General, is a political appointee: he is appointed by the General Assembly upon the recommendation of the Security Council. As was observed in the election of Kofi Annan, one permanent member of the Council can block the election (or re-election) of a particular candidate and obtain the election of its favourite candidate through the threat of the veto.

The Secretary-General has administrative, political and representative functions. As 'chief administrative officer', he prepares and submits the UN programme and budget for the approval of the General Assembly; he creates, reshuffles or abolishes departments and units, appoints and manages staff, allocates funds and is responsible for budget and financial operations, purchases and all other activities required for the effective administrative and physical functioning of a large organization. The UN Charter has limited his political role to a right to 'bring to the attention of the Security Council any matter which in his opinion may threaten the maintenance of international peace and security' (Article 99). However, the Secretary-General may exert significant political influence, depending on his own skills, temperament, competence and hard work, as well as on the world's current political climate, the attitude of member states, political opportunities and luck. He uses his good offices in order to initiate or maintain negotiations. Recent examples of the Secretary-General's political activism include Javier Pérez de Cuéllar's initiatives in promoting a regional peace process in Central America in the 1980s, and Kofi Annan's risky but successful mission of February 1998 to Iraq, which found a diplomatic solution to the weapons inspections stand-off, forestalling military confrontation, at least for a time. Finally, the Secretary-General has an everyday public relations job: he represents the UN in the world and is expected to explain and promote the current positions and programmes of the Organization and his own vision of the Organization's future.

Through the sheer pressure of international politics, all secretaries-general have had to give most of their time and energy to their political and public relations functions, often to the detriment of their role as executive head responsible for the management and motivation of their staff. Hence the need for the Secretary-General to be assisted by competent and loyal deputies in the administrative and management areas.[3]

National administrations are often criticized by citizens for their overbearing bureaucracy, lack of adequate response to their needs, excessive numbers and costs. They are subject to downsizing, some of their functions are privatized. The UN Secretariat, together with many other IGOs, is currently the object of similar criticisms on the part of some of its member states, and is subject to financial pressures and staffing cuts.

The UN Secretariat and its head, the Secretary-General, are a convenient scapegoat for governments that dislike some of the Organization's positions, resolutions, programmes or management. The UN Secretariat is an especially exposed target for at least three reasons. First, it is the administration of a political organization that was subject to the tensions of the Cold War, and now to the enduring conflicts between industrialized and developing countries. Second, UN Headquarters is especially exposed and visible because of its location in the USA, open to the scrutiny of Congressmen hostile to multilateralism and intent on reducing the role and finances of the Organization, and of media investigations focusing more on abuses than on achievements. Third, some of the criticisms addressed to the Secretariat's failings are justified.

The UN Secretariat has been charged in some quarters with overstaffing, incompetence, over-generous salaries and pensions, corruption, poor leadership, politicization: such generalized charges, emanating from habitual UN-bashers, cannot be accepted as a global condemnation of the overall performance of the UN Secretariat over half a century, even if some specific criticisms are well founded. What is beyond doubt is that the UN Secretariat has suffered from incompetent management and benign neglect for several decades, which caused many of the shortcomings identified by its critics. Member states have to share some of the blame with UN leaders and staff for some of the past and present failings of the UN Secretariat.

All large, complex organizations must satisfy basic requirements. A clear mission must be defined and realistic objectives must be set by governing boards. A bureaucracy must be created, with an evolving structure and a hierarchy. A large organization should be decentralized, and smaller and more manageable 'profit centres' created, with significant delegation of authority and *post facto* control. While the bureaucracy needs policies, rules and standards, governing boards and senior managers must ensure that the organization maintains its capacity for adaptation to changing mandates, growth or downsizing. The appointment of the Chief Executive Officer should be based on his or her known experience and success in similar high-level positions. He is responsible for leading the organization in the direction decided by the governing board, for fulfilling set objectives. He will personally appoint his senior assistants and he will be accountable for the effectiveness of the organization's planning and control processes, its internal and external communications and external relations.

The UN Secretariat is a large, complex organization to which these basic requirements should apply. However, while the UN mission for peace and security, international co-operation in economic, social, cultural and humanitarian domains and human rights well defines the overall mandate of the Organization, objectives set out in General Assembly or Security Council resolutions are not always precise and realistic, insofar as the Secretariat's performance is dependent on governments' action and many other factors to reach their objectives, and many General Assembly resolutions are only rhetorical. The UN is a political organization and its Secretariat is subject to constant government interference (188 member states, not just one government as for national administrations); the appointment of the Secretary-General is not based on explicit requirements of qualifications, but is mainly the result of political bargaining among the five permanent members of the Security Council; senior posts are usually filled at the discretion of specific governments; political appointments are made at various levels of the hierarchy; the structure is a heavy pyramid with too many layers and little attempt at decentralization and delegation. The management of a multinational and multicultural staff has its own problems, from which evolved the need for defining standards for an international civil service. Finally, the UN and its managers lack the harsh stimulus and judgement of the profit motive.

THE ORIGIN AND EVOLUTION OF THE UN SECRETARIAT

The first international secretariats were created in the nineteenth century in relation to international conferences and institutions. International political conferences and congresses held in Europe, the then political centre of the world, had temporary secretariats during their sessions, directed by national diplomats. The secretariats were initially composed of national civil servants of the host country, while some became multinational. Multinational secretariats became the norm with the Hague Conferences of 1899 and 1907 and the Peace Conference of 1919. However, the multinational concept only applied to senior conference posts attributed to the diplomats of participating countries, who maintained their national status. Second, conferences and congresses were time-limited events. One of the key elements of the future international civil service, permanency, also came about in the nineteenth century through the creation of international 'administrative unions', whose mandate was to increase trade exchanges and facilitate communications through international regulations and co-operation. Among them were the International Telegraph Union (renamed the International Communications Union in 1934) founded in 1865 and the Universal Postal Union, in 1874. Both are now specialized agencies of the UN. The staff of the administrative unions was usually composed of civil servants loaned by the host country and some other member states. The innovation was created by the International Institute of Agriculture, founded in Rome in 1905. The predecessor of FAO obtained an international status for itself and its staff.

The slow transformation from national to multinational to international secretariats finally matured into the latter concept with the League of Nations and the ILO, both created in 1919. The concept of an international civil service was founded on two principles:

- the allegiance owed by staff members exclusively to the international organization that employs them;
- the complementary duty of member states to respect the exclusively international character and responsibilities of the staff.

The first principle was adopted for the League of Nations' staff by the League's Council in May 1920, on the recommendation of the British representative, Arthur J. Balfour. It represented the views of Sir Eric Drummond, the first Secretary-General of the League, views that prevailed over those of Sir Maurice Hankey who had proposed a structure consisting of five national sections, one for each of the permanent members of the Council, working side by side. The Council decided that 'the members of the Secretariat, once appointed, are no longer the servants of the country of which they are citizens, but become for the time being the servants only of the League of Nations. Their duties are not national, but international.'[4]

The United Nations Conference on International Organization held in San Francisco from 25 April to 26 June 1945 confirmed, *inter alia*, the fundamental principles of the independence of international officials. Contrary to the Dumbarton Oaks proposals, which conceived several parallel secretariats, the Secretariat was to be a coherent administrative unit despite the multiplicity of its functions, entirely subordinated to the Secretary-General as sole head of the whole staff. The Secretary-General was given wider responsibilities than the League's Secretary-General: besides his functions as 'chief administrative officer', he was given a right of political initiative under Article 99 of the Charter.

The then US Secretary of State, Edward R. Stettinus, reporting to the US President on the results of the San Francisco conference, wrote:

> The proposed Secretariat of the United Nations will be, in effect, an international civil service. It will be recruited on the basis of competence, promoted on the basis of merit, and selected with due reference to linguistic and geographical considerations. Unlike a national civil service, however, it will not have the policy-making authorities (the General Assembly and all of the Councils) constantly available for reference and guidance. The staff must therefore be able to give effect to the decisions of policy-making bodies by exercising a high degree of good judgment and responsibility. In this concept the Secretariat becomes rightly one of the principal organs of the United Nations.[5]

The Preparatory Commission, which met between August and December 1945 in London, formulated general recommendations, based on the experience of the League, concerning the role of the Secretary-General and of the Secretariat. Among these: 'The Secretariat cannot successfully perform its task unless it enjoys the confidence of all the Members of the United Nations' – a proposition that was soon put to the test.[6]

Both principles of the internationalist concept were included in Article 100 of the UN Charter as follows:

> In the performance of their duties, the Secretary-General and the staff shall not seek or receive instructions from any government or from any other authority external to the Organization ... Each member of the United Nations undertakes to respect the exclusively international character of the responsibilities of the Secretary-General and the staff and not to seek to influence them in the discharge of their responsibilities.

The main rationale for the acceptance of this concept is first that the value of UN staff resides in their impartiality and independence from national or other loyalties, their respect for positions and decisions taken by their governing bodies, their voluntary allegiance to the Organization's interests and their accepted subordination to the head of the international Secretariat. A subsidiary, related reason is of an administrative nature: a secretariat composed of national sections with separate and possibly opposed objectives and interests would be unmanageable. The adoption of the internationalist concept was accompanied by the progressive construction of an autonomous international personnel system, aimed at ensuring that the international organization's staff, being left in a legal and administrative vacuum, were not tempted to call on their national authorities to seek protection.

Salary levels for the staff of the League of Nations were determined by the Noblemaire principle in 1921, a pension scheme was set up in 1923, and an administrative tribunal was established in 1927, to settle disputes between staff and the Organization for which national courts have no jurisdiction. The UN system has confirmed these developments – the Noblemaire principle is still the norm for professional salaries, the UN Joint Staff Pension Fund has replaced the League scheme and an Administrative Tribunal has been established for UN staff, while the League Tribunal became the Administrative Tribunal of the ILO, whose statute has been accepted by most specialized agencies.

The small Secretariat of the League and of the ILO, both created in 1919, gave way to a vast and complex network of UN organizations, with a combined approximate total of 53,000 staff members, a huge increase over the 900 League and 400 ILO employees. This increase included a diversification of professions, skills and functions well beyond the diplomatic and bureaucratic qualifications required for League work. UN staff are expected to respect their international obligations and to possess and demonstrate high qualities of efficiency, competence and integrity. In spite of all efforts to reach these standards, it is unavoidable that a proportion of the 53,000 staff of all UN organizations, and a proportion of the more than 14,000 staff of the UN Secretariat will be unable or unwilling to maintain or even reach these standards. The question is whether the UN Secretary-General and his senior assistants take these requirements seriously, whether 'managers' (supervisors) exercise leadership and control, and whether offenders are sanctioned.

The internationalist concept of the international civil service has been subject to constant attacks. During the late 1920s and in the 1930s, the internationalist obligations of some of the League's staff members were openly breached by a few governments, including fascist Italy and Nazi Germany. In the 1950s, during the McCarthy witchhunts, the first two Secretaries-General had to accept unwieldy US pressures and interference in the Secretariat's internal management. The Soviet Union created severe

public crises in its violent attacks against the same Secretaries-General for
their alleged lack of neutrality. The USSR and other socialist countries,
until the end of the Cold War, maintained close control over the recruitment and terms of employment of their nationals in UN organizations,
demanding that their allegiance be primarily to their own country and to
communist ideology, rather than to the UN Organization and its internationalist mandate. Many other governments apply pressure periodically
on the Secretary-General and other senior officials to enhance the recruitment or promotion of their nationals to high-level positions.

The evolution of the UN Secretariat may be assessed first in terms of
almost constant growth until the 1990s: from 300 persons on temporary
contracts in 1946, Secretary-General Trygve Lie recruited 2,900 new staff
in a few months. This hasty recruitment caused serious geographical
imbalance and staff with uneven, and sometimes untested, qualifications.
This raised the issue of defining recruitment criteria and setting quotas for
geographical distribution.

The staffing of the UN Secretariat[7] rose from 3,237 in 1964, to 11,393 in
1974 and 14,481 in 1984. It reached a peak in 1994 with 14,691 staff
members. In June 1997, it employed 14,136 staff members. Staffing growth
reflected the growth of UN members: from 51 states in 1945, to 159 in
1985 and 188 at present. Newly independent countries from Africa and
Asia, when joining the UN, were entitled to their own quotas to be filled
by their nationals. Their pressures and the lack of post descriptions and
reliable recruitment criteria raised suspicions that geographical representation was prevailing over qualifications and experience, as was the case
later with the Soviet-imposed 'official candidate' procedure. Budget
growth preceded staffing growth: in 1946, the UN regular budget was
$21.5 million. It was $784 million for 1976–77, $1,587 million for 1984–85
and rose to $2,603 million for 1996–97.[8] Staffing and budget growth were
approved by governing bodies on the basis of new or expanded programmes and activities, demands of new or extended intergovernmental
bodies, increased costs due to inflation, currency variations, and staff
costs. For example, the sudden explosion of peacekeeping missions from
1988 and the innovative creation of election-monitoring operations not
only represented a significant evolution in the role of the UN in international peace and security, it also required the back-up services of the
Department of Political Affairs, the Department of Peacekeeping Operations, the Office of Legal Affairs and administrative services among
others.

Administrative reform and changes in the Secretariat structure were
initiated periodically by the Secretary-General on the basis of his own
views. Some were proposed by 'expert' groups either appointed by the
Secretary-General or by member states: for instance, the 1961 Committee

to review the activities and organization of the Secretariat and the 1968 Committee on the reorganization of the Secretariat. In 1980, the General Assembly established a Committee of Governmental Experts to Evaluate the Present Structure of the Secretariat in the Administrative, Finance and Personnel Areas, and in 1985, the Group of High-Level Intergovermental Experts to Review the Efficiency of the Administrative and Financial Functioning of the United Nations, or Group of 18.[9] This Group included among its recommendations a reduction in the Organization's staffing by 15 per cent, the first in the history of the UN. This was the end of the growth era, which was linked to increasing US criticisms and pressures on the Organization.

A CLOSELY MONITORED SECRETARIAT

The management of the UN Secretariat is subject to an array of detailed rules and regulations, formulated or monitored by internal and external bodies. The Secretary-General reports to the General Assembly. His programme budget, staffing and restructuring proposals are reviewed by the Advisory Committee on Administrative and Budgetary Questions (ACABQ), the Committee for Programme and Co-ordination (CPC),[10] and by the Fifth Committee before a decision is taken by the General Assembly. All UN agencies have agreed, through relationship agreements concluded between the agencies and the UN, that the development of a 'single unified international civil service' is a desirable objective.[11] To this end, they have set up a 'common system of salaries, allowances and other conditions of service', a body of obligations which provides in practice that all 'common system' organizations will apply the same salary scales, the same allowances and benefits, the same post classification system and a common Pension Fund. The central 'decider' in important issues is the UN General Assembly. The principal 'personnel' adviser to the General Assembly, and decider in less important benefits matters, is the International Civil Service Commission (ICSC), a body established by the Assembly in 1974.[12] The UN Joint Staff Pension Board plays a role similar to that of ICSC in pension matters.[13] The agencies have set up a co-ordination mechanism in programme and administrative matters: the Administrative Committee on Co-ordination (ACC), supported in administrative and personnel matters by the Consultative Committee on Administrative Questions (CCAQ).[14] Any proposal to increase the salaries of UN professional staff has first to be discussed by CCAQ, agreed by ACC, submitted to ICSC, reviewed by ACABQ and the Fifth Committee, and finally decided upon by the General Assembly. The Organization's accounts and management are verified by internal and external auditors.

The Office of Internal Oversight Services (OIOS), created in 1995, has integrated audit and management consulting, inspection, investigation and evaluation activities. OIOS annual reports and annual reports of the UN Board of Auditors are submitted to the General Assembly, which ensures full disclosure of their findings to member states and the media. An inter-agency body, the Joint Inspection Unit (JIU),[15] has issued a number of critical studies on the management of the UN Secretariat; its reports are also submitted to the General Assembly. Disputes between staff members and the Organization may be referred to Joint (advisory) Appeals Boards and ultimately to the UN Administrative Tribunal. The Tribunal's judgments are issued as open documents. In brief, the UN Secretary-General, as Chief Administrative Officer, has powers limited by common system rules; his management in the administrative, budget, financial and personnel areas is subject to prior scrutiny and authorization and to *post facto* review, evaluation and criticisms by intergovernmental bodies and other groups. But these limitations are no excuse for a lack of leadership and poor management. Senior UN managers should welcome reviews and assessments by internal and external groups: they identify problems and weaknesses, and should trigger reform processes.

A SELECTION OF PROBLEMS AND WEAKNESSES

Inspector Richard V. Hennes of the Joint Inspection Unit noted in 1995:

> Over the past 50 years, there have been various attempts to strengthen United Nations programmes and improve their management, but they have not been well implemented. The unfortunate result has been a growing web of administrative controls and mandates that have enveloped the governing bodies, leadership, and staff of the United Nations in bureaucratic gridlock without providing the intended management culture.[16]

In a summary of efforts to establish UN management systems, the Inspector also noted, *inter alia*, that the General Assembly had first stressed the 'need for careful programme reviews to effectively use available resources' in 1950. In 1975, the Secretary-General acknowledged that there was 'still no systematic evaluation of results, which was the "key problem" which the medium-term plan did not yet cover'. In 1981 and 1985, JIU found that, despite a small central evaluation and monitoring unit finally established in 1980, the UN had fallen behind most other UN system organizations in the assessment of results to improve future programmes. In 1985–86, outside consultants found that internal audit coverage was ineffective and recommended a large increase in audit staff and their skills – which did not occur. The 'Group of 18' urged much greater independence for the internal auditors. In 1990–92, the General Assembly repeatedly urged action to strengthen internal controls and decisive action to deal with fraud. Lack of action on the part of the UN Secretariat or long delays were also experienced in the personnel management domain, considered as a 'patchwork management system . . . poorly administered, very bureaucratic, and costly'.[17] For instance, in 1978, the Secretary-General expressed the intention to establish a career development system, but it remained only an intention. In 1983, 1985 and 1989, the General Assembly had to call on the Secretary-General to complete the development of a comprehensive career development plan which would recognize merit through a rational performance evaluation and reporting system. In December 1993, the General Assembly called for the 'establishment of a transparent and effective system of accountability and responsibility no later than 1 January 1995' and specified that this system should include 'performance evaluation for all officials' (Res. 48/218). In 1994, JIU had found five different attempts to create a sound performance evaluation system in the Secretariat during the past 17 years: 'In spite of some improvements made to the system, however, they all failed because the Secretariat was unable to successfully implement them.'[18] Among the recruitment deficiencies, JIU found the absence of objective, uniform, job-specific criteria, lack of planning, and long delays. There was a tendency for political considerations and favouritism to exert a strong influence on recruitment at levels P.3 and above. The general practice was to identify posts for candidates known in advance instead of seeking to attract large fields of candidates qualified to fill vacant posts. Evidence of the incompetence of personnel managers in the most basic requirements of their discipline was the fact that there was no staffing table for the 11,000 regular budget posts.[19]

This self-inflicted, long-lasting mismanagement, damaging to the Organization's work and image, is probably the result of a lack of interest on the part of the first five Secretaries-General, more concerned with and interested in international diplomacy and relations with member states than with internal management. The absence of effective recruitment and promotion policies and practices, the lack of professionalism and authority of the central Office of Personnel, then Office of Human Resources Management (OHRM), combined with a lack of support by top management, the easy acceptance by senior UN officials of political pressures by governments in favour of unqualified candidates under the guise of 'equitable geographical distribution', created a vicious circle leading to a lowering of quality of selected candidates and uneven performance. Candidates were hired to managerial positions without specific management training or managerial experience. Poor performance was ignored, misconduct did not lead to sanctions, merit was not rewarded. There was a lack of incentive for change as the heavy machinery creaked and occasionally stalled, but most of the essential tasks were fulfilled, albeit at a cost and with delays: some observers wondered that the machine *eppure si muove*, or were satisfied that 'if it ain't broke, don't fix it'!

THE ATTITUDE OF MEMBER STATES

In principle, all member states should be equally concerned with the performance of the UN Secretariat and intent on promoting better efficiency and effectiveness at low cost. However, member states' objectives in this domain differ on account of with what they expect the Organization to deal, with what powers and with what financial and staffing resources. Do they want the role of the UN in international politics and relations to expand, to remain as it is, to wither, or do they really want the UN to disappear from the international scene? Should the UN give priority to multilateral diplomacy, peacekeeping, the making of international law, development, human rights, democracy, the environment or should it 'sub-contract' some of these activities to other organizations – IGOs or NGOs – or leave some of them essentially to governments? Most of the industrialized countries understand and appreciate the value and the limitations of the UN mandate and capacity. Their attitude towards the UN is similar to their attitude towards other IGOs – for instance, OECD, European Space Agency, CERN: they want value for money, clear objectives, zero growth budget, effective management and financial control, no salary increases for the staff and even salary reductions in some IGOs. They do not want the Organization to gain any degree of independence or autonomy in political and budgetary matters.

The attitude of the USA in 1999 was more complex, in view of the differences of positions between the Clinton (Democrat) administration's qualified support for the UN and the US (Republican) Congress's unilateralism. Speaker Newt Gingrich characterized the UN as a failed institution with 'grotesque pretensions, a totally incompetent instrument any place that matters'.[20] The Congress repeatedly used the illegal weapon of budgetary withholdings from their mandatory contributions on various grounds: to protest against UN support for liberation movements, and its condemnations of Israel, or as a rejection of unwanted programmes. In the mid-1980s, the Congress demanded that all UN organizations adopt weighted voting in order to impose budgetary control by the United States and other main contributors: the organizations' governing bodies agreed that budget levels would be approved by consensus, thus giving the USA a *de facto* veto right in this matter.[21] The yearly US withholdings have brought the UN to the verge of bankruptcy. The Congress then linked the partial repayment of their mandatory dues to a series of unilateral conditions. Under the Helms-Biden agreement, payment of the US debt would be subject to, *inter alia*, reducing the US contribution from 25 to 20 per cent, a permanent US seat on ACABQ (which the US lost for the first time in 1996), procedures to allow the US General Accounting Office to examine UN financial data, certifications concerning UN adherence to a negative growth budget, proof of continuing effectiveness of the UN Inspector-General's Office, elimination of 1,000 posts from 1996–97 levels and retention of a continuing vacancy rate of 5 per cent in the ranks of professional staff of the Secretariat. In effect, the US Congress seemed more intent on lowering the UN profile in US foreign policy rather than in increasing the effectiveness of the Organization.[22] These unrealistic demands took no account of the fact that they needed to be negotiated with the other 188 member states.

The lack of any consensus on reform of the UN Secretariat, and more generally reform of the UN, is demonstrated by the views of the 'South' expressed by the President of the 51st session of the General Assembly, Razali Ismail (Malaysia) on 15 September 1997. He said: 'Every aspect of the United Nations remains a stake and a prize in the escalating debate between the North and the South, each side with conflicting claims on fundamental values and perspectives, causing political gridlock in virtually every aspect of reform.'[23] He added that the UN will not be strengthened 'if reform only concentrates on cost-effectiveness, efficiency and better coordination'. Similar views were expressed on 1 March 1995 by Julius K. Nyerere (Tanzania), Chairman of the South Centre at a Forum on the Future of the UN held in Vienna: 'We all want to see the United Nations well managed. But it is not a business; its operations cannot be judged solely by "efficiency" in money terms. I have not heard the argument that attempts to prevent or settle conflicts should be ruled out because very often they do not succeed, and are thus "not cost-effective".'[24] For the South Centre, the UN's problems are primarily political and substantive. They cannot be resolved by reforms that are largely confined to a management approach and the mechanical transplantation of models, techniques and institutional approaches applicable, for example, to transnational enterprises or national administrations. The overall UN performance cannot be assessed on the basis of a cost-benefit analysis. The UN is often used as a scapegoat for the failed policies of one or more powers. The South wants a strong UN.

Mechanisms are needed to ensure payment of dues, and institutional safeguards need to be introduced to prevent abuse involving the use of financial contributions to obtain privilege and special status. In clear terms, the US should stop blackmailing the UN through financial withholdings.

In direct opposition to the US Congress, the South supports new and
stable sources of finance for UN organizations 'detached from the direct
budgetary processes and domestic politics of member states', including
taxes on international transactions. The new direction towards a 'corpor-
ate' mentality should not destroy the fabric of the international civil
service. An independent and high quality international civil service should
be re-established, protected against unilateral pressures from efforts by
individual governments to dominate or even run the UN secretariats. It
should be authorized to express views and make recommendations about
issues on the agenda. To reinvigorate the International Civil Service after
many years of neglect and demoralization, a short-term independent and
representative commission should be established to study the situation
and to recommend policies and programmes to bring the Service up to
the required standards of excellence.

BOUTROS BOUTROS-GHALI'S REFORMS

The first serious reforms were finally carried out by the sixth Secretary-
General, Boutros Boutros-Ghali (Egypt), following almost five decades of
indifference to modern management exigencies. Although his career, prior
to his appointment in January 1992, had been that of a diplomat without
specific experience or interest in management, US financial and other
pressures made him submit to most of the US demands, perhaps more to
save the Organization than in a real appreciation that reform was needed.
In order to carry out the reforms, the Secretary-General surrounded
himself with US-nominated candidates.[25] He appointed three successive
US nominees to head the Department of Administration and Management.
In addition, he appointed two other Americans with the rank of Under-
Secretary-General: one to whom he delegated the role of presiding over
staff management consultations, and the other in charge of UN 50th
anniversary observances. A third American nominee, at the level of
Assistant Secretary-General, was appointed to advise him on media
relations. He selected an American nominee for the post of Director of
UNICEF (Carol Bellamy) in preference to a European candidate, to the
annoyance of European governments: Americans already held executive
heads' posts in both UNDP and WFP. Boutros-Ghali's apparent eagerness
to please the Americans was not rewarded: the United States blocked his
bid for re-election to a second term and imposed their otherwise well-
qualified candidate, Kofi Annan. Boutros-Ghali had become the scapegoat
for all UN failings, and the object of unpleasant ethnic slurs that would
not have been tolerated if addressed to an American public figure in the
USA.

The impact of the Office of Internal Oversight Services

The main successful innovation introduced by Boutros-Ghali, under strong US pressure, was the creation of the Office of Internal Oversight Services (OIOS), approved by the General Assembly on 29 July 1994 (Res. 48/218 B). The Office was given monitoring, internal audit, inspection and evaluation functions, integrating the pre-existing units in charge of these activities. According to an observer, OIOS head, Under-Secretary-General Theodor Paschke (Germany), first had trouble ridding the office of 'dead wood' and getting qualified people to fill the Office's posts.[26] In its second report covering activities for the period from 1 July 1995 to 30 June 1996,[27] the head of the Office noted that an organization that has lived without independent and effective internal oversight for decades had to get used to outspoken criticisms, all the more so in documents submitted to the General Assembly. The OIOS had been confronted with some attempts to slow down, stall or discredit its work, a clear sign of bureaucratic resistance to investigation and transparency. The concept that audit recommendations must be followed up until they are fully implemented was not 'an established part of the management culture of the UN' (no doubt an understatement) prior to the establishment of OIOS. Programme managers were now required to implement OIOS recommendations fully and to report quarterly on the status of implementation.[28]

A 'Lessons Learned Unit' was created in the Department of Peacekeeping Operations in April 1995 in response to OIOS recommendations. Frustration and inefficiency had long been imposed on field operations by the lack of standard operating procedures and policies derived from experience. It appeared that each new operation had to reinvent policies, guidelines and procedures from scratch, and lacked adequate control. Most of the irregularities or wrong decisions, due to an ignorance of or violation of established procedures, or simply to a lack of administrative common sense, or fraud, were found in peacekeeping operations – still the ultimate responsibility of the UN Secretariat – and other UN agencies. Inadequacies in procurement planning and processes, and deficiencies in the routine administration of peacekeeping missions, were particularly noteworthy. A report of the UN Board of External Auditors[29] pointed to extenuating circumstances which alleviated, to a point, the blame assigned to UN managers, namely the rapidity with which the Organization had to adapt to new demands under conditions of extreme political and, increasingly, financial difficulty. The level of peacekeeping expenditures during the 1994–95 biennium exceeded the combined total of all other expenditures under the regular budget, technical co-operation, trust fund and other special activities.

The OIOS' third report, for the period 1 July 1996 to 30 June 1997,[30] identified as another area to be tackled the huge mass of unclear rules and regulations that have piled up over the decades and confuse rather than guide administrative activities, mainly in the fields of financial and human resources management. As an encouraging note, cost savings and recoveries resulting from OIOS action had risen from $15.8 million over 1995–96 to $17.8 million over 1996–97. The implementation rate for audit recommendations had risen from 61 per cent to 71 per cent for the same periods. Among cases recorded by OIOS, in July 1996 the UN Office at Geneva submitted a criminal complaint to the Swiss authorities against a senior UNCTAD staff member, who was arrested pending investigation. The staff member was summarily dismissed. He admitted in a signed confession owing the UN a total amount of CHF 731,645 ($609,704) and agreed to liquidate his entire assets in order to restitute to the UN to the extent his assets made that possible. The UN has recovered about $350,000. A Swiss court judged the defendant guilty and sentenced him to 18 months in jail. The court further directed that the staff member pay the balance due to the UN from his thefts and be prohibited from entering Switzerland for ten years. In this case, the over-protective diplomatic immunity of the official concerned had been waived by the Secretary-General.

While it is premature to assess OIOS' impact over a short period of four years, the creation of the Office and its activities and results show that such an independent and active investigation body was more than necessary: at last, the results of investigations were published in open UN documents; the reality of cases of irregularities and fraud was recognized and follow-up action taken; a significant innovation, a few staff members or former staff members found guilty of fraud were brought to national courts for trial and judgment. The UN culture of administrative improvisation, negligence and impunity was finally shaken for the first time: OIOS is contributing to its evolution towards a culture of accountability. Those who feel that the new openness of findings of abuses and fraud falls as a too easy prey to sensationalist media are wrong.[31] The previous ostrich policy of not responding to charges of abuse, in the hope that they would go away or be forgotten about, was irresponsible. Taxpayers, governments and the media have the right to know that faults are found and investigated, guilty parties are identified and sanctioned, and corrective and preventive measures are carried out. National and international public trust can only be recovered at this cost.

Other reforms

Other moves aimed at building a 'new management culture' in the UN Secretariat, at the urging of the General Assembly and under US pressure, failed to bring positive results in a debilitating and threatening climate of US-caused financial crisis and US-style downsizing, and also as a result of bureaucratic resistance, vested interests and staff scepticism over, yet again, another reform. Among these moves, the Secretary-General's Human Resources Management Strategy was adopted by the General Assembly in 1994 (Res. 49/222). The strategy is generally a catalogue of good management principles and intentions, with the expressed aim of modernizing and re-energizing human resources management. It covers human resources planning based on needs assessments, skill inventory, succession systems, career pathing and counselling, global mobility, innovative recruitment systems, performance assessment and enhanced attrition or buyouts. A redeployment scheme designed to weed out 'dead wood' seemed more to target competent staff members disliked by their chiefs. A new attempt at creating an effective performance appraisal system proved to be as bureaucratic as previous ones, and its accompanying training efforts were derided by the staff as costly and ill-focused.[32]

In November 1995, the Secretary-General created an Efficiency Board to act as a catalyst. According to its September 1996 report, the Board led every department and office in the UN Secretariat to carry out efficiency reviews. Some 400 projects to deliver both better service and better value to member states were identified. Efficiency measures were to contribute to the UN budget situation through reduced staff levels and increased staff productivity. However, this initiative was criticized as being without legislative mandate, the composition of the Board was criticized as being without proper geographical balance and its members of inadequate expertise.[33] In order to improve the internal system of justice in the UN Secretariat, perceived as 'slow, complex, inefficient and self-serving', the Secretary-General proposed another complex system, which was to create ombudsman mediation panels and 'professionalize' the appeal process by replacing the Joint Appeals Boards with an Arbitration Board composed of externally recruited experts, with optional binding awards. In the same vein, the Joint Disciplinary Committee would be replaced by a Disciplinary Board composed of qualified professionals. The new system would probably have been more expensive than the existing one, in view of the salary costs required by outside professionals,[34] but the main objection was to suppress boards composed of representatives of both management and staff, which have provided the UN Administrative Tribunal with useful background information on cases that could not be easily available to outside 'experts'. There was also a risk of overlapping with the power of the Tribunal: its members expressed serious reservations about the proposed reform.[35] The Fifth Committee voted at its 40th meeting in December 1995 to postpone consideration of reforming the internal justice system after the Secretary-General and ACABQ could not agree on

whether to replace the current system. The Chairman of ACABQ
described the proposal to replace the Joint Appeals Board and the Disciplinary Board by a professional Arbitration Board as 'radical and controversial' and concluded that the time was not ripe to implement the
proposed changes. The President of the Staff Committee said that the
proposal lacked due process and equity.[36]

KOFI ANNAN'S REFORMS

On 2 January 1997, Kofi Annan (Ghana) took up his duties as seventh UN
Secretary-General. He was the first long-term UN staff member to be
appointed Secretary-General, (his last post was that of Under-Secretary-
General in the Department for Peacekeeping Operations). All previous
Secretaries-General were 'outsiders', diplomats, politicians or senior civil
servants. In contrast with his predecessor, he showed that he would
depend more on teamwork within the UN and consultation with regional
groups and national delegations. He also showed that he would search
for practical solutions to the Organization's problems and, although he
owed his election to US insistence, that he had 188 masters, not just one.
His first priority was to establish a competent, experienced and dynamic
team. Mid-January 1997, he appointed Maurice Strong (Canada) as Executive Co-ordinator of UN Reform. Mr Strong was to steer a consultative
process, engaging the entire UN system, to assemble a 'comprehensive
package' of reform measures 'acceptable to all Member States'.[37] Annan
appointed in 1997 and 1998 a number of individuals considered as
experienced and competent. Among these, the appointment of Mary
Robinson, former President of Ireland, as High Commissioner for Human
Rights was the most striking. Appointing such an independent, outspoken
and highly qualified candidate to this highly politically sensitive function
was underlining Annan's own belief in the UN's role in the human rights
area, and his own independence in making this choice. Also in January
1997, the Secretary-General reorganized the Organization's work programme around the five areas that comprise the core missions of the UN:
peace and security; economic and social affairs; development co-operation;
humanitarian affairs; and human rights. Executive committees were established in the first four areas, while human rights was designated as cutting
across, and therefore participating in, each of the other four.

The first track

On 17 March 1997, the Secretary-General announced a ten-point initiative
for administrative and management reform of the UN. This was the first

track of a two-track reform process, involving managerial decisions that fell within the Secretary-General's authority and could be taken immediately. The ten points were:

1. Abolish approximately 1,000 posts in the 1998–99 budget. This would contribute to a 25 per cent decline in staffing from peak levels.
2. Submit a 1998–99 budget that is $123 million less than the previous one.
3. Merging of departments.
4. Set up a new Department of General Assembly Affairs and Conference Services, integrating major technical support services for the Assembly, ECOSOC and their subsidiary bodies.
5. Transform the Department of Public Information into an Office of Communications and Media Services.
6. Cut by one-third the proportion of budget resources used for administration costs by the year 2001, and make the savings available for development activities.
7. Strengthen UN Resident Co-ordinators' role in development co-operation and as leaders of UN country teams.
8. Integrate UN Information Centres into the Resident Co-ordinator's Office.
9. Prepare a Code for Conduct requiring the highest standards of competence, independence and integrity of UN staff.
10. Reduce documentation by 25 per cent.[38]

After briefing delegations, Annan reminded UN correspondents that reform was a process and not an event. The 1998–99 budget was approved at $2,532 million, compared to the $2,608 million appropriation for 1996–97. In 1998, the Secretariat had 8,741 regular budget posts, down from 10,012 posts in 1996–97.[39]

The second track: a quiet revolution?

The Secretary-General's overall Programme for Reform, including a few elements of his Track I, was presented to the General Assembly on 16 July 1997.[40] It is an ambitious programme, but politically acceptable with a few exceptions. The ambition was expressed in these words: 'Here the report seeks nothing less than to transform the leadership and management structure of the Organization, enabling it to act with greater unity of purpose, coherence of efforts, and agility in responding to the many challenges it faces. These measures are intended to renew the confidence of Member States in the relevance and effectiveness of the Organization and revitalize the spirit and commitment of its staff.'

Structural changes in the Secretariat

1. A *Senior Management Group* was established to replace the previous *ad hoc* meetings between the Secretary-General and his senior officials. The Group is to ensure strategic coherence and direction in the work of the UN. It serves as the Secretary-General's cabinet, advising him on all matters of policy that affect the Organization as a whole. It will also serve in a crisis management capacity. Formalization of former arrangements should not be controversial, as regular meetings of senior officials are a most basic management requirement for all large organizations, to ensure policy direction, unity of purpose and action, and co-ordination.

2. The post of *Deputy Secretary-General* (DSG) was created (one of the US demands) and could have been challenged as giving too much power to a non-elected official. It is, however, justified by the multiplicity of roles performed by the Secretary-General and their contradictory obligations, the primacy of diplomatic, representational and programme functions, requiring frequent absences from UN Headquarters, and the continuing need for management initiatives and monitoring, requiring a visible presence in New York. A Secretariat paper justified the creation of the post in terms of three needs.[41] First, a managerial need: with 30 or so senior officials reporting directly to the Secretary-General, there is a need for help to ensure managerial oversight and supervision. The second need is as stand-in when the Secretary-General is away from Headquarters. Third, the DSG would ensure attention to issues and concerns that cut across the work of the four Executive Committees. The DSG will be an integral part of the Secretary-General's office and will exercise only such responsibilities and functions as are derived from his own authority, as delegated by him from time to time. The DSG's appointment would not extend beyond the Secretary-General's own term of office. The General Assembly approved the creation of this post on 19 December 1997. In January 1998, Annan appointed Louise Frechette (Canada) to this post: an experienced and capable diplomat, her last post was as Deputy Minister of National Defence.[42]

3. A small *Strategy Planning Unit* was set up in the Secretary-General's Office. It will identify emerging global issues and trends, analyse their implications for the roles and working methods of the UN, and devise policy recommendations for the Secretary-General and the Senior Management Group. This creation responds to the felt need for a think-tank within the Secretariat and recognizes that the Secretariat, as a principal organ of the UN, is not mainly reacting to member states' demands, but has the capacity to undertake research, to analyse and to formulate

issues and prospects on a long-term basis. It should identify areas which the UN could realistically cover, objectives which could be attained and services which the UN would be best placed to provide.

4. A *UN Development Group* is to be constituted, comprising the major UN development programmes and funds, as well as departments and other entities. Its objectives are to facilitate joint policy formation and decision-making, encourage programme co-operation and realize management efficiencies. This change at Headquarters will be reflected at the regional and country levels, where all UN programmes will be integrated within a United Nations Development Assistance Framework. The Group will bring together UNICEF and UNFPA under the leadership of the UNDP Administrator, a grouping that was originally opposed by UNICEF Head Carol Bellamy. Discussions led to the decision that funds and programmes participating in the Group would retain their current distinctiveness and existing structures of accountability, while working as a team.

5. An *Office of the Emergency Relief Co-ordinator*, located in New York, is to replace the Department of Humanitarian Affairs.

6. A single *Office of the High Commissioner for Human Rights* in Geneva will consolidate the Office of the High Commissioner for Human Rights and the Centre for Human Rights.

Human Resources Management

Based on the former Secretary-General's Human Resources Management (HRM) strategy approved by the General Assembly in 1994, Kofi Annan's 'further efforts' are typical of sound management theory and practices in an international organization: staff training, simplification of rules, streamlined recruitment and administrative practices, reaching the goals of geographical representation and gender balance, more effective career development, decentralization and delegation of authority. However, staff training and career development are necessarily restrained in a climate of financial crisis and staffing cuts. One thousand staff posts are to be eliminated and administrative costs reduced by one-third. The UN Secretariat of the future will be 'somewhat smaller, better trained, more versatile, more mobile, better managed and better integrated as a global team'.[43] The ageing staff will be rejuvenated: the average age of UN staff is 49 – at least 4,500 will retire from the Organization over the next decade.

The Secretary-General established a Task Force on Human Resources Management in 1998, which would submit its findings and recommendations to him before the September 1998 session of the General Assembly. Chaired by Ms Rafiah Salim, the Task Force is composed of experts from different regions of the world with a wide diversity of experience in human resources management in the public and private sectors. Within the context of the whole UN system, the Secretary-General has recommended that the General Assembly initiate a review of the International Civil Service Commission, including its mandate, membership and functioning. This responds to a concern of the Federation of International Civil Service Associations (FICSA), which has long criticized the Commission as lacking in professionalism and objectivity, and has proposed that the composition of a new commission be tripartite, with members appointed by governments, UN executive heads and staff representatives. The Secretary-General's main innovation was to submit a Code of Conduct, another response to one of the US demands as a prerequisite for payment of US arrears. The Code was negotiated with the UN staff representatives in New York but raised protests from UN staff representatives in Geneva and from FICSA. The main purpose of the Code is to formalize in more detail the rights and obligations of UN staff members by including it as an integral part of the UN Staff Regulations and Rules. The UN administration, based on the jurisprudence of the UN Administrative Tribunal, felt that there were some loopholes in the existing Regulations and Rules concerning staff obligations.

The *Report on Standards of Conduct in the International Civil Service*, prepared in 1954 by the International Civil Service Advisory Board (ICSAB), is a discussion of expected standards rather than a set of binding rules. FICSA has objected to the 'basic tenor' of the Code. For FICSA, the Code is not an integrity-based set of rules outlining values to which staff are expected, or even assumed, to subscribe. It is a compliance-based book of directives that converts those values deemed necessary to the effective functioning of the Organization into staff rules and regulations with which the staff member must comply or risk disciplinary action. FICSA was 'outraged' that the Code was 'worded in such a way as to imply that international civil servants and their families are potentially capable of wrongdoing'.[44] FICSA's 'outrage' is not warranted: national or international employees are potential wrongdoers, and management is within its rights in setting out clearly what is or is not permitted, and what may be the sanctions applicable in case of misconduct. On the other hand, FICSA has grounds to criticize the Code's restrictive approach to staff representatives' acquired rights to demonstrate, to stop work (actual or symbolic strike), or to lobby member states' representatives or UN organs in support of their salary and other claims.

Budget and finances

The Secretary-General proposes to shift the UN programme budget from a system of input accounting to results-based accountability. The General

Assembly would specify the results they expect the Organization to achieve. The Secretariat would then be held responsible for, and judged by, the extent to which the specified results are reached. While this approach is desirable and applicable in certain areas where results will clearly be due to the Secretariat's work and efforts (holding a meeting, preparing, translating and issuing studies and documents), in many areas – disarmament, peacekeeping, human rights, environment and the like – results depend on many factors well beyond the power or influence of the UN, such as the action of states and other national and international actors, international and national politics, economic and social factors.

The Secretary-General proposes the establishment of a Revolving Credit Fund of up to $1 billion, financed from voluntary contributions or other means that member states may wish to suggest, pending a lasting solution of the Organization's financial situation. This follows similar proposals made by former Secretaries-General Pérez de Cuéllar and Boutros-Ghali. It is most unlikely that member states will be any more willing than before to provide the UN with more resources. The main reason why the UN suffers from a chronic and severe financial crisis is the failure of a number of member states to discharge their Charter obligations regarding prompt and full payment of assessed budgetary contributions. Budgetary withholdings by the US Congress are a political weapon intended to impose US-defined reform on the UN. However, the main reason why other member states delay payment of their financial contributions is their chronic or temporary inability to pay, on account of their economic and financial position caused by their under-development, their political insta-bility, break-up of a state or federation into independent states, civil war, man-made or natural emergencies, or other factors. The only sanction that may be applied to offenders is the loss of their vote in the General Assembly in accordance with Article 19 of the Charter. The reference to 'other means that Member States may suggest' may be an indirect suggestion that the UN could complement its regular budget and extra-budgetary funds by its own resources, on the model of other IGOs (WIPO, the European Union). International taxes on arms sales, international air travel, transnational financial transactions, etc. have been mentioned. The United States has flatly opposed this option; it is, however, supported by a number of developing countries.

Civil society and private business

UN links with NGOs are not new. The number of NGOs granted consul-tative status by ECOSOC has grown from 41 in 1948, to 377 in 1968, to 1,200 in 1977. NGOs play a considerable operational role in UNHCR and UNICEF programmes. The Secretary-General's decision to request all substantive departments of the UN to designate an NGO liaison officer is only a complement to existing arrangements. The more innovative aspect of the Secretary-General's programme in this area is however his acknowledgement of the increasing preponderance of market-based approaches to national and global economic management, and therefore the need for the UN to establish open mechanisms to set up and maintain a dialogue with business representatives, a total turnabout from previous UN attacks against the 'evil' transnational enterprises. Links have been established with the International Chamber of Commerce and the World Economic Forum. Gatherings involving eminent leaders of different sectors of civil society now include private business besides academics, organized labour, NGOs, youth and the foundation community. Finally, the Secretary-General would consult with ACC with a view to establishing a jointly funded interagency business liaison service, the UN Enterprise Liaison Service, patterned along the lines of the existing NGO Liaison Service.

Reforms approved

No reform package can satisfy equally all 188 members of the UN. However, it appears that most of the reforms proposed by the Secretary-General, if approved and properly implemented, would provide a long-needed impetus to the Organization and new motivation to its staff. Initial reactions were dismissive, supportive or guarded. US Senate views were predictably negative, as they did not satisfy its demands point by point. Senator Rod Grams said, inaccurately, that the plan 'represents nothing more than the *status quo*'. On the other hand, Secretary of State Madeleine Albright lauded the package of reforms that 'go a long way toward meeting our concerns'. She said that 'our crusade for reform is not just an effort to save money, but an effort to focus the UN's limited resources on the priorities we share'. With more credibility and a truly multilateralist approach, the New Zealand representative said: 'We are not interested in mere cost-cutting. And we most emphatically disagree with suggestions which would leave the UN with a diminished role in the world.' European Union countries supported the reform proposals, which, according to the French Quai d'Orsay, 'for the main part were supported by the Union'. Developing countries' diplomats feared that change would be limited to cutbacks in development programmes that they strongly support.[45] On 12 November 1997, the General Assembly adopted by consensus a resolution welcoming the Secretary-General's report of 14 July 1997, implicitly allowing him to implement the actions described in his report within his authority, subject to 'full respect for the relevant mandates, decisions and resolutions of the General Assembly' (Res. A/52/12). In a second resolution adopted on 19 December 1997 (Res. A/52/12 B), the General

Assembly established the post of Deputy Secretary-General, created a development account to be funded from savings from possible reductions in administration and other overhead costs and gave UNDP responsibility for operational activities dealing with natural disasters. The Assembly postponed a decision on the $1 billion Revolving Credit Fund by asking for more details.

STRENGTHENING THE UN SYSTEM

The Open-ended High-level Working Group on the Strengthening of the United Nations System submitted its report in July 1997.[46] It refers mainly to the General Assembly's functions, role and powers, and in part to the capacity of the Secretariat to 'carry out effectively and efficiently the mandates of intergovernmental processes with the necessary transparency and accountability'. One recommendation was addressed to the Secretary-General. Clearly dissatisfied with the format of his Annual Reports on the work of the Organization, the Group was telling the Secretary-General how to present his report: an executive summary highlighting the main issues, the main body of the report should be 'comprehensive, informative and analytical in a way that will allow Member States to examine and assess, *inter alia*, through its debate the extent to which mandates given by the General Assembly have been fulfilled, as well as for priority setting by Member States'; and a new forward-looking section describing the specific goals in the year ahead. Addressing both the General Assembly and the Security Council, the Group recommended that the process of selection of the Secretary-General should be more transparent, with due regard given to regional rotation and gender equality. The duration of the term or terms of appointment, including the option of a single term, should be considered before the appointment of the next Secretary-General. Executive heads of programmes, funds and other bodies of the General Assembly and ECOSOC should have uniform terms of office of four years, renewable once. There should be no monopoly on senior posts by nationals of any state or group of states, as periodically requested by the General Assembly. An innovative recommendation was that all levels of senior management would have to make financial disclosures at the time of appointment and on a regular basis. On staffing, a career international civil service was essential for the Organization's core functions, and there was an important role for fixed-term contracts. There should be an appropriate balance between institutional memory, long-term commitment and independence and the ability to bring in fresh insights and expertise, and to dismiss non-performing staff. A planned rotation among different departments as well as between Headquarters and the field

should be developed. The General Assembly is reviewing these
recommendations.

CONCLUSION

The UN Secretariat has grown for more than four decades without
systematic order or adequate control. The morale of the Secretariat suffered from political pressures by the United States and by socialist
countries, as well as from a lack of professionalism in human resources
management by UN administrators and managers. Constant growth, due
to the increase of member states and the uncontrolled increase of *ad hoc*
bodies and programmes, led to the creation of new departments and
services while dead branches were left to decay. The Secretariat suffered
from overlapping of mandates and functions, vague or unrealistic objectives, lack of planning and weak oversight. The principles of the international civil service, inherited from the League of Nations, were
progressively eroded. Geographical representation often prevailed over
competence and merit. The Secretaries-General only offered a weak resistance to governments' interference in personnel management. The administrative failings of Secretariat managers encouraged the General
Assembly in pursuing counter-productive micro-management. The General Assembly, at the urging of the rich countries, froze professional
salaries, while allowing the latter to pay salary supplements to some of
their well-qualified nationals above UN compensation deemed inadequate. The Noblemaire formula is ignored by both the International Civil
Service Commission and the Fifth Committee, in a clear intent to avoid
salary increases. Rich countries second 'gratis' personnel to UN programmes, personnel whose allegiance to the UN is doubtful. There is a
crucial need to reassess staff policy. It is hoped that the task force will
submit innovative ideas.[47] WHO's proposal for a revised personnel policy
(not implemented in 1998) may give some inspiration to the UN. WHO's
new staffing pattern would include a core group of career staff, a number
of other staff with time-limited contracts (without expectation of renewal)
who may also be seconded or on loan from centres of excellence, and
advisers or consultants hired for a short time to complete specific tasks.
Quotas for geographical distribution would not apply to non-core staff.[48]
For the UN, the identification of these three groups would allow more
flexibility in employment conditions, while the core group would retain
all the attributes and characteristics of the traditional international civil
service. This would be a major change, likely to be resisted by the staff
representatives. Kofi Annan, with the support of his Deputy and other
senior officials, is well placed to tackle this challenge – one among many

others. Reform is needed in the UN secretariat, but, as often stated by Annan, reform is a process, not an event. The Secretary-General's own efforts need the firm and persistent support of all those who believe that the UN should be strengthened, not weakened – that is, 'like-minded' member states, pro-UN groups and individuals and informed public opinion.

NOTES

1. This chapter is written in a personal capacity. The views and assessments are the author's own responsibility.
2. The UN Secretariat is composed of UN Headquarters in New York, the UN Office at Geneva, the UN International Drug Control Programme (UNDCP) and the Crime Prevention and Criminal Justice Division, both located in Vienna, the Economic Commissions for Africa (ECA), for Europe (ECE), for Latin America and the Caribbean (ECLAC), the Economic and Social Commission for Asia and the Pacific (ESCAP), for Western Asia (ESCWA) – UN subsidiary bodies such as UNICEF, UNHCR, UNDP, UNCTAD, ITC, the UN Centre for Human Settlements, UNEP, UNU and UNRWA are usually treated as separate entities although their staff is subject to the UN Staff Regulations and Rules.
3. The UN Secretaries-General were Trygve Lie (Norway), 1946–53; Dag Hammarskjöld (Sweden), 1953–61; U. Thant (Burma), 1962–66; Kurt Waldheim (Austria), 1972–81; Javier Pérez de Cuéllar (Peru), 1982–91; Boutros Boutros-Ghali (Egypt), 1992–96. Kofi Annan (Ghana) was appointed in January 1997.
4. Georges Langrod, *The International Civil Service* (Dobbs Ferry, NY: Oceana, 1963), p. 51 and League of Nations, *Official Journal*, June 1920, 137.
5. US Department of State Publication no. 2349, Conference Series no. 71, quoted in UN Doc. ACC/1997/PER/R.2, 22 January 1997.
6. Langrod, *op. cit.*, p. 166.
7. These figures are shown in the CCAQ Annual Statistics for the UN, excluding UNDP, UNFPA, UNHCR, UNICEF, UNRWA and ITC. They include professional and general service staff appointed for one year or more, assigned to Headquarters, other established offices and projects.
8. UN *Press Release* SG/2034 ORG/1236, 27 May 1997. Budget figures are those of periods indicated.
9. Yves Beigbeder, *Management Problems in United Nations Organizations: Reform or Decline?* (London: Frances Pinter, 1987), chs 3 and 11.
10. ACABQ, a subsidiary organ of the General Assembly, is composed of experts of 16 countries chosen by the Assembly. CPC is a main subsidiary organ of ECOSOC and the General Assembly. It has 34 members designated by governments.
11. In accordance with Articles 57 and 63 of the UN Charter, 14 specialized agencies have relationship agreements with the UN. For instance, see the 'Agreement between the United Nations and the World Health Organization' in WHO *Basic Documents*, 41st edn. (Geneva: WHO, 1996).

12. ICSC has 13 members of whom two, its Chairman and Vice-Chairman, serve full-time. They are appointed by the General Assembly on the proposal of the Secretary-General 'in their personal capacity as individuals of recognized competence who have had substantial experience of executive responsibility in public administration or related fields, particularly in personnel management'.
13. The Board is composed of 33 persons, 12 from the UN (one-third chosen by the Assembly and the governing bodies of the other organizations, one-third by the executive heads, one-third by the participants) and 21 from the other member organizations.
14. ACC is composed of the agencies' executive heads under the chairmanship of the UN Secretary-General. It generally meets twice a year for two or three days. It has no decision-making power.
15. JIU, created in 1966, is a subsidiary organ of the General Assembly and of legislative bodies of the UN organizations that accept its statute, to which it reports. It consists of 11 inspectors serving in their personal capacity. Inspect ors have the 'broadest powers of investigation in all matters having a bearing on the efficiency of the services and the proper use of funds' (Statute, art. 5.1).
16. UN Doc. JIU/REP/95/8, 1995, p. v and Annex.
17. UN Doc. JIU/REP/96/6, 1996, p. 1.
18. UN Doc. JIU/REP/94/5, 1994, p. iv.
19. UN Doc. JIU/REP/95/1 (Part I), 1995, pp. 21–26.
20. Quoted by Benjamin Rivlin in 'UN reform from the standpoint of the United States' (The UN University, 1996), p. 1. Gingrich changed his views in a November 1996 speech: 'We must reform the UN, but then, frankly, we're going to have to pay for the UN ... We can't end up as a country totally isolated around the world...': *International Documents Review* (hereunder referred to as *IDR*), 18 November 1996, p. 3. On the UN financial crisis, see Y. Beigbeder, 'The continuing financial problems of the United Nations: Assessing reform proposals', in C. de Cooker (ed.), *International Administration*, II.10/ 1–20 (The Hague/Boston/London: UNITAR, Martinus Nijhoff Publishers, 1995).
21. Congressional measures included the Kemp-Moynihan Amendment of 1979 prohibiting the USA to pay its share of UN funds for liberation movements such as the PLO, and the Kassebaum Amendment of 1985 prescribing a 20 per cent cut in US contributions to international organizations until weighted voting was introduced. See Rivlin, *op. cit.*, pp. 11–12.
22. See Steven A. Dimoff, 'Helms-Biden: Congress looks to micromanage the US', *The Inter-Dependent*, Summer 1997, pp. 7–11.
23. UN *Press Release* GA/9293, 15 September 1997.
24. 'Reforming the United Nations: A View from the South', (Geneva: South Centre, March 1995). See also *FICSA Newsletter*, January 1997, p. 4.
25 See *International Documents Review* (*IDR*), 31 December 1996, p. 1.
26. *IDR*, 24 February 1997.
27. Doc. A/51/432, 30 September 1996 and Annexe.
28. *Ibid.*, Preface and para. 3.
29. Doc. A/51/5.
30. Doc. A/52/426, 2 October 1997.
31. On media reports, see, for instance, *Tribune de Genève*, 3 October 1997; *Le*

Monde, 16 October 1997; *Sunday Times*, 2 November 1997; *International Herald Tribune*, 3 November 1997.

32. *UN Staff Report*, June/July 1997, p. 16.

33. See *IDR*, 21 October and 31 December 1996. The Efficiency Board was replaced in 1997 by a Management Reform Group established in the Department of Administration and Management.

34. UN Doc. A/C.5/49/60, 18 March 1995.

35. See Doc. A/C.5/49/60, 18 March 1995. See also Y. Beigbeder, *The Internal Management of United Nations Organizations: The Long Quest for Reform* (Basingstoke: Macmillan, 1997), ch. 11.

36. Doc. A/C.5/50/SR.40, 14 December 1995, paras 38–41, 69.

7. Mr Strong has successfully undertaken several UN assignments, including that of Secretary-General of the first Conference on Human Environment held in Stockholm in 1972.

38. Doc. A/51/829, 17 March 1997, and A/INF/51/6 and Corr.1.

39. *Secretariat News*, January–February 1998.

40. Doc. A/51/950, 14 July 1997.

41. Doc. A/51–950/Add 1.

42. *International Herald Tribune*, 14 January 1998.

43. UN Doc. A/51/950, 14 July 1997, para. 229.

44. *IDR*, 24 November 1997, p. 1.

45. *International Herald Tribune*, 18 July and 27 October 1997, US *Daily Bulletin*, Geneva, EUR504, 19 September 1997.

46. Doc. A/51/24.

47. Doc. A/51/950, p. 74.

48. WHO Doc. EB99/16, 26 November 1996, p. 4.

CHAPTER 8

STATES GROUPS AT THE UNITED NATIONS AND GROWTH OF MEMBER STATES AT THE UNITED NATIONS

Sally Morphet[1]

INTRODUCTION

This chapter considers the groups of states that use or have used the UN system (which had 51 member states in 1946 and 188 by the end of 1999) and discusses why they were set up and, in certain cases, why they collapsed. It also discusses how they pursue or have pursued their aims, both within the UN electoral group system, and in terms of their own political and economic interests and their need to take the changing global, regional, political and economic context into account. It then attempts to assess their successes and failures, similarities and differences.

Groups' activities range and have ranged from the development of norms of international law, agenda setting, and the making of ECOSOC, General Assembly and Security Council resolutions to help resolve major political and, occasionally, economic problems. Groups also work in the UN specialized agencies (e.g. attempting to expel South Africa from a number of these: or trying to join them to help achieve statehood), as well as at major UN conferences. The main Third World preoccupations over the whole period were decolonization, nuclear disarmament, economic development, Palestine and South Africa, as well as the seating of the People's Republic of China in the UN (achieved in 1971).

The chapter argues that most states found it essential to promote their interests (both political and economic) more effectively at a global level by forming groups that could work both within and, sometimes, outside the UN system. This political necessity was given more weight by the fact that states had to ensure that they had their fair share of electoral posts in part in terms of the equitable geographical distribution laid down in the UN Charter. Most states were well aware that legitimacy could be given to causes that were exposed to the UN system. Over the years a number of groups were formed with bases both geographical and ideological for electoral political and economic reasons. None of the groups discussed, except at some points the Eastern Europeans (including the Soviet Union), could normally be described as blocs in the sense that they always voted together. Other groups could be split in certain circumstances or even bought. The more powerful Third World states (e.g. Egypt, India and, up until 1990, Yugoslavia) proved more able to pursue their own interests despite opposition by major powers. Those less happy with the status quo were normally those who took the most initiatives. This is why particular attention has been given to Third World groupings and to the different ways they tried to achieve maximum influence, as well as to the ways in which they were blocked.

Decision-making within the groups, insofar as it can be ascertained, revolves more around achieving consensus (weak or strong) than any use of majority voting. The non-aligned, for instance, approved recommendations on strengthening co-operation at their 1979 Havana summit.[2] They noted that 'consensus is both a process and a final compromise formula, shaped by prior consultations, discussions and negotiations into a generally agreed position', and laid down a number of methods for its promotion. Expressions of dissent are often noted in summit documents (e.g. the Durban summit in 1998 elicited seven such expressions from six countries[3]). There is normally some sort of pattern for changing the leadership from one summit to another (again by consensus within and often across geographical groups), on a regular basis. In the case of the non-aligned this is usually done geographically. The Asians (Bangladesh) will take over from the Africans (in this case South Africa, 1998–2001) in 2001; the South Africans took over from the Latin Americans (Colombia) in 1998. The non-aligned Europeans, with the exit of Yugoslavia from the scene following the Jakarta summit in 1992, are no longer part of this system. In contrast, the Group of 77 has different systems for leadership in New York and Geneva though both are based on geographical rotation. In the case of the EU the change is made through the use of alphabetical names of each country in their own language. Sometimes they have other tasks. The non-aligned Chair to be has to provide the first draft of the summit documents which are sent to other non-aligned countries some six weeks before the summit. The chairpersons, as in other groups, also provide leadership at the UN and elsewhere when necessary, particularly in New York and Geneva.

The role of major powers, particularly the United States but also China, and how they obtain support is also considered. One main role for both since 1945 has been 'coalition building' both in the General Assembly and the Security Council.[4] The United States has benefited from the ending of the Cold War though it remains uncertain about its policy towards the

UN in general. China too has created a strong base since it became an observer within the non-aligned in 1992 as Indian opposition to this move faded with the break-up of its patron, the Soviet Union.

The new UN, which began in 1946, was designed to provide some benefits for all its member states, as well as provide a fruitful context for them to work in, given UN Charter principles. It was meant to be 'an Alliance of the Great Powers embedded in a universal organization'.[5] Roberts and Kingsbury suggest that 'The UN finds roles for itself in those areas of activity which are most appropriately tackled either on a truly multilateral basis, or by individuals representing, not a particular state, but the collectivity of states.'[6] This may be an end result. But this has often been achieved (or shown as not then possible) through the interaction between the different groupings that have been set up to pursue the interests of some states within and outside the UN. One major carrot the UN can provide is legitimacy: this was very important in the cases of both South Africa and Namibia.

THE CONTEXT

The context for the setting up of electoral and political groups was provided both by the UN Charter agreed at San Francisco in June 1945 and by the work of the UN Preparatory Commission in London between August and December 1945, during which the first major UN political and electoral grouping – the Latin American group – was formed.

San Francisco, June 1945

The British commentary on the UN Charter, agreed at San Francisco in June 1945, stated: 'It is not suggested that all this machinery, however impressive it may be, can by itself preserve the peace or increase the welfare of the peoples of the world. That depends on *how governments use such machinery* [my italics].'[7] 'The very basis of the scheme [of setting up the UN],' Gladwyn Jebb (one of the main negotiators) noted in July 1945, 'namely, continued co-operation between the Great Powers, and notably between the Soviet Union, the United States and the United Kingdom, had its origin in this country.' He went on to state that 'the United States, we hope, will shortly be committed to intervene if trouble breaks out anywhere in the world. The Soviet Union will shortly be bound by the most solemn obligations, which it must surely hesitate to repudiate. And, finally, the position of the smaller states, their independence and integrity, have all been made vastly more secure than they would have been if no

Organisation had been agreed upon.'[8] The latter suggestion was more prescient than the former.

The UN Preparatory Commission and the formation of the Latin American group, August to December 1945

The development of the first distinct group of UN actors, the Latin Americans, was instigated by the Colombian delegate to San Francisco, Eduardo Angel, who subsequently became Colombia's special represent-ative to the UN Preparatory Commission which was held in London. In his unpublished memoirs[9] he states that he drew one important conclusion after talking to Jebb on his arrival: 'If we Latin Americans, as happened in the League of Nations, are splintered into a myriad of viewpoints, we will receive nothing other than the crumbs other nations choose to give us. If, on the other hand we work together with solidarity, we can obtain for each of the 20 delegations an honored position on the Preparatory Commission and at the General Assembly.' He went on to discuss these ideas with his Latin American colleagues and gave them a feasible plan 'provided we worked as a team'. This gave the group 20 votes which were supplemented by six[10] from King Faisal, 'who dominated the Pan-Arab Movement' (the Arab League had been founded in 1945) and 'realized the convenience of uniting with the Latin American countries . . . Thus we were in control of 26 votes – a majority of the 51 member countries.'

Senor Angel became President of the Preparatory Commission and subsequently the initial President of the General Assembly. As he states dryly, 'Naturally the great powers were not overly pleased that their delegates had to follow the Colombian delegate around like lap dogs in their quest for votes – since it was he who presided over the meetings of the Latin American group.' He then describes how he allied with the Soviet Union's Gromyko to try to ensure that five Latin American judges were elected to the International Court of Justice, not two as the United States wished. Four were subsequently elected[11] in February 1946: one lost on a Security Council technicality.

The original electoral and political groupings, 1946

The earliest emergence of groups within the General Assembly[12] revolved around decisions as to who should be the President of the General Assembly, the seven Vice-Presidents and the Chairmen of the six main committees. These together were to compose the important General Com-mittee which controls the General Assembly agenda and therefore had to have a representative character. The General Assembly elected seven Vice-

Presidents at its third plenary meeting. They were all five permanent members plus South Africa and Venezuela. The Chairmen of the original six main committees also elected *inter alia* on the basis of equitable geographical distribution, comprised Commonwealth 1, Eastern Europe 2, Middle East 1 and Latin America 2. Western Europe was represented by the President of the General Assembly, M. Spaak. A similar 'gentleman's agreement' was made over the distribution of non-permanent seats in the Security Council.[13] The final decision was that non-permanent seats of the 11-seat Security Council should be distributed according to the following pattern: Commonwealth 1, Eastern Europe 1, Middle East 1, Latin America 2 and Western Europe 1. They were complemented by the five permanent members: the United States, the Soviet Union, China (then represented by the Kuomintang), France and the United Kingdom.

The United Nations was also affected by the creation of political groupings outside the system (as has already been noted, the Arab League in 1945 followed by the Organization of American States including the United States in 1948). A similar attempt to set up an Asian grouping through the New Delhi Asian Relations conference of 1947 was less successful. An Asian Relations Organization was set up but it had lost any influence it had by 1952. The Asian countries did get together in New Delhi in January 1949 to try to find a solution to the colonial problem of Indonesia after the second Dutch police action against it in December 1948. They considered that the Security Council resolutions did not adequately condemn the Dutch action and *inter alia* called for the transfer of power by 1 January 1950. Black Africa at that time did not come into the picture as it was only represented in the UN by Ethiopia and Liberia, apart from the special case of South Africa (a Commonwealth member). The growing strength of the Soviet Union was reflected in the Eastern European group at the UN, although this group also had to deal with the defection of Yugoslavia (see below). Western Europe remained more divided despite the fact that the Western parties to the regional Brussels Treaty (1948), which had reaffirmed their faith in fundamental human rights and in the other ideals proclaimed in the Charter of the United Nations,[14] agreed, in London in May 1949, to establish the Council of Europe. At the UN the United Kingdom played a role in the Commonwealth group while continental European states were involved in the Western Europe group.

THE THIRD WORLD: EMERGENCE OF THE ARAB–ASIAN GROUP, 1946–54

Within the UN system the subsequent development of the Arab–Asian group was stimulated by the increase in UN membership from Asia and the Middle East (9 in 1946[15] to 15 in 1950) as well as the need to address, from their perspective, such important political issues as Palestine and Korea. It was helped by its growing relationship with Yugoslavia after Yugoslavia was expelled from Cominform in 1948.

The first important votes: Palestine and the Human Rights Declaration, 1947–48

The interplay between the changing groups and rifts within groups can be seen in certain important votes of the period. The votes on Palestine showed the First and Second Worlds combining against the Arab–Asian group (the Third World). Iraq and Saudi Arabia failed in their attempt to inscribe an additional item on the agenda of the April–May 1947 General Assembly special session on Palestine calling for 'The termination of the mandate over Palestine and the declaration of its independence'. At the end of November 1947 three resolutions were rejected by the *ad hoc* committee. The first raised the question of the competence of the UN to recommend any solution contrary to the UN Charter and against the wishes of the majority of the people of Palestine and suggested that an ICJ advisory opinion be sought on a number of questions including 'whether the indigenous population of Palestine has not an inherent right to Palestine and to determine its future constitution and government'. The second called for international co-operation over the resettlement of Jewish refugees in their countries of origin, and the third called for the establishment of an independent, unified Palestine.

Israeli claims to part of Palestine were immeasurably strengthened by the subsequent General Assembly partition resolution of November 1947 (GAR 181 (II)), which recommended the division of Palestine into two states with Jerusalem as a *corpus separatum*[16] by 33 for (the necessary two-thirds majority) to 13 against, with 10 abstentions. India (with its large Muslim population) and Pakistan (two Asian Commonwealth states) joined the six Arab states (Egypt, Iraq, Lebanon, Saudi Arabia, Syria and Yemen) and the other Islamic states (Afghanistan, Iran) and Turkey[17] in voting against the resolution (the others were Cuba and Greece). They saw this as a straightforward colonial issue.[18]

One of the main surprises was the Russian support for Zionism, which was overall probably due to 'the overriding Russian aim' of the disruption of the British Empire. 'Without the endorsement of the eastern bloc

[Byelorussia, Czechoslovakia, Poland, Soviet Union, Ukraine – but *not* Yugoslavia which, interestingly, abstained] the United Nations could not have voted in favour of the creation of a Jewish state.' Huge pressures were put on other states.[19] The Commonwealth split: the mainly white Dominions (Australia, Canada, New Zealand and South Africa) voted for a Jewish state; the United Kingdom as the previous Mandate holder abstained. The vote was also one of the first indications of the future demise of the Commonwealth group as a United Nations collective actor, which had occurred by the end of the 1950s.

Meanwhile Western European states (Belgium, Denmark, France, Iceland, Luxembourg, the Netherlands, Norway and Sweden, but not Greece), no doubt influenced by the Holocaust, voted for. The Latin Americans, some of whom were concerned about colonialism, were the most split – Bolivia, Brazil, Costa Rica, Dominican Republic, Ecuador, Guatemala, Haiti, Nicaragua, Panama, Paraguay, Peru, Uruguay and Venezuela voted for; Cuba voted against; and Argentina, Chile, Colombia, El Salvador, Honduras and Mexico abstained. China (the Koumintang version) abstained, as did the African Ethiopia, while Liberia with its strong American connections voted for, as did, of course, the United States. Siam (now Thailand) was diplomatically absent.

This vote gave legitimacy to the Israeli claim to statehood and was used as one of the two bases for its declaration of independence in May 1948.

In contrast, the Universal Declaration on Human Rights was adopted in December 1948 by 48 to 0, with 8 abstentions. The eight votes of abstention were those of six Eastern Europeans including the Soviet Union,[20] South Africa and Saudi Arabia, the latter concerned about marriage rights and the right to change religion. All other Third World countries then in the UN (15) voted for the resolution. They were concerned about human rights, in particular the right of self-determination, as will be seen below.

Indonesia, Korea and the Yugoslav Connection, 1948–51

A significant development in the late 1940s was the forming of a partnership between Yugoslavia (expelled from the Cominform in 1948 but voting with the Third World on Palestine as early as 1947)[21] and India and Egypt, who were to join it on the Security Council in 1950. Yugoslavia began to seek security in relationships with non-communist countries who could be like-minded friends and to whom it could relate politically and economically, both to gain influence and a new role in world affairs, and for support against future threats to its existence and stability. These three major founders of the Non-aligned Movement began to work together to some extent, once they joined the Security Council. On 25 June 1950 Egypt and India voted for the Security Council resolution condemning North

Korean aggression (the Soviet Union was absent and Yugoslavia abstained). The three were the only abstainers on the General Assembly resolution of 7 October, which obliquely approved UN action north of the 38th parallel. On the subsequent 'Uniting for Peace' General Assembly resolution of 3 November, only India abstained since the United States persuaded other Arab and Asian states to vote in the affirmative. Yugoslavia also voted for the resolution since it wished the General Assembly to have the power to recommend action, in the face of a great power veto in the Security Council, on account of its fear of the Soviet Union.

The Chinese intervention in North Korea in late November and early December 1950 transformed the military balance in Korea. This highlighted the efforts of the Indian delegation, who made contact with the representatives of the People's Republic of China who came to New York to address the Security Council at the end of November. What is described as the first meeting of the Arab–Asian group[22] (Afghanistan, Burma, Egypt, India, Indonesia, Iran, Iraq, Lebanon, Pakistan, the Philippines, Saudi Arabia, Syria and Yemen) at the UN was held on 5 December 1950.[23] The participants appealed to the North Korean authorities and the People's Republic of China to declare that no forces under their control would cross south of the 38th parallel of latitude. The same 13 states subsequently put forward two General Assembly resolutions on 12 December, although the Philippines did not sponsor the second. The first, requesting the Indian President of the General Assembly to set up a group to determine the basis for a satisfactory cease-fire, was approved by 52–5–1 on 14 December; the second, which would have asked certain governments to make recommendations for the peaceful settlement of existing issues, was ultimately not put to the vote. Egypt and Yugoslavia abstained and India voted against the General Assembly resolution of 1 February 1951 which *inter alia* found that the Chinese People's Republic had committed aggression in Korea. The basis for future Yugoslav co-operation with India had been achieved by the end of 1950. Rubinstein notes:

> Prior to June 1950 the belief was widespread among Yugoslav officials that India, though nominally independent, was part of the West. But India's position on Korea made it evident that India was in fact an independent country. Yugoslavia came to appreciate the independent stand of these new nations, not only on this issue, but on disarmament and colonial questions, on the seating of Communist China, and on the urgency of promoting the economic development of the less-developed countries.[24]

The period December 1950 to January 1951 gave the Arab–Asian group 'a moral stature and political impetus that endured for several years',[25] although the group had only acted as a group in real moments of crisis,

and India often acted alone, particularly after Mr Khrishna Menon
replaced Sir Benegal Rau as Indian Permanent Representative in 1952.
Asian–Arab co-operation on colonial issues and on the ill treatment of
underdeveloped countries was remarked on by Western observers. Mr
Dean Acheson wrote to President Truman in October 1952 that 'the
outstanding fact of the Assembly so far, is its dominance by the Arab–
Asian bloc.'[26]

Negotiation on the right of self-determination, 1950–54

The Arab–Asian group was, not surprisingly, passionately interested in
developing anti-colonial norms, in part by proclaiming the right of self-
determination. The UN Charter merely mentions the principle of self-
determination. Article 1, on the right of self-determination in both the two
human rights covenants (on civil and political rights the International
Covenant on Civil and Political Rights (ICCPR), and on economic, social
and cultural rights the International Covenant on Economic and Social
Rights (ICESCR)), stems from the early 1950s. The three main resolutions
involved (see below) were masterminded by two persistent Permanent
Representatives at the UN: Mr Baroody, a Lebanese Christian representing
Saudi Arabia, and Mr Pazhwak representing Afghanistan.[27]

Both representatives avoided becoming involved with the Soviet proposal on the right to national self-determination which was rejected in
November 1950.[28] They then submitted a joint amendment to the draft
Covenant in the General Assembly requesting the Human Rights Commission study ways and means of ensuring the right of peoples and nations
to self-determination. This was adopted by 38–7–12 in December 1950,
despite Western dissent as part of GAR 421 (V). John Humphrey, the first
Director of the UN's Division of Human Rights, considered that these
'decisions marked the beginning of the politicisation of the covenants. The
developing countries were in revolt, and new voices were beginning to be
heard.'[29]

The Human Rights Commission found it impossible to prepare recom-
mendations for consideration by the General Assembly by its 1951 session.
Consequently, the 13 members of the Arab–Asian group drew up a draft
resolution proposing that the General Assembly should insert in the
Covenant an article on the right of peoples to self-determination. This
GAR 545 (VI) was adopted in February 1952 by 42 to 7 (Australia,
Belgium, France, Luxembourg, New Zealand, United Kingdom and
United States), with 5 abstentions.

The draft Article was subsequently debated in the Third Committee in
1954. All the delegations that had sponsored GAR 545 (VI), except Iran,
plus Bolivia, Chile, Greece, Haiti, Liberia, Thailand, Uruguay and notably

Yugoslavia, jointly submitted a draft resolution proposing that the right of self-determination be maintained in both Covenants. In the end no vote was taken and the fraught question was discussed again in the Third Committee in 1955. The tension surrounding the question had been made evident on 11 October 1955 when the UN Secretary-General suggested that the Assembly should appoint an *ad hoc* committee to try to reach agreement on basic principles; this would then be incorporated into a General Assembly declaration. The Secretary-General had hoped to help the United States proposal to have a study on self-determination as an alternative to the two Covenants recommended by the Human Rights Commission. However, the ploy did not succeed. Instead a working party was eventually set up to prepare a new text of Article 1. Their final text was adopted in the Third Committee by 33 (including 11 of the 13-strong Arab–Asian group[30]) to 12 (the white Commonwealth and Western Europe), with 13 abstentions. This, with very minor adjustments, became the final text of Article 1 of the Covenants that were put forward for signature in 1966 and came into force in 1976.

BANDUNG, APRIL 1955

Note: An * identifies the original 13 Arab and Asian members. All attended.

The growing complexity of group interaction within the United Nations was given further cohesion by the seminal Asian–African Bandung conference of April 1955, which was crucial to the setting up of the Non-aligned Movement in 1961. The Conference was convened by Burma*, Ceylon, India*, Indonesia* and Pakistan* and attended by Afghanistan*, Cambodia, China, Egypt*, Ethiopia, the Gold Coast, Iran*, Iraq*, Japan, Jordan, Laos, Lebanon*, Liberia, Libya, Nepal, the Philippines*, Saudi Arabia*, Sudan, Syria*, Thailand, Turkey, the Democratic Republic of Vietnam, the State of Vietnam and Yemen*.

The participants discussed the position of Africa and Asia, and the ways and means by which their peoples could achieve the fullest economic, cultural and political co-operation. The main items on the agenda were Economic Co-operation, Cultural Co-operation, Human Rights and Self-Determination, Problems of Dependent People, Other Problems including Palestine, and the Promotion of World Peace and Co-operation. The final communiqué specifically noted that the 'representation of the countries of the Asian–African region on the Security Council, in relation to the principle of equitable geographical distribution, was inadequate'. It expressed 'the view that as regards the distribution of the non-permanent seats, the Asian–African countries which, under the arrangement arrived at in London in 1946, are precluded from being elected, should be enabled to serve on the Security Council'.

The Asian–African conference[31] also declared its full support for the fundamental principles of human rights as a common standard of achievement for all peoples and nations. It took note of UN resolutions on the right of peoples and nations to self-determination, which was a prerequisite of the full enjoyment of all fundamental human rights. The policies and practices of racial segregation and discrimination were deplored. Colonialism in all its manifestations was an evil that should speedily be brought to an end. The subjection of peoples to alien subjugation, domination and exploitation constituted a denial of fundamental human rights and was contrary to the UN Charter.

The continuing debate on the right of self-determination subsequently became less fraught. As early as 1958 John Humphrey noted: 'I was now more optimistic about the future of the Covenants; so many dependent territories were becoming independent that the political implications of the articles on self-determination seemed less important.'[32] It was also illustrated by the fact that in 1960 the nine countries (Australia, Belgium, Dominican Republic, France, Portugal, South Africa, Spain, United Kingdom and United States) that could not subscribe to the seminal Declaration on the Granting of Independence to Colonial Countries and Peoples (GAR 1514) adopted by 89–0–9, only abstained rather than voted against the Declaration.

THE SECOND WORLD, 1947–60

As the Cold War became more intense, with the blockade of Berlin in 1948, the Second World – the Eastern European group (then the Soviet Union, Byelorussia, Czechoslovakia, Poland and the Ukraine) – consolidated its positions. Yugoslavia, which did not always follow their example (e.g. in its abstention on the partition resolution on Palestine), was expelled from Cominform in 1948.[33] It remained a member of the Eastern European Group for electoral purposes only. The Soviet Union and its Eastern European allies did not, as has already been noted, always vote in the same way as the emerging Third World.

Second World–Third World differences, 1956–60

This pattern continued. Yugoslavia and India did not, for instance, go along with the Soviet Union's proposal in 1957 for a declaration on peaceful coexistence after the invasion of Hungary in 1956. A similar Indian draft on Peaceful and Neighbourly Relations among States was passed by 77–0–1 as GAR 1236 (XII). These countries, plus the 16 black African states admitted in 1960, were also hostile to the 1960 Soviet proposals for replacing the UN Secretary-General by a triumvirate representing all three blocs, as well as to their proposal for a declaration on colonialism. Third World countries also noted that Soviet attitudes to setting up or expanding institutions within the UN with the aim of furthering economic development, particularly as regards finance, were either similar to, or even more restrictive than, those of Western countries.

THIRD WORLD REGIONAL GROUPS, 1958–72

Groups most involved in taking the initiative on particular questions were often those closest to the problems. Both the Arab group and the African group (formed in 1958) took initiatives in the late 1950s on their major issues of concern, both of which had been highlighted at Bandung: the rights of the Arab people of Palestine and racial discrimination. And in 1969 an Islamic group was formed in the context of concern over Jerusalem.

The Arab group within the Arab–Asian group

The Arab group took the initiative on Palestine from the West in the late 1950s.[34] Previously certain states in the Western group had put forward resolutions based on the idea that the refugee problem needed to be resolved by resettlement outside former Palestine rather than being a matter for the right of self-determination and the right of return. The previous normal pattern of operation can be illustrated by the year 1958.[35] Iraq as usual made sure a Palestine Arab refugee addressed the Special Political Committee, but the only draft resolution put forward was sponsored by the United States plus the United Kingdom, the Netherlands and New Zealand. This emphasized resettlement rather than repatriation and was passed as GAR 1315 (XIII) by 57–0–20.

The new positive attitude by Arabs and Muslims towards the problems of Palestine both inside and outside the UN (the Palestinian National Liberation Movement, Fatah, was being set up at this time, probably with the support of the Algerian nationalists who had themselves learned how to use the UN) is first noticeable in 1959. The ten Arab states at the UN circulated a report in October on the Secretary-General's proposals concerning UN assistance to Palestine refugees. This reaffirmed their stand on behalf of the Arab people of Palestine and the right of Arab refugees to return to their homeland. It also rejected proposals for resettlement. Indonesia and Pakistan from the Asian group then put forward a draft resolution that gave more emphasis to repatriation and compensation for the refugees than resettlement. An amended version was approved by 80–0–1, GAR 1456 (XIV), in 1959. The main paragraph, which was adopted by 54–1–18 in Committee, requested the UN Conciliation Committee for Palestine to make further efforts to secure the implementation of paragraph 11 of GAR 194 (III) (on the right of return).

An Islamic group – the Organization of the Islamic Conference – formed 1969

Even more attention was focused on the Palestine problem after the 1967 war, but SCR 242 did not mention the question of Jerusalem – a city of great importance to three of the world's major religions. This showed up the differences between the United States and the Europeans on the issue of Israel/Palestine. The ambivalence of the United States on the question was shown in May 1968 when it abstained with Canada on a Security Council resolution (SCR 252) which deplored Israel's failure to comply with two of the emergency special session resolutions on Jerusalem and considered that all administrative measures taken by Israel to change Jerusalem's legal status were invalid. The United States did join in a unanimous resolution in July 1969 (SCR 267) censuring Israel for all measures taken to change the status of Jerusalem. But it subsequently abstained on SCR 271 (September 1969) which noted the Council's concern at the damage caused following the arson attempt on the Al Aqsa mosque; called on Israel to refrain from causing any hindrance to the discharge of the established functions of the Supreme Moslem Council of Jerusalem; and condemned Israel for its failure to comply with the resolutions passed in the General Assembly and the Security Council on Jerusalem since the 1967 war.

After the Al Aqsa mosque incident Arab League Foreign Ministers decided to convene a conference of Islamic Foreign Ministers. The PLO was present as an observer at the first summit (September 1969) of the Organization of the Islamic Conference (OIC), which has presented the Islamic view ever since, both inside and outside the United Nations. Interestingly Islamic and non-aligned states rather than the Arab states took the lead for the first time in the General Assembly that year in sponsoring a resolution (eventually GAR 2535) recognizing that 'the problem of the Palestine Arab refugees has arisen from the denial of their inalienable rights under the Charter of the United Nations and the Universal Declaration of Human Rights'. This was the beginning of a long campaign to persuade the Security Council to give support to Palestinian rights as it had already done partially over Jerusalem.

The African group formed 1958

The question of South African racial policies was raised in the UN as early as 1946 when India complained about discriminatory treatment of South African residents of Indian origin. GAR 44 (I) recommended that South Africa treat Indians in conformity with international agreements and the UN Charter. South Africa countered by maintaining that these policies were part of the domestic jurisdiction of a state. Bandung (with five African participants – Egypt, Ethiopia, Gold Coast, Liberia and Sudan) 'was the first international gathering outside the UN to deal with the apartheid issue in a substantive fashion', as well as demonstrating the 'impact that outside coordination could have on the progress of an issue in the UN'.[36]

The first Conference of Independent African States in Ghana in 1958 established the UN African group to co-ordinate 'all matters of common concern to the African states'.[37] This group became more powerful with the admission of 16 black African states into the UN in 1960. As Bissell notes, 'the African bloc' possessed 'the initiative during 1961–2 without organized opposition'.[38] The concerted African campaign against South Africa in the specialized agencies led, in the first instance, to the South African decision to withdraw from the FAO in 1963 and the ILO and WHO in 1964. Organizational efforts were completed with the setting up of the Organization of African Unity in 1963.

Human rights aspects of racial discrimination were not forgotten. The General Assembly called unanimously in 1962 for a declaration on racial discrimination. The 1963 Declaration was followed by the Convention on the Elimination of All Forms of Racial Discrimination adopted, with one abstention, in 1965. It was the first of the current six major UN human rights conventions to come into force. The Ghanaian delegate, Mr Lamptey, played the major role in the negotiations.[39]

THE NON-ALIGNED, 1961–72

As has already been noted, Third World countries remained determined not to align with either the United States or the Soviet Union in the early 1950s, a trend further confirmed by the Soviet Union's invasion of Hungary in 1956. In 1957 Third World countries also attempted to extend relations with Latin American states, a number of whom were poised between the First and Third Worlds. In 1958 two delegations from Arab countries visited Latin America and Scandinavia prior to the General Assembly with the aim of winning sympathy for the cause of Algerian independence. In 1959 Yugoslavia sent a large goodwill mission to Argentina, Bolivia, Brazil,

Colombia, Costa Rica, Cuba, Ecuador, Haiti, Honduras, Peru and Venezuela. One example of their resultant co-operation was the fact that a
number of Latin American states moved from abstaining in Committee to
voting against in Plenary on a resolution (GAR 1379 (XIV)) in late 1959
requesting France to refrain from nuclear testing in the Sahara. President
Castro met Nehru, Sukarno, Nkrumah, Nasser and Sihanouk when he
visited the General Assembly in 1960.

The admission of 16 black African states into the UN in 1960 also
helped. Their views and those of other putative non-aligned countries
were not necessarily in harmony: this was the case with regard to the
Congo – a major preoccupation of the General Assembly. Their views did,
however, coincide on decolonization, and this question, as before, continued to provide the main strand of unity in the formation of the Non-
aligned Movement. They also continued to oppose many Soviet proposals.

A crucial factor in favour of a non-aligned conference was the search by
middle-rank powers for organizational ways of influencing the United
States and the Soviet Union, a dominant theme going back to the Asian–
Arab intervention in the Korean crisis of the early 1950s. In 1959 and 1960
Yugoslavia intensified its campaign to secure non-bloc participation at
high-level conferences between East and West, and with the approach of
the May 1960 summit conference, Nehru and Presidents Nasser and
Sukarno joined President Tito in calling for such participation in meetings
on disarmament. Following this abortive summit, a five-power resolution
(sponsored by Ghana, India, Indonesia, the United Arab Republic and
Yugoslavia), calling for the restoration of direct contact between the
leaders of the two blocs, was put before the General Assembly on 29
September 1960. This was opposed by the Western powers, partly on
procedural grounds, and subsequently withdrawn.

This setback spurred President Tito on to greater efforts to co-ordinate
non-aligned countries, efforts which initially encountered resistance from
Nehru and President Nasser. He sought to win over the newly independent African countries during his first tour of black Africa in early 1961
when he visited Ghana, Guinea, Liberia, Mali and Togo, besides Morocco,
Tunisia and the United Arab Republic. However, after the Bay of Pigs
invasion, which occurred when President Tito was in Cairo, President
Nasser became more interested in a non-aligned conference. On 2 April
1961 they issued a joint communiqué expressing their anxiety over the
international situation and called for consultations among uncommitted
countries in order to strengthen world peace, preserve the independence
of all nations, and remove the danger of intervention in the internal affairs
of other countries. A preliminary meeting was subsequently held in Cairo
in June.

Non-aligned politics, 1961–72

The first non-aligned summit conference opened in Belgrade on 1 September 1961 against a sombre background of East–West tension, due in part to the erection of the Berlin Wall on 13 August, but in larger measure to the Soviet Union's resumption of nuclear testing on 31 August (an action that unilaterally abrogated an informal moratorium that had been in existence between the United States and itself). The participants were Afghanistan, the Algerian National Liberation Front, Burma, Cambodia, Ceylon, Congo, Cuba, Cyprus, Ethiopia, Ghana, Guinea, India, Indonesia, Iraq, Lebanon, Mali, Morocco, Nepal, Saudi Arabia, Somalia, Sudan, Tunisia, United Arab Republic, Yemen and Yugoslavia.[40] The three observer states were Bolivia, Brazil and Ecuador. Their main preoccupations, which were very similar to those voiced at Bandung, were great power disarmament, the elimination of colonialism, economic development and the right of all nations to self-determination, as well as the restoration of all rights to the Arab people of Palestine and the condemnation of apartheid. They recommended the expansion of the Security Council and ECOSOC, and particularly noted that they did not wish to form a new bloc and could not be a bloc. They considered it essential that the non-aligned should participate in solving outstanding international issues. They argued that the extension of the uncommitted area of the world constituted the only possible and indispensable alternative to the policy of total division of the world into blocs.

The co-operation of many of those who had attended the Belgrade summit over the next three General Assembly sessions had the effect of expediting action on many of the issues discussed at Belgrade. Immediately following the 1961 General Assembly, the United States and the Soviet Union finally put forward a statement of agreed principles for disarmament negotiations, and by 13 December they were able to endorse an agreement on the formation of an enlarged Disarmament Committee of 18, containing 4 non-aligned African–Asian countries. They also managed to secure the adoption of a draft resolution setting up a special committee of 17 (to become better known after its expansion in 1962 as the Committee of 24) to examine the implementation of the 1960 Declaration on Colonialism. The 1962 General Assembly set up a special committee on the Policies of Apartheid of the Government of South Africa to keep South Africa's racial policies under review and to report, as appropriate, to the General Assembly, or the Security Council, or both. And in 1963 the General Assembly recommended the expansion of the Security Council and ECOSOC.

Internal problems then began to dent the effectiveness of the movement. President Nasser and Mrs Bandaranaike became particularly active proponents of a second summit in October 1963 in the face of Indonesian proposals for a second radical Bandung. The battle between Tito and Sukarno underpinned the second summit in October 1964. Tito championed 'nonalignment, active and peaceful coexistence, and co-operation throughout the United Nations as the main political organization of the international community'. Sukarno wanted a movement 'exclusively predicated on racial and ethnic ties among Afro/Asian states, unremitting struggle against "reactionaries" and the West, and the creation of a new militant organisation of Afro-Asians outside the UN framework of the UN'.[41] President Sukarno, however, failed, as did his successors, to shift the movement into more radical channels and away from its original objectives. The participants supported the Joint Declaration of the Group of 77 at UNCTAD and called for harmonization of policies within the Group before UNCTAD II. No further non-aligned meeting was held until 1969. The relative inaction can be partially explained by the fact that much attention was then being focused on the problems of Vietnam, which was handled outside the UN, and that the Group of 77 maintained its predominance on economic matters within the UN system.

Tito then tried again to encourage non-alignment to help resolve Third World problems. A special meeting at Belgrade in July 1969 agreed that those countries interested in non-alignment, particularly those that had become independent since 1964 and all OAU members, should also be invited to future gatherings on the principles and criteria observed at the Belgrade and Cairo conferences. A specific resolution was passed on strengthening the role of non-aligned countries. This set up machinery to 'provide for continuity, maintain contacts between member states and ensure the implementation of the decisions' of non-aligned conferences by entrusting the Chairman with the function of 'taking all necessary steps' to ensure the above. Non-aligned representatives in UN bodies were requested 'to co-ordinate and harmonise their efforts'. In 1972 the Georgetown Foreign Ministers Conference decided that annual meetings of non-aligned countries should be held at ministerial level in the last week of September in New York. These have continued ever since.

The People's Republic of China finally took over the Chinese seat in the Security Council UN in 1971 after the Third, Second and certain First World countries combined to achieve a two-thirds majority vote (76–35–17, GAR 2758) and thus overrode US opposition.

THE GROUP OF 77, 1963–72

One expert on the North–South dialogue suggests that the pursuit of the 'development imperative' was an immediate post-war priority, given the fact that the UN Charter was guided by the principle that the maintenance of peace requires economic and social co-operation with permanent international machinery to back it up, and that governments had a significant measure of responsibility for the management of their economy and international economic relations.[42] It is significant that Bandung gave pride of place in its communiqué to economic co-operation. This recommended the early establishment of the Special United Nations Fund for Economic Development – the allocation by the World Bank (a UN specialized agency) of a greater part of its resources to Asian–African countries – and the early establishment of an International Finance Corporation, as well as the vital importance of stabilizing commodity trade in the region. The participants also suggested that, without forming a bloc, there was a need for prior consultation of participating countries in international fora to further their mutual economic interest.

These views were to some extent shared by many Latin American countries that were combating the relative decline in their influence as a voting bloc as the UN continued to extend its membership, particularly to newly independent countries. They also wished to propagate more widely certain ideas on economic development which had gained currency under the leadership of Dr Prebisch of the regional UN Economic Commission for Latin America. Their lobbying for an increase in the size of ECOSOC had begun in 1956, but had been resisted. At the 1958 General Assembly certain Latin American countries therefore combined with the Arab and Asian countries to sponsor a draft resolution requesting the Secretary-General to study the fields in which private capital could best be used by underdeveloped countries. This was followed in 1959 by a resolution sponsored by Brazil and 32 others, proposing the establishment by ECOSOC of a Commission for Industrial Development to take account of the growing interest in industrialization and economic diversification among underdeveloped countries, which was eventually adopted unanimously. Another link between Latin America and the Arab world began in 1960 when Venezuela joined with Iran and three Arab countries to form the Organization of Petroleum Exporting Countries (OPEC). From the late 1950s the Latin American group began to see itself overall as part of the Third World rather than part of the First World.

Latin American concern with economic issues and influence

One important Latin American contribution to the formation of both the non-aligned group and Group of 77 was a resolution sponsored by Argentina at the summer meeting of ECOSOC in 1961 (i.e. before the first non-aligned summit took place). This resolution (later revised in the General Assembly) called for international conferences to find solutions to

the problems encountered by less-developed countries in securing a
steady expansion of their external trade. It was not therefore surprising to
find that eight Latin American countries[43] attended the 1962 Cairo non-
aligned conference on the Problems of Economic Development. This aired
worries about the growing disparity of standards in living in different
parts of the world, called for the convening of a UN world trade
conference in 1963 and proposed a series of mutual consultations and
studies before the conference.

Continued Latin American influence on the forthcoming UNCTAD I
was strengthened by the appointment of Dr Prebisch as its Secretary-
General during the first session of the Preparatory Committee in early
1963. Yugoslavia, which had been the driving force behind the setting up
of the Non-aligned Movement in 1961, also played an important role on
this Committee and was, unprecedently, in 1964 included by the Committee in the African–Asian group as a developing country. This meant
that it was, ultimately, included in Group A of UNCTAD – African and
Asian states and Yugoslavia – rather than Group D, Eastern Europe.
President Tito, visiting Latin America for the first time, went to Brazil,
Bolivia, Chile and Mexico in September 1963.

Emergence of the Group of 77, 1963–64

The development of the Group of 77 in 1963–64 helped bring about the
formation of UNCTAD. It contained three regional groups, African, Asian
and Latin American, the few European members were incorporated in
these groups. It was similar to but larger than the non-aligned, dealing
almost exclusively with economic issues. Latin American states continued
to need allies to make their presence felt, given the increase of the number
of states in the UN to 100 by the end of 1960. The first appearance of the
Group of 77 can be seen in a draft General Assembly resolution put
forward by 75 member states in October 1963. This welcomed the joint
declaration of the developing countries prepared in the Preparatory
Committee, stressed the importance of the forthcoming conference for the
economies of developing countries and the world economy as a whole,
and insisted that the domestic efforts of these countries needed to be
supplemented by adequate international action. The second part emphasized the desirability of a new international division of labour with new
patterns of production and trade. This, it argued, was the only way in
which the economic independence of developing countries could be
strengthened. This was approved unanimously as GAR 1897 (XVIII). The
call for the New International Economic Order really appears to begin
here. Of the 75 states participating, 21 came from Latin America and the
Caribbean, 31 from Africa (regarded as a geographical entity) and 20 from

Asia (including the Middle East). The other 3 were Cyprus, New Zealand and Yugoslavia.

One major battle in UNCTAD I (March–June 1964) concerned its possible institutionalization. Western countries were forced to accept the idea of some such organization but determined to prevent any consequent diminution of ECOSOC's powers and functions. A compromise proposal was eventually agreed over the question of voting procedures and membership of standing committees, and UNCTAD was unanimously established as an organ of the General Assembly by GAR 1995 (XIX) in December 1964. The Group of 77 came into the limelight with the making of a joint declaration at the end of the conference, noting that although this was a new era, they did not consider that the progress made in each of the major fields was adequate or commensurate with their essential requirements.

The Bretton Woods institutions, 1966–72

Third World groupings were able to play a greater part in the Bretton Woods institutions (both the IMF and IBRD are specialized agencies of the UN) in the 1960s. A decision was taken in September 1966 that joint meetings on improving the international payments system would be held for the first time between deputies of the Group of 10 (the main Western industrial states) in the IMF and the Executive Directors of the Fund including representatives from developing countries. The process continued after the collapse of the Bretton Woods monetary order, which was triggered by the US decision in August 1971 to cease allowing the dollar to be convertible into gold. At UNCTAD III (April–May 1972) the Group of 77 elected 15 countries to represent them. One of the main results was agreement to include the less-developed countries in a new IMF Committee (sometimes called the Group of 20) to negotiate international monetary reform and to replace the Group of 10. This was possible because of Western division: the United States had begun to fear the European strength in the Group of 20.[44] The Group of 77 did not, however, succeed in gaining agreement for a direct link between Special Drawing Rights and development financing.

WEOG, GROUP B, THE EUROPEAN COMMUNITY AND THE CSCE, 1957–75

The West, like the Third World, has not always been united. The Commonwealth, both Western and Third World body, and Western European groups were supplanted by the Western European and Other States group

(WEOG) and the Asian–African group as early as 1957, the year the European Economic Community was founded. And the EEC, particularly after it was joined by three new members including the United Kingdom in 1973, became an influential political grouping in both New York and Geneva. It did not always agree with the United States on either economic or political issues. First World Europeans (plus the United States and Canada), together with Third World Europeans, were able to begin negotiating with the Second World in the early 1970s through the CSCE process.

Electoral changes, 1957–63

The most important electoral changes ever in the UN system took place between 1957 and 1963. They were spearheaded by the Third World (as noted at Bandung), helped by the increase in numbers in the General Assembly from the original 51 to 82[45] and supported by the Second World. The Commonwealth electoral group at the UN was replaced by the Asian–African group and the Western European and Others States group (WEOG) – the Others being the old British Dominions: Australia, Canada and New Zealand, with the notable exception of South Africa[46]). WEOG itself was much influenced by the foundation of the European Economic Community in 1957, followed by EFTA in 1960 and the Western economic think-tank, and co-ordinator of the OECD, in 1961.

All this had to be reflected in the important General Committee. The General Assembly therefore decided by GAR 1192 (XII) of 1957 passed by 49–1–27 (France, United Kingdom, United States) that the number of Vice-Presidents in the Assembly should be increased from 8[47] to 13 as follows: 4 from Asia and Africa; 1 from Eastern Europe; 2 from Latin America and 2 from Western Europe and Other States, besides the 5 permanent members. The resolution also stated that at least one of the Vice-Presidents among the Asian and African and the Western Europe and Other States groups, or the President or one of the Chairmen of the main committees, should be from a Commonwealth country without altering the geographical distribution of seats in the General Committee[48] as defined by the resolution. This was the last time the Commonwealth was noted as a specific electoral group in the UN. The question of apartheid (and economic issues) had split the Commonwealth[49] by the next time the number of General Assembly Vice-Presidents was increased in 1963. (The United States is a member of WEOG for electoral purposes only.)

The subsequent changes made in UN electoral patterns in 1963 to accommodate the Asian–African group remain the most fundamental ever to have been made in the UN system. GAR 1991 A (XVIII) was passed by 97 to 11 (France, Soviet Union) to 4 (United Kingdom, United States), despite the fact that only one permanent member (China–Taiwan) of the Security Council voted for it. This decided that the Security Council should be expanded from 11 to 15 (a Charter amendment) and that non-permanent members in this enlarged Council should be elected as follows: 5 from Africa and Asia; 1 from Eastern Europe; 2 from Latin America; and 2 from WEOG. A further resolution, GAR 1991 B (XXVIII), decided by 96 to 11, (France, Soviet Union) to 5 (China, United Kingdom, United States) that ECOSOC should be enlarged from 18 to 27 members (a further Charter amendment) and that the nine additional members of ECOSOC[50] should be elected, with 7 from Africa and Asia; 1 from Latin America; and 1 from WEOG.

Meanwhile the number of Vice-Presidents in the General Assembly was increased from 13 to 17 by GAR 1990 (XVIII) (111–0) as follows: 7 from Africa and Asia; 1 from Eastern Europe; 3 from Latin America; and 2 from WEOG. It was also decided that the seven Chairmen of the main General Assembly committees should be elected as follows: 3 from Africa and Asia; 1 from Eastern Europe; 1 from Latin America; 1 from WEOG. The seventh chairmanship would rotate every alternate year between the last two groups. This was the last time Asian and African groups were linked. They have been separately listed ever since.

The General Assembly increased the number of its Vice-Presidents from 17 to 21 in 1978 (GAR 33/138). This marked the final separation of the Asian and African groups. The numbers were: 6 from Africa; 5 from Asia; 1 from Eastern Europe; 3 from Latin America; 2 from WEOG, as well as the 5 permanent members.

WEOG as a political grouping, Group B of UNCTAD and the expanding EEC (later EU), 1963–74

In New York WEOG does not act as a political grouping. It has always been eclipsed politically by the European Economic Community (later European Union – EU). In Geneva both Group B (the Western group), which was set up by UNCTAD in 1964, and the EU also work as political groupings. The European Community collectively was a significant factor in UN economic discussions, not least because of Community competence in trade matters. Political co-operation agreed by the European Community in 1972 enhanced Western European co-operation at the United Nations. This was further enhanced by the admission of the Irish Republic, Denmark and the United Kingdom into the Community in 1973 and the admission of the Federal Republic of Germany (and its Eastern counterpart) into the UN the same year. Although the EU (then EEC) could not and does not operate in the UN Security Council,[51] European Community co-operation in the UN as a whole has become stronger.

The other members of WEOG have often found this difficult to cope with and have, in certain cases, formed alternative groupings on specific issues (e.g. the Cairns Group[52] on agriculture formed in 1986) to press their interests more effectively. Both the EEC and the Council for Mutual Economic Assistance were given observer status at the General Assembly in 1974 because of the increased attention given by the Assembly to economic problems. As Peter Marshall notes, 'The joint positions taken by the Community [in 1974] ... came naturally to dominate the Group B position [in UNCTAD], especially as the United States' disenchantment and hostility to the UN process became more marked and the US contribution less influential. Community coordination has become a regular feature of the UN gatherings.'[53]

Palestine and Europe, 1970–72

Differences between the United States and the European Community within the First World have often surfaced in the context of Palestine. France, for instance, before the OPEC price rise, added a clause to a resolution in 1970 (eventually GAR 2628 (XXV)) reaffirming SCR 242 and recognizing 'that respect for the rights of the Palestinians is an indispensable element in the establishment of a just and lasting peace in the Middle East'. This resolution was passed by 57 (France, Soviet Union) to 16 (United States) to 39 (United Kingdom). This clause was added again to a further draft resolution in 1972 (ultimately GAR 2949 (XXVII)) which, for the first time, contained a decision to transmit the resolution to the Security Council for appropriate action. European solidarity was emphasized by the fact that the United Kingdom and other major European countries joined France and the Soviet Union in voting for the resolution, which was passed by 86–7–31.

The voting also showed clearly the first major positive switch of Latin American opinion on Palestine. Cuba and Chile had voted for this kind of resolution before. They were joined for the first time by Argentina, Ecuador, Guyana, Honduras, Jamaica, Mexico, Peru and Trinidad and Tobago. Radical Arab dissension was shown by the fact that Algeria, Iraq and Syria did not participate in the vote.

The CSCE process, 1973–75

Meanwhile a larger potential grouping began to be formed with the negotiations on Security and Co-operation in Europe in conformity with the purposes and principles of the United Nations, which began in 1973 and was agreed in 1975.[54] The participants included representatives of East and West including the United States and Canada, besides the

European neutrals and the European non-aligned (Cyprus, Malta and Yugoslavia). The emphasis given to communications and national minorities was prescient. Environment too was included, despite the fact that the Soviet bloc did not participate on the first major UN conference on the environment at Stockholm in 1972. Interestingly but not surprisingly, the neutrals and non-aligned played a similar role in this process 'as constructive participants, mediators and bridge builders',[55] as they sometimes tried to do within the UN system.

FIRST WORLD–THIRD WORLD INTERACTION, 1973–82

The pervasive influence of Algeria, the host to the fourth non-aligned summit (September 1973), was to dominate economic developments in regard to developing countries to the end of 1975. Seventy-five countries took part: these now made up half the member states of the international community and between them represented the majority of the world's population. On the economic side, the conference resolved to press for a UN special session on development, to establish a non-aligned economic and social development fund, and seek special measures in favour of the least developed countries. Imperialism was stated to be the greatest stumbling-block to the advancement of developing countries. At the same time socialist countries were asked to grant more favourable terms to the non-aligned in the fields of trade and scientific co-operation.

The Economic Declaration stated that the trend towards *détente* had not had much effect on the development of the developing countries and on international co-operation, and that the increasing trend towards closer economic relations between developed countries should in no way adversely affect the basic interests of developing countries. The parties agreed to give priority to the elaboration of a charter on the economic rights and duties of states at the next General Assembly. The Action Programme of economic co-operation stated *inter alia* that the non-aligned should act as a catalytic force in the Group of 77 in order to increase the effectiveness and solidarity of the developing countries.

The General Assembly accepted the proposal for a special session to be held in 1975. However, in January 1974 President Boumediénne put forward a proposal for a sixth special session of the UN General Assembly on raw materials and development. This action, taken after the raising of oil prices by OPEC following the Arab–Israeli war in October 1973, was in part due to a desire to prevent a wedge between the oil producers and other developing countries. The Group of 77 submitted a draft programme of action for this session (based on the Algiers non-aligned summit) for the establishment of a New International Economic Order (NIEO). This was eventually adopted without a vote, although many Western countries had substantial reservations on some of its contents. The session represented the height of the confrontation between the developed and developing countries. The Charter of Economic Rights and Duties of States was subsequently passed in the General Assembly by 120 to 6 (Belgium, Denmark, the Federal Republic of Germany, Luxembourg, the United Kingdom and the United States) to 10. Major areas of disagreement included nationalization and compensation for nationalization, permanent sovereignty over natural resources, and relations betwen states and companies and the rights of each.

This 1974 General Assembly also saw the beginning of what has become known as the North–South dialogue.[56] In October, the French President proposed the convening of an international conference on energy between producers, consumers and developing states as oil was regarded by the Group of 77 as outside the competence of the General Assembly. A meeting in April 1975 to discuss the agenda, attended by delegates from the EEC, the United States, Japan, Algeria, Brazil, India, Iran, Saudi Arabia, Venezuela and Zaire, failed because of a disagreement between the industrialized countries, who wished to discuss energy exclusively, and the Group of 77 representatives, who wanted a broader agenda. This disagreement provided the backdrop for the non-aligned Foreign Ministers' meeting in Lima in August 1975, one of the main purposes of which was to co-ordinate action for the seventh special session of the General Assembly, for which the 1973 non-aligned summit had called. The special session was able to adopt a consensus resolution on Development and Economic Co-operation since the United States took a less hard-line position.

Continuing North–South dialogue, 1977–78

Ministers from North and South finally met in Paris at the Conference on International Economic Co-operation (significantly a conference held outside the UN framework for the reasons explained above) in May–June 1977. Consumer countries agreed to contribute to a special action programme to help individual low-income countries to establish a common fund, to finance buffer stock, and to increase their volume of official aid. Although consensus was achieved on some of the broad issues discussed, no agreement on such key subjects as the relationship between the price of oil and its supply was reached.

Under pressure from the Group of 77, the General Assembly decided in 1977, without a vote, to hold a special session in 1980 to assess progress made in the UN system on the establishment of the NIEO and *inter alia* to establish an inter-sessional Committee of the Whole (COW), which first met in 1978 to monitor and encourage work on North–South issues, besides adopting a report on restructuring the economic and social sectors of the UN. Differences of opinion between the developed countries and the Group of 77, which wished to see it used as a negotiating forum, soon led to its adjournment. It was finally agreed in late 1978 by GAR 33/2 that it would negotiate with a view to adopting guidelines on central policy issues, as well as achieving agreement on fundamental issues underlying problems relating to international economic co-operation.

Splits in the Group of 77 over energy, 1979

At the following Group of 77 ministerial meeting at Arusha in February 1979 President Nyerere stressed the need for the Third World to build its own power base through national and collective self-reliance, and called for continuing unity of opposition. He laid emphasis on the unequal interdependence of developing countries with the developed. The Declaration deplored new protectionist trends and asked the Group of 24 to intensify its work on fundamental reform of the international monetary system.

Agreement in principle on the setting up of a Common Fund was finally reached in March 1979, but the run-up to UNCTAD V (Manila, May–June 1979) was dominated by awareness of the continuing instability and recession in the world economy. UNCTAD V was marked by open disagreement among the Group of 77 on the discussion of energy. Latin American countries led by Costa Rica sought to discuss this against the wishes of OPEC members. The Group of 77 was profoundly disappointed by the failure of the conference which, they thought, was due primarily to the negative attitude of the developed countries, particularly Group B (i.e. WEOG). The Group subsequently decided at a meeting held in Sri Lanka at Foreign Minister level just after UNCTAD V, that energy should be properly discussed in global North–South negotiations.

At the subsequent Havana non-aligned summit (August–September 1979) the Economic Declaration was revised even more substantially, representing a victory for OPEC as regards the South–South dialogue. A resolution endorsed the Sri Lanka proposal for global North–South negotiations at the 1980 UN Special Session on raw materials, energy, trade and development, and finance as a contribution to the implementation of the International Development Strategy was taken to the COW meeting in New York the following week and presented there by the Group of 77.

The final stages of the North–South dialogue, 1980–82

The North–South dialogue was enhanced by the 1980 Brandt Commission report calling for a North–South meeting which gave birth to a summit (organized by Austria and Mexico) at Cancun in October 1981[57] at which most heads of government, with the exception of the United States, were concerned to achieve global negotiations. This was given additional momentum at the G7 meeting at Versailles in 1982. 'At French behest the G7 agreed to launch the global negotiations on the basis of the latest G77 text, subject to four amendments. The Group of 77 in New York felt able to accept two of these amendments but rejected the other two [on the specialized agencies and the nature of the detailed work of the conference].'[58]

The US position under the conservative Reagan administration, which came into office in 1981, was that 'extraneous politicization was precluding much-needed technical agreement in one functional area after another to the point where the UN system ceased to be either useful or true to its original principle of universality'.[59] Others note 'that U.S. policy has been the only insurmountable obstacle to the initiation of the Global Negotiations. Much more broadly, the United States is the leader of resistance to change in the global economic order.'[60] Much of the United States' disillusion and perhaps misunderstanding of the UN system dates from this period.

Third World politics, 1973–81

The political as opposed to the economic side of Third World politics was also eventful in these years. At the 1973 Algiers non-aligned summit two significantly different views of non-alignment were expressed. President Gaddafi of Libya announced that he supported socialism not communism and sided neither with East nor West. President Castro announced Cuba's breaking of relations with Israel during the conference. He also denounced the theory that there were two imperialist powers led by the United States and the Soviet Union and stressed the need for the 'closest alliance amongst all the world's progressive forces'. The final political Declaration maintained that the balance of forces of the world had been profoundly changed as a result of the strengthening of 'the forces of peace, independence and progress'. It also noted that the people of the non-aligned countries must consolidate independence against any hegemony, a formula which had often been used to denote the influence of the Soviet Union.

The Declaration emphasized the need for more resolute action by the non-aligned countries to solve Third World conflicts stemming from imperialism and colonialism and stressed the need for *détente* between the great powers. A further Declaration on the struggle for national liberation agreed on the creation of a fund to support and strengthen the effectiveness of liberation movements. A 15-member bureau was set up to make preparations for future conferences and to co-ordinate governmental positions, particularly at the UN. At the next non-aligned summit at Colombo (August 1976) the political Declaration assessed the role of the non-aligned since 1961 (again dismissing the idea that security could be ensured by countries joining power blocs) and noted the increased role of the non-aligned in the solution of international problems. Mrs Bandaranaike described the underlying philosophy of the non-aligned in September 1976 as 'the deliberate choice by a large number of nations not to be drawn into the politics of confrontation implicit in the system of hostile military alliances, a refusal to contribute to the division of the world into camps. The world should not fear and distrust a movement which came into being as a creative alternative to mutual suspicion, recrimination and hate.'

Meanwhile the non-aligned had, at their Foreign Ministers meeting at Belgrade in July 1978, become concerned by the impending leadership of the movement by Cuba. Leading countries within the movement, particularly Yugoslavia, feared an attempt by Cuba to swing the movement more in the direction of the Soviet bloc on the premise that the socialist countries were the natural allies of the non-aligned. Yugoslavia, India and others wished to continue to stress the movement's traditional stance of keeping its distance from both blocs.

The sixth summit was, in fact, marked by a strong but ultimately unsuccessful attempt by the Cubans and some other Marxist countries to align the movement more closely with the Soviet bloc. The theoretical parts of the final Declaration were heavily amended by the Yugoslavs and Indians to reflect non-aligned theory, while regional groups rewrote many of the paragraphs on regional issues. Non-aligned resentment of Cuba was shown at the subsequent General Assembly by the battle between Colombia, a non-aligned observer, and Cuba for a Latin American seat on the Security Council for 1980–81. After some 124 inconclusive ballots the Soviet invasion of Afghanistan in late December 1979 forced both countries to withdraw and the seat was won by the new contender, Mexico. In January 1980, 54 non-aligned countries voted for the resolution condemning the invasion and only 9 voted against (Afghanistan, Angola, Cuba, Democratic Yemen, Grenada, Ethiopia, Laos, Mozambique and Vietnam); 17 abstained and 8 were absent (four others were not members of the UN).

The non-aligned were not always at odds with the United States. SCR 435 on Namibia in 1978 was voted for by six non-aligned states and the

United States. US diplomacy in Southern Africa was put on the path to success when the American negotiators decided in 1981 'to operate within a UN framework and to retain Resolution 435 as the basis and pivot for a settlement', which provided 'indispensable credibility'.[61]

THE GROUP OF 7, 1975–77

These movements were part of the background to what can now be seen as the formation of the Group of 7 and its first meeting at Rambouillet in November 1975. Proposals for a multilateral meeting had been put forward by both the United States and France since 1971.[62] The original players at Rambouillet were France, West Germany, Italy, Japan, the United Kingdom and the United States (Canada joined in 1976 to make a Group of 7). This 'Western' group primarily discussed their macro-economic policies, international trade and monetary issues, as well as energy, relations with developing countries and East–West trade. Their preoccupations were very Western. The major book on the subject does not even state how energy and relations with the developing countries were dealt with at Rambouillet, although it mentions they were discussed. Against this background it is not surprising that the CIEC conference of December 1975 at ministerial level only announced the decison to initiate 'intensified international dialogue' through four commissions (on energy, raw materials, development and financial affairs).

These continuing differences in expectations between G7 and developing countries could be seen at UNCTAD meeting after meeting. The Group of 77 kept together in its pre-UNCTAD negotiations in 1976 despite the fact that its three main regional groups differed over the question of which commodities should be included in the integrated programme and on preferential access to the EEC. However, they were once again disappointed at UNCTAD IV (Nairobi, May 1976). The industrialized countries were only able to reaffirm that the debt problem of developing countries would be considered constructively in a multilateral framework, even though they finally agreed that a negotiating conference for a Common Fund should be held before March 1977.

THE PERMANENT MEMBERS GROUP AND
THE NON-ALIGNED, 1986–99

The main overarching groupings of states at the UN and elsewhere (the Third World/non-aligned/Group of 77/South; the First World/West/ North and Second World/East) began to change in the mid-1980s (i.e.

before the ending of the Cold War) when the distinctive contribution of the Soviet Union and Eastern Europe on the Security Council began to disappear.[63] Instead, a new group consisting of the five permanent members began to be formed in late 1986. The permanent members began to work closely together (at first on trying to find a solution to the Iran–Iraq question culminating in the unanimous Chapter VII SCR 598 in July 1987) and, fairly often but certainly not always, with the non-aligned. The non-aligned itself also changed to meet changing circumstances.[64] Harare in 1986 was the last of the old-style summits: new more action-oriented thinking was noticeable at the next major Foreign Ministers meeting in Nicosia in 1988.[65] The non-aligned on the Security Council had worked more closely together after they formalized their relationship under the guidance of Kuwait in 1979, when the six non-aligned members plus one non-aligned observer agreed to form a group with a rotating monthly chairmanship.[66] The same year the non-aligned put forward a draft Security Council resolution suggesting the expansion of non-permanent members of the Security Council from 10 to 14. The first major Contact Group on Namibia set up in 1977 had already shown the advantage of *ad hoc* coalitions within this framework. These and the device of friends of the Chair were already becoming more extensively used.[67]

Before the end of the Cold War, 1986–90

These changes were reflected in voting patterns. Between 1980 and 1985, the permanent members voted together on 75 out of 119 Security Council resolutions. Their converging interests were illustrated by the fact that they voted together on 68 out of the 79 resolutions passed between 1986 and July 1990 as the Cold War came to an end. They differed on such subjects as Afghanistan, Palestine/Israel, Cyprus, the Falklands, the Gulf, Iran/Iraq, Lebanon, Namibia and South Africa. Vetoes were cast by four different permanent members (China was the exception) on some of the subjects noted above, as well as US intervention in Grenada, Iran and Nicaragua. Non-aligned interests changed less. They voted together on 113 of the 119 resolutions passed between 1980 and 1985 and on 79 of the 79 resolutions passed between 1986 and July 1990. Both groups voted together more than they differed: the two groups voted on 72 resolutions out of 119 between 1980 and 1985 and on 68 resolutions out of 79 between 1986 and July 1990.

   In the mid-1980s the differences and convergences on rights between the non-aligned and some in the West were expressed through the vote in the General Assembly on the right to development in December 1986. The vote, 146 to 1 (United States) to 8 (Denmark, Finland, Germany, Iceland, Israel, Japan, Sweden and the United Kingdom) showed that the non-aligned continued to take these human rights issues seriously. Both groups were also aware of the legitimacy that could be given if one worked through the UN. This route, as has already been noted, was used by Chester Crocker in the context of the negotiations over Namibia from 1981 onwards. Namibia became a member of the UN in 1990.

After the Cold War, 1990–99

The Iraqi invasion of Kuwait ushered in the beginning of a new era after the end of the Cold War. Both groups continued to vote more together than separately. Overall, they voted together on 552 out of the 625 Security Council resolutions passed between August 1990 and the end of 1999. The permanent members voted together on 572 and the non-aligned voted together on 586. On Chapter VII resolutions, of which an amazing 158 were passed between August 1990 and December 1999, they agreed on 123. This shows strikingly the change induced by the demise of the Second World/Eastern European bloc. Only 17 Chapter VII resolutions were passed between 1946 and 1989.

Among the permanent members, there were disagreements on 33 Chapter VII resolutions – obviously through abstentions, otherwise the resolutions would have been vetoed. Within the non-aligned there were disagreements on 22. In contrast, there were only seven vetoes between August 1990 and December 1999. Russia vetoed resolutions on Cyprus peacekeeping finance in 1993 and on the movement of goods from Bosnia in 1994. The United States vetoed one resolution on the expropriation of land in East Jerusalem in 1995 and two, in 1997, on settlement activities in the occupied territories, including East Jerusalem. China vetoed a resolution in 1997 attaching military observers to MINUGUA in Guatemala because of Guatemala's relationship with Taiwan and, for similar reasons, in 1999 refused to extend UNPREDEP in Macedonia.

The enthusiasm for certain types of Security Council action, particularly if it meant paying for peacekeeping operations, began to run out after the US débâcle in Somalia within UNOSOM II in October 1993. Nevertheless it is interesting to note the number of Chapter VII resolutions per year since August 1990 following the Iraqi annexation of Kuwait: 9 in August–December 1990, 13 in 1991, 10 in 1992, 27 in 1993, 23 in 1994, 21 in 1995, 12 in 1996, 17 in 1997, 22 in 1998 and 13 in 1999. It is also interesting to note that since November 1994 there has only been one example of non-aligned dissension on a Chapter VII resolution within the Security Council. This was a vote threatening travel sanctions on Iraqi officials (SCR 1134, October 1997) in which non-aligned Egypt and Kenya abstained in the company of three permanent members: China, France and Russia.

During this period the non-aligned continued to meet at regular summits: Jakarta in 1992, Cartagena in 1995 and Durban in 1998.[68] South Africa was triumphantly admitted to non-aligned membership at the Cairo non-aligned Foreign Ministers meeting in 1994.[69] Jakarta overcame internal political divisions about the future role of Yugoslavia. On economic issues the non-aligned were united in their concern to put economic growth and the eradication of poverty at the forefront of the global agenda. They appealed in their Call from Colombia (1995) for 'peace and development of our peoples' and co-operation not confrontation. They noted that there had been a 'progressive evaporation of the expectations following the end of the Cold War' and considered that globalization and interdependence had mainly benefited industrialized countries and, additionally, made problems for them in the areas of environmental degradation and illicit drugs. They requested the Colombian President (as they had also asked President Suharto at Jakarta) to convey these views and others to the Group of 7, besides promoting South–South co-operation.

Other issues of concern included UN reform, nuclear testing, peacekeeping and other finance and human rights, but with others they remained aware of a frustrating, prevailing stalemate, especially in their relations with the United States. This feeling of frustration continued at their Durban summit (August–September 1998) despite the fact that the United States was invited (and attended) as a guest for the first time. Apart from economic issues – they were particularly concerned to understand the Asian economic crisis as well as find out how to make globalization work for them – they spent most of their political time trying to find acceptable ways to deal with the first Indian and Pakistan nuclear tests earlier in the year.

In 1999 the pressures on the permanent members as a group increased in the context of Kosovo. Although three Chapter VII resolutions had been passed on the issue in 1998, it became clear that a veto by Russia or China might well be the outcome of any attempt to authorize the use of force in the Security Council against the Yugoslav Serbs on account of their attacks on the Kosovo Albanians. The NATO bombing campaign against Yugoslavia was ultimately started without explicit Security Council authorization. Subsequently, on 26 March, a draft resolution demanding an immediate cessation of the use of force against Yugoslavia failed to pass the Security Council since it did not gain the requisite number of votes. Three countries, China, Namibia and Russia, voted for it. The rest of the Security Council voted against it. The permanent members group is certainly much less cohesive than it was.

THE RISE OF THE UNITED STATES, 1986–99

The United States does not constitute a group in the UN and only plays a part in the electoral side of WEOG. By the end of 1986 it had been part of both the Group of 7 and the CSCE process since the mid-1970s. It then became part of the new permanent members group and also (see below) ensured that decisions about the budget in the General Assembly should be agreed by consensus. Its attitudes to the UN over the years have been, and remain, very variable. As Anthony Parsons noted in 1987, 'the trend in the 1980s has been for the major powers to address both political and economic problems bilaterally or in regional or functional groups, thus avoiding the tumult and shouting of the United Nations, which has been inexorably pushed to the outer margin of events'.[70] This situation was reversed in the early years of the post-Cold War era following the UN's successful enforcement activities in 1991 against Iraq in Kuwait.

This successful engagement with the United Nations lasted, as discussed in the previous section, until the peace enforcement débâcle in Somalia in October 1993. Since then the US relationship with the United Nations has become more fraught, in part because of its attitude to its financial obligations to the UN (see below). It is significant that the United States has an easier and more productive relationship with other members of the G7/8 today than it has with certain other permanent members, particularly China and Russia. Nevertheless, as has been noted, the post-1945 international role of the United States 'has quite largely been one of coalition building', which makes 'the UN Security Council a critically important area'.[71] The United States continues to need to use the UN system as a whole, and the Security Council in particular, some of the time.

UN finance, 1986–99

United States attitudes to the UN were compounded in the 1980s under the Reagan administration by new concerns expressed both by Congress and by certain pressure groups (e.g. the Heritage Foundation) over aspects of the UN system including its financing. In 1985 the Kassebaum Amendment to the Senate Foreign Relations Act of August 1985 required 'that the United States should pay no more than 20% of the assessed annual budget of the United Nations or any of the Specialized Agencies that do not adopt weighted voting procedures on "matters of budgetary consequence".[72] This was followed by underpayment by the United States of its assessed financial contributions until a range of reforms in budgetary procedures judged acceptable by the US administration had been introduced, despite the fact, as Paul Taylor notes, that 'by 1986 total contributions in real terms had only returned to the 1973–4 level'.[73] The US view was that it was paying too much. By GAR 41/213 of December 1986 it was agreed, by consensus, that decisions about the budget would be taken by consensus.[74]

The agreement had run into trouble by 1990 when the Group of 77 began to wonder if they were to continue to uphold what they considered had been the bargain in 1986 – their agreement against the US return to full funding. Nevertheless, it has staggered on. Negotiators in Congress, when nearing a possible compromise in November 1997, were pre-empted by a successful attempt by others (also in Congress) to get the budget bill caught up with the tense debate in the United States on abortion issues. This led to its barring by President Clinton. Congress and Clinton finally agreed a compromise on arrears (containing a series of congressional conditions over the next three years – many unacceptable to other UN members) in November 1999 since the United States could have lost their vote in the General Assembly in January 2000 under Article 19 (for those two or more years in arrears with their payment of their dues). It remains to be seen whether these conditions will be accepted by the UN membership as a whole.[75]

CHINA, THE NON-ALIGNED AND THE PERMANENT MEMBERS GROUP, 1992–99

China, a potential superpower, has also adjusted its attitudes in the post-Cold War world. At the end of 1991 it announced in Peking[76] that it wished to become an observer in the Non-aligned Movement. The Chinese government had been interested in increasing its links with the movement for some time, but had been blocked by the Indians, who had a long-standing association with the Soviet Union. However, the situation had changed with the breaking up of the Soviet Union: Russia took over the permanent seat in the Security Council in January 1992. China was accepted as an observer at the preparatory meeting for the Jakarta summit held in Bali in May 1992. The Chinese Foreign Minister spoke to the summit in September 1992. He noted that the two main issues of peace and development facing mankind had not been resolved. China regarded closer South–South co-operation as an important part of its policy of opening up and reform.

China has continued to develop its relationship with the non-aligned while also keeping its links with the other permanent members as a group. It has only used its veto twice (1997 and 1999) in the Security Council since the end of the Cold War. Both vetoes were designed to ensure that Taiwan failed in its attempt to assert its independence from China. Otherwise China has gone along (sometimes indicating differences by abstentions) with the vastly increased number of Chapter VII Security Council resolutions passed since August 1990. Between August 1990 and the end of 1999 China, through abstention, differed from the permanent members as a group on 48 Security Council resolutions and voted with them on 625. The main subjects on which they sometimes differed were aspects of Iraq, Haiti, Libya, and former Yugoslavia including Kosovo, as well as war crimes tribunals and sanctions.

THE G7/8 AND THE GROUP OF 15, 1989–99

The decision to establish a small summit-level group of developing countries was announced at the end of the 1989 Belgrade non-aligned summit. The original members of the Group of 15 were Algeria*, Argentina, Brazil, Egypt*, India*, Indonesia*, Jamaica*, Malaysia*, Mexico, Nigeria*, Peru*, Senegal*, Venezuela*, Yugoslavia* and Zimbabwe* (the non-aligned are asterisked – all were members of the Group of 77). The Group was established to promote South–South co-operation and a more positive and productive North–South dialogue. Since then Yugoslavia has been suspended and the Group has been joined by Chile*, Kenya* and Sri Lanka*. The Group has held summits nearly every year since then, its latest being Jamaica (its ninth) in February 1999. Over the years it has continued, with varying success, to promote dialogue with the G7/8. Indonesia, as Chair of the non-aligned, was invited to the pre-summit dinner in Tokyo in 1993 by Japan and the United States.[77]

As its current Chairman, the Prime Minister of Jamaica noted at the conference that 'the G-15 represents an important group that stands ready to contribute to the international consultative process which must be established, so that the reform architecture accommodates the differences which undoubtedly exist'.[78] They will work together at the WTO to ensure their objectives, besides requesting the ILO to consider a comprehensive employment strategy. They continue to maintain their position that social safety nets to meet the basic needs of the poorest and most vulnerable must be regarded as integral parts of development policies. On South–South issues they agreed to adopt a new strategic sector approach focusing on biotechnology, information technology and infrastructure development. The South Commission in Geneva remains their think tank.

Meanwhile the Group of 7/8, which now discusses political as well as economic issues, remains more concerned about Western problems than negotiating with the Group of 15 or the non-aligned. It can be argued that there has been a return to the US 'disenchantment and hostility to the' political side of the 'UN process'[79] which was so evident on economic matters in the early 1970s. The Middle East peace process is now being conducted outside the UN framework, which makes for problems in the context of legitimacy. There still seems very little meeting of minds on issues such as economic development, peacekeeping and Palestine.

THE EASTERN EUROPEAN GROUP, 1990–99

As the Soviet Union broke up and changed (Russia took over the Security Council seat in January 1992) the role of the Eastern European group also changed. A number wished to join WEOG on the grounds that their ideologies were now similar, but WEOG declined to accept them as it considered that this could be detrimental to its electoral interests. There are many examples of different groupings with similar ideologies (e.g. Groups A and C at UNCTAD). It is obvious, however, that with any EU expansion new solutions will have to be worked out for European groupings in the UN and elsewhere. Estonia is the only eligible UN member that still declines to join the Eastern European group.

CONCLUSION

The subjects that engrossed Middle Eastern and Asian countries in 1946, and subsequently the Third World as a whole, have not changed much over the last 54 years. They continue to include decolonization, disarmament and economic development; rights to support their cause, in particular self-determination; and justice for Palestine. Added to these was a concern with other mainstream issues such as Korea in the late 1940s and early 1950s and, subsequently, attempts to influence disarmament negotiations between the superpowers and, later, environmental issues. There have been two success stories: the seating of the People's Republic of China in the Chinese permanent seat in the Security Council in 1971 and the liberation of South Africa in 1993–94.

What has changed more has been the range of methods employed to try and win their cause. These have ranged from setting up and using electoral and political groups effectively (as the Latin Americans did at the UN Preparatory Commission in 1945), to trying to ensure important votes go your way (e.g. on Palestine in 1947), to attempts to make international legal norms that help your case and to use them (e.g. the right of self-determination and the major treaties negotiated in such areas as environment and human rights). Other tactics employed have included setting up major conferences, such as Bandung outside the UN and the series of UN conferences dealing with social issues in the 1990s, which achieve agreement on major issues, getting groups of countries to work together on prominent issues both inside and outside the UN (the non-aligned), attempting to increase the size of important bodies in order to gain more influence (e.g. the Security Council), setting up bodies based on General Assembly voting patterns (e.g. UNCTAD), and trying to find ways of setting up groups in bodies with restricted voting (e.g. the IMF and World Bank) which can be used to reflect Third World concerns. Radical decisions to leave the UN (Indonesia) and to press for the New International Economic Order have often been seen as ultimately counter-productive.

The role of initiative-taking has been crucial in all the groups, although the West has been more likely to try to maintain the status quo. Western initiatives have often been taken when there is disagreement within the West: the French initiatives on Palestine in 1970–72 were not welcome to the United States. Nor were some of the US moves on economic issues welcome to its European partners. The West, when reasonably united and determined not to do much, has spent great tracts of time suggesting that a negotiation is not a negotiation but a discussion (over North–South issues) and has not been inclined to provide much finance for development. In this it was tacitly supported during the Cold War by the Soviet bloc countries. Third World initiatives have covered both their own concerns (e.g. Palestine in 1947) and certain world issues (e.g. Korea and disarmament).

One response to some of the initiatives has been to show their hollowness by not putting them into practice, for example the New International Economic Order. Others have been countered mainly in and by the West, or North, through the use of the veto, through the use of financial measures such as the refusal to pay certain dues (a US tactic but one that has also been used by three other permanent members on peacekeeping finance: China, France and the Soviet Union/Russia), and also through a refusal to discuss certain subjects (e.g. Vietnam by the United States, Kashmir by the Indians) within the UN system.

However, it has often proved impossible to keep subjects outside the UN system since the UN has the power of granting legitimacy (peace with justice) to appropriate solutions (e.g. South Africa). As Robert Jackson noted in 1983, 'the non-aligned have been successful in keeping Namibia and Palestine before the public through recourse to the Council and General Assembly. Without illusions that UN resolutions could lead to a breakthrough in either case, they have viewed the process as a long term form of pressure on the West to intervene with South Africa and Israel.'[80] This concern with legitimacy also explains why Chester Crocker chose, in

1981, to 'operate within a UN framework and to retain Resolution 435 as the basis and pivot for a settlement' which provided 'indispensable credibility'.[81] This worked in the context of Southern Africa. Negotiations outside the UN on the major issue of Israel and Palestine have not led, as yet, to a peaceful and just settlement.

None of this implies that the Third World and the West have nothing in common. In fact they are often united in their concern for Charter principles and, even in terms of the Security Council, have agreed far more than they have differed over the years. The role of the now defunct Second World seems to have been very much that of blocking initiatives through vetoes in the Security Council, although this has also been true of the United States, particularly on Israel/Palestine. The Soviet bloc was not able to make the Third World their natural ally. And on human rights they took the most negative view in the 1940s and 1950s, although members of that group ultimately became parties to both the major Covenants on Civil and Political, and Economic, Social and Cultural Rights.

Groups of states work when they empower their individual members, as the Latin Americans showed in 1945 and the EEC (now EU) has done since the early 1970s. They continue if they are useful, but they may break up over controversial questions, as the Commonwealth group did in the UN, in this case over race. The United Nations, and sometimes its specialized agencies, have also enabled other voices such as NGOs[82] and those operating within the arena of 'civil society'[83] to be heard, and wider negotiations to take place. But groups trying to find economic answers[84] in the context of the UN and its institutions have, up until now, had less success than those seeking political redress, stability and legitimacy in certain areas including Southern Africa (both Namibia and South Africa itself). In other areas such as Palestine/Israel, the groups remain far apart. Placing and keeping issues on the agenda, and developing new ideas, are therefore crucial until the time is ripe.

Table 8.1 Growth of African, Asian, European, Latin American and other membership of the United Nations, 1945–99 (Names are those in use in 1999.)

Date	Africa	Asia and Pacific	Europe	Latin America and Caribbean	Other	Total
1945	Egypt[i]	China[ii]	Belarus[iii]	Argentina	Australia	51
	Ethiopia	India[iii]	Belgium	Bolivia	Canada	
	Liberia	Iran	Czechoslovakia[iv]	Brazil	New Zealand	
	S. Africa	Iraq	Denmark	Chile	United States	
		Lebanon	France	Colombia		
		Philippines[iii]	Greece	Costa Rica		
		Saudi Arabia	Luxembourg	Cuba		
		Syria[v]	Netherlands	Dominican R.		
		Turkey	Norway	Ecuador		
			Poland	El Salvador		
			Russia[vi]	Guatemala		
			Ukraine[iii]	Haiti		
			United Kingdom	Honduras		
			Yugoslavia[vii]	Mexico		
				Nicaragua		
				Panama		
				Paraguay		
				Peru		
				Uruguay		
				Venezuela		
1946		Afghanistan	Iceland			55
		Thailand	Sweden			
1947		Pakistan				57
		Yemen				
1948		Burma				58
1949		Israel[viii]				59
1950		Indonesia				60
1955	Libya	Cambodia	Albania			76
		Jordan	Austria			
		Laos	Bulgaria			
		Nepal	Finland			
		Sri Lanka	Hungary			
			Ireland			
			Italy			
			Portugal			
			Romania			
			Spain			

Table 8.1 (*continued*)

Date	Africa	Asia and Pacific	Europe	Latin America and Caribbean	Other	Total
1956	Morocco Sudan Tunisia	Japan				80
1957	Ghana	Malaysia				82
1958	Guinea					83
1960	Benin Burkina Cameroon Central African Rep. Chad Congo Congo DR Gabon Ivory Coast Madagascar Mali Niger Nigeria Senegal Somalia Togo		Cyprus			100
1961	Mauritania	Mongolia				104
1962	Algeria Burundi Rwanda Uganda			Jamaica Trinidad & Tobago		110
1963	Kenya Zanzibar[ix]	Kuwait				113
1964	Malawi		Malta			115
1965[x]	Gambia	Maldives Singapore				118
1966	Botswana			Barbados Guyana		122
1967		Yemen (S)				123
1968	Equatorial Guinea Mauritius Swaziland					126
1970		Fiji				127

Table 8.1   (*continued*)

Date	Africa	Asia and Pacific	Europe	Latin America and Caribbean	Other	Total
1971		Bahrain Bhutan Oman Qatar United Arab Emirates				132
1973			German (E)[xi] Germany (W)	Bahamas		135
1974	Guinea-Bissau	Bangladesh		Grenada		138
1975	Cape Verde Comoros Mozambique São Tomé & Principe	Papua New Guinea		Surinam		144
1976	Angola Seychelles	Samoa				147
1977	Djibouti	Vietnam				149
1978		Solomon Is.		Dominica		151
1979				St Lucia		152
1980	Zimbabwe			St Vincent		154
1981		Vanuatu		Antigua Belize		157
1983				St Kitts & Nevis		158
1984		Brunei				159
1990[xii]	Namibia		Liechtenstein			159
1991		Korea (N) Korea (S) Marshall Is. Micronesia	Estonia Latvia Lithuania			166
1992		Kazakhstan Kyrgyzstan Moldova Tajikistan Turkmenistan Uzbekistan	Armenia Azerbaijan Bosnia Croatia Georgia San Marino Slovenia			179

Table 8.1   (*continued*)

Date	Africa	Asia and Pacific	Europe	Latin America and Caribbean	Other	Total
1993	Eritrea		Andorra			184
			Czech Rep.[xiii]			
			Slovakia			
			Macedonia			
			Monaco			
1994		Palau				185
1999		Kiribati				188
		Nauru				
		Tonga				

NB: The Holy See and Switzerland are noted in UN sources as 'Non-member States maintaining permanent observer missions at Headquarters' while Palestine is listed under the rubric of 'Entities having received a standing invitation to participate in the sessions and the work of the General Assembly and maintaining permanent observer missions at Headquarters'.

i. Egypt merged with Syria between 1958 and 1961: they then separated.
ii. In 1971 the General Assembly restored all rights to the People's Republic of China and recognized its government representatives as the only legitimate representatives of China in the UN.
iii. At the time of joining the United Nations these members were not fully sovereign in the normally accepted sense but subsequently became so.
iv. Czechoslovakia was divided into two states in 1993.
v. Syria merged with Egypt between 1958 and 1961; they then separated.
vi. Russia joined as the Soviet Union. The 11 members of the Commonwealth of Independent States agreed that it should take the place of the Soviet Union in 1992.
vii. In 1992 the General Assembly considered that the Federal Republic of Yugoslavia (Serbia and Montenegro) could not automatically continue membership of the UN. It decided that it should not participate in the work of the General Assembly.
viii. Israel has not yet been accepted by the Asian group. This is not surprising given its policies towards the Palestinians and other states in the area. It first tried to join WEOG in the early 1960s.
ix. Zanzibar merged with Tanganyika in 1964 to become the United Republic of Tanganyika and Zanzibar, later Tanzania.
x. Indonesia withdrew from membership of the UN in 1965 and resumed full participation in 1966.
xi. The two German states merged in 1990.
xii. The two Yemens merged in 1990, as did the two German states.
xiii. Czechoslovakia was divided into two states: the Czech Republic and Slovakia.

NOTES

1. The opinions expressed are the author's own and should not be taken as an expression of official United Kingdom policy.
2. Volume 1 *Twenty-five Years of the Nonaligned Movement 1961–1982* (New Delhi: Ministry of External Affairs, 1986), Annex 1: Decision Regarding Methods of Strengthening Unity, Solidarity and Cooperation among Non-Aligned Countries, pp. 471–74.
3. See documents of the Twelfth Conference of Heads of State or Government of Non-Aligned Countries, A/53/667, 13 November 1998.
4. See foreword by Adam Roberts, in David M. Malone, *Decision-Making in the UN Security Council: The Case of Haiti* (Oxford: Clarendon Press, 19980, p. x.
5. See chapter 'The founding of the United Nations: principles and objects', by Lord Gladwyn, in Erik Jensen and Thomas Fisher (eds), *The United Kingdom– The United Nations* (London: Macmillan, 1990).
6. See A. Roberts and B. Kingsbury (eds) *United Nations, Divided World* (Oxford: Oxford University Press, 1993), p. 61.
7. Cmd 6666, Commentary on the UN Charter.
8. Despatch of 25 July 1945, paras 3 and 6, printed in *British Policy Overseas*, Series I, Vol. I, no. 407 (London: HMSO, 1984).
9. 'How Latin America shaped the U.N.: the memoirs of a Colombian statesman', *Americas*, Eduardo Zuleta Angel, Sept/Oct 1982, vol. 34. no. 5.
10. These were Egypt, Iraq, Lebanon, Saudi Arabia and Syria – all Arab League members – and probably Iran.
11. *The Yearbook of the United Nations* 1946–7, p. 62.
12. *Ibid.*, pp. 56–58. See also the essay by Sam Daws on 'The Origins and Development of UN Electoral Groups', in Ramesh Thakur (ed.), *What Is Equitable Geographic Representation in the Twenty-first Century?* (The United Nations University, 1999).
13. *Ibid.* p. 60. See also Sydney Bailey and Sam Daws, *The Procedure of the Security Council*, 3rd edn (Oxford: Oxford University Press, 1998), pp. 143–44.
14. Geoffrey Marston, 'The United Kingdom's part in the preparation of the European Convention on Human Rights 1950', *International and Comparative Law Quarterly*, vol. 42, October 1993, p. 800.
15. The other three countries were India, the Philippines and Turkey.
16. An important perspective on this resolution is given in Walid Khalidi, 'Revisiting the UNGA Partition Resolution', *Journal of Palestine Studies* XXVII, no. 1 (Autumn 1997) pp. 5–21.
17. Pakistan and Yemen had become UN members on 30 September 1947.
18. This is discussed in greater detail in Walter Zander, *Is this the Way? A Call to Jews* (Victor Gollancz Ltd, 1948). As he notes (p. 15), 'The votes on the Palestine question in the General Assembly were an exact reflection [of Jewish violation of the rights of the native population – the Palestinian Arabs] and all peoples whoever in the past, directly or indirectly, were the objects of colonial policy were in opposition to the establishment of a Jewish state.'
19. *Ibid.*, pp. 484–93.
20. The other East Europeans were Byelorussia, Czechoslovakia, Poland, Ukraine and, interestingly, Yugoslavia.

21. For more detail see Alvin Z. Rubinstein, *Yugoslavia and the Non-aligned World* (Princeton: Princeton University Press, 1970), ch. 1.

22. G. H. Jansen in *Afro-Asia and Non Alignment* (London: Faber and Faber, 1966), p. 102 calls this the real beginning of Afro–Asian group action. This is not correct given the 1947 vote against Palestinian partition. It also seems more sensible to call this the Arab–Asian group, as Egypt was the only participant from the African continent and is Arab. The United Nations normally includes Arab countries, with the exception of those located in Africa, in the Asian group.

23. Sir Benegal Rau, the Indian Permanent Representative, noted that the appeal 'gave the first indication to a distracted world that the countries of Asia had taken the initiative . . . to prevent the outbreak of hostilities in the East'. *Ibid.*, p. 106.

24. Alvin Z. Rubinstein, *op. cit*, p. 33.

25. G.H. Jansen, *op. cit*, p. 109.

26. Dean Acheson, *Present at the Creation* (New York: Norton, 1969), p. 699.

27. Much of this is taken from my chapter on Article 1 in Dilys M. Hill (ed.), *Human Rights Covenants in Human Rights and Foreign Policy Principles and Practice* (Basingstoke: Macmillan, 1989).

28. This is one example of the tendency of Third World countries to keep their distance from the Soviet Union, even if they agreed with much of the content of the Soviet Union's proposals.

29. J. P. Humphrey, *Human Rights and the United Nations: A Great Adventure* (Dobbs Ferry: Transnational Publishers, 1984), p. 129.

30. The two that did not vote were Burma and Iran.

31. For more background see George McTurnan Kahin, *The Asian–African Conference* (Ithaca, NY: Cornell University Press, 1956).

32. Humphrey, *op. cit.*, p. 252.

33. After a number of Soviet vetoes on membership questions, Bulgaria, Hungary and Romania plus certain other states joined the United Nations in 1955.

34. See comment on the domination of the process of initiating resolutions by the Africans and Asians in Robert O. Keohane, 'Political influence in the General Assembly', *International Conciliation*, March 1966, p. 24.

35. See Foreign Policy Document 223, 'The United Nations: does the rhetoric matter? A case history: Palestine 1947–1983', October 1983, Research Department, Foreign and Commonwealth Office.

36. Richard E. Bissell, *Apartheid and International Organizations* (Boulder, CO: Westview Press, 1977), pp. 20–21.

37. *Ibid.*, pp. 22–23.

38. *Ibid.*, p. 31.

39. Michael Banton, *International Action Against Racial Discrimination* (Oxford: Clarendon Press, 1996), pp. 66–67.

40. This included all the members of the original Arab–Asian group except for Iran and the Philippines. Syria was then part of the United Arab Republic.

41. Rubinstein *op. cit.*, pp. 301–2.

42. See chapter by Peter Marshall, 'North–South Dialogue: Britain at odds', in Erik Jensen and Thomas Fisher (eds), *The United Kingdom – The United Nations* (London: Macmillan, 1990), pp. 160 and 164.

43. See Foreign and Commonwealth Office Research Department Memorandum of 1980 on 'The Non-Aligned Movement and the Group of 77', Annex 3. The Latin American participants were Bolivia, Brazil, Cuba and Mexico. Observers were Chile, Ecuador, Uruguay and Venezuela.
44. 'UNCTAD: Intervener between poor and rich states', *Journal of World Trade Law* 1973, p. 546.
45. Of these, 29 now came from Asia and Africa compared with 11 in 1946 (excluding South Africa).
46. South Africa joined the Western caucus in 1965 according to Bissell, *op. cit.*, p. 106.
47. There were originally only seven Vice-Presidents.
48. This included both the Vice-Presidents and the Chairmen of the main committees.
49. The Commonwealth subsequently made 'a contribution to global efforts to reshape international arrangements in the economic, financial and trade fields so as to make them more equitable'. See 'International Economic Issues, Contributions by the Commonwealth 1975–1990', Commonwealth Secretariat, 1990.
50. ECOSOC was expanded once more from 27 to 54 by GAR 2847 (XXVI) December 1971 as follows: 14 from Africa; 11 from Asia; 10 from Latin America; 13 from WEOG and 6 from Eastern Europe.
51. This was last reaffirmed in the 1992 Maastricht Treaty.
52. The members are Argentina, Australia, Brazil, Canada, Chile, Colombia, Fiji, Indonesia, Malaysia, New Zealand, Paraguay, the Philippines, South Africa, Thailand and Uruguay.
53. Peter Marshall in 'The United Kingdom – The United Nations', *op. cit.* pp. 190–91.
54. *Selected Documents Relating to Problems of Security and Cooperation in Europe 1954–77*, HMSO, Cmnd 6932, p. 145.
55. Hanspeter Neuhold (ed.), *CSCE: N+N Perspectives*, Austrian Institute for International Affairs, Laxenburg Paper 1987, p. 147.
56. There is a wealth of material on this subject. Useful books include Robert Mortimer, *The Third World Coalition in International Politics*, 2nd edn (Boulder, CO: Westview Press, 1984); Charles A. Jones, *The North–South Dialogue: A Brief History* (London: Frances Pinter, 1983); I. William Zartman (ed.), *Positive Sum: Improving North–South Negotiations* (New York: Transaction Books, 1987).
57. See 'Cancun 1981 Framework, Debates and Conclusions of the International Meeting on Cooperation and Development', (Mexico: Secretaria de Relaciones Exteriores, 1982), and Sir Peter Marshall, 'The North–South Dialogue: Britain at Odds' in Erik Jensen and Thomas Fisher (eds), *The United Kingdom – The United Nations* (London: Macmillan, 1990), pp. 177–78.
58. Sir Peter Marshall, *ibid.*, p. 178. See also 'Hanging Together', p. 136.
59. Charles A. Jones, *op. cit.*.
60. Robert Mortimer, *op. cit.*, p. 174.
61. Chester Crocker, *High Noon in Southern Africa: Making Peace in a Rough Neighborhood* (New York: Norton & Company, 1993), p. 454.
62. See Robert D. Putman and Nicholas Bayne, *Hanging Together: Cooperation and Conflict in the Seven-Power Summits*, 2nd edn (Cambridge, MA: Harvard University Press, 1987), pp. 27–29. As they state (p. 14), growing economic inter-

dependence had 'ineluctably dissolved the barriers between foreign and domestic economies and hence between foreign and domestic politics'. See also Peter I. Hajnal, *The G7/G8 System: Evolution, Role and Documentation* (London: Ashgate, 1999).

63. See Sally Morphet, 'The influence of states and groups of states on and in the Security Council and General Assembly, 1980–94', *Review of International Studies* (1995), 21.

64. See Sally Morphet's chapter on 'Three Non-Aligned Summits: Harare 1986, Belgrade 1989 and Jakarta 1992' in David H. Dunn, *Diplomacy at the Highest Level: The Evolution of International Summitry* (London: Macmillan, 1996).

65. Sally Morphet, 'The Non-Aligned Movement and the Foreign Ministers' meeting at Nicosia', *International Relations*, vol. IX, no. 5, May 1989.

66. Richard L. Jackson, *The Non-Aligned, the UN and the Superpowers* (New York: Praeger Special Studies, 1983), pp. 116–19.

67. See Margaret Karns, 'Ad hoc multilateral diplomacy: The United States, the Contact Group and Namibia', *International Organization*, vol. 41:1, 1987 and Helen Leigh-Phippard, 'Coalitions and Contact Groups in Multilateral Diplomacy', Leicester University Discussion Paper 21, September 1996.

68. The next Summit Chair, Bangladesh, will take over from South Africa in 2001.

69. For more detail on Jakarta see David H. Dunn, *op. cit.*, and on Cartagena see Sally Morphet, 'The Non-Aligned and their 11th summit at Cartagena, October 1995', *Round Table* (1996), 340, (455–63).

70. Douglas Williams, *The Specialized Agencies and the United Nations: The System in Crisis* (London: C. Hurst & Co. 1987), p. vi.

71. David Malone with Foreword by Adam Roberts, *Decision-Making in the UN Security Council: The Case of Haiti 1990–1997* (Oxford: Clarendon Press, 1998), p. x.

72. Douglas Williams, *op. cit.*, p. 65.

73. Paul Taylor, 'The United Nations system under stress: financial pressures and their consequences', *Review of International Studies* (1991), p. 368.

74. See also Anthony McDermott, *The New Politics of Financing the UN* (London: Macmillan, 2000).

75. Edward C. Luck, *Mixed Messages: American Politics and Organization 1919–1999* (Washington DC: Brookings Institution Press, 1999).

76. See Sally Morphet, 'The Non-Aligned in "The New World Order": the Jakarta Summit, September 1992', *International Relations*, vol. XI, no. 4, 1993.

77. See Hajnal, *op. cit.*, p. 28.

78. The South Letter, vols 1 & 2, 1999, pp. 16–17.

79. Marshall, *op. cit.*, pp. 190–91.

80. Jackson, *op. cit.*, pp. 128–29.

81. Chester Crocker, *op. cit.*, p. 454.

82. See Peter Willetts (ed.), *The Conscience of the World: The Influence of Non-Governmental Organisations in the U.N. System* (London: C. Hurst & Co., 1996). NGOs predate the UN. Article 71 of the UN Charter provided for them to make consultation arrangements with ECOSOC.

83. See Michael Edwards, *Future Positive: International Cooperation in the 21st Century* (London: Earthscan, 1999) and Inge Kaul, Isabelle Grunberg and Marc

A. Stern (eds), *Global Public Goods: International Cooperation in the 21st Century* (Oxford: OUP, 1999).

84. See Kenneth Dadzie, 'The UN and the Problem of Economic Development', in Adam Roberts and Benedict Kingsbury (eds), *United Nations, Divided World: The UN's Roles in International Relations* (Oxford: Clarendon Press, 1993).

CHAPTER 9

NGOs AND THE PRINCIPAL ORGANS OF THE UNITED NATIONS

Carolyn M. Stephenson[1]

Non-governmental organizations (NGOs) were not mentioned in the original drafts of the United Nations Charter. By the time of the signing of the Charter in San Francisco, however, NGOs had a place in the UN Charter related to the Economic and Social Council. Over the roughly 55 years since then, the number of NGOs has increased tremendously and the role of NGOs has become increasingly significant in global governance, in and out of the UN. In the context of the UN principal organs, NGOs have expanded their UN relationship beyond ECOSOC and they continue to do so. The relationship between NGOs and the UN General Assembly *ad hoc* mega-conferences, which began in the early 1970s, has been important in this expansion of the NGO role with respect to the other principal organs of the UN, particularly the General Assembly. NGOs have made important contributions to the UN and have played a significant role in the evolution of the principal organs.

Non-governmental organizations are not a homogeneous group. The long list of acronyms that has accumulated around NGOs can be used to illustrate this. People speak of NGOs, INGOs (International NGOs), BINGOs (Business International NGOs), RINGOs (Religious International NGOs), ENGOs (Environmental NGOs), QUANGOs (Quasi-non-governmental Organizations – i.e. those that are at least partially created or supported by states), and many others. Indeed, all these types of NGO and more are among those having consultative status at the UN. Among the 1603 NGOs that have consultative status with ECOSOC in 1999 are the Academic Council on the UN System, the All India Women's Conference, the Canadian Chemical Producers Association, CARE International, the World Young Women's Christian Association, the World Wide Fund for Nature International, the World Wide Fund for Nature (Malaysia), the Union of Arab Banks, the Women's International League for Peace and Freedom, the World Energy Council, the World Federation of Trade Unions, and the World Veterans Association. Thus it is difficult to generalize about NGOs at the UN.

While it is often argued that NGOs are the voice of the people, representing grass-roots democracy, a counter-argument is made that NGOs have tended to reinforce rather than counter existing power structures, having members and headquarters that are primarily in the rich northern countries.[2] Some also believe that NGO decision-making does not provide for responsible, democratic representation or accountability.

While the term 'NGOs' is sometimes used interchangeably with 'grass-roots organizations', 'social movements', 'major groups', and 'civil society', NGOs are not the same as any of these. Grass-roots organizations are generally locally organized groups of individuals which have sprung up to empower their members and take action on particular issues of concern to them. Some NGOs are grass-roots organizations. Social movements are broader and more diffuse than organizations; a social movement encompasses a broad segment of society which is interested in fomenting or resisting social change in some particular issue area, such as disarmament, the environment, civil rights, or women's movements.[3] A social movement may *include* NGOs and grass-roots organizations. 'Major groups' is a term coined at the time of the 1992 Rio 'Earth Summit' as a part of Agenda 21 to encompass the societal sectors that were expected to play roles, in addition to nation-states and intergovernmental organizations, in environment and development. NGOs are identified as one of these sectors, but in fact NGOs overlap with many of the other sectors; there are women's NGOs, farmers' NGOs, labour NGOs, and business NGOs, among others.[4] Finally, 'civil society' is a term that became popularized at the end of the Cold War to describe what appeared to have been missing in state-dominated societies: broad societal participation in and concern for governance, but not necessarily government. Civil society is thought to be the necessary ingredient for democratic governance to arise. NGOs are one part of civil society. NGOs themselves can be domestic or international. International NGOs, according to an early decision of the United Nations, are international organizations that have not been created by an agreement among governments.[5] Historically, most NGOs accredited to the UN Economic and Social Council have been international, but contrary to the popular wisdom, even the first group of NGOs accredited to ECOSOC in the 1940s included some national NGOs.

Both the number of non-governmental organizations and their involvement in national and international policy-making have increased tremendously over the last half a century and especially the last several decades. At the time of the foundation of the United Nations in 1945 there were 2865 international non-governmental organizations (INGOs), while by 1990 that number had increased to 13,591.[6] This compared to 3443 international intergovernmental organizations (IGOs) and roughly 200 states. But, more important, in the 1990s there began to be a recognition of the import of the NGO role. In human rights, development, environment and even disarmament, NGOs had begun to be recognized for their role in influencing public policy at the UN.[7]

WHAT DID THE 'FOUNDING FATHERS' INTEND FOR NGOS?

Non-governmental organizations were instrumental in calling for and developing public support for the First World Disarmament Conference held in 1932. Feminist, pacifist and other organizations in the United States had made the Conference a central part of their programme during the several years preceding this Conference.[8]

NGO activities in the areas of both disarmament and human rights generated controversy for governments that were active in the League of Nations. Certain governments, however, saw the activities of NGOs to be useful to their own position. Thus, during the formative conference of the United Nations, some countries advocated writing into the Charter some consultative roles for NGOs.

Neither the original 18 July 1944 'US Tentative Proposals for a General International Organization', nor the Dumbarton Oaks proposals put forth by the four major powers (the US, UK, Soviet Union and China) on 7 October 1944, contained any reference to the role of non-governmental organizations, but only to what would become the specialized agencies of the UN system.[9] At the San Francisco conference, however, during discussion of the relationship to be established with the specialized agencies, a Canadian amendment unwittingly entered into a conflict between the UK and the USSR over relationships with certain labour organizations. The UK had sought to have the ILO recognized by name for a special relationship with the UN, while the Soviet Union sought similar status for the World Trade Union Congress, a non-governmental organization established in rivalry to the ILO. The Canadian amendment defined specialized agencies as 'intergovernmental', thus ruling out the WTUC. The USA, partly to avoid domestic conflict with the American Federation of Labor (AFL), a supporter of the ILO, and the Congress of Industrial Organisations (CIO), a member of the WTUC, opposed both the giving of an official relationship to any non-governmental organization and the naming of any intergovernmental organizations in the Charter.[10] The drafting committee provided a way out of the impasse by providing for the establishment of a relationship between the Economic and Social Council and the non-governmental organizations, formalizing the League practice of consultation with NGOs. Thus the two related paragraphs 70 and 71, dealing with relationships with the specialized agencies and with NGOs, became a package that satisfied the Soviet Union on the issue of the

WTUC and the British government agreed to drop the request to name the ILO in the Charter.

The Dumbarton Oaks proposals were immediately published, with the US Department of State distributing approximately 1,900,000 copies of the text domestically, and public response was enormous. As a result, the US delegation to the San Francisco conference included representatives of 42 national organizations as consultants. These included organizations in the fields of labour, law, agriculture, business and education, plus women's, church, veterans' and civic organizations. The purpose was both to inform them on the conference and to secure their advice. Other organizations also sent representatives to San Francisco, and briefings were also held for this wider group.[11]

While the US Report to the President suggests that a recommendation by consultants representing major US agricultural, business, educational and labour organizations for a paragraph providing for consultation between NGOs and ECOSOC led directly to Article 71, it seems clear from Russell's history of the Charter that this simply played into the international dynamics over the representation of the ILO and the WTUC. The support of the American consultants did lead to a change in the US position, which now came to support what became Article 71. However, the American consultants wanted such a relationship for both national and international NGOs (as many of them were national organizations), and the American delegation succeeded in inserting this modification into the article.[12] Thus Article 71 of the United Nations Charter came to read: 'The Economic and Social Council may make suitable arrangements for consultation with non-governmental organizations which are concerned with matters within its competence. Such arrangements may be made with international organizations and, where appropriate, with national organizations after consultation with the Member of the United Nations concerned.'

THE EARLY DEVELOPMENT OF THE NGO–UN CONSULTATIVE PROCESS

As early as the first year of the development of the process of consultation between NGOs and the United Nations, there began to be a realization, both that states had different views of the nature of the consultative process and, that the term 'non-governmental organization' encompassed a wide variety of organizations which differed in such factors as size, representativeness, scope, expertise, funding and purpose, among others. The disparities between organizations have been one of the factors responsible for continuing difficulties in the consultative process. Much of this can be traced back to the period when methods for consultation were being set up. As this was not done at the San Francisco conference, the General Assembly, at its meeting of 14 February 1946, recommended that the Economic and Social Council adopt arrangements for consultation, to which the Council responded by setting up a 12-member Committee on Arrangements for Consultation with Non-Governmental Organizations.

At its first session on 20 February 1946, the Committee proposed some criteria for NGOs to be admitted to consultative status. It suggested that 'research, scientific, educational, cultural, informational, professional, and philosophical' organizations and those that represented a substantial proportion of the interests present within the field represented would be appropriate. Part I, section 5 also suggested that an organization should be 'international in its structure'.[13] In the Summary Record of the fourth Meeting, however, following on a discussion of US representative Kotschnig's categories of NGOs (in which, incidentally, he made the case that the AFL was international, since it had members from Canada and Mexico), governments agreed to make no distinction between international and national organizations for purposes of consultation.[14]

The report of the Committee on Arrangements for Consultation with Non-Governmental Organizations, which was adopted by ECOSOC on 21 June 1946, exhibits evidence of the double goals of consultation, stating that the establishment of consultative status was 'on the one hand for the purpose of enabling the Council or one of its bodies to secure expert information or advice from organizations having special competence on the subjects for which consultative arrangements are made, and, on the other hand, to enable organizations which represent important elements of public opinion to express their views'. Thus consultative status was to encompass both organizations with particular expertise in areas of ECOSOC attention and organizations that purported to represent the public. A third goal, and thus a third type of organization that might qualify for consultative status, was brought up during ECOSOC discussion of the report by representatives of the United States and the United Kingdom. The US delegate stressed the representation of a public opinion function. The British delegate added: 'Unless we can capture the power of the organized movements of the world behind this United Nations, then in the long run it will fail.'

Thus a third purpose of consultative status was to develop support for the programme of ECOSOC and for the United Nations itself. While there are other roles played by NGOs with respect to the United Nations today, these continue to be probably the most obvious. Today, however, organizations that primarily serve this third purpose tend rather to be on the list of organizations associated with the UN Department of Public Information than have consultative status, although all three purposes, and all three types of organization, are represented among those holding consultative status. This mixture of the purposes of consultative status has tended to confuse the understanding of the role of NGOs with respect to the United Nations. While different categories of consultative status were set up, these categories were not mutually exclusive, and indeed could not be, as some organizations served only one of these functions, while others served a number of them.

Original categories of consultative status were Categories A, B and C, which were similar, in both type and organization included and privileges accorded, to today's General and Special and Roster organizations. A report commissioned by the Interim Committee of Non-Governmental Organizations having Consultative Status with ECOSOC in 1949 already gave notice of the problems of lumping together organizations that could provide expertise with those that could represent public opinion or transmit information back to the public, and recommended that consultative status be accorded only to the former category, while the latter category be served by the Department of Public Information. To a large extent, that recommendation has been followed, but the multifunctional nature of many NGOs has meant that the list of NGOs with consultative status continues to contain a mixture of organizations. Resolution 288B(X), of 27 February 1950, established procedures that have since been revised several times, but there has been no substantial change from early practice.

NGO RELATIONS WITH THE SECRETARIAT

Three main bodies have overseen the UN–NGO relationship since early in the UN's history. The Committee on NGOs, a standing committee of ECOSOC, was established by ECOSOC Resolution 3 (II) of 21 June 1946. The Committee, which began with a membership of seven states, today has a membership of five African states, four Asian states, two Eastern European, four Latin American and Caribbean, and four Western European and Other states. It considers NGO applications for consultative status, reviews NGO quadrennial reports, and monitors the NGO–UN consultative relationship. Until recent years the Committee met every two years, but with the increase in NGO applications in the 1990s, it now meets twice a year.

The NGO section of the Department of Economic and Social Affairs provides Secretariat support to the Committee. It also serves as a focal point for all matters related to the consultative relationship. It issues NGO passes, and provides conference services related to NGO participation.

The other UN section that oversees NGOs is the NGO section of the Department of Public Information (DPI). When the General Assembly established DPI by Resolution 13 (I) in 1946, it instructed it to assist both governments and non-governmental organizations interested in spreading information about the United Nations. The DPI defines an NGO as 'any non-profit, voluntary citizens group which is organized on a local, national or international level', and it publicizes UN activities and promotes UN observances. It maintains the NGO Resource Centre, provides tickets for open meetings, and holds an annual conference in September and weekly briefing sessions. The DPI–NGO Executive Committee, 18 members elected from NGOs associated with DPI, provides for consultation.

THE DEVELOPMENT OF NGO NETWORKS: CONGO

NGOs have often banded together in networks to enhance their influence. In 1948 a small group of the non-governmental organizations that had been granted consultative status with ECOSOC met in Geneva with a member of the UN Secretariat to discuss enlarging and implementing rules for NGO participation at the UN. Out of this consultation came the organization that in its early years was called the Conference of NGOs in Consultative Status with the United Nations Economic and Social Council, or CONGO.[15] The organization's basic mission has been 'to ensure that NGOs in consultative status enjoy the fullest opportunities and all appropriate facilities for performing their consultative functions'. While CONGO does not take positions on substantive issues, it eventually developed 27 substantive issue committees, which provide a forum for dialogue among NGOs and between NGOs, states and the Secretariat. While other networks of organizations grew up over time, usually focused on specific issues, CONGO consistently played a role focusing on improvement of the NGO–UN relationship itself.

EVOLUTION OF THE UN-NGO RELATIONSHIP, 1965–95

A year after the 1965 membership increase on ECOSOC from 18 to 27, the Committee on NGOs, which decided which NGOs would be granted what level of consultative status, also increased its membership from 7 to 13 member states elected on the basis of geographical distribution.[16] This new committee in 1967 compiled a list of the NGOs granted consultative status since the beginning of the UN. By that date there were 12 organizations in Category A, 135 in B and 43 on the register.[17]

Non-governmental organizations were buffeted by Cold War politics in the UN. The Women's International Democratic Federation, an Eastern bloc organization that had initially been granted Category B status, had lost that status in 1954 and was regranted it in 1967, shortly after the enlargement of the Committee on NGOs. During the 1970s, Cold War politics also divided CONGO, with turf battles causing division between its Geneva and New York offices in ways similar to the tensions between East and West in the United Nations.[18]

RESOLUTION 1296 OF 1968

Until the mid-1990s, arrangements for consultative status were provided for under Resolution 1296 of the 44th session of the Economic and Social Council, adopted on 23 May 1968. There were three major parts to this resolution. Part one dealt with principles, decreeing that consultative status may be set up for organizations concerned with 'matters falling within the competence' of ECOSOC, that is with 'international economic, social, cultural, educational, health, scientific technological and related matters and to questions of human rights'.

Part two stressed the distinction to be maintained between the rights of states and UN agencies on the one hand, and NGOs on the other, and went on to reiterate almost the same twofold purpose we have already noted in the original 1946 attempt of ECOSOC to define consultative status: that of provision of expertise as well as balanced representation of world public opinion.

Part three went on to define differences in eligibility requirements for Categories I and II and the Roster. Category I may contain:

> Organisations which are concerned with most of the activities of the Council and can demonstrate to the satisfaction of the Council that they have marked and sustained contributions to make to the achievements of the objectives of the UN in the fields set out, and are closely involved with the economic and social life of the peoples of the areas they represent and whose membership, which should be considerable, is broadly representative of major segments of population in a large number of countries.

Thus Category I did not contain one or other of the two purposes of consultative status, but included organizations that could perform both of these functions. Category I required expertise, not in one limited area, but over the broad range of ECOSOC interests.

Category II, in contrast, was to contain: 'Organisations which have a special competence in, and are concerned specifically with, only a few of the fields of activity covered by the Council, and which are known internationally within the fields for which they have or seek consultative status.' Category II contrasted with Category I on *both* of the criteria that constitute the purposes of consultative status; organizations need not have either broad competency in ECOSOC's fields *or* broad representativeness. This category, then, was relatively discrete, intending to contain those organizations with a well-defined and well-recognized expertise in some of ECOSOC's fields of activity.

The third category of NGOs under Resolution 1296, that of the Roster, was another composite category, consisting of

> other organisations which do not have general or special consultative status but which the Council, or the Secretary-General of the U.N., in consultation with the Council or its Committee on Non-Governmental Organisations, considers can make occasional and useful contributions to the work of the Council or its subsidiary bodies or other U.N. bodies within their competence.

The Roster thus did not need to reflect the ability to contribute over the long term, as Categories I and II did. It also contained those organizations that had consultative status with another UN agency or body.

Resolution 1296 also provided for those procedures of consultation for the different categories of NGOs. All NGOs could send representative observers to ECOSOC meetings. Categories I and II could also submit written statements for circulation to member states. Category I organizations could also propose agenda items, and could in certain cases make oral interventions. Formerly, consultative organizations were entitled to receive by mail all unrestricted Council documents, but the costs of this proved prohibitive. Even now the cost of providing documentation to consultative organizations is large in some issue areas, given the rise in the number of organizations with consultative status.

CHANGES IN NGO RELATIONS WITH THE SECRETARIAT

At the same time as ECOSOC promulgated Resolution 1296, it also called on the Department of Public Information (DPI), in Resolution 1297 of 23 May 1968, to associate NGOs with it, in order to help them gain access and disseminate information about the UN. By 1997 roughly 1500 NGOs were associated with DPI. There is some overlap between the ECOSOC and DPI lists.[19] The perspectives from which the two offices deal with non-governmental organizations are very different, with the NGO section relying on the threefold consultative status definition and thus seeing itself as a facilitator for both the provision of expertise and representation functions of NGOs, while the DPI section sees itself more as the dispenser of information to NGOs that will carry out that third function: that of publicizing and developing support for the activities of the UN and for the UN itself. This led to some strains within the UN bureaucracy in early periods.

To co-ordinate UN Secretariat dealings with NGOs, the Secretary-General created the internal Inter-Departmental Working Group on NGOs in 1984.[20] The group invited officers of CONGO and the DPI–NGO Executive Committee to participate. It alternated activity with dormancy until it was revived, with NGO participation, in the 1990s, although invitations to NGOs were not continued after 1998. During the mid-1990s, Secretary-General Annan's reform process made the office of Assistant Secretary-General for External Affairs, Gillian Martin Sorenson, responsible for chairing the IDWG, while a similar group met in Geneva. A CONGO resolution of 26 February 1999 expressed concern that NGOs should not be dealt with as 'external' to the UN.[21]

NGOS AND THE ADVENT OF THE *AD HOC* MEGA-CONFERENCES

In 1968 at the time of the UN conference in Teheran celebrating the twentieth anniversary of the UN Declaration of Human Rights, a substantial NGO presence at UN conferences was not permitted. CONGO therefore organized an NGO Conference on Human Rights in Paris. This NGO conference was in some ways a prototype for the NGO fora which were to accompany all the major UN General Assembly conferences from 1972.[22]

Following that event CONGO lobbied for UN conferences to include an invitation to NGOs with consultative status, to allow NGOs to speak and to submit documents. According to the Chief of the NGO Unit in the Secretariat from 1976 to 1989, CONGO also encouraged governments to allow non-consultative NGOs at the conferences. The Conference on New and Renewable Sources of Energy in 1979 was the first to be open to non-consultative NGOs.[23]

In 1972 the UN Conference on the Human Environment was held on issues that arose from NGO concerns. This time NGOs in consultative status were officially there to observe. For those organizations that did not have consultative status, Swedish non-governmental organizations held an NGO forum to accompany the official conference, and large numbers of NGOs attended. One NGO produced a daily newspaper. Both the forum and the daily newspaper became a pattern in all the *ad hoc* mega-conferences of the 1980s and 1990s.

In some cases it was NGOs that were the actual initiators of these UN conferences. In 1972 a group of NGOs under the leadership of a representative of the International Federation of Business and Professional Women asked ECOSOC's Commission on the Status of Women (CSW) to call for an International Women's Year. At the 24th session of the CSW, from 14 February to 3 March 1972, ten NGOs signed a statement calling for such a year.[24] The General Assembly subsequently declared 1975 International Women's Year and held the International Women's Year Conference in Mexico City. The ten NGOs that had signed the statement at the CSW came together to run the Tribune, the equivalent of the fora that had been held at other conferences, for NGOs not allowed to attend the formal UN conferences.[25]

In subsequent UN conferences on women, held in Copenhagen in 1980, in Nairobi in 1985 and in Beijing in 1995, the numbers of NGOs attending both the official UN conference and the NGO fora grew significantly. In Mexico City, there were 113 NGOs at the UN conference and 7200 NGO participants at the Tribune; at Copenhagen there were 134 NGOs at the conference and 8022 NGO participants at the NGO forum. In Nairobi, 163 NGOs participated in the conference, while 13,500 NGO participants attended Forum '85.[26] Roughly 4000 NGOs participated in the Beijing conference, and almost double the Nairobi number attended the NGO forum.

Women who attended out of concern for women's issues came away aware of the potential role of the United Nations and, as with the case of the environment, this increased the number of NGOs seeking access to the UN. Similar patterns were apparent in the food and population conferences in 1974, and in the other conferences of the 1970s on water, desertification, technical co-operation among developing countries, and science and technology for development.

THE NON-GOVERNMENTAL LIAISON SERVICE (NGLS)

In 1975, as development became a major thrust of the UN and as NGO participation in global conferences began, the Non-Governmental Liaison Service was established to foster co-operation between the UN system and NGOs on development education and sustainable development issues. Begun as a joint effort of several UN agencies and programmes, NGLS is now a jointly financed inter-agency unit with a staff of roughly ten located in offices in Geneva and New York. It collaborates with almost 20 UN agencies and departments which sponsor its activities, especially UNICEF and UNCTAD. NGLS reports annually to the Joint UN Information Committee and, through it, to the Administrative Committee on Co-ordination.[27]

By the mid-1980s, ECOSOC had placed 30 organizations in Category I, 204 in Category II, and 133 on the Roster. The Roster also contained another 28 organizations placed there by the Secretary-General, and 212 that were there because of their consultative status with another UN agency or body. These organizations related primarily to the NGO Section of the Secretariat, which at that time handled the procedures for consultative status with only two professional staff.

While the Charter only provided for consultative status for NGOs with ECOSOC, the relationship of NGOs to the UN system has expanded far beyond ECOSOC. NGOs have participated in committees of the General Assembly, especially the Special Political and Fourth Committees, where they have given oral testimony, as well as in the Special Committee Against Apartheid, the Special Committee on the Situation with Regard to the Implementation of the Declaration on the Granting of Independence to Colonial Countries and Peoples, and the Tenth and Twelfth Special Sessions of the General Assembly (on Disarmament) and their preparatory committees. They took part in 11 UN conferences between 1972 and 1980 and in their follow-up conferences and special sessions in subsequent decades. They developed consultative relationships with UN bodies and specialized agencies, including FAO, IAEA, IFAD, ILO, ITU, UNICEF, UNCTAD, UNESCO, UNRWA, WHO and WIPO, and developed informal relationships with some others.

CONGO was instrumental in the late 1980s in expanding the ability of NGOs to address committees of the General Assembly. After failing to find anything in the General Assembly rules that might allow this, they obtained an opinion from the legal counsel that there was nothing in the General Assembly rules to prevent an NGO speaking, so long as the bureau of the committee approved. CONGO also tried to get the NGO section of the Secretariat moved from the Department of International Economic and Social Affairs to the office of the Secretary-General, but was unsuccessful. This would have symbolized expansion of the NGO role beyond ECOSOC.[28]

By the 1980s, a number of perceived problems led to a call for a review of future activities by the Committee on Non-Governmental Organizations. In addition to the problem of lack of clarity between the functions of the two UN offices dealing with NGOs, and the shortage of staff to handle the large number of NGOs, other reasons occasioned the need for a review of current practice. A draft resolution put forth on the subject by Chile, Ghana, Kenya, Pakistan and Sweden in May 1981, cited three main reasons for the need for such a study: (1) the number of NGOs with consultative status is growing; (2) there is a wide variety of NGOs, and their contribution to UN activity, particularly in the area of development, has been important and increasing; (3) there have been numerous *ad hoc* arrangements for NGOs in UN conferences and bodies, and there is a need for harmonized procedures. Such calls for reviews of the UN–NGO

Table 9.1   Number of non-governmental organizations in consultative status with the UN Economic and Social Council

Year	General	Special	Roster	Total
1948	7	32	2	41
1968	12	143	222	377
1991	41	354	533	928
1993	42	376	560	978
1995	69	436	563	1068
1996	81	499	646	1126
1997	88	602	666	1356

Source: UN/ECOSOC. 'Work of the Non-Governmental Organisations Section of the Secretariat, Report of the Secretary-General', 8 May 1998 (E/1998/43).

relationship have occurred periodically in UN history, but have in general not produced major changes in procedures.

THE 1990S: NGO GROWTH AND THE UN RESPONSE

Matters came to a head in the 1990s. On the one hand, the United Nations' visibility had increased, both with the end of the Cold War and through the rise of the UN global conferences, and this brought demands for access from more NGOs. On the other hand, fears of unlimited numbers of NGOs on the part of some states and parts of the UN, plus successes of certain NGO efforts in influencing international political issues, led to attempts to curtail NGO access.

The number of NGOs seeking and receiving consultative status with ECOSOC had indeed risen, although the burdens that some feared in terms of actual attendance at meetings did not occur, except perhaps at the 1992 Rio 'Earth Summit' and the 1995 Beijing Fourth World Conference on Women. In 1999 there were 1603 NGOs in consultative status with ECOSOC. Table 9.1 shows the increase in consultative status:

The Global Concerences of the 1990s

The global conferences, whose rules of procedure had accredited many NGOs to them in an *ad hoc* fashion, led to an increased demand for NGO access as the work of the conferences, and later five-year reviews of their work, was institutionalized in the UN system. As at the 1972 Stockholm conference, there was substantial NGO demand for access to the 1992 UN

Conference on Environment and Development (UNCED) in Rio, as well as its preparatory meetings and, later, to the annual spring meetings in New York of the Commission on Sustainable Development which had been created by UNCED. While NGOs had feared reduced access to the Rio conference, the conference enjoyed unusually co-operative relationships between NGOs, states and the conference secretariat, and this was to spill over to UN work on environment subsequent to Rio.

The regional meetings were among the first to contribute to the UNCED process. In the course of the Bergen regional ministerial meeting sponsored by the UN Economic Commission for Europe in May 1990, there was an unusual display of governmental and non-governmental organization co-operation, which went so far as to allow joint chairing of certain meetings by governmental and non-governmental organization representatives. The high degree of successful co-operation became known as the 'Bergen process' and was to have an influence on later arrangements for NGO participation.

At the first substantive session of the Preparatory Committee (PrepCom) in August 1990 in Nairobi, the basic outlines of the preparatory process and the conference began to take shape. With a fairly small number of NGOs, roughly 40, those that were there were an integral part of the process. The PrepCom agreed that NGOs with 'relevance' and 'competence' in the issues of UNCED could apply to take part in the UNCED process.[29] This was approved by the UN General Assembly in December 1990.[30]

At the fourth Preparatory Committee session in New York in March 1992, only three months before the Rio 'Earth Summit', UNCED Secretary-General Maurice Strong noted that non-governmental organizations had made 'extremely important substantive contributions' to the preparatory work of UNCED and expressed his hope that 'every effort will be made to facilitate their attendance as observers' at this final PrepCom. More significantly, he noted that there were many new organizations, especially in developing countries, which existing accreditation arrangements did not take into account.[31] Sessions during this PrepCom ranged from formal meetings, to which NGOs could have access, informal meetings, to which they were eventually granted limited access, and informal informal meetings, where the hard political bargaining took place and from which they were clearly excluded.

Some 1420 NGOs were accredited to the Rio conference itself, while perhaps 25,000 NGO participants from 9,000 NGOs attended the NGO global forum. Agenda 21, at the behest of UNCED Secretary-General Maurice Strong and NGOs, included an entire section on the role of 'major groups', highlighting the importance of NGOs and civil society in the achievement of environmental goals.[32] The notion of social partnership embedded in Agenda 21 eventually led to what came to be called 'stakeholder dialogues', organized with the co-operation of states, NGOs and the UN Secretariat, within the framework of the Commission on Sustainable Development.

Following on from the Rio UN Conference on Environment and Development, many of the NGOs that had been granted accreditation to the conference but did not have regular consultative status with ECOSOC wanted to be able to attend and influence the newly created Commission on Sustainable Development (CSD), which they had been in part responsible for creating. The practices of UNCED became in essence the practices followed for NGO participation in the CSD. This essentially meant a contraction of rights for the traditional ECOSOC consultative status NGOs, and an expansion of rights for previously non-consultative organizations, as those NGOs that did not have ECOSOC consultative status gained access to the CSD with rights similar to those in Rio. A certain amount of rancour developed within the NGO community during this period, with each side claiming to be opening up the UN to NGOs. The 'CSD list' of roughly 550 non-ECOSOC NGOs wishing to be accredited to the CSD – including 481 that had been accredited to UNCED – was approved as a whole in time for the first session of the CSD in 1993.[33] After much debate over whether this list was to be limited to participation in the CSD, the list was added to the regular ECOSOC Roster on 29 July 1994.[34]

The Commission on Global Governance

In 1995, at the height of the post-UNCED enthusiasm for NGOs, the Report of the Commission on Global Governance devoted a section to global civil society. Arguing that 'NGOs are helping to set public policy agendas, it highlighted proposals for a People's Assembly, initially an assembly of parliamentarians, initially elected by parliaments and subsequently by direct election, expanding on the role the NGOs Inter-Parliamentary Union and Parliamentarians for Global Action already played'.[35] It suggested beginning with an annual Forum of Civil Society with 300 to 600 'organs of global civil society', to meet prior to the General Assembly opening, to 'inform' the discussion of the General Assembly. It called for a new 'right of petition' to the Security Council for international civil society for 'action to redress wrongs that could imperil people's security'.[36] The Commission did not face the difficult question of exactly how a civil society of NGOs should be related to UN organs, nor did it address the question of how civil society organizations might be chosen. While most of these proposals have lain fallow, the Millennium NGO Forum, which was to be held 22–26 May 2000 as a companion to the UN

Millennium General Assembly of 6 September 2000, was in a sense a derivative of the civil society forum notion.

The Exapnsion of NGO Roles in the other Principal Organs

Constant references began to appear in the 1990s in UN negotiating documents and in speeches and reports of the Secretary-General to the importance of NGOs. In development and in humanitarian relief, NGOs had become major players, particularly in implementation of aid projects. On environment and on the advancement of women, NGOs had often been initiators bringing issues into the UN, as well as inserting language into UN documents. In crime and drug control, NGOs were accepted partners. Even in disarmament, NGOs had begun to play important roles. While rules did not change, NGO access to the International Court of Justice and to the Security Council changed in practice.

The World Court Project:
NGOs in the General Assembly and the International Court of Justice

While consultative status has been important to NGOs, the role they have played in other principal organs where they did not have consultative status has also been significant. In the World Court Project, NGOs played a major role with respect to another of the principal organs, the International Court of Justice. In the early 1980s Sean MacBride of the International Peace Bureau suggested getting an advisory opinion of the World Court on the legality of nuclear weapons. In 1986 the World Court Project began in New Zealand to get countries to request such an opinion. The International Physicians for the Prevention of Nuclear War (IPPNW), which had received a Nobel Peace Prize in 1985 for its work on nuclear weapons, sponsored a resolution at its World Congress in 1988. The practice of states including NGOs on their national delegations enabled a citizen adviser on the New Zealand delegation to the Third UN Special Session on Disarmament to spread the idea to other delegates. The project spread to the World Congress of the International Association of Lawyers Against Nuclear Arms (IALANA), and to other states, with the aid of newsletter coverage by the Parliamentarians for Global Action.

Using Article 66 of the Charter, which allows other organs in addition to the UN General Assembly to request World Court advisory opinions, the IPPNW convinced the World Health Organization to adopt a resolution on the subject on 14 May 1993.[37] The Lawyers' Committee on Nuclear Policy, the US affiliate of IALANA, pushed for the adoption of a resolution by the UN General Assembly First Committee. Having achieved the support of the Non-aligned Movement, the resolution was adopted on 18

November 1994. In December 1994 the resolution was adopted by the General Assembly.[38] Within days the case arrived at the World Court, which decided to consider WHO and General Assembly questions separately but simultaneously. The World Court delivered its decision on 8 July 1996, finding threat or use of nuclear weapons contrary to the law of armed conflict, and in particular international humanitarian law, but not concluding in the case of self-defence.[39]

NGOs in this case used access through states and through consultative status with ECOSOC, coupled with legal expertise and social movement organizing, to obtain a result from the International Court of Justice that powerful nuclear states had opposed. This pattern was echoed in several other cases outside the realm of economic and social issues. Secretary-General Kofi Annan has repeatedly indicated how important the role of NGOs has been with respect to the development of the International Criminal Court and the land mines treaty.

NGO co-operation with some states on these and other issues has angered other states, which moved to limit NGO access. In particular, certain states raised the extensive work NGOs had done on human rights since the beginning of the UN. At the June 1999 session of the UN Committee on NGOs, Christian Solidarity International lost its consultative status after an incident in which a rebel Sudanese leader the organization had allowed to speak made accusations against a government before the UN Commission on Human Rights.[40] Others were particularly disturbed at the success of the International Campaign to Ban Landmines, which proceeded to win the Nobel Peace Prize in 1997 for its work on the Ottawa process.

NGO Relations with the Security Council and other organs

Informal dialogues have become an important mechanism linking NGOs with the UN. The co-ordination of humanitarian aid and security questions in complex emergencies led to discussion between Security Council members and certain humanitarian organizations, especially focusing on Africa in 1997. The roughly 30 NGOs in the NGO working group on the Security Council have met increasingly with members of the Security Council since then.[41]

The Inter-Agency Steering Committee, as the central humanitarian policy-making body, is chaired by the Emergency Relief Co-ordinator, and includes heads of UN agencies, including the Office for the Co-ordination of Humanitarian Affairs in the Secretariat, as well as both Red Cross organizations and three consortia of NGOs. One of these, the Steering Committee for Humanitarian Response, has developed a code of conduct for NGOs, to which 144 NGOs have adhered.[42] Informal co-operation may be as important as consultative relations in these cases, but with the proviso that lack of formalization means that the access provided through such co-operation could disappear in a minute.

ECOSOC Resolution 1996/31

In 1993 ECOSOC requested a general review of NGO consultative arrangements in order to revise Resolution 1296 and to introduce coherent rules for NGO participation in UN conferences, as well as to improve the practical arrangements of both the Committee of NGOs and the NGO section of the Secretariat.[43]

On 25 July 1996 the 49th plenary meeting of ECOSOC approved a new resolution revising the arrangements for consultation with non-governmental organizations set out in Resolution 1296 of 1968. While there was a great deal of fanfare about how this resolution expanded consultative status from just international NGOs to include regional and national NGOs, in fact the criteria were almost entirely a seamless web with those found in 1296 and in Resolution 288B (X) of 1950 before it. The resolution re-emphasized the principle that NGOs admitted to consultative status would be those concerned with the business of ECOSOC rather than the UN as a whole (Part I, para. 1). It reaffirmed that consultative relationships could be established with international, regional, sub-regional and national organizations – 'after consultation with the member state concerned' – and encouraged greater participation of NGOs from developing countries and from economies in transition (Part I, paras 4–8). It emphasized that an organization should have the authority to speak for, and mechanisms for accountability to, its members (Part I, paras 11–12). It emphasized that 'consultation' was not the same as the 'participation without vote' accorded to non-member states and specialized agencies and stressed that two principles shall govern decisions on consultative status: (1) the provision of expert information and advice, and (2) the enabling of organizations representative of 'important elements of public opinion' to express their views (Part II, paras 18, 20).

In Part III of Resolution 1996/31, the Council resorted to what amounted to simply renaming the categories of consultative relationships. Category I was renamed 'general consultative status', with the only language change being the additional requirement of being representative of 'different regions of the world'. Category II became 'special consultative status'. The Roster category remained the same (Part III, paras 22–24).

The resolution also provided rules for consultation with the Council (Part IV) and with commissions and other subsidiary organs of the Council (Part V). Organizations in general and special consultative status may observe meetings of the Council and subsidiary bodies, and may

submit written statements on subjects on which they have special competence under certain specified conditions, while Roster organizations may
observe meetings 'within their field of competence' and may submit
written statements at the initiative of the Secretary-General. Organizations
in general consultative status may also propose to the Committee on
NGOs that the Secretary-General place items on the provisional agenda
and, if such an item has been included, may make an oral presentation
(Part IV, paras 28, 32b). The Committee is also to recommend which
organizations in general, and in some cases special, consultative status
should make oral presentations to the Council (Part IV, para. 32a).

Part VII of ECOSOC Resolution 1996/31, which addresses NGO participation in UN conferences and their preparatory processes, places the
accreditation process squarely in the hands of the preparatory committee
of member states (Part VII, para. 41). While organizations in consultative
status will as a rule be accredited, other NGOs may also be accredited on
the basis of the competence of the organization and its work's relevance
to the conference, based on specified information to be provided (Part VII,
paras 42, 44a–g). Accreditation to a preparatory session also allows
attendance at the conference itself, but neither provides 'a negotiating
role' (Part VII, paras 49–50). Oral NGO statements are at the discretion of
the Chair and the conference (Part VII, paras 51–52). While accredited
NGOs may make written presentations, accreditation to a conference does
not guarantee regular ECOSOC consultative status, but documents used
for conference accreditation may be used for the ECOSOC application
(Part VII, para. 53). This part of the resolution essentially codified the
procedures that had grown up around the participation of NGOs in
conferences and the transition to participation in permanent bodies created by such conferences, in particular the Commission on Sustainable
Development (CSD) created by the Rio conference. In the case of the CSD,
however, the whole list had been admitted together in a single action.

Finally, in Part VIII the resolution provided procedures for suspension
and withdrawal of consultative status, based on 'a pattern of acts contrary
to the purposes and principles' of the UN Charter, influence of criminal
activity, or no positive contribution during three years (Part VIII, para.
57).

Part IX updates the procedures of the Council Committee on NGOs,
while Part X provides access for NGOs to the Secretariat, to UN documents, to UN libraries, and to seating and documents during General
Assembly meetings in economic and social and related fields. Perhaps
most importantly, Part XI requests the Secretary-General to provide
adequate Secretariat support. This provision led to a much-needed
increase in the staffing of the NGO office in the Secretariat.

Following the passage of ECOSOC 1996/31, CONGO proposed that similar arrangements be extended to the General Assembly.[44] In 1997 CONGO changed its name to the Conference of Non-Governmental Organizations in Consultative Status with the United Nations, symbolizing its expanded role and its desire for the expansion of the NGO–UN relationship beyond ECOSOC.

THE WAY AHEAD: UN REFORM AND THE SECRETARY-GENERAL'S REPORTS

The question of the NGO role now proceeded to the General Assembly and the office of the Secretary-General. At the same time as 1996/31, ECOSOC Decision 1996/297 of 25 July 1996 recommended that:

> the General Assembly examine, at its fifty-first session, the question of the participation of non-governmental organizations in all areas of the work of the United Nations, in light of the experience gained through the arrangements for consultation between non-governmental organizations and the Economic and Social Council.

When the Open-Ended High-Level Working Group on the Strengthening of the UN System began its work, Ambassador Razali Ismail of Malaysia, who had worked closely with NGOs in the very open atmosphere of the first years of the CSD, and was by then President of the 51st General Assembly, named Pakistani Ambassador Ahmed Kamal as Chair of the sub-group on NGOs. Governments were unable even to agree on the mandate for the sub-group after ten meetings. The Final Report of the Open-Ended Working Group on Strengthening the UN System, 31 July 1997, stated that the sub-group on NGOs recommended early 52nd General Assembly consideration of the question of participation of NGOs in the work of the UN in accord with ECOSOC 1996/297.[45]

At the July 1997 ECOSOC meeting the USA circulated a 'non-paper' that recommended an extension of some NGO access to the General Assembly and a report of the Secretary-General on NGO arrangements and practices in the General Assembly and elsewhere in the UN.[46] Facing substantial opposition, ECOSOC deferred consideration of the draft resolution and recommended early General Assembly consideration of the issue.[47]

This failure of the General Assembly to come to agreement on NGO issues led it to request a report from the Secretary-General.[48] The Secretary-General's 1998 Report on 'Arrangements and practices for the interaction of non-governmental organizations in all activities of the United Nations system' noted a growing operational partnership and growing participation of NGOs from all regions. It noted that 'national

NGOs now account for the majority of applications for consultative status', and that UN mechanisms would need to be developed in this area.[49] In large part, however, the report effectively sidestepped one question the General Assembly had asked – that of the financial implications of NGO participation – with the exception of noting a need for funding and raising the issue of a trust fund to facilitate NGO participation from developing countries and countries in transition.[50]

Criticism about lack of consultation in the construction of the report led the General Assembly to ask the Secretary-General to seek the views of states, specialized agencies and IGOs and NGOs.[51] On 8 September 1999 the Office of External Relations issued a new report of the Secretary-General on these views.[52] Most responding states found NGOs 'a driving force in the conceptualization and implementation of decisions taken at major United Nations conferences'. While states differed on the expansion of the NGO role beyond ECOSOC, the majority agreed that states should not bear any related additional financial burden. Access to information, including the use of the UN's Optical Disc System, and document distribution, and access to UN headquarters, were big issues for NGOs.[53] While both the reports were judged useful, they did little to address questions of the further development of the NGO relationship to the principal organs other than ECOSOC, or of the co-ordination of NGO relations in the UN system. Thus ECOSOC 1996/31 remained the fundamental document governing NGO relations with the principal organs, with changes being largely informal and incremental.

ASSESSING THE NGO ROLE

NGOs have long been important as providers of information about the UN and as providers of expertise to the UN. They have increasingly become implementers of UN policy in development and even in the security-related area of humanitarian intervention. Largely as a result of the UN global conferences since the 1970s, they have initiated and influenced UN policy-making and monitored resultant state policies and actions. According to the Secretary-General's 1998 Report, NGOs 'are no longer seen only as disseminators of information, but as shapers of policy and indispensable bridges between the general public and the intergovernmental process'.[54] The Secretary-General's second report in 1999 finds that some member states 'consider that access for non-governmental organizations would contribute to a significant increase in transparency and accountability in the United Nations, and improve the quality of such decision-making'.[55]

The notion that NGOs can represent the voice of the people, however, is another question. NGOs represent the interests of their members, and even then imperfectly. NGOs do not include all members of global civil society. Although states may also imperfectly provide democratic representation, it is at least their task to do that, while NGOs have no such obligation. Does this mean that NGOs have no place in the principal organs of the UN except for ECOSOC? On the contrary, their role has expanded and is likely to continue to do so because they provide, not democratic representation, but an important alternative and often unheard voice. In that sense they have become an important part of the overall development of global governance through the principal organs of the United Nations.

NOTES

1. This chapter is part of a broader project on non-governmental organizations and UN conferences. The author gratefully acknowledges the support of a Research and Writing Grant from the John D. and Catherine T. MacArthur Foundation for the project.
2. See for example Elise Boulding, *Women in the Twentieth Century World* (New York: John Wiley, 1977), pp. 165–218, for the argument that NGOs represent the voice of the people in a landscape of money and power.
3. For definition and discussion of these and other social movements see Roger S. Powers and William B. Vogele (eds.), *Protest, Power and Change: An Encyclopedia of Nonviolent Action from ACT-UP to Women's Suffrage* (New York: Garland Publishing Inc., 1997).
4. Section 3, chapters 23–32, 'Strengthening the role of major groups', includes women, children and youth, indigenous people, NGOs, local authorities, workers and trade unions, business and industry, the scientific and technological community, and farmers. See United Nations Department of Public Information, *Earth Summit Agenda 21: The United Nations Programme of Action from Rio*, New York: UN DPI/1344, April 1993, pp. 219–45.
5. See Harold Jacobson, *Networks of Independence* (New York: Alfred A. Knopf, 1984), pp. 4–13, for a good discussion of the complexities of defining INGOs.
6. Compiled by author from *Yearbook of International Organisations, 1990–91*, table 4, pp. 1665–68.
7. One of the first major news articles on NGOs at the UN was Paul Lewis, 'Fixing world crises isn't just a job for diplomats', *New York Times*, 5 April 1992, section 4, p. 4, which looked at NGOs in the context of the UNCED PrepCom.
8. Charles DeBenedetti, *The Peace Reform in American History* (Bloomington: Indiana University Press, 1980).
9. See first text in US Department of State, *Postwar Foreign Policy Preparation*, 1939–1945, Publication 3580 (February 1950) Appendix 38, pp. 595–606. See second text in 'Dumbarton Oaks proposals for the establishment of a general international organization', in US Department of State, *Dumbarton Oaks Documents on International Organization*, Publication 2257 (1945), pp. 5–16.

10. Ruth Russell, *History of the United Nations Charter* (Washington, DC: Brookings Institution, 1958), pp. 798–802.

11. *Charter of the United Nations: Report to the President on the Results of the San Francisco Conference by the Chairman of the United States Delegation, the Secretary of State*, Department of State Publication 2349, Conference Series 71 26 June 1945), pp. 26–28.

12. Russell, *op. cit.*, p. 801; and Report to the President, *op. cit.*, pp. 120–21.

13. UN Document E/NGO/2 (14/V/46), Part I, section 5.

14. UN Document E/NGO/6 (21 May 1946).

15. Conference of Non-governmental Organizations in Consultative Relationship with the United Nations (CONGO), *CONGO at Fifty: A Reaffirmation of Commitment* (New York: CONGO, 1998), pp. 1, 13, 27.

16. UN ECOSOC Resolution 1099, Official Records 40th Session, 1, 415th meeting, 4 March 1966.

17. 'List of Organisations Granted Consultative Status by the Council, the Date Granted, and Country of Headquarters,' UN Document E/4321, Annex III, May 1967.

18. CONGO, *op. cit.*, pp. 16–17.

19. Of the organizations with ECOSOC consultative status, 164 were also listed in the May 1982 NGO/DPI list of 'Non-Governmental Organisations Associated with the Department of Public Information'. This list also contained 215 other organizations associated with DPI.

20. Secretary-General, Bulletin ST/SGB/209 of 21 December 1984.

21. Report of the Secretary-General: 'Arrangements and practices for the interaction of non-governmental organisations in all activities of the United Nations system.' United Nations, 53rd session, A/53/170, 10 July 1998, paras 14, 74, 75. Also Global Policy Forum, 'NGOs and the United Nations: Comments for the Report of the Secretary-General,' New York, June 1999, pp. 14–15.

22. *Ibid.*, p. 23.

23. Virginia Saurwein, 'The United Nations and non-governmental organisations: creating an enabling environment', in CONGO, *op. cit.*, pp. 27–28.

24. E/CN.6/NGO/244.

25. CONGO, *op. cit.*, p. 52.

26. Author's participant observation and interviews at each conference and also United Nations, World Conference of the International Women's Year, Report of the Conference (E/CONF.66), and United Nations Report of the World Conference of the United Nations Decade for Women (A/CONF.94/35).

27. United Nations, 'Arrangement and practices for the interaction of non-governmental organisations in all activities of the United Nations system: Report of the Secretary-General', 10 July 1998 (A/53/170), para. 53.

28. CONGO, *op. cit.*, pp. 18–19.

29. A/CONF.151/PC/L.8 of 13 August 1990 became Decision 1/1. It can be found in A/45/46 of 25 January 1991, the official report of the PrepCom.

30. General Assembly Resolution 45/211, 21 December 1990, which extended the NGO provisions to all the UNCED PrepComs. The second Preparatory Committee took place in Geneva in March 1991, with a total of 187 NGOs in attendance. By the time of the third Preparatory Conference in Geneva in October 1991, NGOs totalled 348.

31. UN GA, Preparatory Committee for the United Nations Conference on Environment and Development, Introductory statement made by the Secretary-General of the Conference at the fourth session of the Preparatory Committee, A/CONF.151/PC/97/Add.1 (4 March 1992), pp. 10–11.
32. Agenda 21: Report of the United Nations Conference on Environment and Development A/CONF.151/26, 14 August 1992, Section 3. For a listing of 'major groups' and an easily accessible version of Agenda 21, see also note 4 of this chapter.
33. ECOSOC Decision 1993/220, 26 May 1993.
34. ECOSOC Decision 1994/300.
35. Report of the Commission on Global Governance, *Our Global Neighborhood* (New York: Oxford University Press, 1995), pp. 254, 257–58.
36. *Ibid.*, pp. 259–61.
37. By a vote of 73–40, with 10 abstentions.
38. First Committee vote was 77–33, with 21 abstentions and 53 not voting. General Assembly vote was 78–43, with 38 abstentions and 25 not voting.
39. Kate Dewes and Robert Green, *Aotearoa/New Zealand at the World Court* (Christchurch, New Zealand: Disarmament and Security Centre, 1999), pp. 20–39.
40. Paul Lewis, 'U.N. Committee, under pressure, limits rights groups', *New York Times*, 22 June 1999.
41. Global Policy Forum, *op. cit.*, p. 2.
42. A/52/170, paras 36–37.
43. ECOSOC Resolution 1993/80, 30 July 1993.
44. Global Policy Forum, *op. cit.*, p. 12.
45. A/51/24 of 31 July 1997.
46. The revised US draft was circulated as E/1997/L.51.
47. email 27 July 1997 from INGLIM/WFM/CDIL.
48. General Assembly Decision 52/453 of 19 December 1997.
49. A/53/170 of 10 July 1998. See especially para. 67.
50. *Ibid.*, para. 79.
51. Decision 53/452 of 17 December 1998.
52. Report of the Secretary-General: 'Views of member states, members of the specialized agencies, observers, intergovernmental and non-governmental organizations from all regions on the report of the Secretary-General on arrangements and practices for the interaction of non-governmental organisations in all activities of the United Nations system.' A/54/329. (Based on comments of 27 states (plus the EU), 10 specialized agencies and IGOs and 130 NGOs.)
53. *Ibid.* See especially paras 7, 16, 18, 46, 58–62.
54. A/53/170, para. 57.
55. A/54/329, para. 30.

CHAPTER 10

THE INSTITUTIONS OF THE UNITED NATIONS AND THE PRINCIPLE OF CONSONANCE: AN OVERVIEW

Paul Taylor

INTRODUCTION

The nature of United Nations institutions can be analysed at several levels. The focus throughout this volume has been on the emergence, structure and functioning of the machinery, but it should not be forgotten that there were at least two other levels of concern. One is the level of resources available to carry out the decisions of the institutions: for instance, how much money, and other inputs, has been provided for peacekeeping and various forms of help for humanitarian assistance and disaster relief? (These specific and serious problems are not discussed in detail here.) A second is the *will* of member governments to act through the institutions.

Obviously the three levels are related and sometimes the relationship has worked in surprising ways. For instance, the shortage of finance – the squeeze – was certainly a major source of difficulty, but it also had positive aspects.[1] At the time of writing, in late 1999, the USA had come close to losing its vote in the General Assembly, following Article 19 of the Charter, because of its failure to pay what it owed the organization. In December 1999 it paid enough to avoid this happening in January 2000. But a positive effect of the financial stringency was that the agencies, and other organizations, were generally persuaded to be more system oriented – to accept more co-ordination – so that they could get a larger piece of the smaller pie. The collapse of the Soviet Union, which in a united stable form in the late Gorbachev period had been a positive factor for the United Nations, also helped the agenda of democratization in developing countries. They were less resistant to pressures to build better civil societies and promote human rights, and were more prepared to accept changes to achieve greater efficiency in key institutions. But the weakening in the late 1990s of the Soviet Union's successor state, Russia, made it more difficult, rather than easier, for the Security Council to act effectively, as was evident in the Kosovo crisis. A new factor making for dissent was the increasing Russian anxiety about its status and the resulting determination to get its way to show it could stand up to the other permanent members, especially the United States. (This point is explored further below.)

In the phase of development of the international economic system after the collapse of the Iron Curtain, which combined the domination of liberal capitalism with budgetary constraint, it became apparent that developing states needed to attract private money. This was more likely to be available if societies were more open and more stable. This was of course often a dangerous game: openness was too often at the expense of mass unemployment which in turn could create civil unrest. Even the development of the new global systems had positive, as well as negative, implications from the point of view of entrenching multilateralism, i.e. strengthening the system of informal rules that governed relationships between states. The revolution in information technology was a part of the destabilizing process, with such developments as the computerization of currency speculation weakening governments' ability to maintain a stable system. But at the same time the evolution of the global village meant that peace was now indivisible, and gross violations of human rights were likely to be brought to the attention of a wider public, for moral reasons but also for reasons of international peace and security. This was part of the process of softening the old distinction between national interest and moral action. It was more likely that the national interest would be served by acting morally, as not to do so would lead to a loss of status and the appearance of weakness, and this change inevitably increased the weight of expectations focused on the institutions of the UN. Put another way, global problems make it clearer that community interest is an integral part of self-interest.

THE BURDEN OF NEW TASKS FOR THE INSTITUTIONS

The late 1990s saw a number of scholarly conferences on the Treaties of Westphalia – and with good reason: there was a useful comparison to be made between the situation which the emerging states faced in the early seventeenth century and that faced by states in the final years of the twentieth century. In the first case states were faced with the problem of how to deal with fading transnational systems, in particular the secular empire of the Catholic Church, as state power increased and as they gathered the appurtenances of sovereignty. In the latter case states were faced with the problem of relating their statehood and continuing sovereignty to emerging transnational forces. As Langhorne put it:

In the first case, those developments had to do with secularisation following the Reformation in Europe, the successful establishment of independently acting states and the retreat of non-state jurisdictions and universalist ideas. The result was the gradual construction of an international system based on the principle that states alone had the right to be actors. What followed was a long period in which that principle was unchallenged and allowed the international system to exert pressure to conform on the actors: a reversal of what had happened during the emergence of the system. In the present case, *raison de système* has ceased to operate, or at least to operate reliably, and once again it is factors external to the system which have the whip hand: an international system consisting only of states or organisations which are the creatures of states cannot cope with developments and pressures which, because of the effects of the global communications revolution, extend horizontally across state boundaries and evade the controlling policies of their governments. Only when the process of change has produced a *really new world order* [my italics] reflecting the realities of the distribution of power among both the old and the new possessors of it, will a new system develop able to extrude similar pressures to conform.[2]

The development of the institutions of the United Nations has to be considered in the context of the need for such a 'really new' world order. The preceding chapters indicated that the organization could be seen as a part of the transformation, helping with the entrenchment of multilateral rules, procedures and decision-making centres, so that global mechanisms for managing the global systems were developed. But its relationship with the environment of the society of states was also important. It could be assisted by the constellation of power or it could be enfeebled by changing structures and circumstances. The UN could help with the development of an international structure in which governments would find it easier to cope with the new horizontal pressures. But alongside this was concern with the optimum organization of the UN itself (how might it be best governed, and what was the ideal pattern of relationships between its constituent institutions and between them and international society?) so that it emerged as an effective actor in the new order. The latter is closely related to the former, and therefore care needs to be taken – often missing – to relate plans for the reform of the institution to the preferred pattern of evolution of international society.

The relationship could be a negative or a positive one. Plans for internal reorganization in the UN could be negated by an adverse international society, as is shown below; but, if properly conceived, they might also help a more supportive international society to develop. In sum, internal institutional changes needed, as always, to be related to the emerging world order. This chapter, like its predecessors, concentrates on the institutional mechanisms and the operational principles, but it attempts to relate arguments about internal change in the UN to the context in the international system. What is not discussed are the details of operational impact within particular states, or the shortfalls of resources in specific contexts.

Two approaches to the problem of controlling the transnational forces are conceivable (they could be used together). First, the international mechanisms could be strengthened to maximize the potential for common control by states, which would inevitably be limited to the extent that their interests differed. Second, the ability of the states to withstand disturbances generated by the transnational forces could be augmented: to the extent that the universal mechanisms fell short the local mechanisms needed to be strengthened. The best strategy for achieving the latter in the late 1990s remained the further development of the dominant structural trend of the second half of the twentieth century, namely progress towards denser organization at the regional level.[3] Until countervailing global systems emerged, only further consolidation of regional organization could create circumstances in which the social, local interests of citizens could prevail over the global, profit-maximizing interests of multinational companies and other systems that could be tempted to pursue asocial strategies.

Paradoxically, however, enhancing the strength of the regions was also a way of strengthening the global mechanisms. Stronger regions could more effectively resist multinationals but also make better, more densely constructed, building-blocks of a stronger set of international institutions, including the United Nations. The general requirement was that a *consonance* was required between the institution, how it was arranged, what it did, and its setting in society. The characteristics of instruments of governance had to fit the society to which it referred, and international society was no exception. But this worked both ways in that society could itself be shaped to suit the available instruments of governance.

Consonance is seen as having two levels. Internal consonance is when the sub-institutions are consonant with each other: the structure, processes and roles in one sub-institution complement and reinforce the structure, processes and roles in other sub-institutions. External consonance is when the overall set of institutions is consonant with its environment in international society: its internal consonance, as defined above, is promoted by the structure of international society, which is its primary environment, and the sub-institutions together promote a favourable structure of international society. Therefore it is necessary to avoid changes in one sub-institution which create contradictions in other sub-institutions in that their structure, processes and roles are in consequence reduced in efficiency and effect, and nothing should be done which gets in the way of the development of a more supportive international society or which inhibits the implications of the positive aspects of international society for internal consonance.

Obviously to carry out a full examination of the UN with these principles in mind would be a massive enterprise; in this chapter they are outlined and illustrated. This is at least a first step towards understanding how it could be made a more effective player in the current international system, able to contribute positively to the 'really new world order'. Three elements of the institutions within the United Nations were selected for closer examination. First was the structure of the membership, defined in terms of members' orientation towards the institution in comparison with their status in international society; second, was the form of collective activity undertaken in the various sub-institutions; and, third, was the structure of the institution in terms of its sub-institutions (Security Council, General Assembly, etc.). The points argued here are that each of the elements has features that might be consonant or dissonant in relation to those of the other elements; and a lack of consonance between the features in each of the three elements would lead to tensions and inefficiencies in the institution, i.e. the ideal was overall consonance, both among the sub-institutions of the UN system and between them and the environment of the society of states.

There were, then, two interrelated fundamental questions to be discussed: what were the general guidelines on how to construct the best kind of United Nations and how should it be related to the society of states? The next two sections, 'The pattern of UN membership' and 'The principles of collective action', focus on the first two elements which are relevant to consonance; the third is discussed *passim*. In the third section 'Principles of consonance in the UN', examples of consonance and dissonance are addressed more directly.

THE PATTERN OF UN MEMBERSHIP

The following typology of state memberships in the United Nations is based on two criteria: the orientation of their governments towards the organization and their status in the hierarchy of states at the global and regional levels. Groups of states can be identified which constitute the structure of membership. In the later discussion frequent reference is made to this typology.

1. Status quo powers, having a position in the organization which matched their status in global international society (e.g. the US, China and the former USSR). These were states where governments were

largely supportive of the system and accepted the need to work through it. They saw the UN as an instrument of their foreign policy, and their role and status in the organization matched their perceived position in the international hierarchy. They had major vetoing or promotional capacity in the context of the institution.

2. Status quo powers, having a position in the organization which exceeded their status in global international society, but which could claim to be representative of a region (e.g. the UK, France). These were states that occupied a position in the international hierarchy that was lower than the one they occupied in the structure of the United Nations, but they saw that mismatch as suiting their interests in that their position in the organization added to their status outside it. It was said that the British position in the UN allowed that state to 'punch above its weight', which was also true of France. But there was a coincidence between their regional position and their global institutional one in that the convergence of regional interests was sufficient for their role in the UN to be seen as compatible with a representative element. This convergence, together with their overall contribution, justified their UN status.

3. Reformist states (e.g. Germany, Japan, Italy). These were states that were significant contributors to the organization – they had high informal status – but which saw a mismatch between their emergent global status and their formal status in the organization. They therefore wished to enhance their position in the latter to reflect the former. This interest was not seen as posing any problems for their regional partners, for reasons discussed below, even though the latter might not always positively support it, as with the case of Italy's policy on Germany's claim to membership of the Security Council. (This group is discussed in comparison with others more fully below.)

4. System-reinforcing problem-solvers (e.g. Sweden, the Netherlands, Norway, Finland, Canada). These were countries that made no claims for enhancement in the formal structure of the organization, even though they were significant contributors and had high informal status. They were relatively unconcerned about obtaining a match between their status in the international hierarchy and their formal status in the UN. They had no claims based on regional representation. They were positive about their membership – seeing it as bringing proportionate benefits, and being prepared to contribute positively to its work, and the solving of problems within it – without attaching these to formal promotion in the institutions, e.g. they refrained from demanding special Security Council membership for themselves to reflect their status as good citizens in the UN and in the global international hierarchy. They were significant net contributors to the resources of the

institution in terms of money and/or supportive involvement and policy development. They were privileged in the system and conscious of it.

5. Reformist states. These were states making claims for formal enhancement in the organization which exceeded their general status in the international hierarchy, and which presented a contested claim to represent regions (e.g. Brazil, India, Nigeria). They saw the promotion of their position in the global organization as an instrument for promoting their status among the states of the region to which they belonged, as well as in global international society. For instance, for Brazil, becoming a permanent member of the Security Council would multiply its power but also increase its status in comparison with other Latin American states, in particular Argentina. (This is discussed further below.) Moving up the institutional hierarchy was likely to increase divergence at the regional level. Similar arguments applied to Nigeria and, to some degree, India.

6. System-loading claimants (e.g. failing and non-developed: G77 and most of Africa). These were states that looked to the organization for the solution of their economic, social political problems, were low in the global international hierarchy, and did not claim to represent a region. They made little contribution to the development of the institution's resources, and were generally short of the skills and resources required for efficient administration and the maintenance of a modern civil society, i.e. they were generally claimants and beneficiaries rather than contributors. But they were prepared to work in the existing structures. In the late 1990s this group could be subdivided into two groups: the least developed, which were close to collapse as states, and included states in Africa south of the Sahara; and those that were somewhat more advanced in economic and political terms and which could be fairly described as developing. The latter's claims in some respects got in the way of attempts to solve the problems of the worse off.

7. The new dissatisfied powers were states that saw the institution as being in need of drastic reform in order to meet their interests, but at the same time were claimants on the system (e.g. Yemen, Cuba, Sudan, Malaysia, Indonesia, sometimes Algeria). They were constantly working for system revolution, and had no expectation of position enhancement within it in its existing form. In particular they sought to acquire structural power by actively promoting collective action in the plenary meetings, and thereby enhancing their position in a more populist UN, but they had little regional base.

8. The pariah states (Libya, Iran, Iraq, Burma). These were states that remained members in order to do what they could to prevent further

moves against themselves, and in the late 1990s they could be regarded as semi-detached from the UN. As with the decision to be with or against the Chicago gangster Al Capone in the 1930s: 'If they weren't there it would be worse for them.' Their strategy was the negative one of remaining in the organization, even though they saw no particular 'positive' benefit in this, simply because leaving would risk even greater costs. They had little or no regional status or representative claims.

A further comparison of the orientation of states in Groups 2, 3 and 5 is illuminating. The UK is taken as illustrative of Group 2, Brazil of Group 5 and Germany of Group 3. By the late 1990s the attitude of the UK towards the reform of the UN, particularly the Security Council, was strongly affected by its membership of the European Union. Unlike 1945, arguments about the role of the British and the Brazilians were crucially affected by their relationship with regional institutions in Europe and Latin America. The situation in the late 1990s was that the UK and France still reserved their right to decide for themselves on issues on the UN agenda. They agreed to inform the other members of the EU through the machinery in New York but would not be bound by instructions from their partners. This was protected by agreements in the Single European Act and the Maastricht Treaty. Because of the EU's gradual development of stronger mechanisms for a Common Foreign and Security Policy (CFSP) this position was becoming more difficult to maintain.[4] To the extent that the CFSP became stronger, interests and policies of which the UK approved and which it had helped to shape, would be collectively pursued.

A regional identity in foreign policy would paradoxically make the question of whether the British and French should lose their membership of the Security Council a less sensitive one. If they stayed they could represent the EU; if they went, the EU representative could take over – the difference was not critical. But in the late 1990s, although the British remained unwilling to renounce their ability to act independently on the Council, and to promote their unilateral position in that context, the matter was by no means as sensitive as it would have been if the EU had not existed. Indeed, the whole question of German accession to the Security Council as a veto-bearing permanent member was less important to the extent that the regional partnership made the precise nature of the Union's representation in the Council less sensitive.

In contrast, some countries sought seats in the Security Council for more traditional reasons. Brazil, for instance, saw membership of the Council as one of the steps in its emergence as a ranking power, a confirmation of status and acceptance by the states that mattered. It saw that membership as confirming its leadership of the regional group of which it was a member, MERCOSUR, which aspired in the late 1990s to emulate the EU. Unlike the case with Britain, membership was seen as an aspect of the defining of Brazilian identity, and its role in the world, and could not be mediated through the notion of an emerging regionalism in Latin America. While British attitudes towards protecting its Security Council position were mixed, it was conceivable by the late 1990s that there could be a regional successor or, more likely, a stronger form of mandating of members by the partners. In contrast, Brazil's position was an indication of the weakness of MERCOSUR in that it would help to assert its separate foreign policy identity, especially in relation to Argentina. If anything, Brazilian membership would challenge rather than enhance regional integration, in that it would increase the status of the biggest regional state at a point in the evolution of MERCOSUR when countervailing regionally located institutions and policy-making arrangements were weak.

From the point of view of the reform of the United Nations it was unlikely that the Security Council membership of states such as Brazil and Nigeria, and some other regional aspirants, would be helpful. Such reforms would be unlikely to increase the effectiveness or efficiency of the Security Council. Brazil could not claim to represent a set of regionally agreed interests in the sense that they emerged by consultation in a set of legitimate institutions embodying common interests, as potentially with the CFSP of the EU: membership looked like a form of triumphalism in relations with the Argentine. In the arguments for membership the question of the capabilities of Brazil in performing UN tasks received little attention, though there was some reference to the modest involvement of Brazilian forces in peacekeeping. It was more a question of entitlements and claims: entitlements because of emerging national economic strength, and claims to be promoting international democracy by representing Latin America more effectively in the UN. Both arguments rested on uncertain foundations: would economic recovery continue? In what sense could Brazil represent other Latin American countries that expressed doubts about its right to do so?

By the late 1990s Britain appeared to have accepted without enthusiasm the case for enlargement of the Council to include Germany, Japan and an undetermined number of non-permanent members. Japan had taken the United Kingdom's 'second place' in the International Monetary Fund (IMF), and both Japan and Germany had provided high-ranking international civil servants in WHO, UNESCO and NATO. But the United Kingdom was seen as a reliable member of the Council, with a wealth of experience in multilateral diplomacy – more than the US – and first-rate diplomats in New York. It was acknowledged by other members that the

United Kingdom (and France) were different from countries such as Germany and Japan. The United Kingdom was a nuclear power and had a global military reach surpassed only by the United States and Russia. Moreover, again like France, the United Kingdom had an inclination to act, which if anything was stronger under New Labour than the Conservatives. The British were unique in having both a large number of technical skills, in drafting, committee work, and so on, and great ability in the processes of multilateral diplomacy, and in the possession of a world view. Both countries had extensive trans-regional ties through the Commonwealth and Francophonie.

The question of the resources, tangible and intangible, that candidate and member states could bring to the Security Council was highly significant. In contrast with the members of the first four groups, Group 5 members were more likely to be net consumers than contributors of resources! They were, taken as a group, of uncertain internal stability, with challenges from other states in their regions, and without global experience or interests. In the late 1990s they also had to be taken as lacking a reserve of tangible resources that could be significant additions to the UN's peacekeeping or development capacity; both tasks had greatly expanded so that the resources of the big players were inevitably critical. Placed in the context of the hierarchy of states, it was therefore easy to see that there would be serious dissonance between the formal status of such states in the UN and their actual status in international society, such that they would be more likely to detract from than add to the overall capacity of the institution.

THE PRINCIPLES OF COLLECTIVE ACTION

Three types of collective action are referred to here:

1. A first form included action to initiate major operations for norm maintenance, such as peacekeeping, humanitarian intervention or enforcement under Chapter VII, but could include executive action in other member organizations to initiate forceful – not necessarily violent – action. The main forum of this form of collective action was the Security Council, which could take decisions in the event of threats to international peace and security, and decisions involving significant expenditure in such areas as peacekeeping and enforcement; and approve major expenditures on humanitarian intervention operations.

In the late 1990s the United Nations seemed to be very much improved as regards its mechanisms, but nevertheless the strong impression was that it was not succeeding. There had been relative failures in Rwanda–

Burundi and the Congo, and the Western states were backing away from their commitment to remove chemical, nuclear and bacteriological weapons from Iraq through the UN inspection teams.[5] This was despite the Security Council approval in SC 1284 of a successor to UNSCOM in December 1999 on which Russia, France, China and Malaysia abstained. It was constantly asked who or what was to blame. There was talk of a failure of political will and often the accusation was levelled explicitly at the United States. That country had emerged as the triumphant superpower at the end of the Cold War and yet was seen as being primarily responsible for the failure of the UN to act as the world's policeman. There was no doubt that some of the blame could fairly be attached to the United States, but that was only a part of the picture.

A brief discussion of the more obvious rules of collective action develops this point.

(a) It is a truism to say that action to protect global standards would be more likely if that action coincided with the perceived interests of the states. But the history of the United Nations showed positive developments in this context, as has been argued in the previous chapters: it was more likely that in the late 1990s moral action – to protect a norm – in fact coincided with national interests. It would add to the status of a state in the community of states, would be seen as a qualification for high office in the institutions of international society, and would help a government with its electorate. The role of the mass media in this was crucial. Its cumulative effect was to ensure that for the first time in the development of global society peace was indeed indivisible.

(b) The chance that a large number of actors would agree to take decisive action to enforce global standards – meaning to act firmly, accepting costs, and not merely expressing support for action – was less than was the case with a smaller number of actors. But there were reasons for supposing that a *single* actor, even the most powerful one, would also be unlikely to wish to go it alone. The costs would be relatively high because unshared, and the perception that others were freeloading would be strong; there would be the risk that the acting state would be blamed for failure, would be too exposed to adverse judgement if things began to go wrong, and would get little credit if they went right. Success was rarely clear-cut and in any case was only to be expected if undertaken by a superpower. The risks of going it alone would be high, and others' failure to act would make it look morally acceptable to do nothing, especially as their hesitation would inevitably attract the attention of the media.

(c) The chances of action being taken would be greater if the decision depended upon agreement to act among a small number of states. In this case the risks of incurring the costs outlined in (b) above would be less. It would be easier to get agreement among a small group first and then to persuade others to that position than it would be to get agreement at the outset among the members of the larger group. But even in a small group it would be necessary that a sub-group, possibly of just one, but probably of no more than two, should be prepared to initiate action and to appear to be prepared to risk going ahead of the others. Action could not depend upon the general and equal commitment of members, even of a small group. The expectation of this would lead to paralysis. Someone had to *appear* to be prepared to go ahead. But the conviction had to be general that a failure to follow would be greeted with opprobrium and create serious costs. If no state was prepared to go ahead, the collective will would be undermined, though the conviction that support for the initiator would be forthcoming was essential.

This rather basic piece of reasoning is highly significant from the point of view of understanding the failures of the UN in the late 1990s. The internal problems of the Clinton regime in the United States, which included the difficulties with his private life, as well as the powerful position of anti-internationalist Republicans in Congress, were only one source of the appearance of institutional *lourdeur* in the UN. But equally important was the lack of any other significant actor in the international system which was prepared to support action, to contribute resources that were enough to make a significant difference to the chance of success, and to stay in convoy. The position of the European Union had become a difficulty rather than an asset from the point of view of successful action.

A comparison of circumstances in the early and late 1990s is illustrative. The move towards effective action in the Gulf in 1991–92 had been much helped by the emergence of a close coalition, under US, UK and French leadership, which had been institutionalized in the P5 arrangement. This informal amendment to Security Council practice was initiated by the then British Ambassador, Sir John Thomson, in the mid-1980s, who, sensing a change in mood in the Iran–Iraq war and in Soviet attitudes towards the United Nations, acted as a catalyst. The idea was that the permanent members would meet before full Council meetings to agree proposals if possible. The meetings were weekly or even more frequent, depending on items on the agenda, and were informal, of a confidential character and worked, in English, on the basis of consensus.

The ground rules were that no member should insist on discussing an issue that another member did not wish to have considered. However, any question could be raised. The work, which started at the end of 1986, was on the basis of written documents and came into operation when the Five had a definite objective in mind. It therefore met on demand. There were also occasional meetings of the five foreign ministers with the Secretary-General – another British initiative. Moreover, it was under British chairmanship in January 1992 that the heads of government of the members of the Security Council met in session for the first time – a meeting that invited the Secretary-General to prepare his *Agenda for Peace*. Reflecting on his experience with co-ordinating permanent member co-operation, Sir Crispin Tickell told a University of Georgia audience:

> Two things are necessary for success. First is an identification of common interest and political will to construct joint policies based on it. Second is a good relationship between the Permanent and non-Permanent Members: for while the Five can stop anything, they do not, by themselves, carry a majority in the Security Council. You will note an important point: the negative power of the Five has always been vital; but now we are seeing the development of the positive power of the Five, and that may turn out to be more important still.[6]

The *positive power* of the P5 arrangement was of key importance in the UN's success in the late 1980s and early 1990s: ending the Iran–Iraq war and winning the enforcement action against Saddam Hussein.[7] By the late 1990s, however, the ties of the successful coalition had been much weakened. The failure of the member states of the EU, including Britain and France, to act decisively in the early days of the Yugoslavia crisis was of crucial importance from the point of view of the later failure of the UN. It began a noticeable pattern of failure to achieve in the EU an acceptable consensus on foreign policy, illustrated by the root and branch opposition of some states to majority voting on foreign policy questions in the Council of Ministers. This was aggravated by the determination of some states to widen the EU's membership which, intentionally or not, was bound to lead to a weakening of its central institutions and to lessen the chances of agreement to push effective action in the UN. The EU now began to appear in the unhappy position of not being united enough to act together decisively in 'high politics' aspects of foreign policy, including in relation to Security Council decisions, and in support of the US, but of being united enough for dissent among members to handicap the ability of any one member to act alone.

This was true of the most willing ally, Britain, whose independent military resources in any case were insufficient to act alone, or indeed to make much difference in crises that required the strength of the US. In other words, the failure of the UN in the late 1990s was as much to do with the failure of the EU to push a more integrated foreign policy and to emerge as a significant actor, as it was to do with US failures. For the time being at least the CFSP had become a mechanism for the mutual enfeeblement of its members in the UN context, and in particular of the Security Council. It was strong enough to get in the way of an activist P5 coalition, but not strong enough to provide a reliable partner for the US. And this meant a partner which, in principle, if necessary, was capable of acting effectively alone.

The end of the Cold War was also in the circumstances of the 1990s unhelpful. It provided a context in which the EU would be enfeebled by pressures towards enlargement, and by disagreement over East European policy. At the same time, as events turned out, the new Russia was a broken reed, incapable of acting effectively but strong enough to put large impedimenta in the way of states wishing to do so in the Security Council. By the late 1990s both Russia and the EU had become relatively ineffective in foreign policy.

If one was in the business of attaching blame for the failure of the UN in the late 1990s, it should be attached to those in the EU who failed to appreciate the way in which the regional and global systems fitted together, and the way in which a stronger, necessarily non-enlarged, EU could more effectively act with the US in promoting world order. Russia could conceivably also have done this had it been possible to move more easily from Communism to capitalism. Unfortunately another historical disjunction meant that extreme economic liberalism became the ideological flavour of the 1980s and 1990s and pushed the Russians to destroy their existing systems without having anything to take their place other than a kleptomaniac state. In consequence it made sense to blame the shallow sentimental nationalisms of some of the member states of the EU, and even the orthodoxies of the right-wing supply side economists, as much as the US administration of Bill Clinton, for the failures of the UN in the late 1990s.

2. A second form of collective action was appropriate to a second major type of decision-making in the UN system: those on expenditure out of assessed budget in economic and social decision fora. These were where decisions on expenditure were made for economic and social programmes over the wide range of UN concerns, usually involving an attempt to relate policy decisions with budgetary plans on a biennial basis. The UN central system's main forum for this type of collective action was the Committee on Programme and Co-ordination (CPC), but by the late 1990s almost all the agencies had a similar forum. The introduction and implications of this procedure in General Assembly Resolution A/41/L.49 in December 1986 were an important development which constituted a model for most subsequent decision-making in this

area in the UN system. It was discussed as follows in the author's 1993 account:

> One particular decision in the resolution attracted particular attention, and was regarded as a breakthrough by United States officials. This was the agreement in paragraph 6 [of the resolution] that the CPC should continue its existing practice of reaching decisions by consensus. Paragraph 7 took this further with the stipulation that 'all possible efforts' should be made in the Fifth Committee 'with a view to establishing the broadest possible agreement'. The argument seemed to be that though consensus had been the established way of reaching agreement before the reforms, this was not significant as long as the CPC's role was modest. With the development of that role, however, there was a greater risk that voting would take place, and lines would be drawn between the larger number of smaller contributors, and the smaller number of larger contributors.[8]

Conversely, the requirement of consensus would greatly increase the leverage that could be exercised by the major contributing states over the others. The client states would be more frequently placed in a situation in which either they concurred with the contributing states, or they risked losing the latter's funds. The consensus approach, in other words, was viewed as a weapon in the hands of the rich which could be used to get the poor states to accept the discipline of the medium-term plan. The rich states would also, however, have been able to play a decisive role in shaping the medium-term plan in the CPC: decisions in that process would also be taken on the basis of consensus. The method would make it more difficult, and, from the point of view of the poorer states, even dangerous, to unravel a carefully structured budget, relating resources to priorities, monetary commitments to programmes and intentions, which had already been agreed in the CPC. It was, therefore, more a question of tipping the balance of probabilities in favour of the richer states, of making it easier for them to lead and more difficult for the poorer states not to follow, rather than one of eliminating opposition. It would be a matter of management, not of control.

The procedure found an echo in the reformed arrangements of ECO-SOC. As is pointed out in Chapter 4, decisions about spending were to be considered in the High Level and Co-ordination segments in the context of decisions about policy in common fora which included the major donors, the major spending institutions, and the major beneficiaries. Decisions were taken by consensus. The expectation was that the participants' involvement with each other would create pressures on them in favour of supporting the approved package in other fora. In the case of the CPC process this assumption proved to be correct, in that the Fifth

Committee of the General Assembly accepted the CPC's budget with little
dissent after the new procedure was introduced in December 1986.

3. The third major form of collective action in the UN system was
found when an institution's main functions were, for example, to agree
general policy recommendations, to assert a norm or a broadly defined
objective rather than a precise command. Plenary meetings of international representatives such as the General Assembly were usually not
empowered to take legally binding decisions: their acts had the status of
recommendations. This was also characteristic of advocacy institutions
such as UNCTAD, which were concerned with mobilizing a large group
of states in support of a strategic plan such as the New International
Economic Order. Why was a plenary body such as the General Assembly
not likely to be effective in making decisions to pursue specific goals
energetically and effectively, as was the ideal of Security Council action?
The range of contributions of the Assembly, such as identifying coalitions
of states and promoting quiet diplomacy, were considered in depth; but
rarely the question of what it was *unfit* to do.

The difficulty of agreeing about more precisely defined and targeted
action was likely to increase as the number of members increased. A
plenary body of 200 was very unlikely to achieve consensus on such
action. Indeed, the history of the General Assembly indicated an opposite
inclination. The trend in resolutions of the 1990s was for an increasing
number of decisions to be taken on the basis of consensus or 'approval
without vote', but this reflected more a failure of will than a genuine
agreement. It was a consequence of formulating resolutions in more
general terms, and concealed the level of potential dissent, which would
become more explicit as the wording became tighter. This habit had
certain advantages from the point of view of getting agreement about
general codes or rules. Governments could agree on a general expression,
precisely because they believed they could evade its implications for
actual behaviour in the short term. And in the long term it represented
the beginning of a ratchet process. In time instruments were set up for
pressing more practical and direct application of the codes that had been
approved.

But there were a number of problems when resolutions became more
explicit and directly targeted. One could be called the problem of *false
echo*, when different and contradictory versions of the resolution were
approved. This could result from the difficulty of establishing an agreed
hierarchy of priorities among so many governments. The issue might be
regarded as important by everybody but not equally as the first priority.
The context was an opportunity for the pursuit of individual agendas that
did not precisely overlap, and hence a number of resolutions, each an

imperfect echo of the other, would be pressed, even if one or other of them was pushed to approval by majority vote. This would naturally be likely to cause uncertainty of purpose and irresolution in execution. Another problem was that of maintaining consistency over time among a series of linked resolutions, which, as with the Security Council and the Gulf War in the early 1990s, would be required in the various stages of a protracted operation. It was also likely that new majorities would need to be constructed for each new resolution, increasing the risk of inconsistency among the resolutions over time: this was a problem, even in the Security Council, illustrated by *mission creep*, but the risk would be greater in a larger body such as the General Assembly.

There would also be problems with setting up smaller executive committees on the basis of a transparent procedure open to all members of a plenary body such as the General Assembly. Giving such a committee executive responsibility for a major operation would be dangerous, and underlines the case for a different kind of executive committee, with distinctive membership criteria, such as the Security Council. In the Assembly protracted diplomacy about initial membership would be likely, and the qualification of particular governments to remain members as circumstances changed would be disputed. One reason for a number of these difficulties was the rather more diffuse social cement in the larger bodies compared with the smaller ones. The development of a degree of collegiality, based on personal acquaintance and common experience, often lay at the heart of a sustained consensus in active, and costly, pursuit of specific goals. It would be more difficult for an individual to behave irrationally or inconsistently in a small group as the disapproval would be more personal and direct. In the Security Council pressures towards acting on a collegiate basis were stronger, and when states found it necessary to resist because of their view of their interest they often found it appropriate to act in ways that were not too blatant an infringement of the principle.

These are the three major forms of collective action, each of which is necessary in the overall functioning of the United Nations. It was important to note, however, that each required different ways of making decisions, with regard to different purposes, among different memberships. There was an implied consonance between these various elements in the sense that a different matching would lead to inefficiencies: having a different pattern of memberships, and purposes, and forms of action, would increase the difficulties in the way of effective action. At the same time the relationships of the sub-institutions, thus conceived, to each other fitted a rational overall institutional design. There was an element of executive agency, for instance in the Security Council, and in the implications of the reforms for ECOSOC; there was an element of code-making, and consensus-building, in the various plenary meetings; there was an appropriate mix of contributor and recipient inputs in the budgetary mechanisms; and, as will be argued below, there was an element of distinctive secretariat provision. These, and other elements, added up to an overall structure, the internal elements of which were rationally related to each other by dint of membership, purpose and style of collective action. There were, therefore, good reasons why a particular institution should not behave as if it were another institution, and should not attempt to acquire the coloration of the whole – as one official said about UNCTAD in the 1970s.[9] Decisions about spending had to be taken in institutions that looked like the CPC. Decisions about norms or general principles needed to be taken by institutions such as the General Assembly, which could not, because of its membership and necessary relationship with the other institutions, take binding decisions that were precisely targeted.

The idea that the Assembly could act as a manager of the specialized agencies was therefore misconceived, as was the idea that ECOSOC and CPC should be made up of all members. The reform of ECOSOC to strengthen its co-ordination role, and the ability of CPC to decide the budget, would be obstructed by such a move. But the Security Council was not constructed to define norms and general standards. A lot more could be said about this, but the general principle was clear: the institutions of the UN had to concentrate on doing better what their positions in the system, the nature of their membership, and the style of their activity – each related to the other – indicated they could do. Reforms of the various parts of the system needed to start from the assumption that there was a requirement for consonance between the features of the different elements in the system.

An appropriate differentiation of roles among the institutions, following the principle of consonance, was indicated by the Kosovo crisis in 1999. In the late 1990s the system functions of the UN included the crucial function of acting as a trigger to set in train the processes appropriate to upholding the rules of the system. Over the previous half a century or so these rules had become increasingly numerous and specific, covering an increasing range of the activities of relations between states. Not only were they concerned with commerce, and the protection of the rights of states, but also with the rights of individuals, fulfilling the promise of the Charter. The biggest change of all was probably the latter one, with a number of conventions defining transgressions against the individual person, and beginning to set up remedies if they were demonstrated. The General Assembly played a key role in promoting such conventions.

However, obtaining the agreement of governments to the principles of individual rights was but the first step. It was necessary to find ways of instituting the remedies and of triggering the actions of the relevant instruments. As within states, this was not merely a legal matter: it was also necessary to have an instrument to trigger action when a law had been transgressed. There was in this process an absolute need for an instrument which appeared to embody in some sense the collective will – as with police acting in the name of the collectivity in a stable democracy – and which achieved consistency, and was impartial and reliable. The closest to that in the international system in the late 1990s remained the executive committee of the UN, the Security Council, and it was striking that even the largest states tended to prefer to get its authorization for any action they proposed, as with the US intervention in Haiti.

With regard to Kosovo, the active states were all concerned to demonstrate that they were acting justly according to the Charter and the relevant Security Council resolutions. A number of adjustments in the working methods of the Security Council in this context had been discussed in the literature, and had been proposed by governments: special procedures might be needed to reinforce the impression that the decisions taken represented the collective will. These included stronger qualified majorities in the Council, and a concurrent vote by a qualified or simple majority in the General Assembly. But the normal pattern was for Security Council involvement and it was to that body that even the more powerful states would come to seek authorization. In the late 1990s the states which it was feared might not do so were China and India.

Other ways of establishing the value of the UN stressed the role of this context in what could be called the evolving civil society of governments. The Security Council had become the legitimizer of international agreements, including that of SC 1244 which marked the end of the NATO bombing in Kosovo and Serbia. Its function in this kind of role had become the equivalent in the international system of that of the registrar in civil society. In the late 1990s there was, however, a debate about the limits of the role of the UN which served to distinguish between a range of system functions and their location. The United States had tried to get support for a new strategic concept for NATO in 1998–99: US Secretary of State, Madeleine Albright, proposed that NATO should act in lieu of the UN as an agent for global stability, partly because of the unpopularity of the organization with some groups of Americans, partly because NATO was an effective organization which was in search of a role for itself at the end of the Cold War, and partly because in 1996 Congress approved an Act requiring the administration to get its approval for each and every future US involvement in peacekeeping operations.

The consequence of this was that the US administration for a while promoted action through NATO rather than the UN, as NATO spending was covered by the regular defence budget and dealing with the top people of the UN – who could easily find themselves demonized by the American right wing – could be avoided. The advantage of working through NATO would be that the administration could avoid the requirement for congressional approval. But the US preference was rebuffed. At the NATO Council meeting in March 1999 the US accepted the refusal of other NATO members to hold the US view of the NATO role. They asserted that the UN should have priority, and that NATO should not have a general sweeper role.

This US initiative should, however, be seen as a forlorn and ill-thought-out attempt to relocate a function of the international community, namely the executing of the various tasks linked with the maintenance of international peace and security, rather than an attempt to deny the UN a role. It went along with a number of other developments that were also noticeable in the mid to late 1990s, such as the increasing use of local or regional organizations to carry out that function in some parts of the world, in particular in Africa, and indeed an increasing preparedness to work with non-governmental organizations to achieve UN-approved goals. But it was important to note that those goals were UN approved. US officials and the military wanted the approval of a significant coalition, and the UN mandate was an acceptable, even desirable, example.

PRINCIPLES OF CONSONANCE IN THE UNITED NATIONS

Any attempt to locate the principles that should be taken into account when proposing reforms of the United Nations should respect the need for consonance of the membership structure, the various forms of collective action, and the overall structure of the institution itself. A consonant relationship of this overall structure with its environment in the society of states was also necessary. What follows is a selection of the resulting injunctions.

States that contributed most to funding should have the biggest say in budgets and spending

An implication of this was that the main contributing states could not be required to pay for operations of which they disapproved. This point is not particularly startling, and after the reform of the budgetary arrangements of the UN and of a number of the agencies in the late 1980s it became an accepted principle. What it pointed to was the need to obtain donor approval for operations, and to have in place consensus-maximizing practices. This moved into the area of judgement of proper and acceptable expenditure which was very much a matter of norms and expectations. It was necessary that the arrangements should promote, rather than get in the way of, the development of these. One sure way of increasing the resistance of donors was to have decisions about the budget controlled by beneficiaries, which appeared to be the case before the mid-1980s in many of the budgets of the UN system. In the terminology of this chapter this was a situation of dissonance between activities and the structure of membership.

This is not to deny that the UN and the system were in serious financial difficulties in the late 1990s. Some of the reasons for this were not directly related to the budgetary process and the norms and expectations of expenditure among members. But it was important to create a context in which agreement to return to paying contributions by all members, but particularly the US, could be sustained. The principle of consonance was an essential part of this. The implication for the arrangements of the UN system was that decisions which involving spending, and making item-ized budgets, should be taken in small joint committees of donors, representatives of the beneficiaries, and the spending agencies, on the basis of consensus. The model for this was the CPC, and the emerging pattern of ECOSOC segments.

The specialized character of the various component institutions of the United Nations should be recognized and asserted

The functional and membership differentiation had been built into the original design but had been maintained precariously over the years in response to various *ad hoc* challenges. In the late 1990s claims to make the UN more democratic, i.e. to make all decisions in plenary meetings on the basis of majoritarian democratic principles, were still being pressed; and, at the other end of the spectrum of opinion, were still those, of decreasing weight and number, who held that their superpower of choice should act unilaterally regardless of the views of the UN membership. These were the clashing visions mediated in several of the chapters in this book.

A specific example of the confusion of procedural principles – of dis-sonance between structure, activities and procedure – was when an organ-ization, such as an agency, or a fund or programme like UNCTAD, began to move from its original function as a forum of policy development, into direct operational activities.[10] When this happened, hopes were raised for the majoritarians that decisions about expenditure would be made in ways other than those recommended here, i.e. by committees dominated by beneficiaries or by agencies anxious for self-aggrandizement. Such devel-opments would inevitably lead to deadlock. The first two kinds of collective action should always involve maximum non-binding consultation with the other categories of state. But they must be led by states in Groups 1, and 2, not the states from other groups, and they could only be effective if the diplomatic patterns reflected the principles of collective action outlined above.

The international hierarchy of states should be reflected consistently in relation to the three forms of collective action across the UN's component institutions

States should not have a higher status with regard to diplomatic and political decisions than they had with regard to economic and social decisions. In plain English: it would get in the way of effective action if a beneficiary, system-reformer state could command decisions on sanctions in the Security Council. Effective leadership by countries that were the major donors and the main contributors to the UN was essential. Although the full implications of the list of different forms of state member in the UN have not been examined here, it is clear that differences in the character of states fit them for different roles in the UN institutions. The pretence that any state is fit for any role is likely to lead to dissonance.

Enlarging the Security Council to include countries in Group 5, such as Brazil, raised the issue of whether this was compatible with other aspects of the reform of the UN system. Would it produce consonance or dissonance? How would this help to solve the problems of the Security Council, which in the late 1990s were judged to include the poor definition of mandates, the production of vague resolutions that were deliberately couched in general terms to facilitate a consensus of members, the problem of 'mission creep' and the difficulty of agreeing to provide enough resources to pay for the agreed policies?

Enlargement was at best irrelevant to these problems and it could exacerbate them. Was it likely that the states contributing the overwhelming majority of resources for peacekeeping would accept decisions about military activity shaped by some developing countries? But there was also the problem of the relationship between the Security Council and the economic and social areas of the UN. The complex crises of the late 1990s demanded the co-ordination of peacekeeping activities, political activities, development activities and humanitarian activities. Maintaining consistency between these various sectors was likely to be undermined by placing control in each in the hands of varying coalitions of states, especially when a major beneficiary from activity in one sector was instrumental in generating activity in another. The major donor states would feel unhappy about footing the bills for peacekeeping or humanitarian assistance operations that had been set up by coalitions of minor contributors. Different hierarchies in different institutions with regard to collective action would lead to increased problems of system-wide co-ordination.

Supranational management principles should be avoided

This injunction emerged clearly from the discussions of ways to obtain a more effective global policy on issues such as population control and how to manage the humanitarian aid process.[11] The structure of the international system, and of the system of international institutions, was polycentric and any central organization claiming authority over the systems would inevitably be resisted. Proposals for reconstituting the agencies to bring them under more effective centralized control flew in the face of the logic of the system.

It would be impossible to get sufficient agreement among member states to achieve fundamental reforms of this kind. And the proposals could not achieve a safe answer to the question of who or what would do the controlling. The different categories of states had their own client institutions, and reform always raised the spectre that some other state category could gain control. Similarly the fact that this was a society of sovereign states meant that compromises between effectiveness and autonomy had to be made continuously. The best that could be hoped for was, therefore, enhanced consonance and in this context more effective co-ordination. This was precisely what was sought in the reformed ECOSOC and in the humanitarian arrangements under OCHA.[12]

The UN should reflect in its internal reform process the need to encourage the emergence of an international society that was more favourable to its work

This meant helping with the emergence of stronger multilateral frameworks, but also stronger sub-units. For example, there was a need for UN organizations to reflect and encourage regional consolidation: any claim to promotion, for example, to membership of the Security Council, should be based on the ability of the candidate to enhance or reflect regional solidarity as well as to contribute resources to UN activities. The idea that non-permanent members of the Security Council should satisfy these criteria was already widely accepted in the late 1990s: those states that did were likely to return to membership more frequently. But as Bertrand pointed out, regions in the UN should be more consistently and rationally organized: different principles on groupings in different institutional settings encouraged division. It also got in the way of consolidating regional arrangements among the members of the regions outside the UN. The UN should be positively involved in strengthening the qualifications of states for promotion within the institution, by encouraging real regional representation, as well as the more obvious enhancements, such as development.

*The donor states needed to multilateralize their leadership
functions in the system*

The few main contributor governments should develop their *mutual* consultation procedures and also those to co-ordinate policy towards the UN system *within* themselves. A part of the problem of UN co-ordination was a lack of donor agreement and of agreement among departments of the same government. It was remarkable that the main donor countries had not initiated more substantial mechanisms for co-ordinating their plans for spending among themselves, and, at the same time, for linking those with developing a consensus on policy so that multilateral arrangements would be strengthened. The Geneva Group was a long-standing institution, which brought the donor states together to talk about keeping control of the budget. But this had never been linked with a mechanism for building donor country consensus on a formal rational overall plan for the programmes of the various spending institutions. There was a very important connection here: such co-ordination would confront donor states squarely with the problem of co-ordinating policy within and between the range of organizations in the system, which would in turn imply a stronger commitment to the resulting multilateral frameworks. The effort to co-ordinate more widely and more deeply between national administrations would strengthen common rules, i.e. it would entrench multilateralism.

A brief sketch of the UK arrangement in the late 1990s indicates the kind of problem and the stage of development of UN co-oordination in the government. Although many home ministries maintained direct relations with the specialized agencies, as did British-based INGOs and NGOs, the organizational hub was the UN Department (UND) in the Foreign and Commonwealth Office (FCO), which fell under the remit of an Assistant Under-Secretary responsible for a range of departments in the FCO. It was a relatively small department, in part because the FCO's structure tended to give priority to issues over particular institutions. In the 1950s and early 1960s, the United Kingdom even had two ambassadors at the United Nations in New York, one of whom was solely concerned with Fourth Committee and Trusteeship Council affairs. There was then a long period during which Her Majesty's Government considered that the United Nations' role on the issues that mattered was marginal and consequently the UND was then not a front-rank FCO department.[13]

This changed as governments came to feel that the United Kingdom could use the United Nations positively, especially the Security Council.

Indeed as Britain's power in the world declined, increasing stress was placed on doing well in the UN to make the most of what was left. However, the geographical and functional departments generally took the lead, and the role of the UND was to get them to think of the UN angle, a way of working which indicated that UN policy was a secondary, not a primary, concern of co-ordination. In the new climate after the end of the Cold War the UND made more policy suggestions and policy in the United Nations was no longer a damage limitation exercise. Nevertheless, the African department, for example, would lead on the Great Lakes problems, and the same was true of the Middle East, the problem of drugs, and the like. From the outside it did not seem likely that the UND would be strong enough in relations with the geographical or functional departments to ensure overall co-ordination of relevant UN system policies.

The UND did not, therefore, have a central position in the FCO, but there was a trend towards task expansion and a greater prominence for UN questions. This account illustrates the general proposition that failures of co-ordination in the UN system are often a reflection of the lack of co-ordination about UN issues within states. There was dissonance between the way in which governments were organized and *expectations* about the organization of the United Nations. It was simply not possible for the latter to be more effectively organized than the former.

There was a need for improved, more consonant administrative arrangements: an international institution has at its core a secretariat

Indeed, there was a sense in which that Secretariat *was* the international institution, in that it was its single permanent feature. What did the principle of consonance suggest about the pattern of reform of the Secretariat? Were there any general principles that could be added to the frenzy of reform of the 1980s and 1990s, from Boutros-Gahli to the Track I and II of Kofi Annan? Some of those reforms were beneficial, producing the banal judgement that the institution was now leaner but fitter. The lead governments lost no opportunity to get at the UN's civil servants, leading to a series of sackings and a loss of around a thousand staff in the central system over a five-year period, with the prospect in 1997 of another thousand lost (A/51/950, para. 2). And there were a number of reorganizations of departments and offices in the central system, many of which have been discussed in the preceding chapters.

But the effects of the reforms of the Secretariat were not entirely positive, and some more advisable reforms had not been stressed, such as the need for improved overall management. This implied an executive committee for the institution involving the heads of the various sections in frequent meetings to discuss overall activity and resolve problems. A start on this had been made by Secretary-General Annan with the setting up in January 1997 of four executive committees (A/51/950, July 1997, para. 28). It remained to be seen how this would work, but the case for a single committee, with real powers, meeting frequently, remained persuasive. What was needed was a Secretariat that was the best possible support for the activities and government committees of the United Nations: the most consonant interaction between government representatives and international civil servants. This required a highly qualified personnel, loyal to the organization, and with skills matched to the job specification. This implied a greater degree of staff mobility, and flexibility: the ability to move the right people to the right job. It also meant being more proactive in finding and keeping the best people. As it was, in the late 1990s, some of the best people had been lost because of the indiscriminate scaling down. More attention had been paid to reducing the numbers than to retaining and indeed recruiting the most able.

One element of consonance was, therefore, getting as close a fit as possible between personnel, their skills and the requirements of the job, and between the international civil servants and the governmental representatives with whom they were required to deal. Another was getting as wide a range as possible of relevant experience input into the central system. One of the major weaknesses in a number of areas was that the number of exchanges between field and headquarters personnel was limited. In some areas, such as humanitarian assistance and economic development, an attempt had been made in the late 1990s to tackle this problem. The point was made that the perspective of headquarters personnel was likely to be different from that of those with field experience. As the UN's range of operations became wider in the 1990s, it became increasingly necessary to find a compromise between the longer planning period, usually five years, of the headquarters people, and the shorter perspective of the field people, who were more concerned with getting an immediate and effective response. Indeed, the more active UN of the 1990s required a modified personnel strategy: consonance of staffing with activities required a flexible, mobile staff, with high technical skills, and hands-on field experience.

The kind of adjustments that had taken place were too often unhelpful from that perspective, though a beginning had been made in some areas. What further reforms could have helped? Among the rather basic points is the idea that all levels of the Secretariat should be filled through neutral, professional procedures; that is, through procedures that did not involve barter among states, but rather a professional search and evaluation, with the doctrine of equitable geographical representation being a secondary consideration. This is what the wording of the relevant article in the

Charter (Article 101, para. 3) indeed stipulates: 'the paramount consideration in the employment of the staff and in the determination of the conditions of service shall be the necessity of securing the highest standards of efficiency, competence and integrity. Due regard shall be paid to the importance of recruiting the staff on as wide a geographical basis as possible.' It is clear that the first principle has priority over the second. The recommendations of Urquhart and Childers on the Secretary-General's appointment were very much on the right lines.[14] The UN needed stricter controls of appointments and a more flexible approach to the principle of equitable geographical representation if there were no candidates of suitable calibre from a particular state or group. It was important to avoid simply filling posts with West European and other people, but groups could be asked to approve suitable people from their area. It was, moreover, very important to have a regular rotation of staff, so that no institution could be identified, as ECOSOC had been, as a poor performer because of the quality and attitudes of its staff.

By extending the idea that good standards of performance were required among national government delegates, and that there should be international ways of monitoring these, the general interest in optimum system performance would be underlined. International procedures for maintaining good technical standards could be extended outwards, from full-time international civil servants, to those on secondment from national governments, and, beyond that, to national delegates. The latter would be at least encouraged to achieve good professional standards, even when instructed to be obstructive in a particular diplomatic setting, and at best would be motivated to a more professional reconciliation, wherever possible, of particular and general interests. At the same time the UN could make a contribution to improving national standards of technical competence among national officers, and even political elites. The fact was that, at the turn of the millennium, the UN had a high number of committed and able staff who deserved recognition, but there were also too many time-servers of low ability. Current staffing practices were not addressing this problem: the UN was becoming not leaner and fitter but thinner and weaker.

CONCLUSIONS

In this chapter some of the general rules that applied at the millennium to the work of the institutions of the UN, the relations between them and between them and member states, have been discussed. What could be done, and what should not be done to make it work effectively? They have been placed under the general heading of consonance, meaning the existence of relationships between key parts of the system which were mutually supportive: they were conducive to effectiveness and efficiency. The overall institutional structure of the UN was taken as a given; that is, no alterations in the constitutive parts of the institution have been suggested, nor were they necessary. The requirement was for what existed to be improved.

At the end of the day there was a natural limit to what could be done, because that depended upon the will of governments and the resources and time they were prepared to commit. The relationship of the institution to its environment in the society of states was also important. The pattern of development of that society was a variable subject to a degree of human control. It was of great importance for the success of the United Nations that there should be other powerful actors in the Security Council in addition to the United States. Hence the future of the European Union, whether it enlarged and became less effective as an international actor, or developed a more effective Common Foreign and Security Policy among a smaller number of members, was directly relevant to the future of the UN.

The rules can be organized into four clusters concerning the three types of collective action in the UN system and the nature of the relationship between the institutions and international society.

1. The first type of collective action depended upon general agreement among the members of a small group. It had to involve those states recognized as having the resources and the commitment to act effectively together to defend the system. The members of the small group also had to be committed to norm maintenance. Action was more likely if they were all generally positive about the role of the Security Council.

   Leadership would be weakened when small group members were exploiting membership to enhance their individual status at the regional level, or if they were perceived to be doing this. In this case such states would be attaching greater importance to the power struggle at the regional level than to the development of collective action in the United Nations. As argued above, within the small leadership group it was also necessary that a sub-group of risk-takers be prepared to go ahead of the others. They were more likely to do this, however, if their governments judged that the act of moving ahead would persuade the other, more cautious, members to follow. Conversely, the more cautious states were more likely to convert to activism in response to the initiative of the risk-takers.

2. Decisions on the second type of collective action, such as the budgetary process, must be responsible. They must involve the donors at an early stage, and not involve procedures through which their disagreement

with particular spending could be evaded by groups of beneficiaries. Similarly beneficiaries should not be in a position in one part of an institution to push decisions that obliged donors in other parts of the system to spending that they would otherwise refuse. For example, it would create serious problems, and the reduction of the commitment of donors, if beneficiary states took decisions with regard to the management of humanitarian crises which then required donors to foot the bill. This danger was reminiscent of the situation that arose in the 1960s when decisions to set up peacekeeping operations were linked with a general obligation to pay.

3. The third type of collective action involved the whole membership, or the majority of members. The norm of collective action for them rested on their right to be consulted with regard to category one and two collective actions, and not to be faced with decisions already taken by the members of the smaller lead group. This was a problem which had led to some concern among the non-permanent members of the Security Council after the emergence of the P5 group of permanent members in the late 1980s. In response the permanent members wisely took care to avoid presenting the results of their consultations as decisions to the plenary Security Council meetings. It was also a fear which motivated the response of the beneficiary states to the main donor's push in the mid to late 1980s to increase their control over the budget. The bargain they accepted was to exchange enhancement of the power of the donors in the budgetary process for a guarantee of consultation and a promise to take decisions by consensus in the controlling committees. They acknowledged their supplicant status and that they would inevitably be subject to pressure to conform if the donors were in agreement, but they retained the right to impose limits on what they considered unacceptable action: the right to say 'no'. The meetings of the general membership of the institutions agreed broad questions of principle and purpose, but were unsuited to taking on direct control of specific programmes or issuing specific instructions. The system of international institutions was like the system of states in that it was essentially multi-centred, and required to be persuaded into co-ordination rather than ordered by a central institution.

4. In the relationship between the institution and international society the important point was not to introduce internal alterations that weakened the sources of support for the institution in that society, and to have in mind the need to relate the institution to the changing system. It was necessary to have a consistent image of the most favourable structure of international society, which, it is proposed here, is a society organized into regional groups of states.

This is not the place to rehearse again the arguments about the development of stronger regional arrangements in international society after the Second World War.[15] There is a whole range of qualifications of the effectiveness of regional arrangements as actors in international organizations and as performers of particular functions such as the maintenance of international peace and security. But two points are clear. First, that following the example of the European Union, there were more of them dealing with regional economic matters, and sometimes with regional security questions. Second, it was increasingly a matter of prescription in economic matters and security matters that regional organizations should be encouraged. By the late twentieth century it was common for United Nations planning to include reference to a regional dimension, and there was recognition that security maintenance could usefully involve partnership between regional organizations and the central UN system. It was also recognized that the social and economic costs of globalization could only be recovered by greater organization at the regional level. Groups of states were more likely to be able to push profit-maximizing global corporations into accepting the need to respect social welfare standards.

There was therefore a need to respect and reflect the development of regional organizations in thinking about the development of the institutions of the United Nations. These were the likeliest general basis of acceptable collective action, given that the alternatives were either unacceptable and impractical (the leadership of the United States) or unrealizable (the will of the global international community). The first was fast declining into the ineffectual and the second was fast evolving into a world of irresponsible private monopolies.

Thinking about the reform of the United Nations at the end of the twentieth century needed to take into account the kind of international society most likely to sustain it. That society was most likely to be one dominated by regional groupings of states. The United Nations was unlikely to succeed in the twenty-first century if it had to operate in a globalized or unipolar world as currently conceived. A number of simple maxims follow: proposals for the UN should reflect regional consolidation and promote it where possible. Proposals for the UN, such as those for changes in the membership of the Security Council, should not have the effect of increasing or reflecting existing divisions within regions.

One element in consonance was the way in which alterations in one part of the system might be assisted or frustrated by the lack of matching changes in other parts of the system. Conversely they might lead to changes elsewhere which were positive in their impact on the reform. The way in which the whole system was interconnected needed to be borne in mind when considering reform and this was often forgotten by designers of change. One link, mentioned in the opening paragraphs of this chapter, was the one between the arrangements in the United Nations, and other international institutions, and the structure of international society. That link had to be placed in the context of overall system change, the primary element of which was the declining capacity of individual states to control their environment. The United Nations could become an element in an arrangement which achieved that control, though in the course of that evolution it could also respond to and create favourable changes in international society.

The United Nations should be seen, therefore, as a framework within which multilateral rules would be progressively strengthened, and super-ordinate interests in the 'really new' world order defined. But it should also be a framework for the consolidation of a system of regional group-ings of states which could pursue welfare for individuals more effectively, especially the classical Keynesian purpose of full employment, in the face of increasingly anti-social global forces. The relationship of the United Nations to the regions was a vital consideration: it should not get in the way of their consolidation; it should promote their emergence; it should reflect them rationally and effectively, and consistently, in its internal arrangements.

NOTES

1. See Report of the Secretary-General, A/50/666/Add.4/Corr.1, 2 April 1996. For updated reports see the annual *A Global Agenda: Issues before the General Assembly of the United Nations*, the UN Association of the USA (New York: University Press of America).
2. Richard Langhorne, 'Full circle: new principles and old consequences in the modern diplomatic system', unpublished paper, written for the Westphalia Conference at Enschede, Netherlands, 16–19 July 1998, p. 2.
3. See the evaluation of regionalism in Lousie Fawcett and Andrew Hurrell (eds), *Regionalism in World Politics* (Oxford: Oxford University Press, 1995). See also Paul Taylor, *International Organization in the Modern World* (London: Pinter, 1993), chs 1 and 2; and the special issue on the UN and regionalism in *Review of International Studies*, vol. 21, no. 4, October 1995.
4. For an account of the development of the CFSP see Desmond Dinan, *Ever Closer Union? An Introduction to the European Community* (Basingstoke: Macmillan, 1994), ch. 17.
5. On the faltering record of the UN see David Malone, 'Goodbye UNSCOM: a sorry tale in US–UN relations', *Security Dialogue*, vol. 30, no. 4, December 1999.
6. Crispin Tickell, 'The role of the Security Council in world affairs', The Sibley Lecture 1989, delivered to the University of Georgia, Athens, 2 February 1989.

7. See Paul Taylor and A. J. R. Groom, *The Gulf War*, Discussion Paper no. 38, Royal Institute of International Affairs, London, February 1992.
8. Paul Taylor, *International Organization in the Modern World, op. cit.*, pp. 154–56.
9. *ibid.*, p. 138.
10. *Ibid.*, ch. 5, for a discussion of this tendency.
11. *Ibid.*, ch. 8.
12. *Ibid.*, ch. 2.
13. See A. J. R. Groom and Paul Taylor, 'The United Kingdom and the United Nations', in Chadwick F. Algen, Gene M. Lyons and John G. Trent, *The United Nations System: The Policies of Member States* (Tokyo: United Nations University Press, 1995).
14. Erskine Childers and Brian Urquhart, 'Renewing the United Nations system: the international civil service', *Development Dialogue* (Hammarskjöld Foundation, 1994), pp. 159–70; and their 'A world in need of leadership: tomorrow's United Nations', *Dialogue*, 1990, pp. 23–30.
15. See Louise Fawcett and Andrew Hurrell (eds), *Regionalism in World Politics: Regional Organization and International Order* (Oxford: Oxford University Press, 1995).

SELECT BIBLIOGRAPHY

(prepared by Yuji Uesugi)

The Charter

Six principal organs
General Assembly
Security Council
Economic and Social Council
Trusteeship Council
International Court of Justice
ICJ reports
Secretariat

Non-governmental organizations

UN system

Future of the UN

Member states

Consonance

The Charter

Amer, R., *The United Nations and Foreign Military Interventions: A Comparative Study of the Application of the Charter*, Uppsala, Uppsala University, Department of Peace and Conflict Research, 1992.

Asrat, B., *Prohibition of Force under the UN Charter: A Study of Art*, Uppsala, Iustus, 1991.

Bailey, Sydney D., *The Secretariat of the United Nations*, 2nd edn, Westport, Greenwood, 1978.

Bennett, A. LeRoy, *International Organization*, 5th edn, Englewood Cliffs, Prentice-Hall, 1991 (also 2nd edn, 1980).

Clark, Grenville and Louis B. Sohn, *World Peace Through World Law*, London, Oxford University Press, 1958 (also 2nd edn revised, 1960; 3rd edn enlarged, 1964).

Claude, Inis L. Jr, *Swords into Plowshares: The Progress and Problems of International Organization*, 4th edn, New York, Random House, 1971 (also 3rd edn revised, 1964).

Drzewicki, K., 'Human Rights in the United Nations Charter and the Universal Declaration of Human Rights', *Polish Quarterly of International Affairs*, vol. 7, no. 3, Summer 1998.

Dubois, Charles, *Le Droit des gens et les rapports de grandes puissances avec les autres états avant le pacte de la SPN*, Paris, Paros Plon, 1921.

Goodrich, Leland M., 'From League of Nations to United Nations', *International Organization*, vol. 1, 1947.

Goodrich, Leland M. and Edvard Hambro, *Charter of the United Nations: Commentary and Documents*, 2nd edn, Boston, World Peace Foundation, 1949.

Goodrich, Leland M. and Davis A. Kay (eds), *International Organization: Politics and Process*, Madison, University of Wisconsin Press, 1973.

Goodrich, Leland M. and A. P. Simons, *Charter of the United Nations: Commentary and Documents*, 3rd revised edn, New York, Columbia University Press, 1969.

Goodspeed, Stephen S., *The Nature and Function of International Organization*, 2nd edn, New York, Oxford University Press, 1967 (also 1959).

Halderman, J. W., *The United Nations and the Rule of Law: Charter Development Through the Handling of International Disputes and Situations*, Dobbs Ferry, Oceana Publications, 1966.

Hawden, J. G. and J. Kaufmann, *How United Nations Decisions are Made*, 2nd revised edn, New York, Oceana Publications, 1962 (also 1960).

Hoffman, Stanley, *Organisations Internationales et Pouvoirs Politiques des Etats*, Paris, Colin, 1954.

Jacobson, Harold Karan, *Networks of Interdependence: International Organizations and the Global Political System*, 2nd edn, New York, Alfred A. Knopf, 1984 (also 1979).

Kay, David A. (ed.), *The United Nations Political System*, London, John Wiley, 1967.

Kelsen, Hans, *The Law of the United Nations: A Critical Analysis of its Functional Problems*, London, Stevens and Sons, 1950; New York, Praeger, 1951.

Khare, S. C., *Use of Force under UN Charter*, New Delhi, Metropolitan, 1985.

Luard, Evan, *A History of the United Nations: The Years of Western Domination*, London, Macmillan, 1982.

Mangone, Gerard J., *A Short History of the United Nations Charter*, New York, McGraw-Hill, 1954.

Mitrany, David, *A Working Peace System*, Chicago, Quadrangle Books, 1966.

Riggs, Robert E. and Jack C. Plano, *The United Nations: International Organizations and World Politics*, 2nd edn, Belmont, CA: Wadsworth, 1994 (also, Chicago, Dorsey, 1988).

Russell, Ruth B. assisted by Jeanette E. Muther, *A History of the United Nations Charter: The Role of the United States 1940–1945*, Washington, DC, The Brookings Institution; London, Faber, 1958.

Savitri, K., 'The United Nations Charter Framework for Conflict Resolution: procedures and practices of pacific settlement of disputes,' *India Quarterly*, vol. 3, nos 3–4, July–December 1997.

Simma, Bruno (ed.), *The Charter of the United Nations: A Commentary*, Oxford, Oxford University Press, 1994.

United Nations, Secretariat, *Consideration of Principles of International Law United Nations, Library, A Bibliography of the Charter of the United Nations*, New York, United Nations, 1955.

United Nations, Office of Public Information, *Guide to the Charter of the United Nations*, New York, United Nations, 1958.

Concerning Friendly Relations and Co-operation among States in Accordance with the Charter of the United Nations, New York, United Nations, 1963.

Six principal organs

General Assembly

Alker, H. R. and B. M. Russett, *World Politics in the General Assembly*, New Haven, Yale University Press, 1965.

Archibugi, Daniele, 'From the UN to cosmopolitan democracy,' in Daniele Archibugi and David Held (eds), *Cosmopolitan Democracy: An Agenda for a New World Order*, Cambridge, Polity Press, 1995.

Armstrong, David, Lorna Lloyd and John Redmond, *From Versailles to Maastricht: International Organization in the Twentieth Century*, New York, St Martin's Press, 1996.

Asamoah, Obed Y., *The Legal Significance of the Declarations of the General Assembly of the United Nations*, The Hague, Nijhoff, 1966.

Baehr, Peter R., *The Role of a National Delegation in the General Assembly*, New York, Carnegie Endowment Occasional Paper, no. 9, 1970.

Bailey, Sydney D., *The General Assembly of the United Nations: A Study of Procedure and Practice*, 2nd edn, Westport, Greenwood, 1978 (also New York, Praeger, 1964, revised edition).

Bertrand, Maurice, *Reporting to the Economic and Social Council*, Joint Inspection Unit, JIU/REP. 84/7, Geneva, United Nations, 1984.

Browne, M. A., *Credentials Considerations in the United Nations General Assembly: The Process and its Role*, Washington, DC, US Government Printing Office, 1983.

Claude, Inis L. Jr, *The Changing United Nations*, New York, Random House, 1967.

Claude, Inis L. Jr, *Swords into Plowshares: The Progress and Problems of International Organization*, 4th edn, New York, Random House, 1971 (also 3rd edn revised, 1964).

Cot, Jean-Pierre and Alain Pellet, *La Charte des Nations Unies: Commentaire Article par Article*, 2nd edn, Paris, Economica, 1991.

Eilan, A, *The General Assembly: Can it be Salvaged?*, Washington, DC, Heritage Foundation, 1984.

Finley, Blanche, *The Structure of the United Nations General Assembly, its Committees, Commissions, and Other Organisms, 1946–1973*, Dobbs Ferry, Oceana, 1977.

Finley, Blanche, *The Structure of the United Nations General Assembly: An Organizational Approach to its Work, 1974–1980s*, White Plains, Unipub/Kraus International Publications, 1988.

Fomerand, Jacques, 'UN conferences: media events or genuine diplomacy?', *Global Governance*, vol. 2, no. 3, September–December 1996.

Gerbet, Pierre, *Le Rêve d'un ordre mondial*, Paris, Imprimerie Nationale, 1996.

Goodrich, Leland and Edvard Hambro, *Charter of the United Nations: Commentary and Documents*, 2nd edn, Boston, World Peace Foundation, 1949.

Goodrich, Leland and Anne Patricia Simons, *Charter of the United Nations: Commentary and Documents*, 3rd edn, New York, Columbia University Press, 1969.

Hadwen, J. and J. Kaufmann, *How United Nations Decisions are Made*, New York, Oceana Publications, 1960.

Jackson, Robert, *A Study of the Capacity of the United Nations' Development System*, Geneva, United Nations, 1970.

Jacobsen, Kurt, *The General Assembly of the United Nations: A Qualitative Analysis of Conflict, Inequality and Relevance*, Oslo, Universitetsforlaget, 1978.

Joyner, Christopher C., 'The United Nations as international law-giver', in Christopher C. Joyner (ed.), *The United Nations and International Law*, Cambridge, Cambridge University Press, 1997.

Kaufmann, Johan, *United Nations Decision-making*, Alphen aan den Rijh, Sjithoff and Noordhoff (also Leyden, Sijthoff), 1980.

Kelsen, Hans, *The Law of the United Nations: A Critical Analysis of its Functional Problems*, London, Stevens and Sons, 1950; New York, Praeger, 1951.

Lie, Trygve, *In the Cause of Peace*, New York, Macmillan, 1954.

Martin-Bosch, Miguel, 'How nations vote in the General Assembly of the United Nations', *International Organization*, vol. 21, no. 4, 1987.

Peterson, M. J., *The General Assembly in World Politics*, Boston, Unwin Hyman, 1990 (also Allen & Unwin, 1986).

Riggs, Robert E., *Politics in the United Nations: A Study of United States Influence in the General Assembly*, Urbana, University of Illinois Press, 1958.

Rothstein, Robert, *The Weak in the World of Strong: The Developing Countries in the International System*, New York, Columbia University Press, 1977.

Russell, Ruth B. assisted by Jeanette E. Muther, *A History of the United Nations Charter: The Role of the United States 1940–1945*, Washington, DC, The Brookings Institution, 1958.

Schachter, Oscar, 'The UN legal order: an overview', in Christopher C. Joyner (ed.), *The United Nations and International Law*, Cambridge, Cambridge University Press, 1997.

Schechter, M. G. (ed.), *Future Multilateralism: The Political and Social Framework*, Tokyo, United Nations University Press, 1999.

Segall, J., 'A UN Second Assembly', in F. Barnaby (ed.), *Building a More Democratic United Nations*, London, Frank Cass, 1991.

Smouts, Marie-Claude, *La France à l'ONU*, Paris, Presses de la Foundation nationale des sciences politiques, 1979.

Smouts, Marie-Claude, 'Les délégations à l'Assemblée', in CEDIN, *La France aux Nations Unies*, Paris, Montchrestien, 1985.

Smouts, Marie-Claude, 'International organizations and inequality among states', *International Social Science Journal*, 144, June 1995.

Smouts, Marie-Claude, 'La construction équivoque d'une "opinion mondiale",' *Revue Tiers Monde*, 151, July–September 1997.

South Centre, *For a Strong and Democratic United Nations: A South Perspective on UN Reform*, Geneva, The South Centre 1996.

Taylor, Paul, 'The origins and institutional setting of the UN special conferences', in Paul Taylor and A. J. R. Groom, *Global Issues in the United Nations' Framework*, London, Macmillan, 1989.

Tomlin, Brian W., 'Measurement validation: lessons from the use and misuse of UN General Assembly Roll-Call votes', *International Organization*, vol. 39, no. 1, 1985.

United Nations, Department for Disarmament Affairs, *Disarmament: The United Nations General Assembly and Disarmament 1988*, New York, United Nations, 1989.

United Nations, Department of Public Information, *Uniting for Peace: How the General Assembly Arrived at its Momentous Resolution, with the Test of the Resolution, Excerpts from the Debate, and the Conclusions of the Collective Measures Committee*, New York, United Nations, 1952.

Zamora, Stephen, 'Economic relations and development', in Christopher C. Joyner (ed.), *The United Nations and International Law*, Cambridge, Cambridge University Press, 1997.

Security Council

Abi-Saab, Georges, *The United Nations Operation in the Congo 1960–1964*, New York, Oxford University Press, 1978.

Alvarez, Jose E., 'Provocations: the once and future Security Council', *Washington Quarterly*, vol. 18, no. 2, Spring 1995.

Bailey, Sydney, D., *Voting in the Security Council*, Bloomington, Indiana University Press, 1969.

Bailey, Sydney, D., 'New light on abstentions in the UN Security Council', *International Affairs*, vol. 50, no. 4, October 1974.

Bailey, Sydney, D., *The Procedure of the UN Security Council*, 2nd edn, Oxford, Clarendon Press, 1988 (also, Oxford University Press, 1975).

Bailey, Sydney D., *The UN Security Council and Human Rights*, Basingstoke, Macmillan, 1994.

Bailey, Sydney, D. and Sam Daws (eds), *The Procedures of the UN Security Council*, Oxford, Oxford University Press, 1998.

Bourantonis, D., 'Reform of the UN Security Council and the non-aligned states', *International Peacekeeping*, vol. 5, no. 1, Spring 1998.

Boyd, Andrew, *Fifteen Men on a Powder Keg: A History of the UN Security Council*, London, Methuen, 1971.

Clark, Anthony and Robert J. Beck, *International Law and the Use of Force: Beyond the UN Charter Paradigm*, London, Routledge, 1993.

Clark, Jeffrey, 'Débâcle in Somalia: failure of the collective response', in Lori Fisher Damrosh (ed.), *Enforcing Restraint: Collective Intervention in Internal Conflicts*, New York, Council on Foreign Relations, 1993.

Claude, Inis L. Jr, *Power and International Relations*, New York, Random House, 1964.

Claude, Inis L. Jr, 'The Security Council', in Evan Luard (ed.), *The Evolution of International Organization*, London, Thames and Hudson, 1966.

Commager, Henry Steele (ed.), *Documents of American History*, 7th edn, New York, Appleton-Century-Crofts, 1963, vol. 2.

Diehl, Paul F. (ed.), *The Politics of Global Governance: International Organizations in an Interdependent World*, Boulder, Rienner, 1997.

Goodrich, Leland M., 'The UN Security Council', *International Organization*, vol. 12, no. 3, 1958.

Goodrich, Leland M. and Edvard Hambro, *Charter of the United Nations: Commentary and Documents*, 2nd edn, Boston, World Peace Foundation, 1949.

Goodrich, Leland M. and Anne P. Simons, *The United Nations and the Maintenance of International Peace and Security*, Washington, DC, Brookings Institution, 1955.

Gross, Leo, 'Voting in the Security Council: abstention from voting and absence from meetings', *Yale Law Journal*, vol. 60, 1951.

Gross, Leo, 'The double veto and the four-power statement of voting in the Security Council', *Harvard Law Review*, vol. 67, 1953.

Haas, Ernst, 'Regime decay: conflict management and international organizations, 1945–1981', *International Organization*, vol. 31, no. 2, Spring 1983.

Higgins, Rosalyn, 'The place of international law in the settlement of disputes in the Security Council', *American Journal of International Law*, 70, December 1976.

Higgins, Rosalyn, *United Nations Peacekeeping 1946–1967: Documents and Commentary*, New York, Oxford University Press, 1980.

Hiscocks, Richard, *The Security Council: A Study in Adolescence*, London, Longman, 1973.

James, Alan, 'The Security Council: paying for peacekeeping', in David P. Forsythe (ed.), *The United Nations in the World Political Economy: Essays in Honour of Leon Gordenker*, London, Macmillan, 1989.

Jimenex de Arechage, Eduardo, *Voting and the Handling of Disputes in the Security Council*, New York, Carnegie Endowment for International Peace, 1950.

Johnstone, I., *Aftermath of the Gulf War: An Assessment of UN Action*, International Peace Academy Occasional Paper Series, Boulder, Lynne Rienner Publishers, 1994.

Kahng, Tae Jin, *Law, Politics, and the Security Council*, The Hague, Martius Nijhoff, 1964.

Kelsen, Hans, 'Organization and procedure of the Security Council', *Harvard Law Review*, vol. 59, 1946.

Kelsen, Hans, *The Law of the United Nations: A Critical Analysis of its Fundamental Problems*, London, Stevens, 1950.

Kennedy, Paul and Bruce Russett, 'Reforming the United Nations', *Foreign Affairs*, vol. 74, no. 5, September–October 1995.

Krauthammer, Charles, 'The unipolar moment', *Foreign Affairs: America and the World 1990/91*, vol. 70, no. 1, 1991.

Lall, Arthur, *The Security Council in a Universal United Nations*, New York, Carnegie Endowment for International Peace, 1971.

Lee, Dwight E., 'The genesis of the veto', *International Organization*, 1947.

Leigh-Phippard, Helen, 'Remaking the Security Council: the options', *The World Today*, Royal Institute of International Affairs, August–September 1994.

Malone, D., *Decision-Making in the UN Security Council: The Case of Haiti, 1990–1997*, New York, Clarendon Press, 1998.

Matanle, E., *The UN Security Council: Prospects for Reform*, London, Royal Institute of International Affairs, 1995.

McCarthy, Patrick A., 'Positionality, tension, and instability in the UN Security Council', *Global Governance*, vol. 2, no. 1, January–April 1996.

Meisler, Stanley, *United Nations: The First Fifty Years*, New York, Grove/ Atlantic, 1995.

Morphet, Sally, 'Resolutions and vetoes in the UN Security Council: their relevance and significance', *Review of International Studies*, vol. 16, no. 1, 1990.

Nicol, Davidson (ed.), *Paths to Peace: The UN Security Council and Its Presidency*, New York, Pergamon Press, 1981.

Nicol, Davidson with Margaret Croke and Babatunde Adentran, *The United Nations Security Council: Towards Greater Effectiveness*, New York, UN Institute for Training and Research, 1982.

Russell, Ruth B., assisted by Jeanette E. Muther, *A History of the United Nations Charter*, Washington DC, The Brookings Institution, 1958.

Sarooshi, D., *The United Nations and the Development of Collective Security: The Delegation by the UN Security Council of its Chapter VII Powers*, New York, Oxford University Press, 1998.

Seara-Vasquez, Modesto, 'The UN Security Council at fifty: midlife crisis or terminal illness?', *Global Governance*, vol. 1, no. 3, September–December 1995.

Sohn, Louis B., 'The Security Council's role in the settlement of international disputes', *American Journal of International Law*, vol. 78, no. 2, 1984.

Sutterlin, James S., 'United Nations decision-making: future initiatives for the Security Council and the Secretary-General', in Thomas G. Weiss (ed.), *Collective Security in a Changing World*, Boulder, Lynne Rienner Publishers, 1993.

United Nations Security Council, *Provisional Rules of Procedure of the Security Council*, New York, United Nations, 1952.

Urquhart, Brian, *A Life in Peace and War*, New York, W. W. Norton & Company, 1991 (also London, Weidenfeld & Nicolson, 1987).

Urquhart Brian, *Hammarskjöld*, New York, Knopf, 1972.

Wallensteen, Peter, 'Representing the world: a Security Council for the 21st century', in Paul F. Diehl (ed.), *The Politics of Global Governance: International Organizations in an Interdependent World*, Boulder, Lynne Rienner Publishers, 1997.

Wallensteen, Peter (ed.), *Preventing Violent Conflicts: Past Record and Future Challenges*, Uppsala, Uppsala University, Department of Peace and Conflict Research, 1998.

Weiss, Thomas G. (ed.), *Collective Security in a Changing World*, Boulder, Lynne Rienner Publishers, 1993.

White, N. D., *The United Nations and the Maintenance of International Peace and Security*, Manchester, Manchester University Press, 1990.

Wilcox, Francis, 'The rule of unanimity in the Security Council', *Proceedings of the American Society of International Law*, 1946.

Economic and Social Council

Camps, Miriam with Catherine Gwin, *Collective Management: The Reform of Global Economic Organization*, New York, McGraw-Hill, 1981.

Cox, Robert W., Harold K. Jacobson, *et al.*, *The Anatomy of Influence: Decision Making in International Organization*, New Haven, Yale University Press, 1973.

Dadzie, Kenneth, 'The United Nations and the problem of economic development', in Adam Roberts and Benedict Kingsbury (eds), *United Nations, Divided World: The UN's Roles in International Relations*, 2nd edn, Oxford, Clarendon Press, 1993.

Finer, H., *The United Nations Economic and Social Council*, Boston, World Peace Foundation, 1946.

Forsythe, David P. (ed.), *Human Rights and World Politics*, 2nd edn, Lincoln, University of Nebraska Press, 1989.

Hill, Martin, *United Nations System: Co-ordinating its Economic and Social Work*, Cambridge, Cambridge University Press and UNITAR, 1978.

Kaufmann, Johan, 'The Economic and Social Council and the New International Economic Order', in David P. Forsythe (ed.), *Human Rights and World Politics*, 2nd edn, Lincoln, University of Nebraska Press, 1989.

Keohane, Robert O., *After Hegemony: Cooperation and Discord in the World Political Economy*, Princeton, Princeton University Press, 1984.

Renninger, John P., *ECOSOC: Options for Reform*, New York, UNITAR, 1981.

Righter, Rosemary, *Utopia Lost: The United Nations and World Order*, New York, Twentieth Century Fund Press, 1995.

Roberts, Adam and Benedict Kingsbury (eds), *United Nations, Divided World: The UN's Roles in International Relations*, 2nd edn, Oxford, Clarendon Press, 1993.

Ruggie, John Gerard, *Constructing the World Polity: Essays on International Institutionalization*, London, Routledge, 1998.

Sharp, W. R., *The United Nations Economic and Social Council*, New York, Columbia University Press, 1969.

Taylor, Paul, *International Organization in the Modern World: The Regional and Global Process*, London, Pinter, 1993.

Taylor, Paul, 'Options for the reform of the international system for humanitarian assistance', in John Harriss (ed.), *The Politics of Humanitarian Intervention*, London, Pinter and Save the Children, 1995.

Taylor, Paul and A. J. R. Groom (eds), *Global Issues in the United Nations Framework*, London, Macmillan, 1989.

United Nations, *Economic and Social Council: Rules of Procedure of the Functional Commissions of the Economic and Social Council*, New York, United Nations, 1953.

United Nations, Office of Public Information, *For Human Welfare: A Study on the Work of the Economic and Social Council*, 2nd edn, New York, United Nations, 1959.

Young, Oran, *International Governance: Protecting the Environment in a Stateless Society*, New York, Cornell University Press, 1994.

Trusteeship Council

Barrett, D. W., *The Law of International Institutions*, 4th edn, London, Stevens, 1982.

Bennett, A. LeRoy, *International Organization*, 2nd edn, Englewood Cliffs, Prentice-Hall, 1980.

Boyd, Andrew, *The UNO Handbook*, London, Pilot Press, 1946.

Claude, Inis L. Jr, *Swords into Plowshares: The Progress and Problems of International Organization*, 4th edn, New York, Random House, 1971 (also 3rd edn revised, 1964).

El-Ayouty, Yassin, *The United Nations and Decolonization: The Role of Afro-Asia*, The Hague, Martinus Nijhoff, 1971.

Finkelstein, Lawrence S., *Somaliland Under Italian Administration: A Case Study in United Nations Trusteeship*, New York, Woodrow Wilson Foundation, 1955.

Goldblatt, I., *The Mandated Territory of South West Africa in Relation to the United Nations*, Cape Town, Struik, 1961.

Groom, A. J. R. and Paul Taylor, 'The role of the UN in Kosovo', in Albrecht Schnabel and Ramesh Thakur (eds), *Kosovo and the Challenge of Humanitarian Intervention: Selective Indignation, Collective Action and International Citizenship*, Tokyo, United Nations University, 2000.

Haas, Ernst B., 'Attempt to terminate colonialism: acceptance of U.N. Trusteeship system', in David A. Kay (ed.), *The United Nations Political System*, London, Wiley, 1967.

Luard, Evan, *A History of the United Nations*, vol. II, London, Macmillan, 1989.

Riggs, Robert E. and Jack C. Plano, *The United Nations: International Organizations and World Politics*, 2nd edn, Belmont, CA, Wadsworth, 1994 (also Chicago, Dorsey, 1988).

Rivlin, Benjamin, 'Self-determination and dependent areas', *International Conciliation*, no. 501, January 1995.

Sears, Mason, *Years of High Purpose: From Trusteeship to Nationhood*, Washington, DC, University Press of America, 1980.

Toussaint, Charmian E., *The Trusteeship System of the United Nations*, London, Stevens, 1956 (also Westport, Greenwood Press, 1976).

United Nations, *What the United Nations is Doing for Trust Territories*, New York, United Nations, 1952.

United Nations, Committee on Information from Non-Self-Governing Territories, *Special Study on Economic Conditions in Non-self-governing Territories: Analyses of Information Transmitted to the Secretary-General, 1957–1960*, New York, United Nations, 1960.

United Nations, Department of Public Information, *A Sacred Trust: The Work of the United Nations for Dependent Peoples*, 3rd revised edn, New York, United Nations, 1957.

United Nations, Office of Public Information, *From Dependence to Freedom: The United Nations' Role in the Advance of Dependent Peoples toward Self-government or Independence*, New York, United Nations, 1961.

International Court of Justice

Abi-Saab, Georges, 'The International Court as World Court', in Vaughan Lowe and Malgosia Fitzmaurice (eds.), *Fifty Years of the International Court of Justice: Essays in Honour of Sir Robert Jennings*, Cambridge, Cambridge University Press, 1996.

Anand, R. P., *Compulsory Jurisdiction of the International Court of Justice*, Bombay, Asia Publishing House, 1961.

Bedjaoui, Mohammed, *The New World Order and the Security Council: Testing the Legality of its Acts*, The Hague, Kluwer Law International, 1994.

Bernhardt, R. (ed.), *Digest of the Decisions of the International Court of Justice, 1976–1985*, Berlin, Springer, 1990.

Bloed, A. and P. van Dijk, *Forty Years International Court of Justice: Jurisdiction, Equity and Equality*, Utrecht, Europa Instituut, 1988.

Bodie, T. J., *Politics and the Emergence of an Activist International Court of Justice*, Westport, Praeger, 1995.

Brownlie, Ian, *Principles of Public International Law*, 1st edn, Oxford, Clarendon Press, 1966 (2nd edn, 1973; 3rd edn, 1979. 4th edn, 1990; 5th edn, 1998).

Chaudhri, Mohammed Ahsen (ed.), *The Prospects of International Arbitration*, Karachi, Palistan Publishing House, 1966.

Elias, T. O., *The United Nations Charter and the World Court*, Lagos, Nigerian Institute of Advanced Legal Studies, 1989.

Gamble, John King and Dana D. Fischer, *The International Court of Justice: An Analysis of a Failure*, Lexington, D. C. Heath, 1976.

Goodrich, Leland M., E. Hambro and A. P. Simons, *Charter of the United Nations: Commentary and Documents*, 3rd rev. edn, New York, Columbia University Press, 1969.

Gross, Leo (ed.), *The Future of International Court of Justice*, Dobbs Ferry, Oceana Publications, 1976.

Hambro, Edvard, *The Case Law of the International Court: Individual and Dissenting Opinions 1947–1958*, Leyden, A. W. Sythoff, 1963.
Hatchard, J. and P. Slinn, *Parliamentary Supremacy of Judicial Independence: A Commonwealth Approach*, London, Cavendish, 1999.
Jenks, C. Wilfred, *The Prospects of International Adjudication*, London, Stevens, 1964.
McWhinney, Edward, *The World Court and the Contemporary International Law-making Process*, Alphen aan den Rijin, Sijthoff and Noordhoff, 1979.
McWhinney, Edward, *The International Court of Justice and the Western Tradition of International Law: Paul Martin Lectures in International Relations and Law*, Dordrecht, Martinus Nijhoff, 1987.
Miller, Linda B., *World Order and Local Disorder: The United Nations and Internal Conflicts*, Princeton, Princeton University Press, 1967.
Muller, A. S., D. Raic and J. M. Thuranszky (eds), *The International Court of Justice: Its Future Role After Fifty Years*, The Hague, Nijhoff, 1997.
Nantwi, E. K., *The Enforcement of International Judicial Decisions and Arbitral Awards in Public International Law*, Leyden, A. W. Sijthoff, 1966.
Peck, Connie and Roy S. Lee (eds), *Increasing the Effectiveness of the International Court of Justice: Proceedings of the ICJ/UNITAR Colloquium to Celebrate the 50th Anniversary of the Court*, Geneva, United Nations Publications, 1997.
Pomerance, Michla, *The Advisory Function of the International Court in the League and U.N. Eras*, Baltimore, Johns Hopkins University Press, 1973.
Prott, Lyndel V., *The Latent Power of Culture and the International Judge*, Abingdon, Professional, 1979.
Rosenne, Shabtai, *The International Court of Justice: An Essay in Political and Legal Theory*, Leyden, Sijthoff, 1957.
Rosenne, Shabtai, *The Time Factor in the Jurisdiction of the International Court of Justice*, Leyden, A. W. Sijthoff, 1960.
Rosenne, Shabtai, (ed.), *Documents on the International Court of Justice (Documents relatifs à la Cour internationale de justice)*, Dordrecht, Martinus Nijhoff Publishers, 1991 (also Leiden, A. W. Sijthoff, 1974).
Rosenne, Shabtai, *The Law and Practice of the International Court*, Dordrecht, Martinus Nijhoff, 1985, reprint (also Leyden, A. W. Sijthoff, 1965).
Rosenne, Shabtai, *Intervention in the International Court of Justice*, Dordrecht, Martinus Nijhoff, 1993.
Rosenne, Shabtai, *The World Court: What it is and How it Works*, 5th completely revised edn, Dordrecht, Martinus Nijhoff, 1995 (also Dordrecht, Nijhoff, 1989).
Seyersted, Finn, *United Nations Forces in the Law of Peace and War*, Leyden, Sijthoff, 1966.
Shahabuddeen, M., *Precedent in the World Court*, Cambridge, Cambridge University Press, 1996.
Singh, N., *The Role and Record of the International Court of Justice, 1946–1988: In Celebration of the 40th Anniversary*, Dordrecht, Nijhoff, 1989.
Taylor, Paul, *International Co-operation Today: The European and the Universal Pattern*, London, Elek, 1971.

Thirlway, H. W. A., *Non-appearance before the International Court of Justice*, Cambridge, Cambridge University Press, 1985.

United Nations, Department of Public Information, *The International Court of Justice*, New York, United Nations, 1957.

Yarnold, B. M., *International Fugitives: A New Role for the International Court of Justice*, New York, Praeger, 1991.

ICJ reports

'Barcelona Traction: Light and Power Co. Case', *ICJ Reports*, 1970.

'Corfu Channel (Merits): U.K. v. Albania', *ICJ Reports*, 1949.

'Legality of the threat or use of nuclear weapons, Advisory Opinion of 8 July 1996', *ICJ Reports*, 1996.

'Reparation for injuries suffered in the service of the United Nations', *ICJ Reports*, 1949.

'Questions of interpretation and application of the 1971 Montreal Convention arising from the aerial incident at Lockerbie: Libyan Arab Jamahiriya v. United Kingdom; Libyan Arab Jamahiriya v. United States of America, Provisional Measures, Orders of 14 April 1992', *ICJ Reports*, 1992.

Secretariat

Bailey, Sydney D., *The Secretariat of the United Nations*, 2nd edn, Westport, Greenwood, 1978.

Barros, James (ed.), *The United Nations: Past, Present and Future*, New York, Free Press, 1972.

Beigbeder, Yves, *Management Problems in United Nations Organizations: Reform or Decline?*, London, Pinter, 1987.

Beigbeder, Yves, 'The continuing financial problems of the United Nations: assessing reform proposals', in C. de Cooker (ed.), *International Administration*, The Hague, Martinus Nijhoff Publishers, 1995.

Beigbeder, Yves, *The Internal Management of United Nations Organizations: The Long Quest for Reform*, Basingstoke, Macmillan, 1997.

Boudreau, T. E., *Sheathing the Sword: The UN Secretary-General and the Prevention of International Conflict*, New York, Greenwood Press, 1991.

Dijkzeul, Dennis, *The Management of Multilateral Organizations*, Boston, Kluwer Law International, 1997.

Dimoff, Steven A., 'Helms-Biden: Congress looks to micromanage the US', *The Inter-Dependent*, Summer 1997.

Finger, Seymour Maxwell and Arnold A. Saltzman, *Bending with the Winds: Kurt Waldheim and the United Nations*, Westport, Praeger, 1990.

Finkelstein, Lawrence S., 'The political role of the Director-General of UNESCO', in Lawrence S. Finkelstein (ed.), *Politics in the United Nations System*, Durham, Duke University Press, 1988a.

Finkelstein, Lawrence S. (ed.), *Politics in the United Nations System*, Durham and London, Duke University Press, 1988b.

Franck, Thomas M. and George Notle, 'The good offices function of the UN Secretary-General', in Adam Roberts and Benedict Kingsbury (eds), *United Nations, Divided World: The UN's Roles in International Relations*, 2nd edn, Oxford, Clarendon Press, 1993.

Gordenker, Leon, *The U.N. Secretary-General and the Maintenance of Peace*, New York, Columbia University Press, 1967.

Gordenker, Leon, 'The Secretary-General', in James Barros (ed.), *The United Nations: Past, Present and Future*, New York, Free Press, 1972.

James, Alan, 'The Secretary-General as an independent political actor', in Benjamin Rivlin and Leon Gordenker (eds), *The Challenging Role of the UN Secretary-General: Making 'The Most Impossible Job in the World' Possible*, London, Praeger, 1993.

Jordan, Robert S., ' "Truly" international bureaucracies: real or imagined?', in Lawrence S. Finkelstein (ed.), *Politics in the United Nations System*, Durham, Duke University Press, 1988.

Langrod, Georges, *The International Civil Service: Its Origins, Its Nature, Its Evolution*, trans. F. G. Berthoud, Leiden, Sijthoff, 1963.

League of Nations, *Official Journal*, June 1920.

Meron, Theodor, *The United Nations Secretariat*, Lexington, D. C. Heath, 1977.

Newman, Edward, *The United Nations Secretary General from the Cold War to the New Era: A Global Peace and Security Mandate?*, Houndmills, Macmillan, 1998.

Pérez de Cuéllar, Javier, 'The role of the UN Secretary-General', in Adam Roberts and Benedict Kingsbury (eds), *United Nations, Divided World: The UN's Roles in International Relations*, 2nd edn, Oxford, Clarendon Press, 1993.

Ramcharan, B. G., *Humanitarian Good Offices in International Law: The Good Offices of the United Nations Secretary-General in the Field of Human Rights*, The Hague, Martinus Nijhoff, 1982.

Riggs, Robert E. and Jack C. Plano, *The United Nations: International Organizations and World Politics*, 2nd edn, Belmont, CA, Wadsworth Publishing Co., 1994 (also, Chicago, Dorsey, 1988).

Rivlin, Benjamin, 'The UN Secretary-Generalship at fifty', *Paradigm*, vol. 8, no. 2, Winter 1994.

Rivlin, Benjamin, 'UN reform from the standpoint of the United States', *UN University Lectures 11*, Tokyo, The United Nations University, 1996.

Rivlin, Benjamin and Leon Gordenker (eds), *The Challenging Role of the UN Secretary-General: Making 'The Most Impossible Job in the World' Possible*, London, Praeger, 1993.

Roberts, Adam and Benedict Kingsbury (eds), *United Nations, Divided World: The UN's Roles in International Relations*, 2nd edn, Oxford, Clarendon Press, 1993.

Russell, Bulkeley, 'Depoliticizing the United Nations recruitment: establishing a genuinely international civil service', in 'The United Nations system: Prospects and proposals for reform', *New York University Journal of International Law and Politics*, New York University, vol. 22, no. 4, Summer 1990.

Schechter, Michael G., 'The political role of recent World Bank presidents', in

Lawrence S. Finkelstein (ed.), *Politics in the United Nations System*, Durham, Duke University Press, 1988.

Sutterlin, James S., 'The UN Secretary-General as Chief Administrator', in Benjamin Rivlin and Leon Gordenker (eds), *The Challenging Role of the UN Secretary-General: Making 'The Most Impossible Job in the World' Possible*, London, Praeger, 1993.

Urquhart, Brian, *Hammarskjöld*, New York, Knopf, 1972.

Urquhart, Brian and Erskine Childers, *A World in Need of Leadership: Tomorrow's United Nations*, Uppsala, Dag Hammarskjöld Foundation, 1990.

Non-governmental organizations

Boulding, Elise, *Women in the Twentieth Century World*, New York, John Wiley, 1977.

Conference of Non-governmental Organizations in Consultative Relationship with the United Nations (CONGO), *CONGO at Fifty: A Reaffirmation of Commitment*, New York, CONGO, 1998.

DeBenedetti, Charles, *The Peace Reform in American History*, Bloomington, Indiana University Press, 1980.

Dewes, Kate and Robert Green, *Aotearoa/New Zealand at the World Court*, Christchurch, Disarmament and Security Centre, 1999.

Golobal Policy Forum, *NGOs and the United Nations: Comments for the Report of the Secretary-General*, New York, United Nations, June 1999.

Jacobson, Harold, *Networks of Interdependence*, New York, Knopf, 1984.

Lewis, Paul, 'Fixing world crises isn't just a job for diplomats', *New York Times*, 5 April 1992, section 4.

Lewis, Paul, 'U.N. Committee, under pressure, limits rights groups', *New York Times*, 22 June 1999.

Powers, Roger S. and William B. Vogele (eds), *Protest, Power and Change: An Encyclopedia of Nonviolent Action from ACT-UP to Women's Suffrage*, New York, Garland, 1997.

Report of the Commission on Global Governance, *Our Global Neighborhood*, New York, Oxford University Press, 1995.

Russell, Ruth, *History of the United Nations Charter*, Washington, DC, The Brookings Institution, 1958.

United Nations, *Report of the Secretary-General: Arrangement and Practice for the Interaction of Non-governmental Organization in All Activities of the United Nations System*, New York, UN, 10 July 1998 (A/53/170).

United Nations, *Report of the Secretary-General: Views of Member States, Members of the Specialized Agencies, Observers, Intergovernmental and Non-governmental Organizations from All Regions on the Report of the Secretary-General on Arrangements and Practices for the Interaction of Non-governmental Organizations in All Activities of the United Nations System*, A/54/329.

United Nations Department of Public Information, *Earth Summit Agenda 21:*

The United Nations Programme of Action from Rio, New York, United Nations, DPI/1344, April 1993.

US Department of State, 'Dumbarton Oaks proposals for the establishment of a General International Organization', *Dumbarton Oaks Documents on International Organization*, Publication 2257, 1945.

US Department of State, *Charter of the United Nations: Report to the President on the Results of the San Francisco Conference by the Chairman of the United States Delegation, the Secretary of State*, Publication 2349, Conference Series 71, 26 June 1945.

US Department of State, *Postwar Foreign Policy Preparation, 1939–1945*, Publication 3580, Washington, DC: Government Printing Office, February 1950.

UN system

Ahluwalia, K., *The Legal Status, Privileges and Immunities of the Specialized Agencies of the United Nations and Certain Other International Organizations*, The Hague, Martinus Nijhoff, 1964.

Ainley, E. M., *The IMF: Past, Present and Future*, Cardiff, University of Wales Press, 1979.

Alexandrowiz, C. H., *The Law-Making Functions of the Specialized Agencies of the United Nations*, Sydney, Angus and Robertson, 1973.

Alger, Chadwick F., 'Thinking about the future of the UN system', *Global Governance*, vol. 2, No. 3, September–December 1996.

Ameri, Houshang, *Politics and Process in the Specialized Agencies of the United Nations*, London, Aldershot Gower, 1982.

Aufrich, H., *The International Monetary Fund: Legal Bases, Structure, Functions*, London, Stevens, 1964.

Bardonnet, D. (ed.), *The Adaptation of Structures and Methods at the United Nations (L'adaptation des structures et méthodes des Nations Unies)*, Dordrecht, Nijhoff, 1986.

Brucan, S., 'The UN system and its challenges', *Pacific Community*, vol. 9, no. 3, April 1978.

Cairncross, Alexander Kirkland, *The International Bank for Reconstruction and Development*, Princeton, Princeton University, Department of Economics and Sociology, 1959.

Elmandjra, M., *The United Nations System: An Analysis*, London, Faber and Faber, 1973.

Finkelstein, Lawrence S., 'The political role of the Director-General of UNESCO', in Lawrence S. Finkelstein (ed.), *Politics in the United Nations System*, Durham, Duke University Press, 1988a.

Finkelstein, Lawrence S. (ed.), *Politics in the United Nations System*, Durham, Duke University Press, 1988b.

Forsythe, David P., 'The political economy of UN refugee programmes', in David P. Forsythe (ed.), *Human Rights and World Politics*, 2nd edn, Lincoln, University of Nebraska Press, 1989.

Gordenker, Leon, 'The United Nations and its members: changing perceptions', *International Journal*, vol. 39, no. 2, 1984.

Gordenker, Leon, *Refugees in International Politics*, London, Croom Helm, 1989.

Gordenker, Leon, 'Clash and harmony in promoting peace: overview', *International Peacekeeping*, vol. 5, no. 4, Winter 1998.

Gore, C., Y. Katerere, S. Moyo and G. C. Z. Mhone, *The Case for Sustainable Development in Zimbabwe: Conceptual Problems, Conflicts and Contradictions: A Report Prepared for the United Nations Conference on Environment and Development (UNCED)*, Harare, Environment and Development Activities/Regional of Environmental Experts, 1992.

Gosovic, Branislav, *UNCTAD: Conflict and Compromise: The Third World's Quest for an Equitable World Economic Order through the United Nations*, Leiden, Sijthoff, 1972.

Gregg, Robert W. and M. Barkun (eds), *The United Nations System and its Functions*, New York, Van Nostrand, 1968.

Hambidge, Gove, *The Story of FAO*, New York, Van Nostrand, 1955.

Harrod, Jeffrey and Nico J. Schrijver (eds), *The UN Under Attack*, Aldershot, Gower, 1988.

Hill, Martin, *Towards Greater Order, Coherence and Co-ordination in the United Nations System*, UNITAR Research Report no. 20, New York, United Nations, 1974.

Hopkins, Raymond F., 'Reform in the international food aid regime: the role of consensual knowledge', *International Organization*, vol. 46, no. 1, Winter 1992.

Hopkins, Raymond F., 'Complex emergencies, peacekeeping and the World Food Programme', *International Peacekeeping*, vol. 5, no. 4, Winter 1998.

Imber, M. F., *The USA, ILO, UNESCO and IAEA: Politicization and Withdrawal in the Specialised Agencies*, London, Macmillan, in association with the Centre for International Policy Studies, University of Southampton, 1989.

Imber, M. F., 'Environmental security: a task for the UN system', *Review of International Studies*, vol. 17, no. 2, April 1991.

Jackson, Robert, *A Study of the Capacity of the UN Development System*, New York, United Nations, 1969.

Kaufmann, Johan and Nico Schrijver, *Changing Global Needs: Expanding Roles for the United Nations System*, Hanover, Academic Council on the United Nations System, 1990.

Khan, M. R., 'UN system and global peace and security: an assessment', *BIISS Journal*, vol. 8, no. 4, October 1987.

Kirkpatrick, J. J., 'The United Nations as a political system: a practicing political scientist's insights into UN politics', *World Affairs*, vol. 146, no. 4, 1984.

Kirshnamurti, R., 'Restructuring the UN system', *International Organization*, vol. 34, no. 4, Autumn 1980.

Knight, W. A., 'Beyond the UN system? Critical perspectives on global governance and multilateral evolution', *Global Governance*, vol. 1, no. 2, May–August 1995.

Kruglak, G. T., *The Politics of United States Decision-making in United Nations*

Specialized Agencies: The Case of the International Labor Organization, Washington, DC, University Press of America, 1980.

Laves, Walter H. C. and Charles A. Thomson, *U.N.E.S.C.O.: Purpose, Progress, Prospects*, London, Dennis Dobson, 1958.

Luard, E., 'Functionalism revisited: the UN family in the 1980s', *International Affairs*, vol. 59, no. 4, Autumn 1983.

McLaren, R. I., 'The UN system and its quixotic quest for coordination', *International Organization*, vol. 34, no. 1, 1980.

Marchisio, Sergio and Antonietta DiBiase, *The Food and Agriculture Organization*, Rome, Martinus Nijhoff, 1991.

Michalak Stanley J., *The United Nations Conference on Trade and Development: An Organization Betraying its Mission*, Washington, DC, Heritage Foundation, 1983.

Michalak Stanley J., 'UNCTAD as an agent of change', in David P. Forsythe (ed.), *Human Rights and World Politics*, 2nd edn, Lincoln, University of Nebraska Press, 1989.

Natsios, Andrew S., 'NGOs and the UN system in complex humanitarian emergencies: conflict or cooperation?', in Thomas G. Weiss and Leon Gordenker (eds), *NGOs, the UN & Global Governance*, Boulder, Lynne Rienner, 1996.

Park, S. S., 'Reform of the United Nations system', *Korea and World Affairs*, vol. 20, no. 2, Summer 1996.

Pathy, S., 'The UN system: a discernment from the South', *Social Action* [New Delhi], vol. 45, no. 2, April–June 1995.

Petersmann, E. U., 'How to reform the UN system? Constitutionalism, International Law, and International Organizations', *Leiden Journal of International Law*, vol. 10, no. 3, 1997.

Pietila, H. and J. Vickers, 'The UN system in the vanguard of advancement of women, development and peace', *International Affairs* [Moscow], no. 3, Spring 1995.

Ramsay, Robert, 'UNCTAD's failure: the rich get richer', *International Organization*, vol. 38, no. 2, 1984.

Rembe, N. S., *Africa and the International Law of the Sea: A Study of the Contribution of the African States to the Third United Nations Conference on the Law of the Sea*, Alphen aan den Rijn, Sijthoff & Noordhoff, 1980.

Rivlin, Benjamin, 'Regional arrangements and the UN system for collective security and conflict resolution: a new road ahead?', *International Relations*, vol. 11, no. 2, August 1992.

Rothstein, Robert L., *Global Bargaining: UNCTAD and the Quest for a New International Economic Order*, Princeton, Princeton University Press, 1979.

Schechter, M. G. (ed.), *Future Multilateralism: The Political and Social Framework*, Tokyo, United Nations University Press, 1999.

Siddiqi, J., *World Health and World Politics: The World Health Organization and the UN System*, London, Hurst, 1995.

Sikkink, Kathryn, 'Code of conduct for transnational cooperation: the case of the WHO/UNICEF Code', *International Organization*, vol. 40, no. 4, 1986.

Sjostedt, Gunnar, Bertram I. Spector and I. William Zartman (eds), *Negotiating International Regimes: Lessons Learned from the United Nations Conference on Environment and Development*, London, Graham & Trotman, 1994.

Spaull, H., *The Agencies of the United Nations*, London, Ampersand, 1967.

Stoessinger, J. G. and Associates, *Financing the United Nations System*, Washington, DC, The Brookings Institution, 1964.

Talbot, Ross B., *The Four World Food Agencies*, Ames, Iowa State University Press, 1990.

Talbot, Ross B., *Historical Dictionary of the International Food Agencies: FAO, WFP, WFC, IFAD*, Metuchen, Scarecrow Press, 1994.

Taylor, Paul and A. J. R. Groom (eds), *Global Issues in the UN Framework*, London, Macmillan, 1989.

Tyerman, D., *The Business of Development: An Essay, and a Review of UNCTAD II*, London, Overseas Development Institute, 1968.

United Nations, Department of Public Information, *Teaching about the United Nations and the Specialized Agencies: A Selected Bibliography, Prepared by the United Nations and UNESCO*, New York, United Nations, 1959.

Wallestein, Michel, *Food for War: Food for Peace*, Cambridge, MA, MIT Press, 1980.

Wells, Clare, *The UN, UNESCO, and the Politics and Knowledge*, London, Macmillan, 1987.

Whitman, Jim (ed.), *Peacekeeping and the UN Agencies*, London, Frank Cass, 1999.

Willetts, Peter (ed.), *The Conscience of the World: The Influence of Non-governmental Organisations in the UN System*, London, Hurst, 1995.

Williams, Douglas, *The Specialised Agencies and the United Nations: The System in Crisis*, London, Hurst, 1987.

Yamin, E., *Legislative Powers in the United Nations and Specialized Agencies*, Leiden, Sijthoff, 1969.

Yoder, A., *The Evolution of the UN System*, London, Crane Russack, 1990.

Zacklin, R., *The Amendment to the Constitutive Instruments of the United Nations and Specialized Agencies*, Leiden, Sijthoff, 1968.

Future of the UN

Abiew, Francis Kofi and T. Keating, 'NGOs and UN PKOs', *International Peacekeeping*, Summer 1999.

Agnelli, Enrico and C. Murphy: 'Lessons of Somalia for future multilateral humanitarian assistance operations', *Global Governance*, September 1995.

Alagappa, Muthiah, 'Regionalism and conflict management', *Review of International Studies*, October 1995.

Arnold, G., *World Government by Stealth: The Future of the United Nations*, Basingstoke, Macmillan, 1997.

Arts, Bas, *The Political Influence of Global NGOs: Case Studies on the Climate and Biodiversity Conventions*, Utrecht, International Books, 1998.

Baehr, Peter R. and Leon Gordenker, *The United Nations in the 1990s*, 2nd edn, London, Macmillan, 1994.

Bertrand, Maurice, *The Third Generation World Organization*, Dordrecht, Martinus Nijhoff, 1989.

Bornschier, V. and C. K. Chase-Dunn (eds), *The Future of Global Conflict*, London, Sage, 1999.

Chopra, Jarat, 'Introducing peace maintenance', *Global Governance*, vol. 4, no. 1, 1998.

Chopra, Jarat, *Peace-Maintenance: The Evolution of International Political Authority*, London, Routledge, 1999.

Coate, Roger A. (ed.), *U.S. Policy and the Future of the United Nations*, New York, Twentieth Century Fund Press, 1994.

Donini, Antonio, 'Asserting humanitarianism in peace-maintenance', *Global Governance*, vol. 4, no. 1, 1998.

Doyle, Michael W., *UN Peacekeeping in Cambodia: UNTAC's Civil Mandate*, International Peace Academy Occasional Paper Series, Boulder, Lynne Rienner, 1995.

Doyle, Michael W., I. Johnstone and R. C. Orr (eds), *Keeping the Peace: Multidimensional UN Operations in Cambodia and El Salvador*, Cambridge, Cambridge University Press, 1997.

Finger, Seymour Maxwell, *Your Man at the UN*, New York, New York University Press, 1980.

Fisas-Armengol, V., *Blue Geopolitics: The United Nations Reform and the Future of the Blue Helmets*, trans. by A. Langdon-Davies, London, Pluto Press, 1995.

Franck, Thomas M., *Nation against Nation: What Happened to the U.N. Dream and What the U.S. Can Do about it*, Oxford, Oxford University Press, 1985.

Fromuth, Peter, *A Successor Vision: The United Nations of Tomorrow*, Lanham, University Press of America, 1988.

Glennon, M. J., 'The new interventionism', *Foreign Affairs*, vol. 78, no. 3, May–June 1999.

Gordenker, Leon, 'NGOs: the people's voice in international governance', *University Lecture 15*, Tokyo, United Nations University, 1997.

Gordenker, Leon and Thomas G. Weiss (eds), *Soldiers, Peacekeepers and Disasters*, London, Macmillan, for the International Peace Academy, 1991.

Guicherd, C., 'International law and the war in Kosovo', *Survival*, vol. 41, no. 2, Summer 1999.

Harriss, John (ed.), *The Politics of Humanitarian Intervention*, London, Pinter, 1995.

Helmes, Jesse, 'Saving the U.N.: a challenge to the next Secretary-General', *Foreign Affairs*, vol. 75, no. 5, 1996.

Johnstone, Ian., *Aftermath of the Gulf War: An Assessment of UN Action*, International Peace Academy Occasional Paper Series, Boulder, Lynne Rienner, 1994.

Kaufmann, Johan, Dick Leurdijk and Nico Schrijver, *The World in Turmoil:*

Towards a Renaissance of the United Nations?, Hanover, Academic Council on the United Nations System, 1991.

Kaufmann, Johan and Nico Schrijver, *Changing Global Needs: Expanding Roles for the United Nations System*, Hanover, Academic Council on the United Nations System, 1990.

Mayall, James (ed.), *The New Interventionism, 1991–1994: United Nations Experience in Cambodia, Former Yugoslavia, and Somalia*, Cambridge, Cambridge University Press, 1996.

McKenna, P., 'Who rules? The United Nations: democratic and representative?', *Medicine, Conflict and Survival*, vol. 15, no. 1, January–March 1999.

Morozov, G., 'Renewing the United Nations', *International Affairs* [Moscow], vol. 44, no. 3, 1998.

Moxon-Browne, E. (ed.), *A Future for Peacekeeping?*, Basingstoke, Macmillan, 1997.

Muller, Joachim W., *The Reform of the United Nations*, New York, Oceana, 1992.

Parsons, Anthony, *From Cold War to Hot Peace: UN Interventions, 1947–1995*, London, Penguin Books, 1995.

Picco, G., 'The U.N. and the use of force', *Foreign Affairs*, vol. 73, no. 5, September–October 1994.

Puchala, Donald J. and Roger A. Coate, *The Challenge of Relevance: The United Nations in a Changing World Environment*, Hanover, Academic Council on the United Nations System, 1989.

Ramsbotham, Oliver and Tom Woodhouse, *Humanitarian Intervention in Contemporary Conflict*, Cambridge, Polity Press, 1996.

Ratner, Steven R., *The New UN Peacekeeping: Building Peace in Lands of Conflict After the Cold War*, Basingstoke, Macmillan, 1995.

Renninger, John P. (ed.), *The Future Role of the United Nations in an Interdependent World*, Dordrecht, Martinus Nijhoff, 1989.

Rivlin, Benjamin and Leon Gordenker (eds), *The Challenging Role of the UN Secretary-General: Making 'The Most Impossible Job in the World' Possible*, Westport, Praeger, 1993.

Rochester, J. Martin, *Waiting for the Millennium: The United Nations and the Future of World Order*, Columbia, University of South Carolina Press, 1993.

Schechter, M. G. (ed.), *Future Multilateralism: The Political and Social Framework*, Tokyo, United Nations University Press, 1999.

Simai, Mihaly, *The Future of Global Governance: Managing Risk and Change in the International System*, Washington, DC, United States Institute of Peace Press, 1994.

South Centre, *For a Strong and Democratic United Nations: A South Perspective on UN Reform*, London, Zed Books, 1997.

Taylor Paul, Sam Daws and Ute Adamczick-Gerteis (eds), *Documents on Reform of the United Nations*, Aldershot, Dartmouth, 1997.

Taylor Paul and J. A. Hall (eds), *International Order and the Future of World Politics*, Cambridge, Cambridge University Press, 1999.

Thomas, R. G. C., 'NATO, the UN, and international law', *Mediterranean Quarterly*, vol. 10, no. 3, 1999.

Urquhart, Brian and Erskine Childers, *A World in Need of Leadership: Tomorrow's United Nations*, Uppsala, Dag Hammerskjöld Foundation, 1990.

Wallensteen, P. (ed.), *Preventing Violent Conflicts: Past Record and Future Challenges*, Uppsala, Uppsala University, Department of Peace and Conflict Research, 1998.

Weiss, Thomas G. (ed.), *Beyond UN Subcontracting: Task-sharing with Regional Security Arrangements and Service-providing NGOs*, Basingstoke, Macmillan, 1998.

Weiss, Thomas G. and Cindy Collins, *Humanitarian Challenges and Intervention: World Politics and Dilemmas of Help*, Boulder, Westview Press, 1996.

Weiss, Thomas G., David P. Forsythe and Roger A. Coate, *The United Nations and Changing World Politics*, Boulder, Westview Press, 1994.

Weiss, Thomas G. and Leon Gordenker (eds), *NGOs, the UN and Global Governance*, Boulder, Lynne Rienner, 1996.

Wesley, M., *Casualties of the New World Order: The Causes of Failure of UN Missions to Civil Wars*, Basingstoke, Macmillan, 1997.

Member states

Alger, Chadwick F., Gene M. Lyons and John E. Trent (eds), *The United Nations System: The Policies of Members States*, Tokyo, United Nations University Press, 1995.

Angel, Eduardo Zuleta, 'How Latin America shaped the U.N.: the memories of a Colombian statesman', *Americas*, vol. 34, no. 5, September–October 1982.

Baehr, Peter R. and Monique C. Castermans (eds), *The Netherlands and the United Nations: Selected Issues*, The Hague, I. M. Asser Institute, 1990.

Bailey, Sydney and Sam Daws, *The Procedure of the Security Council*, 3rd edn, Oxford, Oxford University Press, 1998.

Banton, Michael, *International Action Against Racial Discrimination*, Oxford, Clarendon Press, 1996.

Bissell, Richard E., *Apartheid and International Organizations*, Boulder, Westview Press, 1977.

Crocker, Chester, *High Noon in Southern Africa: Making Peace in a Rough Neighborhood*, New York, Norton, 1993.

FCO Research Department,, *The Non-Aligned Movement and the Group of 77 Annex 3*, Memorandum 1980.

FCO Research Department, *Foreign Policy Document 223, The United Nations: Does the Rhetoric Matter? A Case History: Palestine 1947–1983*, October 1983.

Gladwyn, Lord, 'The founding of the United Nations: principles and objects', in Erik Jensen and Thomas Fisher (eds), *The United Kingdom – The United Nations*, London, Macmillan, 1990.

Grassi, S., 'The Italian contribution to the UN's stand-by arrangements system', *International Peacekeeping*, vol. 5, no. 1, Spring 1998.

Groom, A. J. R., Paul Taylor and Andrew Williams, *The Study of International*

Organisation: British Experiences, Hanover, Academic Council on the United Nations System, 1990.

Hajnal, Peter I., *The G7/G8 System: Evolution, Role and Documentation,* Aldershot, Ashgate, 1999.

HMSO, *Selected Documents Relating to Problems of Security and Cooperation in Europe 1954–77,* London, HMSO, Cmnd 6932.

Humphery, John P., *Human Rights and the United Nations: A Great Adventure,* Dobbs Ferry, Transnational Publishers, 1984.

Jackson, Richard L., *The Non-Aligned, the UN and the Superpowers,* New York, Praeger Special Studies, 1983.

Jansen, G. H., *Afro-Asia and Non Alignment,* London, Faber & Faber, 1966.

Jones, Charles A., *The North–South Dialogue: A Brief History,* London, Pinter, 1983.

Kay, David A., *The New Nations in the United Nations 1960–1967,* New York, Columbia University Press, 1970.

Khalidi, Walid, 'Revisiting the UNGA Partition Resolution', *Journal of Palestine Studies,* vol. 27, no. 1, Autumn 1997.

McDermott, A., 'Japan's financial contribution to the UN system: in pursuit of acceptance and standing', *International Peacekeeping,* vol. 6, no. 2, September 1999.

Marshall, Peter, 'The North–South dialogue: Britain at odds', in Erik Jensen and Thomas Fisher (eds), *The United Kingdom – The United Nations,* London, Macmillan, 1990.

Marston, Geoffrey, 'The United Kingdom's part in the preparation of the European Convention on Human Rights 1950', *International and Comparative Law Quarterly,* vol. 42, October 1993.

Maynes, Charles William and Richard S. Williamson (eds), *U.S. Foreign Policy and the United Nations System,* New York, Norton, 1996.

Morphet, Sally, 'Article 1 of the Human Rights Convenants in human rights and foreign policy principles and practice', in Dilys M. Hill (ed.), *Human Rights and Foreign Policy: Principles and Practice,* Basingstoke, Macmillan, 1989a.

Morphet, Sally, 'The Non-Aligned Movement and the foreign ministers' meeting at Nicosia', *International Relations,* vol. 9, no. 5, May 1989b.

Morphet, Sally, 'The Non-Aligned in "The New World Order": The Jakarta Summit, September 1992', *International Relations,* vol. XI, no. 4, April 1993.

Morphet, Sally, 'The influence of states and groups of states on and in the Security Council and General Assembly, 1980–94', *Review of International Studies,* vol. 21, no. 4, 1995.

Morphet, Sally, 'Three non-aligned summits: Harare 1986, Belgrade 1989 and Jakarta 1992', in David H. Dunn (ed.), *Diplomacy at the Highest Level: The Evolution of International Summitry,* Basingstoke, Macmillan, 1996a.

Morphet, Sally, 'The Non-Aligned and their 11th summit at Cartagena, October 1995', *Round Table,* no. 340, October 1996b.

Mortimer, Robert A., *The Third World Coalition in International Politics,* 2nd updated edn, Boulder and London, Westview Press, 1984 (also New York, Praeger, 1980).

Neuhold, Hanspeter (ed.), *N+N Perspectives*, Laxenburg, Austrian Institute for International Affairs, Laxenburg Paper, 1987.

Putnam, Robert D. and Nicholas Bayne, *Hanging Together: Cooperation and Conflict in the Seven-Power Summits*, 2nd edn, Cambridge, MA, Harvard University Press, 1987.

Roberts, Adam, 'Foreword', in David M. Malone, *Decision-Making in the UN Security Council: The Case of Haiti 1990–1997*, Oxford, Clarendon Press, 1998.

Roberts, Adam and B. Kingsbury (eds), *United Nations, Divided World*, Oxford, Clarendon Press, 1993.

Rubinstein, Alvin Z., *Yugoslavia and the Non-aligned World*, Princeton, Princeton University Press, 1970.

Secretaria de Relaciones Exteriores, *Cancun 1981: Framework, Debates and Conclusions of the International Meeting on Cooperation and Development*, Mexico City, 1982.

The South Letter, vols 1 & 2, 1999.

Taylor, Paul, 'The United Nations system under stress: financial pressures and their consequences', *Review of International Studies*, vol. 17, no. 4, 1991.

'UNCTAD: intervener between poor and rich states', *Journal of World Trade Law*, 1973.

United Nations, *The Yearbook of the United Nations*, New York, United Nations, 1946.

Williams, Douglas, *The Specialized Agencies and the United Nations: The System in Crisis*, London, Hurst, 1987.

Zartman, I. William (ed.), *Positive Sum: Improving North–South Negotiations*, New Brunswick, NJ, Transaction Books, 1986.

Consonance

Archer, Clive, *International Organizations*, 2nd edn, London and New York, Routledge, 1992 (also London, Allen & Unwin, 1983).

Armstrong, David, *The Rise of the International Organization: A Short History*, London, Macmillan, 1982.

Barston, R. P., *Modern Diplomacy*, London, Longman, 1988.

Bennett, A. LeRoy, *International Organisations: Principles and Issues*, 5th edn, Englewood Cliffs, Prentice-Hall, 1991.

Boutros-Ghali, Boutros, *An Agenda for Peace*, New York, United Nations, 1992.

Boutros-Ghali, Boutros, *An Agenda for Development*, New York, United Nations, 1995.

Boutros-Ghali, Boutros, *An Agenda for Democratisation*, New York, United Nations, 1996.

Brundtland, Gro Harlem, et al. (The Brundtland Report), *Our Common Future:*

Report of the World Commission on Environment and Development, Oxford, Oxford University Press, 1987.

Brundtland, Maurice, 'The historical development of efforts to reform the UN', in Adam Roberts and Benedict Kingsbury (eds), *United Nations, Divided World: The UN's Roles in International Relations*, 2nd edition, Oxford, Clarendon Press, 1993.

Claude, Inis, L. Jr, *Swords into Plowshares: The Progress and Problems of International Organization*, 4th edn, New York, Random House, 1971 (also 3rd edn rev., 1964).

Fawcett, Louise and Andrew Hurrell (eds), *Regionalism in World Politics: Regional Organization and International Order*, Oxford, Oxford University Press, 1995.

Finkelstein, Lawrence S. (ed.), *Politics in the United Nations System*, Durham, Duke University Press, 1988.

Groom, A. J. R. (eds), *Functionalism: Theory and Practice in International Relations*, London, University of London Press, 1975.

Groom, A. J. R. and Paul Taylor, *Framework for International Cooperation*, London, Pinter, 1990.

Jacobson, Harold Karan, *Networks of Interdependence: International Organizations and the Global Political System*, 2nd edn, New York, Knopf, 1984.

James, Alan, *Peacekeeping in International Politics*, London, Macmillan, 1990.

Jensen, Erik and Thomas Fisher (eds), *The United Kingdom – The United Nations*, London, Macmillan, 1990.

Lyons, Gene M. and Michael Mastanduno, *Beyond Westphalia: State Sovereignty and International Intervention*, Baltimore, Johns Hopkins University Press, 1995.

Roberts, Adam and Benedict Kingsbury (eds), *United Nations, Divided World: The UN's Roles in International Relations*, 2nd edn, Oxford, Clarendon Press, 1993.

Taylor, Paul, *International Organisation: A Conceptual Approach*, London, Pinter, 1978.

Taylor, Paul, *International Organization in the Modern World: The Regional and Global Process*, London, Pinter, 1993.

Taylor, Paul and A. J. R. Groom (eds), *Global Issues in the United Nations' Framework*, London, Macmillan, 1989.

Taylor, Paul and A. J. R. Groom (eds), *International Institutions at Work*, London, Pinter, 1988.

Urquhart, Brian, *A Life in Peace and War*, New York, Norton, 1991 (also London, Weidenfeld & Nicolson; New York, Harper & Row, 1987).

Whitman, Jim (ed.), *Peacekeeping and the UN Agencies*, London, Frank Cass, 1999.

Williams, Douglas, *The Specialised Agencies and the United Nations: The System in Crisis*, London, Hurst, 1987.

INDEX

Abi-Saab, Georges   190
accountability   216–17, 272, 291
Acheson, Dean   232
Administrative Committee on Co-
    ordination (ACC) 109, 116, 124–5,
    132, 134, 203, 218, 281
administrative unions   160, 199
    see also international public unions
Advisory Committee on
    Administrative and Budgetary
    Questions (ACABQ)   48, 116, 203,
    207, 211–12
Afghanistan   47, 81, 147, 251
Afro-Asian group of countries, see
    Asian-African group
Agenda for Peace, An   42, 86–7, 92, 189,
    307
Agenda 21   272, 284–5
AIDS   126
Al Aqsa mosque incident   236
Alabama case   3
Aland Islands dispute   7–8
Albania   184
Albright, Madeleine   218, 313
Algeria   45, 237, 247, 301
Ameri, H.   116
American Federation of Labor (AFL)
    12, 273, 275
Angel, Eduardo   227
Annan, Kofi   53, 55, 129–30, 185, 190,
    196–7, 208, 212, 215, 220–1, 280,
    287, 319–20
Anti-Slavery League   4–6
apartheid   44, 77, 85, 162–5, 171, 178,
    237, 239, 244
Arab League   18, 47, 227–9

Arab-Asian group of countries   231–2,
    235
arbitration   3
Argentina   171, 173, 241, 301, 303
Armenia   146
Arria formula   92
Asian-African group of countries   32,
    233–4, 244
Atlantic Charter   12–13, 62, 148
auditing of UN programmes   203–5,
    209–10
Australia   16–17, 68, 145–6, 166–7
Austro-Hungarian Empire   144
Avenol, Joseph   11

Balfour, Arthur J.   199
Bandaranaike, Sirimavo   239, 251
Bandung conference (1955)   32, 233–7,
    241, 260
Barbados   119
Barcelona Traction case (ICJ, 1970)   183
Bedjaoui, Justice   181–3, 189–90
Beijing conference on women's issues
    (1995)   120, 126, 281, 283
Belarus   26
Belgium   146
Bellamy, Carol   208, 215
Bergen process   284
Berlin, Congress of (1885)   143
Bernadotte, Count   40
Bertrand, Maurice   119–20, 317
Bill of Rights   179
Bissell, Richard E.   237
Bosnia   254
Bouteflika doctrine   34
Boutros-Ghali, Boutros   42, 48, 85–6,
    189, 208–9, 217, 319

boycott action 40, 72, 160
Brandt Commission report (1980) 250
Brazil 10, 303, 316
Bretton Woods conference and
    institutions 13, 105, 243
Britain, *see* United Kingdom
British Empire and Commonwealth
    17, 143, 147–8, 229–30, 244, 261
Brownlie, Ian 193
Bruce Committee report (1939) 4, 10,
    101–2
Brussels Treaty (1948) 228
budget of UN 202, 308–10
budgetary contributions 48
    withholding of 260, 295
    see also United States
Bulgaria 28
Bunker, Ellsworth 167
Burke, Edmund 143
Burma 301
Burton, John 167
Burundi 94, 305
Byelorussia 14

Cairns Group 246
Cairo conference
    on economic development (1962)
    242
    on population questions (1994) 120,
    126
Cambodia 34, 42, 81, 169, 171
Campaign for a More Democratic
    United Nations (CAMDUN) 56
Canada 273, 300
Cancun conference (1981) 250
'capacity' requirement for member
    states 29
Capacity Study (1969) 110–11, 119
Carter, Jimmy 77
Castro, Fidel 238, 250
Cecil, Viscount 12
Charter of Economic Rights and Duties
    of States 46, 248
Charter of the UN 1, 6, 9–11, 14, 16,
    19–20, 69, 95, 102, 150, 155, 159,
    170
    Article 1 187

Article 2 30, 36–7, 43, 150
Article 4 28–9
Article 8 27
Article 9 33
Article 10 10, 26
Article 11 27
Article 12 10, 26
Article 13 50
Article 14 27
Article 15 26
Article 17 27
Article 18 49
Article 19 217, 295
Article 20 35
Article 22 27, 56
Article 23 27, 91, 154
Article 31 76
Article 32 76
Article 39 82
Article 40 86
Article 41 82, 94
Article 42 83–4
Article 43 42, 73, 84, 86
Article 50 86
Article 51 186
Article 55 151
Article 57 103–5
Article 58 49, 103
Article 60 27, 49, 103
Article 61 27
Article 62 103
Article 63 103, 105
Article 64 117
Article 66 285
Article 68 103
Article 71 274
Article 73 151
Article 74 152
Article 76 152, 162
Article 77 152–3
Article 78 153, 172
Article 79 153
Article 80 153
Article 81 153, 158
Article 82 153
Article 83 153
Article 84 153

Article 85   27, 153
Article 86   27, 153-4
Article 87   154
Article 88   154
Article 97   27
Article 99   11, 80, 200
Article 100   200
Article 101   27
Article 108   173
drafting of   65-6
interpretation of provisions   187-8
Special Committee on   174
Childers, Erskine   321
China   8, 13-15, 17, 34, 40-1, 46, 63-4,
   72, 83, 156-7, 160, 171, 224-6, 231,
   240, 254, 257-9, 313
Christian Solidarity International   287
Churchill, Sir Winston   12-14, 62-3,
   71, 148-9
Civil and Political Rights, International
   Covenant on   51, 191-2, 232, 261
civil society   4, 22, 53-6, 132, 174-5,
   261, 272, 284-5, 292, 295, 313
Claude, Inis   11, 28, 50, 162
Clinton, Bill   206, 257, 306, 308
Club of Rome   45
coalition-building   32-3, 225, 256
Code of Conduct for UN staff members
   216
Cold War, ending of   61, 81, 120, 225,
   308
collective action
   principles of   304-14
   types of   322-3
collective security   6-7, 22, 41-2, 73,
   83-5
collective self-defence   184, 249
collegiality   124, 311
Colombia   251
colonialism, see decolonization
Commission on Global Governance
   285-6
Commission on the Status of Women
   127, 281
Commission to Study the Organization
   of Peace   12

Commission on Sustainable
   Development   284-5, 289
Committee on NGOs   276-7, 279, 282,
   287-9
Committee for Programme and Co-
   ordination (CPC)   49, 118, 125,
   134, 138, 203, 308-10, 312, 315
Committee of 24   43, 239
Committee of the Whole (COW)
   248-9
Common Foreign and Security Policy
   (CFSP), European   302-3, 308, 322
Concert system   3, 7, 22
Conference on Security and Co-
   operation in Europe (CSCE)
   246-7, 256
conferences, global   6, 50, 119-20, 122,
   126-7, 131-7, 241, 260, 271, 281-5,
   288-91
conflict prevention   189-90
Congo   74-5, 111, 143, 169, 238, 305
CONGO   277-8, 280, 282, 289-90
Congress of Industrial Organizations
   (CIO)   273
Connally, Tom   69
consensus   31, 49, 75, 133, 138, 225,
   256-7
   on funding   309, 315, 318, 323
Conservative Party   304
consonance   312-24
   internal and external   298-9
   principles of   314-21
Consultative Committee on
   Administrative Questions (CCAQ)
   203
consultative procedures, see Economic
   and Social Council; Security
   Council
contact groups   32
Contra forces   184-5
Cook Islands   170
Copenhagen conference on women's
   issues (1980)   281
core and non-core staff   220
Corfu Channel case (ICJ, 1949)   183, 185
Council of Europe   63, 228

Council for Mutual Economic Assistance 246
Country Strategy Notes 123, 131–40 *passim*
Credentials Committee 34
Crocker, Chester 254, 260
Cross Organizational Programme Analyses (COPAs) 118–19
cross-sectional programmes 135–7
Cuba 83–4, 250–1, 301
customary law 51, 184–5
Cyprus 75, 254

Dadzie, Kenneth 116
de Gaulle, Charles 44, 163
debts of developing countries 252
decolonization 42–3, 74–5, 95, 111, 142–3, 148, 155, 163, 224, 234, 238
delegations to the UN 33–5
democratic institutions and processes 7, 28, 315
Denmark 33
Department of Economic and Social Affairs (ESA) 110, 112, 276
Department of Public Information (DPI) 275–7, 279–80
Deputy Secretary-General (DSG), post of 129–30, 214, 218
détente 247, 251
diplomatic immunity 210
Diplomatic Relations, Convention on 51
dollar convertibility 243
domestic jurisdiction, non-interference in 28, 37, 151, 171, 185–6, 237
donor approval for operations 314–18, 322–3
Drummond, Sir Eric 11, 199
Dulles, John Foster 12
Dumbarton Oaks conference (1944) 13–17, 25–6, 65–7, 200, 273–4

East Timor 169, 171
Eastern European group of countries 234, 259

Economic Commission for Asia and the Far East 110
Economic Commission for Europe 110, 284
Economic Commission for Latin America 44, 241
Economic and Social Council (ECOSOC) 10–11, 14, 18, 25, 27, 49–52, 125–39, 149, 154, 217, 243, 245, 271–4, 281–3, 312, 315, 317, 321
  consultation with NGOs 274–9, 288–90
  Co-ordination segment 125–7, 132, 136, 139, 309
  Operational segment 125, 127–8, 132, 138
Economic, Social and Cultural Rights, International Covenant on 51, 232, 261
Ecuador 84
Efficiency Board 211
Egypt 25, 225, 230–1
elections, monitoring of 202
Enterprise Liaison Service 218
entrenched multilateralism 101, 121, 123, 137–8, 296, 318
environmental issues 187
  Rio de Janeiro conference on (1992) 120, 126, 272, 283–5
environmental programmes 114–15
epistemic communities 4, 54
Eritrea 157–8
Estonia 259
Ethiopia 157–8, 165
European Monetary Union 122–3
European Parliament 56
European Union 32, 121, 128, 131, 147, 217–18, 225, 244–6, 259, 302–3, 306–7, 322–4
  foreign policy 307–8
  see also Common Foreign and Security Policy
Euroscepticism 122
evaluation of UN programmes and officials 204–5, 211
Evatt, Herb 17, 68, 167

Evian Agreements 163
Expanded Programme of Technical Assistance (EPTA) 109, 114
expenditure of UN 202, 308–10
extradition 189

'failing states' 30, 121, 301
Faisal, King 227
Falkland Islands 171–3
'false echo' 310
Federal Council of Churches of Christ in America 12
Federation of International Civil Service Associations 216
financial disclosure by senior UN staff 219
Finland 300
Fitzmaurice, Judge 188
Food and Agriculture Organization (FAO) 13, 47, 100–14 *passim*, 237
Formosa 156–7
see also Taiwan
France 14–17, 25, 27, 37, 42, 71, 73, 145–9, 158, 218, 246, 260, 300–8 *passim*
Frechette, Louise 130, 214
freeloading by UN member states 305
functional commissions 126–39

Gaddafi, Muammar 250
General Agreement on Tariffs and Trade (GATT) 104, 108, 113
General Assembly of the UN 9–10, 14, 17, 21–56, 66, 88, 180, 196, 219–20, 271, 290–1, 310–12
agenda-setting for 35–7, 44, 52–3
budgetary powers of 48–9
competences of 26–7
constitutional function of 49–50
decline of 46–8
economic and social issues considered by 111–20, 126–33, 137
emergency special sessions of 35, 41
evolution from 1945 to 1965 38–44

Fifth Committee 36, 49, 138, 203, 211, 220, 309–10
First Committee 36, 286
first session 1, 19
Fourth Committee 36, 162, 282
functioning of 33–8
future of 54–6
General Committee 36, 227, 244
law-making function of 50–1
President of 37–8, 227–8
resolutions of 31
revitalization of 52–4
Second Committee 36, 128
Sixth Committee 36, 50, 173
Special Committees 282
stagnation in 44–6
Third Committee 36, 128, 232–3
Trusteeship questions 153–6, 161–72 *passim*
types of session 35
Vice-Presidents of 244–5
Geneva Group 318
genocide 182–3, 191
geographic groupings, *see* regional groupings; states groups
Georgetown Conference (1972) 240
Germany 7, 29, 89, 144, 156, 201, 300–4
Ghana 125
Gibraltar 171–3
Gingrich, Newt 206
global conferences, *see* conferences
globalization 163, 255, 324
Goa 171
Gorbachev, Mikhail 81, 295
Grams, Rod 218
grass-roots organizations 272
Greece 145, 147
Gromyko, Andrei 227
Gros, Judge 188
Group B 245–6, 249
Group of 7 (later 8) 128, 190, 250, 252, 255–8
Group of 10 243
Group of 15 258
Group of 18 49, 203, 205
Group of 20 243
Group of 24 249

Group of 77 (G77)   32, 133–4, 138, 225, 240–3, 247–52, 257, 301
Guatemala   254
Gulf War   86, 306–7, 311

Hague, The   3
Hague Peace Conferences   3–4, 177, 199
Haile Selassie   158
Haiti   94, 313
Hammarskjöld, Dag   37–8, 73–4, 163
Hankey, Sir Maurice   199
Havana conference (1947–48)   104
   see also Non-aligned Movement
Helms-Biden agreement   207
Hennes, Richard V.   204
Heritage Foundation   47, 256
Higgins, Rosalyn   188–9
Hiss, Alger   15
Hong Kong   171
Human Environment, the, Conference on (1972)   280
Human Resources Management Strategy   211, 215
human rights   85, 127, 150–2, 171–2, 178–9, 183–4, 191, 212, 215, 234, 237, 254, 287, 295–6
   Paris conference on (1968)   280
   Universal Declaration on   51, 230
   Vienna conference on (1993)   120, 126
Humphrey, John   232, 234
Hungary   28, 234, 237
Hussein, Saddam   82, 84, 307

Iceland   25
idealistic expectations   95
India   163, 171, 225–37 passim, 251, 257, 301, 313
indigenous peoples   171
Indonesia   166–71, 235, 260, 301
initiative-taking   260
Inter-Agency Consultative Board   109
Inter-Agency Steering Committee   287
Inter-American Conference on Problems of Peace and War (Mexico City, 1945)   15

internal affairs of states, see domestic jurisdiction
International Association of Lawyers Against Nuclear Arms (IALANA) 286
International Atomic Energy Authority (IAEA)   104–8 passim
International Bank for Reconstruction and Development (IBRD)   13, 104, 243
   see also World Bank
International Chamber of Commerce 218
International Civil Aviation Organization   13, 104
International Civil Service Advisory Board   216
International Civil Service Commission (ICSC)   203, 216, 220
International Communications Union 199
international community, duties of states towards   183
International Court of Justice (ICJ)   3, 11–19, 27, 29, 165, 177–93, 227, 286–7
   advisory opinions   181–2, 186, 188, 192–3, 229
International Development Association 105
International Federation of Business and Professional Women   280
International Finance Corporation 105, 241
International Institute of Agriculture 199
International Labour Organization (ILO)   13, 23, 100–8, 111, 199, 201, 237, 258, 273–4
International Law, Committee for the Progressive Codification of   177
International Law Commission   50–1, 177
International Maritime Consultative Organization (IMCO)   104, 107–8
International Monetary Fund (IMF) 13, 47, 102, 104, 106, 163, 243, 303

International Network for a UN
   Second Assembly   56
international organization, growth of
   1–6, 11–12, 63
international organizations in general,
   legal personality and competence
   of   187, 192
International Physicians for the
   Prevention of Nuclear War
   286
international public unions   4
   see also administrative unions
International Relief Organization   104
International Seabed Authority   174
International Telecommunication
   Union   104–7, 199
International Union of Official Travel
   Organizations   105
International Women's Year   281
internationalist concept for UN staff
   200–2
INTERPOL   105
Iran   69–73, 147, 301
Iran–Iraq War   81, 253, 306–7
Iraq   79–86, 197, 229, 235, 253–6, 301,
   305–7
Ireland   28
'Iron Curtain' speech   71
Islamic group at the UN   235–6
Ismail, Razali   207, 290
Israel   32, 34, 48, 79, 206, 229–30, 236,
   260–1
Italy   89, 145, 156–9, 201, 300

Jackson, Sir Robert   110, 260
Japan   89, 147, 156–7, 166, 300, 303–4
Jebb, Sir Gladwyn   19, 226–7
Jennings, Sir Robert   180, 182, 193
Jerusalem   236, 254
Joint Inspection Unit (JIU)   116, 119,
   204–5
Jordan   28
jus cogens, principle of   177

Kamal, Ahmed   290
Kant, Immanuel   3
Kassebaum Amendment   47–8, 256

Kingsbury, Benedict   226
Kissinger, Henry   46
Korea   156
Korean airliner, shooting down of   78
Korean War   28–9, 40–2, 72–3, 157,
   230–1, 238
Kosovo   169–72, 175, 255, 295, 312–13
Kurile Islands   156–7
Kuwait   82–3, 86, 253–4

Labour Party   149, 304
land mines   287
Latin American group   227, 230,
   237–8, 241, 246
Law of the Sea, Conventions on   51
Law of Treaties, Convention on   51
Lawyers' Committee on Nuclear Policy
   286
League of Nations   1, 3–14 *passim*,
   22–5, 101–3, 131, 170, 199, 273
   Covenant of   8–11, 23, 144, 177
   Mandate system   142–6, 154–6, 171
League of Nations Union   12
legislation, unconstitutional   179
Lester, Sean   11
liberation movements   251
Liberia   165
Libya   148, 157–8, 189, 301
Lie, Trygve   73, 142, 202
Lima meeting (1975)   248
'Little Assembly'   39
Litvinov, Maxim   13
Lockerbie case (ICJ, 1992)   189, 191
Luard, Evan   167

Maastricht Treaty   121, 302
MacArthur, Douglas   41
MacBride, Sean   286
McCarthy, Joseph   74, 201
Macmillan, Harold   163
Major, John   85
'major groups'   272, 284
Malaysia   166, 301
Maldive Islands   30
Mali   133
Malta   173–4

management structure and culture
  204–15 *passim*, 319
market-based approaches   218
Marshall, Peter   246
Marshall Islands   160
member states of the UN   25, 28–9
  number of   224, 244, 310
  typology of   299–304
Menon, Krishna   232
MERCOSUR   303
Mexico   251
Mexico City conference
  on peace and war (1945)   15
  on women's issues (1975)   281
Micronesia   160
micro-states   30
Military Staff Committee   10, 73
Millennium Assembly   55, 130
Millennium NGO Forum   285–6
'mission creep'   311, 316
Mitrany, David   12
Montenegro   172
Montreal Convention   189
moral pressure   22, 305
Moscow conference (1943)   64
Moynihan, Daniel   77–8
multinational corporations   298
Myrdal, Gunnar   115

Nairobi conference on women's issues
  (1985)   281
Namibia   78, 81, 162–6, 188, 191, 226,
  251–4, 260–1
Nasser, Gamal Abdel   238–9
Nehru, Pandit   163, 238
Netherlands, the   147, 149, 166–9, 300
New Delhi conference
  of Asian countries (1947 and 1949)
    228
  of UNCTAD (1967)   113
New Guinea   166–9
New International Economic Order
  (NIEO)   32, 45–6, 77, 117, 242,
  247–8, 260, 310
New Zealand   145–6, 218, 286
Nicaragua   178, 184–5
Nigeria   301, 303

Noblemaire principle   201, 220
Non-aligned Movement   32, 76–7, 83,
  87–91, 112, 163, 230, 233, 237–42,
  254, 257, 260, 286–7
  Algiers summit (1973)   247, 250
  Belgrade summit (1961)   239
  Colombo summit (1976)   251
  Durban summit (1998)   225, 255
  Harare summit (1986)   253
  Havana summit (1979)   225, 249
  Jakarta summit (1992)   255
Non-Governmental Liaison Service
  281–3
non-governmental organizations
  (NGOs)   4–6, 54, 92, 124, 130,
  135, 217, 261, 271–92, 314
  number of   272, 283
non-intervention, principle of, *see*
  domestic jurisdiction
norms, creation and maintenance of
  51, 304–5, 322
North Atlantic Treaty Organization
  (NATO)   32, 172, 255, 303, 313–14
North Korea   29
North–South dialogue   30, 32, 45–7,
  51, 248–50, 258
Norway   300
nuclear disarmament   187, 224, 286
nuclear weapons
  legality of threat or use of   186–7,
  191, 286–7
  nonproliferation treaty (1968)   51
  testing of   239, 255
Nyerere, Julius   207, 249

observer status   34, 162, 278–9,
  288–9
Office for Programme Planning and
  Co-ordination   118
Office of Internal Oversight Services
  204, 209–10
Okinawa   156–7
Onyeama, Judge   188
open diplomacy   22, 77
Organization of African Unity   171,
  237
Organization of American States   228

Organization for Economic Co-operation and Development (OECD) Development Assistance Committee 133
Organization of Petroleum Exporting Countries (OPEC) 241, 247, 249
Ottoman Empire 144–5
Ottawa Agreement (1932) 147
Ottawa process 287
Otunnu, Olara 79
Outer Space Treaty (1967) 51

Pacific Islands, Trust Territory of 142, 156–63
Pakistan 168, 229, 235
Palau 142, 160, 173
Palestine 40, 77–8, 125, 145, 155–6, 224, 229, 235–6, 246, 259–61
pariah states 310
Paris conference on human rights (1968) 280
Parliamentarians for Global Action 286
Parliamentary Supremacy and Judicial Independence, Colloquium on (1998) 179
Parsons, Anthony 256
Paschke, Theodor 209
peace enforcement 86
peaceful settlement of disputes 67–70, 95–6, 181–2, 189
peacekeeping operations 42, 74–5, 85–6, 95, 202, 209, 254, 313, 323
Pearson, Lester 163
People's Assembly 285
Pérez de Cuéllar, Javier 79–80, 189, 197, 217
Permanent Court of Arbitration 3, 177
Permanent Court of International Justice 8–9, 11, 14, 23, 177
permanent missions to the UN 33
petitions 160, 162, 171, 285
P5 arrangement 306–8, 323
Philadelphia Declaration (1944) 102, 107
plebiscites 168

Poland 15, 72
population, conferences on (1974, 1984 and 1994) 120, 126, 135, 281
Population and Development, Commission on 127
Portugal 28, 149, 169
Prebisch, Raul 113, 241–2
'problem-solving' UN members 300–1
propaganda 78
public opinion 22, 275–6, 278, 288

'qualification', power of 27
quasi-autonomous non-governmental organizations (QUANGOs) 271

racial discrimination 235, 237
see also apartheid
Rambouillet conference (1975) 252
Rau, Sir Benegal 232
Reagan, Ronald (and Reagan administration) 47, 77–8, 81, 250, 256
recruitment of UN staff 205, 320–1
reform
    of Secretariat 319–21
    of Security Council 87–94
    of UN economic and social arrangements 123
    of UN organization 208–21
'reformist' member states 300–1
regime theory 122
regional conflicts 81
regional economic commissions 110–11
regional groupings of states 18, 318, 323–5
Relief and Rehabilitation Administration 13
reparations case (ICJ, 1949) 188
resident co-ordinators 123–5, 130, 136, 213
restitution, principle of 170–1
Revolving Credit Fund 217, 219
Rhodesia 78
right to development 253
right to life 191–2

Rights of the Child Convention   132
Rio de Janeiro conference on the
    environment (1992)   120, 126, 272,
    283–5
Ripert, Michael   116
Roberts, Adam   226
Robinson, Mary   212
Romania   28
Roosevelt, Franklin D.   12–14, 62–6,
    93, 159
Rubinstein, Alvin Z.   231
Ruggie, John   130
rules generated by multilateral
    diplomacy   122, 325
Russell, Ruth   63, 274
Russia   82, 254, 257, 295–6, 308
Rwanda   304

salaries of UN staff   201, 220
Salim, Rafiah   215
Salim, Salim   79
San Francisco conference (1945)
    14–19, 26–7, 61–2, 67–9, 95, 102,
    148, 150, 155, 179–80, 188, 200, 226,
    271, 273–4
sanctions   82–3
Saudi Arabia   229–30
Seabed Arms Control Treaty (1971)   51
Secretariat of the UN   14, 19, 80, 108,
    113, 124–5, 128, 131, 196–221
    criticisms of   197–8, 203–6, 220
    origin and evolution of   199–203
    reform of   208–21, 319–21
    see also Department of Economic and
    Social Affairs; Department of
    Public Information
Secretary-General of the UN   11, 27,
    41–2, 49, 190
    Annual Reports by   219, 290–1
    appointment of   196, 198, 219, 321
    functions of   196–7, 200, 204
    status of   37–8, 74
    see also Annan, Kofi; Boutros-Ghali,
    Boutros; Hammarskjöld, Dag; Lie,
    Trygve; Pérez de Cuéllar, Javier;
    Waldheim, Kurt
Security Council   3, 7–18 passim,
    61–95, 180, 188–91, 196, 285–7,
    305–14
    consultation procedure   76, 79–81
    friends of the Chair   253
    and the General Assembly   21–9
    passim, 33, 35, 40–2, 48, 54
    membership of   75, 82, 87–92, 96,
    300–4, 316
    in the post-Cold War era   81–96
    President of   76
    reform of   87–94
    and states groups   228, 233–4, 245,
    253–61
    supremacy of   10
    and Trusteeship issues   153–9,
    164–5, 169, 172
Segall, Jeffrey   56
self-determination, principle of   170–1,
    191, 232, 234
'semi-detached' UN members   302
Senior Management Group   214
Serbia   172
Shotwell, James   12
Singapore   147
Single European Act   302
Smith, Adam   3
Smuts, Jan Christian   155
Social Development, Commission for
    127
social movements   272
social partnership   285
soft law   51
Somalia   87, 159, 254, 256
Somaliland   157–9
Somavia formula   92
South Africa   32, 34, 37, 77, 81, 145–6,
    149, 151, 155, 165, 191, 224, 226,
    230, 237, 239, 255, 259–60
South Centre   207
South Commission   258
South Korea   29
South-West Africa   149, 151, 155,
    162–5, 178
sovereign equality of nations, principle
    of   30, 64, 172
sovereignty   67, 95, 165
    over natural resources   248

Soviet republics 14, 26, 66
Soviet Union 7–8, 11–17, 24–8, 39–40,
    43, 156–60, 201–2, 273
  and the Security Council 61–72, 78,
    81–2
  and states groups 226–39 *passim*,
    251, 253
  and Trusteeship issues 144, 147–52
    passim, 156–60
Spaak, Paul-Henri 37, 228
Spain 171, 173
Special United Nations Fund for
    Economic Development (SUNFED)
    114, 241
specialized agencies of the UN
    103–6
  co-ordination of 106–15
  locations of 106
Speth, Gus 130–1
staff of UN, numbers of 201–3
stakeholder dialogues 285
Stalin, Joseph 13–14, 25, 29, 68
standards, setting of 4, 103, 170
Standing Committee on Administrative
    Unions 160
states groups at the UN 31,
    224–65
status of UN members, differences in
    299–302, 316, 322
status quo powers 299–300
Steering Committee for Humanitarian
    Response 287
Stettinius, Edward 16, 200
Strategic Trust Territories 153–9,
    162–3
Strategy Planning Unit 214
Strong, Maurice 212, 284
Structural Adjustment Programmes
    47
Sudan 301
Suez crisis 74–5
'sunset provision' 54
superpowers, emergence of 19
Sustainable Development, Commission
    on 127, 174
Sweden 300
'system-loading' UN members 301

Taiwan 258
  see also Formosa
technical assistance 109
Teheran conference (1943) 13, 25
Thailand 42
Thatcher, Margaret 77
Thomson, Sir John 306
Tickell, Sir Crispin 307
Tito, Josip Broz 238, 240, 242
Track I and Track II procedures 130,
    212–13, 319
Truman, Harry 71, 158, 232
Trusteeship Council 10, 18, 27, 130,
    149–75
Trusteeship territories, list of 161
Turkey 144–7

Ukraine 14, 26
ultra vires action 187
unanimity principle 9–10
United Kingdom 3, 11–19, 24–5, 63,
    70, 85, 103, 122–3, 145–50, 155–8,
    172, 184, 229–30, 273–4, 300–7
  Colonial Office 143
  Foreign and Commonwealth Office:
    United Nations Department
    318–19
  Overseas Development
    Administration 139
United Nations Commission on
    Human Rights 232–3, 287
United Nations Conference on Trade
    and Development (UNCTAD) 32,
    45, 47, 104–8, 112–18, 240–52
    passim, 281, 310, 312
United Nations Development
    Assistance Frameworks (UNDAFs)
    129, 131–4, 137, 215
United Nations Development Decade
    45, 133
United Nations Development Group
    (UNDG) 129–33, 139, 215
United Nations Development
    Programme (UNDP) 45, 100, 105,
    109–18, 123–5, 129–31, 163, 208,
    215, 219
  Capital Development Fund 125

United Nations Educational, Scientific
and Cultural Organization
(UNESCO)   15, 47, 104–11, 303
United Nations Environment
Programme (UNEP)   105, 114–15,
174
United Nations Fund for Population
Activities (UNFPA)   100, 114–15,
129, 215
United Nations High Commission for
Refugees (UNHCR)   115, 217
'United Nations houses'   130–1
United Nations Industrial
Development Organization
(UNIDO)   105–8, 112–17, 132
United Nations International
Children's Emergency Fund
(UNICEF)   100, 111–15, 129–32,
208, 215, 217, 281
United Nations Relief and
Rehabilitation Administration
103
United Nations Relief and Works
Agency   40
United Nations system   4–6, 13,
100–1
agencies oriented towards   134, 136,
139, 295
weakness of central authority in
102–3
United States   3, 7–8, 11–17, 103, 128,
184–5, 273–4, 305–8, 324
Advisory Committee on Post War
Foreign Policy   12
Chamber of Commerce   12
Congress   17, 47–8, 65, 147, 206–8,
218, 257, 306, 313–14
Council on Foreign Relations   12
Navy   148, 157
State Department   12, 64–7, 274
and states groups at the UN   225–6,
236, 238, 246, 250–8 passim
and Trusteeship issues   144–52,
156–69 passim
and the UN General Assembly
24–5, 28, 32, 39–49 passim

and the UN Secretariat   201–12
passim, 220
and the UN Security Council   61–9,
73, 77–87, 92–6, 313–14
withholding of budget contributions
48, 111, 120, 206–8, 217, 256–7,
260, 315
'Uniting for Peace' resolution (1950)
10, 35, 40–2, 231
Universal Postal Union   104, 106, 199
universality   27–30, 144, 250
Urquhart, Brian   321
USSR, see Soviet Union
Utrecht, Treaty of   172

Versailles, Treaty of   9, 101
veto power   10, 14, 16–18, 66–9, 73–6,
88–91, 159, 196, 253–4, 261, 300
over membership of UN   28
Vietnam   29, 133
Vietnam War   44, 167, 240
voluntary financing of UN
programmes   114
voting rights   244–5
see also weighted voting

Waldheim, Kurt   79
War Crimes Tribunal for Yugoslavia
4
Weeramantry, Judge   190
weighted voting   48, 206, 256
West Irian   166–71
Western European and Other States
Group (WEOG)   244–6, 249, 256,
259
Western Sahara case (ICJ, 1975)   191
Westphalia, Treaties of   296
Wilson, Woodrow   22, 63, 77, 146
Women's International Democratic
Federation   277
women's issues, global conferences on
120, 126, 281, 283
World Bank   47, 102, 106, 121, 125,
133, 163, 241
see also International Bank for
Reconstruction and Development
World Bank Group   105

World Court, *see* International Court of Justice

World Court Project 286

World Disarmament Conference (1932) 273

World Economic Forum 55, 218

World Food Programme 100, 114, 129, 208

World Health Organization (WHO) 100, 104–11, 220, 237, 286, 303

World Intellectual Property Organization 105–6

World Meteorological Organization 104–7

World Parliament 56

World Peace Foundation 12

World Trade Organization (WTO) 104, 258

meeting in Seattle (1999) 138

World Trade Union Congress 273–4

Wyndham, Sir Eric 113

Yalta conference (1945) 14–15, 26, 67, 150

Yemen 83–4, 301

Yugoslavia 230–1, 234, 237–8, 242, 251, 307

Zionism 31, 229